Georg Büchner

Georg Büchner
The Shattered Whole

JOHN REDDICK

CLARENDON PRESS · OXFORD
1994

Oxford University Press, Walton Street, Oxford OX2 6DP
Oxford New York
Athens Auckland Bangkok Bombay
Calcutta Cape Town Dar es Salaam Delhi
Florence Hong Kong Istanbul Karachi
Kuala Lumpur Madras Madrid Melbourne
Mexico City Nairobi Paris Singapore
Taipei Tokyo Toronto
and associated companies in
Berlin Ibadan

Oxford is a trade mark of Oxford University Press

Published in the United States
by Oxford University Press Inc., New York

© John Reddick, 1994

All rights reserved. No part of this publication may be reproduced, stored in a retrieval system, or transmitted, in any form or by any means, without the prior permission in writing of Oxford University Press. Within the UK, exceptions are allowed in respect of any fair dealing for the purpose of research or private study, or criticism or review, as permitted under the Copyright, Designs and Patents Act, 1988, or in the case of reprographic reproduction in accordance with the terms of the licences issued by the Copyright Licensing Agency. Enquiries concerning reproduction outside these terms and in other countries should be sent to the Rights Department, Oxford University Press, at the address above

British Library Cataloguing in Publication Data
Data available

Library of Congress Cataloging in Publication Data
Reddick, John
Georg Büchner: the Shattered Whole / John Reddick.
Includes bibliographical references and index.
1. Büchner, Georg, 1813–1837—Criticism and interpretation.
I. Title
PT 1828.B6R36 1994 '832'.7—dc20 94-17243
ISBN 0-19-815812-2

1 3 5 7 9 10 8 6 4 2

Typeset by Pure Tech Corporation, Pondicherry, India
Printed in Great Britain
on acid-free paper by
Bookcraft Ltd.,
Midsomer Norton, Bath

For Kate, Adam, and Sarah

(Grass for breakfast, Büchner for lunch; supper may be difficult)

Acknowledgements

MANY friends and colleagues have given invaluable help and encouragement over the long gestation period of this book. Very special thanks are due to those who allowed me to inflict draft chapters on them, and offered such a wealth of advice (though the blame for all errors remains wholly mine): Michael Butler (Birmingham); Barry Nisbet (Cambridge); Jim Simpson (Liverpool); Martin Swales (London); Margaret Jacobs and Jim Reed (Oxford); and the late Peter Stern, so sorely missed.

Quotations

IN order to make this book accessible to all readers, whether or not they are familiar with German, quotations are given throughout both in the original, and in English translation.

The German quotations (which always reproduce the original grammar, spelling, and punctuation) are taken in the main from Werner Lehmann's 'Hamburg Edition', by kind permission of the publisher, Carl Hanser Verlag. In the few cases where quotations are taken from other editions, these are identified by means of abbreviations that are explained in the footnotes, and also in section I (c) of the Bibliography.

The English translations are my own, and are largely borrowed or adapted from my Penguin Classics edition of Büchner's works: Georg Büchner, *The Complete Plays, 'Lenz' and Other Writings*, translated, introduced and annotated by John Reddick (London, 1993).

Contents

Part I: Background

1 The Desperate Mosaic — 3
2 A Rearguard Action — 29
3 Routing the Robots — 43
4 The Quick and the Dead — 60

Part II: *Dantons Tod*

5 A Dance of Delusions — 79
6 Fraud, Futility, Freedom — 93
7 Metamorphosis and Choice — 121
8 Masks and Faces — 145
9 Vénus Noire — 167
10 Vénus Blanche — 186

Part III: *Leonce und Lena*

11 Masquerade — 207
12 Identity and Ennui — 231
13 Epiphany, Death, Transfiguration — 255
14 A Flight into Paradise? — 268

Part IV: *Woyzeck*

15	The Manuscripts	289
16	*Natur* and *Kunst*	303
17	A Question of Seeing	314
18	Emblems and Archetypes	335
19	Choice or Compulsion?	353

Conclusion   371

Bibliography   373

Index   389

Part I
Background

I
The Desperate Mosaic

WHEN this book was first proposed to Oxford University Press, I suggested that Georg Büchner might be a suitable candidate for inclusion in the pantheon represented by the Press's 'Past Masters' series. It came as no real surprise when this suggestion was graciously declined. After all, how could Büchner bear comparison with the one German literary figure then enshrined in the series, the colossal Goethe? Goethe lived to be 82, wrote vigorously for over sixty years, published Complete Edition after Complete Edition, each fatter than the last, and long before his death had become the awesome high priest of a temple of German classicism that he himself had very largely created. In this perspective, Büchner is a figure both puny and profane. He died at 23 (an age at which Goethe had not even produced *Werther*); he left the barest handful of texts; and he impinged little on the consciousness of the century in which he so briefly lived. Not for him the succession of definitive editions, the Eckermanns eager to immortalize each crumb of wisdom from his mouth. His œuvre, already slender enough, was further decimated by the disappearance, perhaps even the physical destruction, of the great majority of his letters,[1] his putative diaries, and possibly an entire play—the mysterious *Pietro Aretino*.[2] Not

---

[1] To date, only 11 autograph letters have come to light; the remainder are either lost, or else survive only in second-hand and excerpted form (i.e. as printed in Ludwig Büchner's 1850 part-edition of his brother's writings; the originals from which these letter-excerpts were taken were destroyed in a fire at the Büchners' home in 1851). Cf. Jan-Christoph Hauschild, *Georg Büchner. Studien und neue Quellen zu Leben, Werk und Wirkung* (Königstein, 1985), 101 ff.; Susanne Lehmann, 'Der Brand im Haus der Büchners 1851', in T. M. Mayer (ed.), *Georg Büchner Jahrbuch*, 6/1986–7, 303–13.—Since this note was written, two further autograph letters have been tracked down; see *Der Spiegel*, 36 (1993), 198–204, and E. Gillmann, T. M. Mayer, R. Pabst, and D. Wolf (eds.), *Georg Büchner an 'Hund' und 'Kater'. Unbekannte Briefe des Exils* (Marburg, 1993).

[2] It was long supposed that Büchner must have left behind a complete or near-complete play manuscript on the subject of Pietro Aretino, and that his fiancée Minna Jaeglé must have destroyed it; it now seems much more likely that the project was planned rather than executed (the negative picture of Minna Jaeglé's attitudes and behaviour in the decades after Büchner's death has also been convincingly

one of his writings was published in his lifetime in authentic and definitive form; even his doctoral dissertation—a *mémoire*, in French, on the cranial anatomy of an obscure fish—though printed just before his death, was not published until just after it.³ For the rest, his work survives only in a more or less conjectural, fragmentary, or reconstituted form. Even today, more than a century and a half after his death, we wait in exasperation for a full historical-critical edition.

In sheer stature, then, Büchner is dwarfed by the monumental figure of Goethe. But monumental stature can exact a heavy price. Goethe looms on his plinth like Nelson on his column, but he is equally remote. For all his true merits, for all the magnificent vitality trapped in the cold stone, he has acquired the status of a curiosity, a monument at once deeply revered and largely ignored. With Büchner it is quite the reverse. This slender, provocative, sharp-edged figure lives more vitally amongst us than ever before. No other German writer before Kafka and Brecht so vividly catches the modern imagination. It is an extraordinary phenomenon that, whereas the nineteenth century was largely deaf to this man's voice, he seems to speak to us now with 'incendiary' force (Günter Grass)⁴ and 'remarkable relevance' (Heinrich Böll)⁵ as if he were alive and well in Munich or Berlin. Political protesters in the Federal Republic have daubed the war-cry of *Der Hessische Landbote* across a thousand banners and squatted houses: 'Friede den Hütten! Krieg den Pallästen!' (*Peace to the peasants! War on the palaces!*) His plays are a mainstay of the contemporary German theatre, and are regularly staged abroad. Werner Herzog, one of the most imaginative directors in the modern German cinema, made a powerful (if capricious) film of *Woyzeck* (and chose a quotation from *Lenz* as the epigraph for *Kaspar Hauser*). Erich Kästner described himself as Büchner's

---

discredited). Cf. Hauschild, *Georg Büchner*, 57 ff.; Jan-Christoph Hauschild, 'Büchners *Aretino*. Eine Fiktion?', in Anon. (ed.), *Georg Büchner 1813–1837. Revolutionär, Dichter, Wissenschaftler* (Basel and Frankfurt, 1987), 353–5. Büchner's interest in Aretino is itself interesting: Pietro Aretino (1492–1556) was a self-styled 'scourge of princes' (*flagello dei principi*) who, besides many other activities including painting, and writing successful comedies and a tragedy, became notorious for his vitriolic satires and his salacious exposés of corruption and carnality in high places, and also for his highly erotic poetry, notably the *Sonetti lussuriosi* (Lewd Sonnets).

³ See Hauschild, *Georg Büchner*, 372–3.
⁴ Anon. (ed.), *Büchner-Preis-Reden 1951–1971* (Stuttgart, 1972), 162.
⁵ Ibid. 183.

The Desperate Mosaic

'pupil and debtor'.[6] For Wolfgang Koeppen 'Büchner was always the closest star in the German firmament'.[7] In the eyes of Christa Wolf, 'German prose begins with Büchner's *Lenz*'; it is her 'absolute ideal', her 'primal experience' ('Ur-Erlebnis') in German literature.[8] For Wolf Biermann, Büchner is quite simply the greatest writer Germany has known ('unser größter Dichter').[9] And we should not forget the revolutionary and revelatory impact that the newly discovered Büchner had on earlier writers: on Gerhart Hauptmann and his fellow Naturalists, on the German Expressionists, on Wedekind and Brecht above all.

Undisputed though the strength and immediacy of Büchner's voice may be, however, there are wild and bitter disputes about what that voice is saying. This is not surprising, for several factors conspire to make him a natural focus of controversy. Most obviously, there is the sheer smallness of scale and the uncertain state of his output. Imagine the jousting ground that would have been afforded to critics if Goethe had left only *Götz*, *Urfaust*, and *Werther*, let us say, and if these had survived only in scrawled, incomplete, often illegible manuscripts, or in printed versions that were variously mutilated, truncated, bowdlerized, or garbled, as well as being largely posthumous and wholly unauthorized. Then there is the richly provocative nature of his concerns. Sex, religion, politics, these taboo topics for all decent folk, are amongst his most urgent preoccupations. From the first lines of *Dantons Tod* with their image of the pretty lady who gives her heart to her husband and her cunt to her lovers, Büchner's 'obscenities' have ensured him the status of *enfant terrible*, and in the process have served to betray the blinkered perspective of countless critics. Gods, God, and spirits are insistently invoked by his characters, to be denied, defied, condemned, entreated—and thus to serve as a constant challenge to believer, agnostic, and atheist alike. Büchner's politics are of course an especially fulminant issue. Here is a man who was one of the

---

[6] Ibid. 56.
[7] Ibid. 116.
[8] Christa Wolf, *Fortgesetzter Versuch. Aufsätze. Gespräche. Essays* (Leipzig, 1979), 64.
[9] Wolf Biermann, 'Der Lichtblick im gräßlichen Fatalismus der Geschichte', *Die Zeit*, 25 Oct. 1991, 73. More recently, Biermann has compared Büchner to Shakespeare, and referred to him as a 'Weltgenie' (genius of world stature); see 'Geschichte kennt keine Moral. Wolf Biermann über die wiederentdeckten Briefe Georg Büchners und ihre Bedeutung für die Gegenwart', *Der Spiegel*, 36 (1993), 207.

6 Background

most radical left-wing thinkers of his age within the German lands, a proto-Marxian revolutionary who, although he entered the fray as a political publicist and activist for only the briefest of periods, remained committed throughout his life to the overthrow of what he saw as an illegitimate, parasitical, and effete ruling class, and the resurgence and emancipation of the cruelly exploited popular mass. Given the paucity both of direct evidence, such as Büchner's correspondence, and of indirect evidence, such as reminiscences of friends and acquaintances, there is much scope for argument even about his precise activities and stance within the political micro- and macro-realities of the time. The fiercest controversy, however, is inevitably provoked by his writing. At one extreme is the view exemplified by Georg Lukács: Büchner as an unswerving Jacobin essentially unaffected by the grim fiasco of *Der Hessische Landbote*: 'Büchner was at all times a rigorous revolutionary'.[10] At the opposite extreme, the view exemplified by Robert Mühlher: Büchner as a man whose abrupt and bitter insights propelled him into 'extreme or absolute nihilism', and in the process depoliticized him and 'thrust him for ever from the liberal and democratic camp'.[11]

The scant and uncertain status of the texts, the inflammatory nature of the issues they contain: these features of Büchner's work are themselves conducive to controversy. But their effect is greatly compounded by a third decisive element: the *manner* of Büchner's art, the language, modes, and structures that he uses to express his concerns. For the flickering image of the world that he evokes is profoundly un- and anti-classical, and consciously remote from the prevailing conventions and expectations of his age. Whether in language, mood, plot, or personae, he offers no steady development, no sense of anything rounded, resolved, or unified. Instead of unfolding in clearly measured rhythm, his works progress through a succession of kaleidoscopic convulsions, enacting what Walter Jens has called a 'law of discontinuity'.[12] Wholeness, when it appears, is always false—a pretence, an illusion, at best a transitory state. It is *particles* that loom large; discrete elements that he highlights in

[10] Georg Lukács, 'Der faschistisch verfälschte und der wirkliche Georg Büchner', repr. in W. Martens (ed.), *Georg Büchner* (Darmstadt, 1965), 201. Lukács's polemic was originally written in Moscow in 1937.
[11] Robert Mühlher, 'Georg Büchner und die Mythologie des Nihilismus', in Martens (ed.), *Georg Büchner*, 260.
[12] Walter Jens, *Euripides. Büchner* (Pfullingen, 1964), 46.

startling isolation, or in disparate clusters and combinations that create a constant sense of paradox, multivalence, and mystery. This is a chief mark of his spectacular modernity: already in the 1830s he is doing the kind of thing that will seem outrageously new when practised by the most avant-garde painters, composers, and writers of the early twentieth century. But it also makes him especially difficult to interpret. In particular, it entails the problem of perspective: being so disparate and discrete, the elements in his work change their aspect and apparent importance quite radically when viewed from different vantage points.

How are we to deal with this systematic discontinuity? As a first step, perhaps, we need to take it seriously. This might seem an easy and obvious measure, but it has eluded many critics.

The most unsubtle way of not taking it seriously is that favoured by certain critics in the English tradition, who have patronizingly applied the yardstick of good old English common sense, and declared Büchner to be insufficiently mature. Thus A. H. J. Knight could assert that 'The perpetual changes of scene in *Dantons Tod* . . . reveal a not unnatural absence of practical dramatic sense in the young author'.[13] Ronald Peacock, likewise referring to *Dantons Tod*, descries a 'disunity . . . that is a symptom both of Büchner's philosophical and of his poetic-dramatic immaturity'.[14] This plain man's approach is severely reductive: the more challenging a complexity, the more likely it is to be branded a defect or mistake—a tendency hair-raisingly exemplified when Knight touches on the Marion episode, one of the most powerful and extraordinary moments in the mosaic of Büchner's work, and baldly dismisses it as 'contributing nothing to the theme of the play'.[15]

A more subtle and more common way of failing to do justice to Büchner's disjunctive and paradoxical mode is to behave as though it did not exist. It is all too easy to don spectacles of this hue or that, and to believe that the particular pattern that they reveal is the only one, or the only one that matters. The basic trouble perhaps is that

---

[13] A. H. J. Knight, *Georg Büchner* (Oxford, 1951), 80.
[14] Ronald Peacock, 'A Note on Georg Büchner's Plays', *German Life and Letters*, NS 10 (1956–7), 191. Peacock's article proved influential, not least in serving as the explicit departure point for Dorothy James's monograph *Georg Büchner's 'Dantons Tod': A Reappraisal* (London, 1982)—a work that is repeatedly weakened by its premiss that *Dantons Tod* demonstrates Büchner's 'immaturity as a dramatist' (25).
[15] Knight, 74.

critics have traditionally been the products of academe who were schooled chiefly or wholly in the traditions of classicism. We are accustomed to seeing works of literature as programmatic and exemplary, as vehicles purpose-built to embody and demonstrate an already fully developed view or ethos. We recognize in the late plays of Schiller, for example, a magnificent complexity, but a complexity like that of a baroque fugue with its rich and balanced elaboration of lucidly stated themes. Such an approach, or such a set of expectations, can only be reductive to the point of distortion when applied to Georg Büchner. He never writes to communicate solutions. Instead, his writing is a kind of happening, a constant search, a dynamic enactment of the very process of argument and conflict, of the collision and interaction of contrary possibilities. His works begin, but never at a beginning, and they come to an end, but not to a conclusion.[16] This means that we should never be tempted to seize on a particular discrete element and single it out as a summation of the whole, or as the definitive fixing of a position—though many critics have done so, hence the persistent misrepresentation of Büchner as being variously a programmatic pessimist and nihilist, a programmatic fatalist, a programmatic Christian, a programmatic Jacobin revolutionary. There is indeed an underlying consistency and unity in Büchner; but it will be found only *within* and *through* the paradoxes and multiplicities of his work—not despite them.

It helps for us to recognize what is perhaps the paradox of paradoxes in Georg Büchner: his disjunctive mode with its relentless insistence on fragments and particles is always the product of a radiant vision of *wholeness*. Again and again, in every area of his existence—his politics, his science, his aesthetics, his art—we find an ardent sense of wholeness, but a wholeness that is almost always poignantly elusive: it *was* but is no longer; or *will* be but isn't yet; or—most poignant of all—it *is* in the present, but can be perceived or possessed only partially or transiently. Büchner is thus forced to be a maker of mosaics. But the more jagged the fragments in these mosaics, the more strident they are in their invocation of the whole;

---

[16] Cf. Helmut Krapp in his seminal study of 1958, *Der Dialog bei Georg Büchner* (Darmstadt, 1958), 145: 'Büchners Position ... ist kein "Entwurf" und keine "Lösung" im überlieferten Sinne, denn das Kontrastschema hat eigentlich keinen Anfang und kein Ende. Kontraste lassen sich unendlich aneinanderreihen' (*Büchner's position ... represents neither a 'blueprint' nor a 'solution' in the traditional sense, for his contrastive scheme of things knows no real beginning or ending. Contrasts can be concatenated ad infinitum*).

The Desperate Mosaic 9

a pattern that is perfectly epitomized in the earliest pages of his work when he has Lacroix define the quest of Danton amongst the whores in just such terms: 'Er sucht eben die mediceische Venus stückweise ... zusammen, er macht Mosaik, wie er sagt'; 'Es ist ein Jammer, daß die Natur die Schönheit ... zerstückelt und sie so in Fragmenten in die Körper gesenkt hat' (20–1;[17] *He's just trying to get the Medici Venus together again piece by piece, he's making a mosaic, as he puts it; It's a crying shame that nature has broken beauty into pieces and stuck it in fragments like that into different bodies.*) Minutes later the theme is echoed and intensified in Danton's yearning response to Marion with its double stress on 'totality': 'Warum kann ich deine Schönheit nicht ganz in mich fassen, sie nicht ganz umschließen?' (22; *Why can't I take your beauty wholly into myself, wholly enfold it within my arms?*) At the beginning of *Lenz* we find the same essential image, even to the extent of a verbal echo: 'er meinte, er müsse den Sturm in sich ziehen, Alles in sich fassen'; 'er wühlte sich in das All hinein' (79; *he believed he should draw the storm right into himself; he burrowed his way into the all*). In *Leonce und Lena* it is the wholeness of love that is fragmented: split asunder into the separate notes of a musical scale, split asunder into the separate colours of a rainbow. But, as always, the emphasis on fragments implies the conviction of wholeness—which indeed is made explicit here in the image of love *beyond* the differentiated spectrum of the rainbow: as 'der weiße Gluthstrahl der Liebe'—a single shaft of white-hot radiance (112). And it is precisely Leonce's experience of a love-inspired totality of being that is celebrated in the fleeting climax of the play: 'Mein

---

[17] Parenthetic page references relate throughout to the so-called Hamburg Edition (plain numbers refer to vol. i, numbers with the prefix 'ii' refer to vol. ii): Georg Büchner, *Sämtliche Werke und Briefe. Historisch-kritische Ausgabe mit Kommentar*, ed. Werner R. Lehmann: i. *Dichtungen und Übersetzungen mit Dokumentationen zur Stoffgeschichte* (Hamburg, 1967); ii. *Vermischte Schriften und Briefe* (Hamburg, 1971). Lehmann's edition has had a sorry and exasperating history. Four vols. were originally planned: the two vols. as published, and two vols. containing the critical apparatus and the promised 'Kommentar'. Not only did the project change publishers (transferring from Christian Wegner, Hamburg, to Carl Hanser, Munich), but the third and fourth vols. never appeared. Although it still constitutes the most authoritative and most widely available complete edition—and is accordingly used as the base-text throughout the present study—most of the main works have since been variously and separately published in editions considerably superior to Lehmann's. A truly historical-critical edition of the entire corpus is in preparation under the editorship of Thomas Michael Mayer; in the meantime we have to wait and make do.

ganzes Sein ist in dem einen Augenblick.' (125; *All my being is in this single moment.*)

The force and central importance of Büchner's vision of wholeness become clearer still when we realize that it also lies at the heart of his work as a scientist-philosopher. Büchner spells this out in his Trial Lecture 'Über Schädelnerven' ('On Cranial Nerves'),[18] which he delivered on 5 November 1836 (less than four months before his death from typhus), and which—astonishingly—he must have written at the very same time as he was working on *Woyzeck*. Trial Lectures were a ritualistic affair, not unlike the modern Inaugural except that they constituted a final hurdle *before* the victim's confirmation in a teaching post, in Büchner's case as a *Privatdozent* in Comparative Anatomy at the brand new University of Zurich. They encouraged a contender to demonstrate his stance as well as his standing; and with an audience of dignitaries that included Lorenz Oken, the University's founding *Rektor*, and one of the most influential and most controversial scientist-philosophers of the age within the German lands, Büchner goes to considerable lengths to define his general standpoint and frame of reference, before launching into his particular argument concerning the skull. And Büchner puts a quite remarkable emphasis in these prefatory pages on his sense of the natural world as an *organic whole* characterized by order, proportion, unity, and essential simplicity. The study of the natural world, he says, has taken on a new shape. Previously, botanists and zoologists, physiologists and comparative anatomists had been confronted by a monstrous chaos of irreconcilable, undifferentiated data—'ein ungeheures, durch den Fleiß von Jahrhunderten zusammengeschlepptes Material, das kaum unter die Ordnung eines Kataloges gebracht war'; 'ein Gewirr seltsamer Formen unter den abentheuerlichsten Namen'; 'eine Masse Dinge, die sonst nur als getrennte, weit auseinander liegende facta das Gedächtniß beschwerten' (ii. 293; *a huge mass of material, laboriously heaped up over the centuries, that had scarcely even been systematically catalogued; a confusion of weird forms under the wildest names; a mass of things that previously weighed heavily on one's memory as so many separate, unconnected facts*). But enormous progress has at last been made ('bedeutender Fortschritt'), and the chaos and con-

---

[18] The title is not Büchner's own. It was coined by Karl Emil Franzos for his 1879 edition of Büchner's works.

The Desperate Mosaic

fusion have resolved in consequence into simple, natural, exquisitely proportioned patterns: 'einfache, natürliche Gruppen', 'schönsten Ebenmaaß'. The essential thrust of this new understanding, in comparative anatomy as in the various kindred subjects, was towards a kind of unity, with all forms being traced back to the supremely simple primordial type, or archetype, from which they were developed: 'In der vergleichenden Anatomie strebte Alles nach einer gewissen Einheit, nach dem Zurückführen aller Formen auf den einfachsten primitiven Typus.'

As we might expect, Büchner tells us that the whole picture in all its richness is not yet fully understood, but that coherent parts of it have taken shape: 'Hat man auch nichts Ganzes erreicht, so kamen doch zusammenhängende Strecken zum Vorschein'. In the similar but more vivid image conveyed earlier in the same paragraph: 'Hatte man auch die Quelle nicht gefunden, so hörte man doch an vielen Stellen den Strom in der Tiefe rauschen' (*Even though one had not found the well-spring, there were nevertheless many places where one could hear the river roaring down below.*) This has a familiar ring, for it echoes the kind of pattern generated in the poetic writing: there, too, the river is never reached, but its roaring can be heard. We have only the fragments of a mosaic, the separate notes of the scale, the scattered colours of the spectrum; but they imply and betoken a vibrant if elusive whole.

The supreme importance to Büchner of this sense of wholeness is evinced even more remarkably a little earlier in the Trial Lecture (ii. 292). What is it that paved the way for this new understanding of the physical world? It is the fundamental postulate that all things in nature are part of a *single organic complex*, a 'gesammte Organisation', and that this rich complex is governed and patterned according to a *single natural law*, a 'Grundgesetz'. Büchner had already begun to define his scientific-philosophical credo in the brief last paragraph of his doctoral dissertation earlier in 1836: his conviction that the grand richness of nature is not due to any kind of arbitrary functionalism, but is the elaboration of a design or 'blueprint' of supreme simplicity: 'La nature est grande et riche, non parce qu'à chaque instant elle crée arbitrairement des organes nouveaux pour de nouvelles fonctions; mais parce qu'elle produit, d'après le plan le plus simple, les formes les plus élevées et les plus pures.' (ii. 125). This is directly echoed, and intensified, in the Trial Lecture: the 'Grundgesetz', the all-informing law of nature, is an 'Urgesetz'—a kind of law-of-laws—'das nach den einfachsten Rissen und Linien die höchsten und reinsten Formen hervorbringt' (*that produces the highest and purest forms according to the simplest patterns and designs*). On this view, everything—form, matter, function—is governed by the one law: 'Alles, Form und Stoff, ist . . . an dies Gesetz gebunden'; 'Alle Funktionen sind Wirkungen desselben [Gesetzes]'. The astonishingly positive nature of Büchner's stance is radiantly clear in these lines. The primal law, the 'Urgesetz' that he sees as the matrix of all things, is to him nothing less than a law of *beauty*, 'ein Gesetz der Schönheit'. And since this law is so benign, and since all things in nature—functions as well as form and matter—are generated by it, the myriad workings of nature not only never conflict with each other: they interact positively together to yield a *necessary harmony*: 'ihr . . . Aufeinander- und Zusammenwirken ist nichts weiter, als die nothwendige Harmonie in den Aeußerungen eines und desselben Gesetzes, dessen Wirkungen sich natürlich nicht gegenseitig zerstören.'

This paean of faith in a universal order of rich simplicity, engendered by beauty and resonant with harmony, can seem bewildering indeed, coming as it does from the pen of a man whom critics of different eras and very different persuasions have variously categorized as 'a most decided nihilist' (Viëtor),[19] 'perhaps the most uncompromising German Nihilist of the nineteenth century' (Closs),[20] an exponent of 'profound pessimism' (Hans Mayer),[21] of 'extreme or absolute nihilism' (Mühlher),[22] of 'an extreme form of pessimism' that is 'deeper and darker than any to be found in the previous history of German thought, with the possible exception of Schopenhauer' (M. B. Benn).[23] This long tradition of depicting Büchner as a nihilist or pessimist has rightly fallen into considerable disfavour.[24] But even if we doubt the many critics of this comple-

[19] Karl Viëtor, *Georg Büchner. Politik, Dichtung, Wissenschaft* (Berne, 1949), 296.
[20] August Closs, 'Nihilism in Modern German Drama. Grabbe and Büchner', in Closs, *Medusa's Mirror: Studies in German Literature* (London, 1957), 157.
[21] Hans Mayer, *Georg Büchner und seine Zeit* (Wiesbaden, [1960]), 104.
[22] Mühlher, 261.
[23] Maurice B. Benn, *The Drama of Revolt: A Critical Study of Georg Büchner* (Cambridge, 1976), 61, 62.
[24] Cf. Gerhard Knapp: 'Es hat sich im Grundsätzlichen erwiesen, daß die Kategorie des Nihilismus . . . für eine Annäherung an das Werk Büchners nicht in Frage kommen kann und sollte. Die Büchner-Forschung sollte diesen Interpretationsgang,

xion, we are still faced with the strident paradox within the texts themselves: the beauteous harmony and order postulated with such faith and confidence in the Trial Lecture—and the bleak visions so frequently and so eloquently evoked in the poetic work: the terrifying cold isolation of Lenz at the end of the story, and of the child in the un-fairytale in *Woyzeck* (100–1; 151); the famous, or infamous, cry of Danton that the world is chaos, and nothingness its due messiah (72); the fear of Leonce that all we see may be mere imaginings masking a reality of blank, bare vacuity (118). Such examples could be multiplied.

Again we face the problem of how to cope with the unremittingly paradoxical nature of Büchner's writing; and again I would insist that we can only begin by taking it seriously. It evades the issue to suppose, as Knight did, that Büchner was simply changing his ground in the last phase of his life, and moderating from his alleged 'total pessimism'.[25] Hans Mayer does not get us much further when he sorrowfully maintains that there is a regrettable discrepancy, a 'dissonance', between Büchner's (radical) view of society and his (conservative) view of nature.[26] And it is quite mistaken, I believe, to allege that the radiant faith expressed in the Trial Lecture is some kind of bogus remedy, a 'nostrum', as J. P. Stern has asserted, hastily contrived 'to repair the shattered fabric of existence'.[27] Büchner's faith in abundant, vibrant wholeness was not a sudden new stance, nor a strange aberration, nor a convenient refuge in adversity: it was fundamental to his existence and to all his doings; and even the most raucous anguish in his writings—*especially* the most raucous anguish—is always born of it.

One of the most extraordinary paradoxes in Büchner is that, whereas the *manner* of his poetic writing is inexorably un- and anti-classical, the faith and vision that underlies it is classical almost to the point of anachronism: if he was spectacularly ahead of his

---

der sich als Aporie erwiesen hat, endgültig *ad acta* legen.' (*It has become clear in all essential respects that the category of nihilism cannot and should not be called upon in any approach to Büchner. Büchner research should once and for all abandon this line of interpretation, which has shown itself to be a complete cul-de-sac*; see also Knapp's endnote).—Gerhard Knapp, *Georg Büchner. Eine kritische Einführung in die Forschung* (Frankfurt, 1975), 120.

[25] Knight, 69, 174–5.
[26] Hans Mayer, *Georg Büchner und seine Zeit*, 372.
[27] J. P. Stern, 'Georg Büchner: Potsherds of Experience', in Stern, *Idylls and Realities: Studies in Nineteenth-Century German Literature* (London, 1971), 35.

time in the one respect, he was unspectacularly but distinctly behind it in the other. We get an inkling of this once we register the gross discrepancy between Büchner's reception as a writer, and his reception as a speculative scientist. As a writer, he notoriously remained largely unrecognized throughout the nineteenth century: there was no framework of reference or of expectations that could begin to accommodate the radical unconventionality of his work. *Dantons Tod*, the only one of his poetic works to appear during his lifetime, could do so only after it had been morally and politically sanitized— even so, it is a mystery how it slipped through the net of an oppressive and efficient censorship—and it met with almost no response at all, except for instance to be savagely castigated by a pseudonymous reviewer as 'filth', 'pestilential impudence', 'excrescences of immorality', 'blasphemy against all that is most sacred', 'degeneracy'.[28] As a comparative anatomist, on the other hand, Büchner was instantly admitted into the fold of international orthodoxy. His doctoral dissertation, *Mémoire sur le système nerveux du barbeau*, published in Strasbourg in April 1837, was immediately welcomed in authoritative circles in France, Germany, and Switzerland: its 'Partie descriptive' was hailed as 'very thorough' and 'entirely correct', and as 'extending knowledge with all desirable precision', while its 'Partie philosophique', containing Büchner's specific argument, was endorsed by Johannes Müller, a like-minded comparative anatomist, but also a physiologist who was to make advances fundamental to nineteenth-century science.[29] Büchner's Trial Lecture, in its turn, met with 'the widest approval' among its local but distinguished audience of established academics, and Oken himself not only made a point of recommending his new young colleague's classes, but sent along his own son.[30]

The problem with the particular scientific-philosophical position that Büchner embraced as wholeheartedly as he rejected its literary

---

[28] Felix Frei [pseudonym], in *Literarisches Notizenblatt der Dresdner Abendzeitung*, 28 Oct. 1835. Cf. Hauschild, *Georg Büchner*, 185 ff. Cf. also Thomas Michael Mayer, 'Büchner-Chronik', in H. L. Arnold (ed.), *Büchner I/II*, special number of *Text + Kritik* (Munich, 1979), 404. Mayer eloquently documents the virulent campaign of the period against 'subversive' writers, orchestrated by the Metternichian hatchet man Wolfgang Menzel—a campaign that culminated in the imprisonment of Büchner's new friend and patron, Karl Gutzkow (ibid. 397 ff.).
[29] Cf. Jean Strohl, *Lorenz Oken und Georg Büchner. Zwei Gestalten aus der Übergangszeit von Naturphilosophie zu Naturwissenschaft* (Zurich, 1936), 59.
[30] T. M. Mayer, 'Büchner-Chronik', 419.

counterpart is that it was rapidly losing its predominance and credibility even as he entered upon it. There is an eloquent irony in the fact that, during the period that Büchner was immersing himself in his dissections and concretizing his received wholist vision of the natural world, Charles Darwin was busily collecting his data on the *Beagle*. By the time his ship returned to England in October 1836, just a few weeks before Büchner's lecture, Darwin had the makings of a theory that would help to make the world-view of which Büchner was such an ardent exponent seem antiquated and irrelevant, an apparent by-water remote from the mainstream of scientific progress—and a deeply suspect one at that. This suspect status was both demonstrated and sharply reinforced in Thomas Henry Huxley's famous Croonian Lecture of 1858, when he set out to discredit precisely that central tenet that lies at the heart of both Büchner's doctoral dissertation and his Trial Lecture, namely Goethe's and Oken's vertebral theory of the skull. The triumphant, sabre-rattling tone is unmistakable when Huxley ridicules 'the speculator' for his conjuror's ability to 'devise half a dozen very pretty vertebral theories, all equally true, in the course of a summer's day', and calls for support from 'Those who, like myself, are unable to see the propriety and advantage of introducing into science any ideal conception, which is other than the simplest possible generalized expression of observed facts'.[31]

We need to appreciate the real enormity of the problems faced by life-scientists in the century or so before Darwin did for biology what Newton had done for physics almost two centuries earlier; even the very word 'scientist'—not coined (by Whewell) until 1840—is an anachronism that tends to beg essential questions. Büchner is not exaggerating when he speaks in his Trial Lecture of a monstrous chaos of disorderly, undifferentiated data. Referring to the great systematizer John Stuart Mill and his attendance at zoology lectures at Montpellier University in 1820, Sir Peter Medawar has remarked that 'there seems no doubt that his thought on

---

[31] T. H. Huxley, 'On the Theory of the Vertebrate Skull', in M. Foster and E. R. Lankester (eds.), *The Scientific Memoirs of Thomas Henry Huxley*, i. (London, 1898), 584–5. Sir Peter Medawar has described Huxley's 1858 lecture as one of the 'very few' cases in the history of science where a theory has been 'utterly discredited' (P. B. Medawar, *Induction and Intuition in Scientific Thought* (London, 1969), 30). But the position is not quite so clear-cut. It can be argued that Huxley's own hypothesis was not all that far removed from the one he so vigorously ridiculed. And even to this day, the theory of the vertebrate skull is still not entirely dead.

methodology was strongly influenced by the study of a subject overwhelmed by a multitude of "facts" that had not yet been disciplined by a unifying theory'; and he continues: 'Coleridge described it [in 1818] as "notorious" that zoology had been "fully abroad, weighed down and crushed as it were by the inordinate number and multiplicity of facts and phenomena apparently separate, without evincing the least promise of systematizing itself by any inward combination of its parts".'[32] Biologists of this period found themselves battling through a teeming jungle of new knowledge. Behind them lay Aristotle-Land, with its clear but no longer adequate model of a fixed and static 'Ladder of Nature'; ahead of them somewhere was that magnificent vantage point that Darwin was ultimately to construct, with its momentous spectacle of an evolutionary pattern in nature both dynamic and explicable. Many crucial stations were established along the way by great speculative and/or systematizing minds like Linnaeus, Bonnet, Buffon, Lamarck, Cuvier; but being on the whole too closely modelled on the Aristotelian 'fixed-and-final' scheme, none of them could sufficiently order or accommodate the riotous growth of new facts and discoveries.

That there was a real fear in this period of being overwhelmed by the welter of 'facts and phenomena' is clear from the comments of Coleridge, and implicit in Büchner's use of language in the Trial Lecture ('ein ungeheures . . . Material, das kaum unter die Ordnung eines Kataloges gebracht war', 'ein Gewirr seltsamer Formen unter den abentheuerlichsten Namen', 'eine Masse Dinge, die . . . als getrennte, weit auseinander liegende facta das Gedächtniß beschwerten'). The fear was a complex one. At its most banal there was no doubt the professional fear of all scholars in all eras that their minds might not be equal to their material. At a much deeper level, the gathering confusion was bound to generate anxious perplexity in an age conditioned by the Enlightenment to believe that all things in existence are systematically patterned, and that man's mind can discern that pattern. At its deepest, however, the fear was existential: what was threatened was man's whole sense of the world in which he lived, and of his place within that world. The ultimate upshot is a matter of history: *On the Origin of Species by Natural Selection* resolved one kind of fear, but confirmed the other: it did

[32] Medawar, 9.

discern a pattern, and it thereby revolutionized biology, and the sciences in general; but in the process it also profoundly affected man's conception of the world in all its dimensions—philosophical, religious, ethical, social, political. In the meantime, though, the earlier systematizers struggled to order the increasing chaos—seeking consciously or unconsciously to put upon it the most comfortable construction that they could.[33]

Both Büchner and Coleridge point to the gravest particular cause of fear: the real threat lay not so much in the sheer extent or bulk of the new 'facts and phenomena', but rather in their disorderliness and, above all, their discreteness: they were 'getrennte, weit auseinander liegende facta', they were 'apparently separate' and showing no promise of an 'inward combination of [their] parts'. This 'inordinate multiplicity' not only resisted Enlightened assumptions about an orderly progression towards the discernment of order in the *natural* world; it also very readily seemed to echo, to symbolize and even to compound the atomistic forces that were tending to disrupt progress towards a better order in the *human* world (as seen from a progressivist point of view), or alternatively to disrupt the human order already prevailing (as seen from a conservative point of view). For approximately a century, cataclysm after cataclysm ensured that no thinking person could easily sustain a clear and stable picture of the world: the devastating Lisbon earthquake of 1755 that so profoundly affected Voltaire; the incessant revolution in scientific data; the Industrial Revolution with its colossal social and economic repercussions; the French Revolution with its magnificent aspirations and horrific reality—precisely the setting of Büchner's first play; the international turmoil of the Napoleonic wars; the bloody spasms of social revolution in 1830 and 1848. This was by far the greatest and the most obsessive age of taxonomy and system-building in human history: like Büchner's Danton, they were 'making

---

[33] One curious monument to this obsession with taxonomy is, of all things, Roget's *Thesaurus*. P. M. Roget, born 1779, was a doctor and natural scientist of considerable repute, a Fellow of the Royal Society and its Secretary for more than twenty years, who not only invented a 'system of verbal classification', but based it—as he explained in the Introduction to the first edition of 1852—on 'the same principle as that which is employed in the various departments of Natural History. Thus the sectional divisions I have formed, correspond to the Natural Families in Botany and Zoology, and the filiation of words presents a network analogous to the natural filiation of plants or animals.' (R. A. Dutch (ed.), *Roget's Thesaurus of English Words and Phrases* (London, 1981), pp. xxi, xxxv.)

mosaics', feverishly trying to assemble the exploded pieces into sensible, significant order. And today we still live to some extent in the long shadow of the twin texts that were the towering culmination of these endeavours, texts that were equally dedicated to the ordering of classes, and to the modes of change to which those classes are subject: *On the Origin of Species*—and *The Communist Manifesto*.

Nowhere was the atomistic threat felt more acutely than in Germany. Not least because there *was* no Germany: in sharp contrast to France or England, there was no kind of political, economic, social, or cultural entity characterized by an 'inward combination of its parts' (to borrow Coleridge's words once again), but instead an 'inordinate number and multiplicity' of states and statelets—the atomization and attendant backwardness of particularism. The hundred years from about 1750 to 1850 saw an astonishing outpouring of genius in German thought and literature (not to mention music) that is without parallel in Europe since the Renaissance. But this great torrent welled up in a fragmented landscape that had lain barren in many respects since time immemorial, and which enjoyed nothing of the clear, well-established, centralized system of channels and reservoirs that offered an instant sense of direction, context, and common endeavour to the gifted Frenchman or Englishman. Referring particularly to literature, W. H. Bruford has observed that 'It is remarkable, as has often been pointed out, that Germany succeeded, in the absence of . . . a national tradition and of political institutions to support it, in producing a literature that came to be looked upon as classical, though it was, in Freytag's phrase, "the almost miraculous creation of a soul without a body".'[34] It was indeed remarkable. But it would have been even more remarkable if the mighty talents of the age had *not* energetically built themselves elaborate constructs to compensate for what was missing.

But what kind of constructs? A fundamental disparity at once begins to appear between the German pattern, and the pattern elsewhere. At its simplest, it is the contrast between empiricism and idealism; between the inductive and deductive modes; between progression from matter to mind, and progression from mind to matter. Given the increasingly evident backwardness and atomization of the

---

[34] W. H. Bruford, *Germany in the Eighteenth Century: The Social Background to the Literary Revival* (Cambridge, 1965), 292.

The Desperate Mosaic

German reality, and the almost non-existent role of the emergent intelligentsia, and its ideas, in the prevailing political structures and processes, it is scarcely surprising that the constructs of thinkers and writers came more and more to be built as it were on stilts, at a deliberate remove from narrow, intractable reality.

The decisive figure here was Immanuel Kant (a man who himself moved from 'matter' to 'mind' in the sense that he taught physics and mathematics before he changed to philosophy). What could the mind know, and how could it know it securely? Kant posited on the one hand a realm of essential reality, of 'things in themselves', of which we can know nothing whatever. But the position is profoundly different with regard to the world of phenomena, of things as they *appear*. Kant's 'Copernican revolution', as he himself described it, was truly revolutionary. Just as Copernicus had shown that the apparent motion of the heavenly bodies was due to the motion of the beholder on his mobile planet, so Kant argued that the world as we know it, the world of appearances, is a function of our vantage point, and is constituted solely by the interaction of our senses and our intelligence: every feature of it, even its thereness in space and time, is ascribed to it by the mind.

The radical epistemology of this 'Transcendental Idealism' took the giant first step towards establishing the mind as the giver of meaning, as the creator in a certain sense of the knowable world— and it thereby prepared the ground for a whole plethora of systems, philosophies, and ideologies that set the human mind or spirit (*Geist*) ever more intensely at the centre of the universe. In terms of philosophy itself, there are the 'Absolute Idealist' systems of Fichte, Schelling, and, above all, Hegel. In the domain of art, there is the High Romanticism of Friedrich Schlegel and Novalis. And in the realm of the natural world, there is *Naturphilosophie*—which is what particularly concerns us in the context of Georg Büchner.

We can enter the fray at a conspicuously benign moment. It is 1794. Goethe and Schiller, these twin giants of Weimar Classicism, are gravely estranged, thanks largely to Goethe's conviction that they are at 'diametrically opposite poles', and separated by such an 'enormous gulf' that there can be 'no question' of their ever being reconciled (x. 540[35]). But they happen to find themselves emerging

---

[35] Volume and page numbers concerning Goethe refer to the 'Hamburg Edition', 14 vols., ed. Erich Trunz *et al.* (Hamburg, 1948–66).

together from a meeting of J. G. K. Batsch's 'naturforschende Gesellschaft' in Jena, and it is Schiller's criticism of the analytical, atomistic tone of this meeting that suddenly sparks their famous friendship. What Schiller objects to is the treatment of nature as so many separate fragments ('eine so zerstückelte Art die Natur zu behandeln', ibid.). Goethe agrees in deeply characteristic terms: instead of nature being regarded as an assemblage of separate bits and pieces, it can readily be shown to be vibrant and alive, carrying its wholeness through into all its parts ('nicht gesondert und vereinzelt . . . sondern . . . wirkend und lebendig, aus dem Ganzen in die Teile strebend', ibid.). What serves to unite these two diametrically different men, therefore, is a shared hostility to what they regard as an excessive and barren empiricism: a concentration on the part, on the particularity of discrete data, that forfeits all sense of the whole. Again there is the Coleridgean spectre of man's ordering mind being swamped by 'facts and phenomena'. This is why Goethe rejects Baconian science: it purports to collate the particular only in order to discern the universal ('Partikularien'/'Universalien'); but it loses itself so completely in individual data that life goes by and all energies are exhausted before any simple essence or any conclusion can be arrived at ('ehe man durch Induktion . . . zur Vereinfachung und zum Abschluß gelangen kann, geht das Leben weg und die Kräfte verzehren sich', xiv. 91). Goethe's crucial point, indeed one of his central articles of faith, is that the whole is always present within the part, and a single fact can therefore serve for thousands in that it contains their essence within itself, all being equally manifestations of the primordial type, the particular 'Urphänomen', that wholly informs them; to fail to grasp this, says Goethe, is to forgo all chance of a joyous or beneficial outcome ('Wer nicht gewahr werden kann, daß ein Fall oft tausende wert ist, und sie alle in sich schließt, wer nicht das zu fassen und zu ehren imstande ist, was wir Urphänomene genannt haben, der wird weder sich noch andern jemals etwas zur Freude und zum Nutzen fördern können.', xiv. 91–2).

In rejecting the Baconian absorption in empirical data, Goethe is by no means turning his back on reality. On the contrary, it is precisely his conviction that true reality is closed to Baconian (or Newtonian) empiricism, which forfeits any chance of seeing the wood through its exclusive concentration on the trees. It is only through a wholist approach, he believes, that one can apprehend reality. He insists on his 'obstinate realism' ('hartnäckigen Realismus', x. 541); and when he conjures up for Schiller his vision of nature as 'wirkend und lebendig, aus dem Ganzen in die Teile strebend', this is to him no abstraction, but something he sees and experiences with his own eye, as he might a table or a chair. Having meanwhile been carried by their conversation into Schiller's house, he not only *exposits* his notion of the metamorphosis of plants, but makes it palpable by actually drawing a 'symbolic plant' ('symbolische Pflanze', x. 540) for the other to physically see with his eyes. But this very nearly ends their friendship before it has begun, for it touches on that 'enormous gulf' that had always separated them: Schiller as a fully fledged Kantian ('ein gebildeter Kantianer', x. 541) cannot accept this assertion of experiential reality: ' "Das ist keine Erfahrung, das ist eine Idee." ' (x. 540; ' *That is not an experience, it is an idea.* ') This was Goethe's self-confessed and blessed 'naïvety': that his thoughts and ideas were literally, palpably visible to his eye (xiii. 26–7). We do not have to be learned Kantians to recognize that Schiller is of course quite right: what Goethe envisions is to his own eye a lived reality, but it nevertheless remains a product of his mind, an ideal—not an inherent and necessary quality of objective reality itself.

This begins to define the central thrust of that contentious but widespread and persistent mode of scientific enquiry that was German *Naturphilosophie*. In essence, and at its best, it was an attempt to syncretize the epoch's two antithetical attitudes of Empiricism and Idealism in order to establish a middle ground in which mind and matter, instead of dominating and diminishing each other, came fully into their own in a kind of rich interplay. In its fundamental wholist tenets it is unquestionably idealist, even metaphysical. As T. J. Reed remarks in his 'Past Masters' book on Goethe: 'The—in some sense—divine ground and wholeness of the world are presupposed, and to that extent Goethe is a metaphysician.'[36] And Strohl has declared that mysticism is plainly the departure point of Lorenz Oken's wholist aspirations in his textbooks of *Naturphilosophie* (*Übersicht des Grundrisses des Systems der Naturphilosophie*, 1802; *Grundriß des Systems der Naturphilosophie*, 1804).[37] But far from rejecting reality and resorting to the pure abstractions and

[36] T. J. Reed, *Goethe* (Oxford, 1984), 47.   [37] Strohl, 12.

fantasies of the Idealist philosophers and the High Romantics, the *Naturphilosophen* used their idealist-metaphysical-mystical postulates as a vantage point from which to comprehend the real workings of the real natural world, to descry imaginatively but also precisely and specifically the order within the otherwise unmanageable chaos of data. Throughout all his scientific-philosophical speculations, Goethe never strayed from detailed and painstaking experimentation and analysis of specimens; Oken published no fewer than thirteen volumes of 'straight' experimental, descriptive 'Naturgeschichte' ('natural history'). But their approach in their laborious experimentation was always deductive and integrative, never inductive and atomistic: whereas the Baconian starts with the part (and in the view of the *Naturphilosophen* can never get beyond it), they begin with the whole—which indeed they believe to be always immanent in every least particle.[38]

By the time it came to Georg Büchner's brief spell in the realm of the sciences in the mid-30s, *Naturphilosophie*, though still predominant, was under severe threat, for the parallel and alternative mode of empiricism was rapidly moving towards that position of supremacy that it still holds to this day (the great dispute between Cuvier and Saint-Hilaire referred to in note 38 is one milestone in this momentous struggle for ascendancy). In the process of the gradual discrediting of *Naturphilosophie*, it attracted much disparagement and even ridicule. This is partly because of the hyperbolization in both expression and conviction that the battle of attitudes forced on its participants. It was engagingly symbolized on the occasion of Oken's Inaugural Lecture at Jena in 1807, a sensational and polemical affair in which Oken felt driven to the climactic and preposterous assertion: 'Der ganze Mensch ist nur ein Wirbelbein.' (*The entire human being is but a vertebra.*)[39]—a dictum that instantly spawned a derisive greeting among the local wags: 'Guten Tag, Herr Wirbelbein!'[40] The polemical intensity of the battle can be readily gauged from the scathing—and no less hyperbolic—tone of Justus von Liebig, the great chemist, who in 1840 attacked the *Naturphilo-*

---

[38] These contrary scientific positions are precisely epitomized by Goethe when he summarizes the attitudes of Cuvier and Saint-Hilaire, the two disputants in the great debate of 1830 in the Paris Academy of Sciences: xiii. 220.

[39] Strohl, 11.

[40] Cf. H. Bräuning-Oktavio, *Oken und Goethe im Lichte neuer Quellen* (Weimar, 1959), 49.

sophen and their doings as 'the pestilence, the Black Death, of the nineteenth century'.[41] Much later Liebig pronounced on *Naturphilosophie* in more moderate, but more devastating terms: 'We look back on German *Naturphilosophie* as though on a dead tree that bore the most beautiful foliage and the most magnificent flowers—but no fruit.'[42] It is no doubt true that some of the extravagances of *Naturphilosophie* were 'fantastic to the verge of insanity'.[43] And one of its most radical exponents was J. B. Wilbrand, professor of Comparative Anatomy, Physiology, and Natural History at Giessen from 1809—and the young Liebig's particular *bête noire* from the moment in 1824 that he took up his own chair in Giessen, where both men were still very active in their antagonistic camps when Büchner arrived to continue his studies in 1833.[44]

It is easy to mock at the excesses of *Naturphilosophie*: at Wilbrand's dogged and absolute denial of the circulation of the blood, and likewise of the interchange of oxygen and carbon dioxide in respiration; at his treatise succinctly entitled 'On the Connection between Nature and the Supernatural, and How a Thorough Study of Nature and its Phenomena Points Ineluctably to the Continuance of Spiritual Life after Death'; at the belief of Oken and others that light is the consciousness of God, ether his self-positing activity, and objects his concretized thoughts; at Goethe's repudiation of Newton's theory of light. For one thing, however, we might bear in mind that Liebig himself, the great empiricist, was trained by *Naturphilosophen*, remained a Vitalist throughout his life, and underpinned the physical with the metaphysical in the motto inscribed over his laboratory: 'God has ordained all things by measure, number, and weight'. It is as easy and convenient for us as it was for the protagonists in the polemic to distinguish categorically between sheep and goats, to see deductivists and speculative idealists on the one hand, and inductivists and rigorous empiricists on the other. In reality, as

---

[41] Cited by Walter Müller-Seidel, 'Natur und Naturwissenschaft im Werk Georg Büchners', in E. Catholy and W. Hellmann (eds.), *Festschrift für Klaus Ziegler* (Tübingen, 1968), 207.
[42] Cited by Raimar St. Zons, *Georg Büchner. Dialektik der Grenze* (Bonn, 1976), 61.
[43] Charles Singer, *A Short History of Scientific Ideas to 1900* (Oxford, 1960), 385.
[44] It has long been customary in Büchner criticism to speak disparagingly—if at all—of Wilbrand. For a long-overdue reappraisal, see Christian Maass, 'Georg Büchner und Johann Bernhard Wilbrand. Medizin in Gießen um 1833/44', in Anon. (ed.), *Georg Büchner 1813–1837*, 148–54.

Popper and Medawar have persuasively argued, there are not two distinct camps in science, but a continuous spectrum linking the opposite and equally unfruitful extremes of 'an inventory of factual information' and 'a totalitarian world picture of natural laws'[45]— with all significant advances in science being made in that mid-range of the spectrum that involves the most fruitful interaction between speculative, imaginative intuition, and careful empirical testing. At its zaniest, *Naturphilosophie* did veer towards a ludicrously absolute and unproductive extreme. Even in its normal, median condition as a classical mode of scientific enquiry enshrined in all the universities of the land, its subordination of experiment to a priori ideology ensured that it could not survive against the professional scepticism, the questioning subjection of hypotheses to experimental testing, that increasingly became the hallmark of nineteenth-century science.[46] Nevertheless, *Naturphilosophie* did make a very real contribution to the development of science, both in the general and in the particular: it considerably extended the realm of the thinkable; and it either made, or provided the stimulus for, a whole range of specific discoveries. As to the general: its dare-to-speculate mentality greatly furthered science in its quantum leap from the physics-derived fixed-mechanism model of the world in the eighteenth century, to the transformational, evolutionary model so characteristic of the nineteenth. The out-and-out empiricists found this imaginative leap very difficult to make. Cuvier, for instance, clung tenaciously to his view of the biological realm as fixed and unalterable; faced with the fossil data produced by the revolutionary new science of palaeontology, his now comical explanation was that the world must have experienced a succession of great catastrophes, the last being the Flood, and the devastated areas had then been repopulated each time from parts of the globe as yet unknown to science. At the level of specifics: Oken with his doctrine of primordial 'sacs' ('Bläschen') paved the way for cell biology; Johannes Müller made great advances in physiology and embryology; Carus helped significantly to open up the new discipline of gynaecology; Schelling's principle

---

[45] Medawar, 59.
[46] The corrective or normative effect of internationalism is highly important here: German political, social and economic structures, and German philosophy and literature, developed in their own relatively isolated and idiosyncratic way in the 19th c.; but science increasingly transcended national frontiers, and the history of German science in the period is in a sense a history of accelerating internationalism.

of polarity led Schönbein to discover ozone, and considerably influenced Berzelius and Volta; Goethe's stress on comparative anatomy and 'morphology' (a word that he himself coined), as distinct from straight anatomy on the one hand, and Linnaean comparing of external characteristics on the other hand, was an important stimulus in the development of evolutionary theory.[47]

This, then, is the kind of context within which Büchner and his science-cum-philosophy belong, and within which we need to try to locate and understand him. Its most crucial characteristic is its 'continuous spectrum' quality: Büchner criticism has been—and continues to be—bedevilled and distorted by that inveterate tendency to polarization that sees only separate, mutually exclusive camps of empiricists-materialists-realists, and speculative idealists. Such a tidy dichotomy may conceivably be relevant to the realms of abstract philosophy and literary fantasizing, both of which offered an alluring refuge from reality during this period; but it is mischievously irrelevant to the realm of scientific enquiry—and hence also to the writing of Georg Büchner. For the beliefs and practices that inform his science equally inform his art. Not only in the commonplace sense that the laboratory dissector is also the literary dissector, but in the much more important sense that there is in both a profound and essential interaction of the Real and the Ideal. For the devotees of polarization, it has to be either/or, and what they inevitably do is to hustle Büchner into the empiricist-materialist camp, which is of course by definition anti-idealist. This is a tendentious travesty, whether in the crass form exemplified by Walter Müller-Seidel with his depiction of Büchner as wholly anti-idealist and wholly 'scientific',[48] or in the subtle form proffered by Raimar Zons with his claim that Büchner held to the notions of *Naturphilosophie*—but only as an expedient heuristic category, not a set of beliefs; only as a 'methodological postulate', a kind of handy toolkit to help him deal with the world.[49]

---

[47] Cf. Strohl, 28 ff.; Singer, 384 ff.
[48] Müller-Seidel, 210 and *passim*. Müller-Seidel has his wires crossed throughout his confused and question-begging essay, not least in his claim that Büchner is a cynical and fatalistic Schopenhauerian, but above all in his assertion that the approach that this entails reflects the general mood and practice of modern science as it was then evolving. The screams of anguish in Georg Büchner's works are those of a passionate, wounded idealist, not a cool, enquiring empiricist.
[49] Zons, 69 ff. Cf. also T. M. Mayer, 'Büchner-Chronik', 419.

This surely is the crux, the teasing but critical question that every serious student of Büchner has to confront. Do we credit the radiantly positive vision—Goethean and *naturphilosophisch* in its essence—that he voices in the preamble to the Trial Lecture? Do we believe that he believed in a primal law of beauty, in simplicity as the fount of rich complexity, in pure harmony as the necessary outcome of the primal law throughout the natural world? Or do we decide that the vision is uncharacteristic and illusory—a strategem perhaps, a piece of ritual rhetoric, a contrived nostrum, an act of calculated ingratiation, an inexplicable and dismissible aberration? Both alternatives are problematic. To take the latter is generally to find oneself in a familiar logical bind: Büchner is a fearless speaker of unidealized truth, therefore it cannot be the truth when he speaks of ideals. To prefer the other alternative is to collide at once with the fact that harmonious beauty and rich simplicity are scarcely the most resonant message of his poetic work. Nevertheless I believe this alternative to be incontrovertibly the right one: Büchner did mean every warm and positive word of his preamble; and so completely was he blessed and cursed by an inherited sense of natural harmony that even the slightest discord, the slightest departure from received pitch, was for him an agony. His misfortune—and in consequence our delight—is that he happened, like Hoffmann's Ritter Gluck, to be a man of richest harmonies in a world increasingly dominated by scratchers and scrapers and mechanical contraptions grinding out the same old cracked, broken, excruciating tunes.

Fanciful language, perhaps? But it echoes Büchner's own, in a memorable letter to his beloved Minna Jaeglé in March 1834 (ii. 424). Even the reference to Hoffmann is there (though not specifically to *Ritter Gluck*): 'Ich hätte Herrn Callot-Hoffmann sitzen können, nicht wahr' (*I could have sat* [as a model] *for Herr Callot-Hoffmann, couldn't I*).[50] So, too, is the strident duality of natural harmony and desperate mechanical grinding. He has just been outside in the open, he writes: 'Ein einziger, forthallender Ton aus tausend Lerchenkehlen schlägt durch die brütende Sommerluft, ein schweres Gewölk wandelt über die Erde, der tiefbrausende Wind klingt wie sein melodischer Schritt.' (*A single resonant tone from the throats of a thousand larks bursts through the brooding summer air,*

---

[50] The 'Callot' is an allusion to Hoffmann's *Fantasiestücke in Callots Manier* (of which 'Ritter Gluck' happens to be the first).

a heavy bank of cloud wanders over the earth, the booming wind rings out like its melodious tread.) This is his vibrant, melodious present. But until the outside air served to free him and give him life again, he had been long transfixed by a kind of rigor ('Starrkrampf'), by a sense of being already dead ('Gefühl des Gestorbenseins'), so that he and all around him seemed like deathly puppets with glassy eyes and waxen cheeks. And at this point Büchner suddenly launches into a characteristically thrilling cadenza of despair (one wonders what poor Minna made of it all):

> und wenn dann die ganze Maschinerie zu leiern anfing, die Gelenke zuckten, die Stimme herausknarrte und ich das ewige Orgellied herumtrillern hörte und die Wälzchen und Stiftchen im Orgelkasten hüpfen und drehen sah,—ich verfluchte das Concert, den Kasten, die Melodie und—ach, wir armen schreienden Musikanten, das Stöhnen auf unsrer Folter, wäre es nur da, damit es durch die Wolkenritzen dringend und weiter, weiter klingend, wie ein melodischer Hauch in himmlischen Ohren stirbt? Wären wir das Opfer im glühenden Bauch des Peryllusstiers, dessen Todesschrei wie das Aufjauchzen des in den Flammen sich aufzehrenden Gottstiers klingt?

> and then, when the whole machinery began to grind away, with jerking limbs and grating voice, and I heard the same old barrel-organ tune go tralala and saw the tiny prongs and cylinders bob and whirr in the organ box—I cursed the concert, the box, the melody—oh, poor, screaming musicians that we are—could it be that our cries of agony on the rack only exist to ring out through cracks between the clouds and, echoing on and on, die like a melodious breath in heavenly ears? Could it be that we are the victims roasted in the belly of Perillus' bull, whose screams as they die ring out like the jubilant roars of the bull-god as it is devoured by the flames?

An unnerving antiphon: in nature—the wind and the larks and their liberating melody; among men—a deathly mechanical rasping, and tortured screams extracted perhaps by some distant deity for his melodious titillation. And it is precisely this drastic antiphon that Büchner uses nine months later to ring in the crescendo marking the grand-opera climax of *Dantons Tod*:

> PHILIPPEAU. Meine Freunde man braucht gerade nicht hoch über der Erde zu stehen um von all dem wirren Schwanken und Flimmern nichts mehr zu sehen und die Augen von einigen großen, göttlichen Linien erfüllt zu haben. Es giebt ein Ohr für welches das Ineinanderschreien und der Zeter, die uns betäuben, ein Strom von Harmonien sind.

DANTON. Aber wir sind die armen Musicanten und unsere Körper die Instrumente. Sind die häßlichen Töne, welche auf ihnen herausgepfuscht werden nur da um höher und höher dringend und endlich leise verhallend wie ein wollüstiger Hauch in himmlischen Ohren zu sterben? (etc.; 71)

PHILIPPEAU. My friends, one doesn't have to stand very far above the earth to see no trace any more of all this shifting, shimmering chaos, and to behold instead a simple, great and godly outline. There is an ear for which the cacophony and clamour, so deafening to us, are a stream of harmonies.

DANTON. But we are the poor musicians and our bodies the instruments. Are the ugly, vamping sounds bashed out on them just there to rise up higher and higher and gently fade and die like some voluptuous puff of breath in heavenly ears?

It would be easy to conclude—as innumerable critics have done—that Philippeau is simply a stooge, a foil of fatuous optimism serving to silhouette the 'true' negativity in the ensuing chorus of grandiloquent despair. But this would be quite wrong. For one thing—as I shall argue in due course—the chorus of despair is itself a desperate illusion. More to the point here: Philippeau's 'stream of harmonies' is profoundly real to Büchner. When he heard its melody among the wind and the larks in Giessen, it brought him back from figurative death (thus inaugurating a central topos of death and resurrection that runs throughout his work). And it is, above all, the measure that makes the sounds given out by the human 'instrument' seem by contrast so ugly, so raspingly mechanical.

The essential question is *why*, for Büchner, men have become so drastically, so agonizingly out of tune, so remote from the 'stream of harmonies', from that 'necessary harmony' that the primal law of beauty bestows so readily upon the rest of nature.

2
A Rearguard Action

AT one point in his essay on Georg Büchner, Walter Müller-Seidel tells us that Danton recognizes the 'fatalism of history' (an axiomatic notion for Büchner, so Müller-Seidel inevitably supposes); and he then continues: 'But this very insight into the deterministic nature of things is itself the first step on the road to holding one's own against history. *It is thought and cognition [Denken und Erkennen] that make this possible.*'[1] This is a monumental misconception that turns Büchner on his head. Let us suppose a contrary state of affairs. Let us suppose that, for Büchner, there is no fatalism in history; that there is no determinism operating upon mankind; and that the workings of the mind, far from being man's salvation, are the very agent of his misfortune, the fundamental cause of his alienation from the unfailingly harmonious and beautiful processes that define the natural world in its entirety. On the face of it, this is a ludicrous proposition. One only has to think of Büchner's most notorious, most commonly quoted pronouncement (in a letter to Minna Jaeglé only days after the one cited in the previous chapter): his sense of being annihilated by 'dem gräßlichen Fatalismus der Geschichte' (*the hideous fatalism of history*); his vision of life as a ridiculous struggle against an iron law, to control which, he declares, is impossible: insight into its reality is the most we can aspire to ('ein lächerliches Ringen gegen ein ehernes Gesetz, es zu erkennen das Höchste, es zu beherrschen unmöglich', ii. 425–6). But it is a common and crude mistake to abstract this all too famous 'fatalism' passage from its living context and, taking it at face value, to turn it into a considered and definitive philosophical statement. On the contrary, it is the sonorous trumpeting of a transient mood—'Katzenmusik', as Thomas Michael Mayer has aptly called it.[2] And its words are startlingly belied by deeds: at the very time that he wrote

---

[1] 'Aber schon die Einsicht in die Determiniertheit ist ein erster Schritt auf dem Wege, sich [der Geschichte] gegenüber zu behaupten. *Die Möglichkeit liegt im Denken und Erkennen.*'; Müller-Seidel, 224 (emphasis added).
[2] T. M. Mayer, 'Büchner-Chronik', 374.

this letter, Büchner—far from resigning himself to the passive contemplation of a deterministic iron law—was busy founding his revolutionary activist cell, the 'Gesellschaft der Menschenrechte', and within a week he had also started work on his call to action, *Der Hessische Landbote*.[3] Given the ebb and flow of feelings, the 'Schweben und Senken im menschlichen Gemüth' (37), to which Büchner—like anyone else—was prone, he certainly had his moments of doubt and bleak despair. But he was wholly, extravagantly positive and harmonistic in his fundamental assumptions. And what matters particularly to us at this stage: in his analysis of the causes of dissonance and discord in the human sphere, it was indeed the *mind* that he saw as the constant culprit.

It is yet another paradox that this heir of the Enlightenment, this dedicated scientific enquirer, this voracious intellectual, this budding academic who had wanted above all to lecture at Zurich on philosophy, was deeply scornful of human reason, and particularly of its manifestations in rationalist philosophy. In his letters he speaks of 'die Verirrungen eines durch philosophische Sophismen falsch geleiteten Geistes' (ii. 451; *the aberrations of a mind misled by philosophical sophisms*); he disparages the language of philosophy as 'artificial' and 'odious' ('abscheulich'), and adds: 'ich meine für menschliche Dinge müsse man auch menschliche Ausdrücke finden' (ii. 421; *for things human, I believe, one must also find human expressions*); his study of philosophy, he tells Gutzkow, gives him fresh insight into the poverty of the human mind ('die Armseligkeit des menschlichen Geistes', ii. 450); 'Der *Verstand*', he assures his family, 'ist nur eine sehr geringe Seite unseres geistigen Wesens' (ii. 422; *the* intellect *is only a very minor aspect of our mental [or: spiritual] being*). In the preamble to the Trial Lecture he is cuttingly dismissive when he refers to 'dem Dogmatismus der Vernunftphilosophen' (ii. 292; *the dogmatism of rationalist philosophers*), and declares:

Daß es bis jetzt gelungen sei, zwischen letzterem und dem Naturleben, das wir unmittelbar wahrnehmen, eine Brücke zu schlagen, muß die Kritik

---

[3] This is the chronology proposed by Thomas Michael Mayer, who suggests that the letter was written between 9 and 12 Mar. 1834, or possibly a little later (loc. cit.). More recently, Jan-Christoph Hauschild has plausibly argued that the letter was written as much as two months earlier, viz. between 10 and 20 Jan. 1834: Hauschild, 'Neudatierung und Neubewertung von Georg Büchners "Fatalismusbrief" ', *Zeitschrift für deutsche Philologie*, 108 (1989), 526.

verneinen. Die Philosophie a priori sitzt noch in einer trostlosen Wüste; sie hat einen weiten Weg zwischen sich und dem frischen grünen Leben, und es ist eine große Frage, ob sie ihn je zurücklegen wird. (ii. 292–3)

It cannot be denied that no one has so far managed to bridge the gulf between the latter, and the living nature that we directly apprehend. A priori philosophy still finds itself in a hopeless desert; a long road separates it from fresh, exuberant life, and it is highly questionable whether it will ever manage to make the journey.

Büchner then rounds off the paragraph with the sardonic observation that, for all its immensely clever attempts to make some progress along the road from 'desert' to 'life', rationalist philosophy will have to resign itself to striving for striving's sake—for its goal will ever be beyond its reach.

It is a mark of Büchner's practice in his poetic writing that parenthetic, seemingly digressive and superfluous episodes tend to be particularly highly charged (the Marion sequence, Camille Desmoulins's divagation on the theatre etc., Lenz's on art and literature, are three such examples). The same principle applies here, too. The paragraph that contains Büchner's laconic dismissal of rationalist philosophy is a sheer parenthesis, indeed it somewhat disrupts his general run of argument; but it serves not only to demonstrate the fervour of his conviction by the very fact of its intrusion, but also to intimate what lies at the heart of those convictions. Why is rationalist philosophy hopelessly arid and remote in Büchner's eyes? Because it bears no relationship to the prime and absolute datum that is Life, that natural and exuberant vitality that we perceive directly, without any mediation through the mind ('dem Naturleben, das wir unmittelbar wahrnehmen'). Like Goethe in his antithesis to Schiller the Complete Kantian, Büchner, too, insists on a kind of 'obstinate realism': he sees essential life as 'Erfahrung', not 'Idee'; as immediate lived experience, not a notion of the mind.

It is precisely this standpoint that forms the basis of Büchner's critique of Descartes and his rationalist 'battlecry' ('Feldgeschrei', ii. 140) of *cogito ergo sum*. In a remarkably revealing passage in *Cartesius* (his long and complex commentary on Cartesian philosophy), he distinguishes categorically between 'Seyn' and 'Denken', between 'being' and 'thinking'. What matters is our Being: thought is merely a 'secondary affair'. The defining characteristic of Being is its immediacy: Büchner repeatedly uses the word 'unmittelbar' (already familiar to us from the Trial Lecture passage). Our Being affords us 'immediate' (or 'unmediated') truths and knowledge; it affords us a spontaneous, natural 'awareness that the self exists'. This primary realm of Being is not only *independent* of rationalistic thought processes, it is—in Büchner's radical view—quite *inaccessible* to it.[4] The relevant passage is full of that 'artificial language' ('Kunstsprache') that Büchner abhorred in philosophy, but it is so fundamentally important, and so rarely (if ever) adduced by critics, that it needs to be quoted at some length:

Der Grundcharakter aller unmittelbaren Wahrheit ist das Poniren, das Affirmiren schlechthin, durch das secundäre Geschäft des Denkens gar nicht vermittelt, wesentlich nicht einmal berührt. Die Existenz seiner und der Dinge außer uns wird auf rein positive, unmittelbare, von der Function des Denkens unabhängige Weise erkannt. Man fragt: ist das philosophirende Subject? Nach Cartesius sagt man: es kann nicht denken, wenn es nicht ist, also ist es; nach dem unmittelbaren Wissen ist es, bevor es philosophirt d. h. es ist positiv dem Bewußtseyn gegeben, daß das Ich ist und dießes Seyn ist dem Denken unzugänglich, es kann gar nicht zu der positiven Bejahung desselben gelangen. (ii. 140)

The basic characteristic of all unmediated truth is postulation and affirmation pure and simple, without its being mediated in any way, or even touched in any essential respect, by the secondary activity of thought. Our own existence and that of things outside us is apprehended in a purely positive, immediate way, independently of the function of thought. The question arises: does the philosophizing self exist? In Descartes's terms, he cannot think if he does not exist, therefore he exists; in terms of unmediated knowledge, he exists before he philosophises, i.e. it is positively vouchsafed to our consciousness that the self exists, and this being is inaccessible to thought, indeed the latter can attain to no positive affirmation of it whatsoever.

Büchner—so often billed as the supreme negativist—lays extraordinary stress here on 'positing' and the 'positive': 'Poniren', 'Affirmiren', three times the word 'positiv'. Half a page later he stresses this again—and specifically attacks the *negativity* of Descartes:

Es wird nach Cartesius also nur erkannt, daß es unmöglich zu denken sey, der Denkende sey nicht. Dieß ist etwas bloß Negatives und der Grundcha-

---

[4] Cf. ii. 179–80, where Büchner notes the inability of Descartes's system to resolve the problem of the relationship between body and mind, between being and thinking: 'er [begegnete] zu großen Schwierigkeiten, das Verhältniß zwischen Körper und Geist, zwischen Seyn und Denken mit seinem System in Einklang zu bringen'.

rakter aller unmittelbaren Wahrheit ist, wie schon gesagt, das Positive, das Poniren, das Affirmiren schlechthin. (ii. 141)

All that may be known, according to Descartes, is that it is impossible to think that a thinking mind does not exist. This is wholly negative and, as already said, the basic characteristic of all unmediated truth is the positive, positing [or: postulation], affirmation pure and simple.

Given the primacy of this positive, unmediated, authentic Being, and its absolute inaccessibility to ratiocination, the entire edifice of Cartesian rationalism appears suddenly false, its pretensions hollow—the pretension, above all, that logical thought is the only path that can carry us to truth: 'Die der Cartesianischen Philosophie zu Grund liegende Ansicht, daß man durch Demonstration allein zu Allem gelangen könnte' (ii. 213). This pretension finds its apotheosis in Spinoza, for whom, as Büchner tells us in his commentary on the post-Cartesian, 'die Vernunft (*intellectus*) unser höchstes Gut ist' (ii. 268; *the intellect is our supreme possession*). Spinoza even outdoes his master ('ja er ist kühner als Cartesius', ii. 269), for he extends the prerogative of demonstrative logic even further, and asserts that 'the demonstrative intellect is everything, and is equal to everything' ('der demonstrirende Verstand ist Alles und ist Allem gewachsen', ii. 269); for Büchner, however, Spinoza's 'intellectual knowledge' ('intellektuale Erkenntniß', ii. 268) can know nothing whatsoever of our true existence, which is apprehensible only by our *intuitive* knowledge (cf. ii. 276: 'intuitive Erkenntniß'). Rationalism is accordingly a set of sheer fictions constructed by, and in, the logical mind, and separated by an unbridged and probably unbridgeable gulf from the authentic living reality of our immediate intuition, the 'Naturleben, das wir unmittelbar wahrnehmen'.[5]

That is already damning enough. But Büchner also suggests that rationalist logic is incapable even of dealing adequately with those philosophical abysses over which it proves to be entirely constructed. This applies especially to the key elements in both Spinoza and Descartes: their supposed proofs of God. What does Spinoza do (ii. 239–40)? He painstakingly argues a case for an eternal and

---

[5] Büchner was of course far from alone in the post-Enlightenment period in adopting such a position. E. T. A. Hoffmann is a classic case in point, as when he speaks in *Prinzessin Brambilla* of 'the unmediated intuition of all existence' ('die unmittelbare Anschauung alles Seins'), and of intuition being destroyed by thought ('Der Gedanke zerstört die Anschauung'); E. T. A. Hoffmann, *Späte Werke* (Munich, [1965]), 251, 257.

infinite 'Substanz' (*substance* or *essence*)—a 'Substanz', however, that is not God, but something that even any straight-thinking atheist must readily acknowledge ('sie ist nicht Gott... —sie ist nichts anders, als was jeder Atheist selbst, wenn er einigermaßen consequent verfahren will, anerkennen muß'). But then Spinoza quite suddenly introduces God into his argument like a rabbit out of a hat; and in arbitrarily deifying the self-containing and all-encompassing essence, so Büchner declares, he is no longer acting as a philosopher ('Hier hört der Philosoph auf und er vergöttert willkührlich das, was in sich und worin Alles ist.') However hard he tried, we are told later (ii. 287), Spinoza never managed to bridge the 'gulf' that yawns between the finite and the infinite (a gulf terrifyingly familiar to the Hauptmann in *Woyzeck* as he spread-eagles himself between moment and eternity, 'Augenblick' and 'Ewigkeit', 171).

In the case of Descartes, Büchner's critique is especially mordant. The Cartesian God, he declares, is a purely expedient mechanism, a dubious *ad rem* device conjured up to fill the void; to bridge the abyss; to serve as a ladder of escape from the 'grave of philosophy':

Gott ist es, der den Abgrund zwischen Denken und Erkennen, zwischen Subject und Object ausfüllt, er ist die Brücke zwischen dem *cogito ergo sum*, zwischen dem einsamen, irren, nur einem, dem Selbstbewußtseyn, gewissen, Denken und der Außenwelt. Der Versuch ist etwas naiv ausgefallen, aber man sieht doch, wie instinctartig scharf schon Cartesius das Grab der Philosophie abmaß; sonderbar ist es freilich wie er den lieben Gott als Leiter gebrauchte, um herauszukriechen. (ii. 153)

It is God that fills the abyss between thinking and knowing, between subject and object, he is the bridge between the *cogito ergo sum*, the lonely, lost mind certain only of its self-awareness, and the external world. The attempt turned out to be a little naïve, but nevertheless one can see with what instinctive precision Descartes measured out the grave of philosophy; what is certainly peculiar is the way he used God as a ladder to crawl out of it again.

God as a 'void-filler', a 'bridge', a 'ladder': Büchner in due course adds a further image: God as a 'lifeline'. In the process he makes it clear that Descartes's God is in his view not merely an incidental expedient, but a desperate last resort: his sole means of clambering out of the 'abyss of doubt', and the slender thread withal upon which the entire system of his thought depends: 'Es blieb ihm also um sich aus dem Abgrund seines Zweifels zu retten nur ein Strick, an den er sein ganzes System hängte und hakte, *Gott.*' (ii. 155).

Quite apart from the arbitrariness and expediency of the Cartesian and Spinozan God, the fundamental flaw for Büchner is that it is a mere intellectual construct, quite remote from our immediate and real experience as human beings. This is made especially clear in the only passage in the philosophical commentaries that is at all well known (ii. 236–7). Büchner begins by citing Spinoza's proposition that God exists necessarily, together with the particular proof that Spinoza appends to it: 'Ist proof. Let whosoever denies [the proposition] understand, if that be possible, how God cannot exist. In that case His being does not entail existence, which is nonsensical.' Büchner's response is characteristic: the logic may be compelling, but what compels us to accept the logic?

Dießer Beweis läuft ziemlich auf den hinaus, daß Gott nicht anders als seyend gedacht werden könnte. Was zwingt uns aber ein Wesen zu denken, was nicht anders als seyend gedacht werden kann?[6] Wir sind durch die Lehre von dem, was in sich oder in etwas Anderm ist freilich gezwungen auf etwas zu kommen, was nicht anders als seyend gedacht werden kann; was berechtigt uns aber deßwegen aus dießem Wesen das absolut Vollkommne, Gott, zu machen?
Wenn man auf die Definition von Gott eingeht, so muß man auch das Daseyn Gottes zugeben. Was berechtigt uns aber, dieße Definition zu machen?
Der *Verstand?*
Er kennt das Unvollkommne.
Das *Gefühl?*
Es kennt den Schmerz.

This proof is much the same as that which says that God can only be thought as existing. But what compels us to think a being that can only be thought as existing?[6] It is true that the doctrine of 'that which is in itself or in something else' forces us to arrive at something that can only be thought as existing; but what justifies us in therefore turning this being into absolute perfectness, i.e. God?
If one accedes to the definition of God, then one must also concede the existence of God. But what justifies us in making this definition?
The *mind* ?

---

[6] Cf. also *Cartesius,* ii. 144: 'freilich muß ich, sobald ich Gott setze auch das Seyn desselben setzen, aber was zwingt mich denn Gott überhaupt zu setzen?' (*once I posit God I must of course also posit his existence, but what compels me to posit God in the first place?*)

It knows unperfectness.
The *emotions*?
They know pain.

But why should any of this matter? Why can't Cartesian rationalism simply be left to its own specious, gratuitous devices in its remote wasteland? Here lies the crucial problem for Büchner: however hopelessly remote systematic rationalism may be from that throbbing, vibrant reality that we directly perceive all around us ('dem Naturleben, das wir unmittelbar wahrnehmen'), its false constructs—and others of the same ilk—are threatening to prevail: they are threatening to condition, and thereby to distort, our perception of the world. This becomes particularly clear in Büchner's own field of biology. Under the deadening hand of Descartes, with his mechanistic logic of mathematics and physics, the living body is reduced to a mere machine held together by nuts and bolts: 'der *homme machine* wird vollständig zusammengeschraubt'; in Descartes's *De homine*, his treatise on physiology, the vital organs are all represented as so many mechanical bits and pieces, as 'bolts, prongs, and cylinders' ('Schrauben, Stifte und Walzen'; ii. 179)—language that clearly echoes the 'melodious nature/rasping barrel-organ' letter to Minna with its vision of human beings as a 'Maschinerie' full of 'Wälzchen und Stiftchen'.

This at once brings us back to the Trial Lecture. For in it Büchner attacks rationalism not only in its 'pure' sense as a (dogmatic, arid, and remote) philosophy, but equally in its 'applied' sense as a (grossly reductive) mode of approach to the problems presented by the natural world (ii. 291f.). In the very first sentence of the Trial Lecture, Büchner identifies two 'antithetical basic viewpoints' ('zwei sich gegenüberstehende Grundansichten') within contemporary physiology and anatomy. And part of his critique of the viewpoint that he opposes is in effect identical to his critique of *De homine*; even the essential vocabulary is the same: he says of the opposing scientific camp, as he said of Descartes, that it sees the living organism as a 'Maschine' (*machine*), as 'künstlich' (*artificial*), as an assemblage of mechanical 'Apparate' (*apparatuses*).[7] The relevant passage is illuminating indeed, for it documents not only the mech-

---

[7] Cf. Goethe who, in his commentary on the Cuvier–Saint-Hilaire dispute of 1830, objected to the living world being seen in terms of 'mechanischer, materieller, atomistischer Ausdrücke' (xiii. 246; *mechanical, material, atomistic expressions*).

A Rearguard Action

anistic Cartesian approach—but equally the contrasting metaphysical and mystical approach that is Büchner's own. In the face of this astonishingly revealing exposé, it is difficult to see how anyone could seriously seek to detach Büchner from the *Naturphilosophie* tradition, and locate him instead in the camp of materialist science:

> Jeder Organismus ist für sie eine verwickelte Maschine, mit den künstlichen Mitteln versehen, sich bis auf einen gewissen Punkt zu erhalten. Das *Enthüllen der schönsten und reinsten Formen im Menschen*, die *Vollkommenheit* der *edelsten* Organe, in denen *die Psyche fast den Stoff zu durchbrechen und sich hinter den leichtesten Schleiern zu bewegen scheint*, ist für sie nur das Maximum einer solchen Maschine. Sie macht den Schädel zu einem künstlichen Gewölbe mit Strebepfeilern, bestimmt, seinen Bewohner, das Gehirn, zu schützen,—Wangen und Lippen zu einem Kau- und Respirationsapparat,—das Auge zu einem complicirten Glase,—die Augenlider und Wimpern zu dessen Vorhängen;—ja die Thräne ist nur der Wassertropfen, welcher es feucht erhält. Man sieht, es ist ein weiter Sprung von da bis zu dem *Enthusiasmus*, mit dem *Lavater* sich glücklich preist, daß er von so was *Göttlichem*, wie den Lippen, reden dürfe. [my emphasis, except 'Lavater']

> For the proponents of this view, every organism is a complex machine, provided with functional devices enabling it to survive over a certain span of time. The *revealing in mankind of the purest and most beautiful forms of nature*, the *perfectness* of the *noblest* organs, in which *the spirit almost seems to break through the barrier of matter, to be actively present beyond the slenderest of veils*, these things are to them merely the optimal attributes of such a machine. They turn the skull into an artificial vault-like structure equipped with buttresses, dedicated to protecting its occupant, the brain; cheeks and lips become an apparatus for chewing and breathing; the eye becomes a complex lens; eyelids and eyelashes become its curtains; even our tears become simply the water-droplets that keep it moist. It is clearly a far cry from that to the *enthusiasm* with which *Lavater* praises his good fortune in being able to speak of something so *divine* as the lips. [my emphasis, except 'Lavater']

This is winsome prose. We are readily seduced by Büchner's putdown of reductivist science; by his lyrical vision of the spirit dancing behind diaphanous veils; by his idealist belief in the absolute purity and beauty of forms in the supreme species of man, and in the perfection of man's noblest organs; by his final, climactic stress on the godlike nature of the body, and on enthusiasm (in the contemporary sense of 'enspiritedness', of being 'possessed by a sense of the divine'). We should not be seduced too far, however; neither by the affective language, nor by our received and almost subliminal tendency to regard Georg Büchner as a radical progressive in all imaginable respects. For nothing demonstrates more surely than do these few lines how gravely and fundamentally Büchner was behind the times. He was wholly if nobly backward-looking in his reliance on idealist, poetical, mystical notions, in his enlistment of Lavater, an eighteenth-century irrationalist and mystical pantheist. This is a lecture on cranial nerves, by an aspiring scientist, in the year 1836. But European science, including the work of the most advanced and pioneering German scientists such as Liebig, had long since been moving in a different direction—and as such was far more in accord with the real temper and character of the age. In his spirited defence of the ideals of the long-dead Lavater, the recently dead Goethe, the elderly Oken, Büchner was fighting a hopeless rearguard action. It is enticing but futile to wonder how he would have developed had he enjoyed the longevity characteristic of his parents and siblings (his brother Alexander survived into the twentieth century, dying only in 1904); but one can be sure that in his science, at any rate, he would have been forced sooner or later into a drastic reappraisal of his position. In the very thesis of his Trial Lecture and his dissertation, after all, he was seriously out of step with the wisdom of the new age. It would be presumptuous to assert that he was *objectively* wrong in his general idealist-mystical stance, especially given the late-twentieth-century reversion to 'alternative' and holistic notions concerning (medical) science, ecology, more 'organic' communities. But it is anyway essentially irrelevant whether or not he was objectively right or wrong. What matters is that he was drastically out of tune with the music of his time, and the outcome could only be a jangling, incessant dissonance—'ach, wir armen schreienden Musikanten'.

In the same paragraph in which Büchner attacks the 'dogmatism' of rationalist philosophy, he also refers fleetingly, almost coyly, to the opposite philosophical mode of the 'intuition of the mystic' ('die Anschauung des Mystikers'). This precisely defines his own stance (however scandalous such a notion may be to those modern materialists who seek to claim him entirely for their own). We can say of his whole vision of nature what Schiller said of Goethe's enthusiastic portrayal of the metamorphosis of plants: it is not an actual empirical experience, it is an 'idea'. It is, indeed, intuitional and mystical, born of that 'intuitive knowledge' ('intuitive Erkenntniß', ii. 276) that Büchner exclusively values as against the pitiful secondary insights of the ratiocinative intellect. All his driving beliefs in the Trial Lecture belong within this ambit: the 'primordial type' to which all forms in nature are supposedly traceable; the 'metempsychosis of the foetus' ('die Metempsychose des Fötus', ii. 293—the belief that a soul migrates into the developing foetus); above all, of course, the 'Grundgesetz für die gesammte Organisation',[8] the 'Urgesetz' that is a 'Gesetz der Schönheit' and which, in the process of governing all functions, forms, and matter in nature, generates a 'nothwendige Harmonie'. His vision is magnificent in all its benign mysticism, but it is achieved only by looking insistently backwards, by remaining splendidly but disastrously hostile to the specific and ever intensifying logic of the epoch. Büchner accused rationalist philosophy of being hopelessly remote from the vibrant reality of life; but he was himself hopelessly remote from the prevailing spirit of his time.

To some extent he realized this himself: at the outset of the Trial Lecture he acknowledges that the mechanistic approach to science is dominant in England and France. How could it have been otherwise in societies already experiencing a phenomenal process of mechanization? (The Liverpool–Manchester railway was already fully operational while Büchner was still in his teens.) Only a culture as grossly backward in machine-age terms as the German lands could enable a pre-mechanistic philosophy of science to survive so far beyond its time—and even so, it was already severely under attack when Büchner so briefly championed it. We have already seen how Goethe's and Oken's vertebral theory of the skull was ridiculed by Thomas Henry Huxley in 1858. But consider also another central and much more far-reaching postulate of Büchner's. This is touched on when he attacks the mechanist-functionalist school for their representation of the living organism as a machine so equipped that it is enabled—within the limits of its lifespan—to 'survive' ('mit den . . . Mitteln versehen, sich . . . zu erhalten'). It is also implied in the preceding sentence when he speaks of the mechanists' view of the individual organism as striving only to ensure its own survival vis-à-vis the external world, both as an individual and as a species: 'Sie kennt das Individuum . . . nur in seiner Bestrebung,

---

[8] This directly echoes the title of one of J. B. Wilbrand's textbooks of *Naturphilosophie*: *Darstellung der gesamten Organisation*.

sich der Außenwelt gegenüber theils als Individuum, theils als Art zu behaupten.' In due course, in the context of his postulation of a 'Grundgesetz' etc., Büchner declares his own position unequivocally: the whole corporeal existence of the individual is *not* brought about just as a means of ensuring the latter's survival, but rather because it is a manifestation of the primordial law of beauty (etc.): 'so wird für die philosophische Methode das ganze körperliche Dasein des Individuums nicht zu seiner eigenen Erhaltung aufgebracht, sondern es wird die Manifestation eines Urgesetzes, eines Gesetzes der Schönheit [etc.]'. What a touchingly humane and positive interpretation of nature this is. But how ominously remote it is from the mechanists' 'survivalist' interpretation that so well reflects the realities of the age—and which is perfectly encapsulated in the title of that central document of the nineteenth century, *On the Origin of Species by Means of Natural Selection, or the Preservation of Favoured Races in the Struggle for Life.*

None of this would really matter—and we could have spared ourselves the bother of talking about it at such length—if it were merely a parochial, scholastic row about alternative philosophies of science. But it goes far deeper than that. Büchner was a dedicated wholist in *all* respects. His science was not in some separate and autonomous compartment of his life: it was all of a piece with the rest of his being. His scientific idealism thus corresponds exactly to his social idealism; both are equally expressions of his idealism concerning existence in general. Furthermore, the mechanistic mode of science was itself—whether wittingly or unwittingly—a reflection of the social mechanisms of the machine age. It is therefore not altogether surprising when we discover that in defending his science against the reductivism of the mechanists and functionalists, Büchner was also defending his life values against the reductivism of an increasingly mechanistic, functionalistic world.

These essential values are clearly evinced within the Trial Lecture itself. One of them we have already identified: his belief in the absolute primacy of natural, vigorous, unmediated Life—'das frische grüne Leben', the 'Naturleben, das wir unmittelbar wahrnehmen', that realm of vitality and being that is separate from, and inaccessible to, the reasoning mind and its specious constructs. But this vibrant life is no remote abstraction: it is richly present in every individual living being. And it needs to be honoured and safeguarded in every least individual being. Karl Viëtor, one of the founding fathers of modern Büchner criticism, declared it to be a fact that 'For Büchner it is not a question of the individual and his rights. He already thinks in the new *social* categories.' His sole focus of interest, Viëtor claims, is the 'anonymous mass'.[9] This seems to me to be a classic and ruinous misconception. Büchner was indeed a revolutionary believer in the crying need and the enormous potential of the exploited mass. But at the risk of being burnt in effigy by parleys of un-like-minded critics, I would assert that for Büchner the glory of the mass lay *not* in any kind of merged, collective identity, but in the vibrant, even sacred individuality of each of its constituent members; and furthermore that he was unswervingly, implacably hostile to anything—from any quarter whatsoever—that tended to infringe or deny that individuality.

Again and again we shall encounter this as one of Büchner's most driving concerns. And we find it here forming the very heart of the preamble to the Trial Lecture. Why is he so completely opposed to the mechanistic view of living things? Precisely because, in systematically functionalizing every element in the living process, it denies the individual any own, intrinsic worth, and reduces him atomistically to the status of a cog-wheel existing solely to be of use to the mechanism as a whole, and to serve a purpose that lies beyond itself: the mechanist school, Büchner declares, 'findet die Lösung des Räthsels in dem *Zweck*, der *Wirkung*, in dem *Nutzen* der Verrichtung eines Organs. *Sie kent das Individuum nur als etwas, das einen Zweck außer sich erreichen soll*' (ii. 291; my italics). For the mechanist there is but a single law manifest in nature: the entirely functionalistic law of 'maximum fitness for purpose': 'Die *größtmöglichste Zweckmäßigkeit* ist das einzige Gesetz der teleologischen[10] Methode' (ii. 292; Büchner's italics). This to Büchner is a complete

---

[9] Viëtor, *Georg Büchner*, 51.
[10] Büchner's term 'teleological' is an unhappy one in that it makes for great confusion. The word 'teleology' was coined by Christian Wolff in 1728 to define his metaphysical, theistic belief that whilst living organisms were indeed 'machines' (as Descartes had argued), they were machines generated by God, and directed towards the fulfilment of his purposes, just as *all* phenomena in the world were in Wolff's view directed towards the realization of God's wise ends. The metaphysical dimension of the word has remained dominant in normal usage to this day. As empirical science began to develop, however, the word 'teleology' and its derivatives soon came to be used in a non-metaphysical, even *anti*-metaphysical sense reflecting the attempt to understand and explain biological phenomena purely in terms of their functional, mechanistic purposes. The conflicting usages are well demonstrated by 19th c. examples cited in the OED, e.g.: 'This is the doctrine of Teleology: i.e. the doctrine

perversion of the truth. For him, nature does not behave according to the dictates of extrinsic purposes, does not fritter itself away in an endless succession of purposes that mutually determine one another; instead, it is wholly and directly sufficient unto itself in each and every one of its manifestations: 'Die Natur handelt nicht nach Zwecken, sie reibt sich nicht in einer unendlichen Reihe von Zwecken auf, von denen der eine den anderen bedingt; sondern sie ist in allen ihren Aeußerungen sich unmittelbar *selbst genug.*' (ibid.; Büchner's italics). At this point he consummates his argument with a maxim that is never cited by critics, and yet is arguably one of the most revealing pronouncements that he ever made: 'Alles, was ist, ist um seiner selbst willen da.' (*Everything that exists, exists for its own sake.*) This maxim expresses what I believe to be Büchner's most fundamental article of faith, the existential premiss upon which his whole ontology is based. Indeed it is precisely at this point that he launches into his ontology, his metaphysic of being, firstly declaring the goal of 'philosophical' science to be 'Das Gesetz dieses Seins zu suchen' (*seeking to discover the law of this existence [or: being]*), and then instantly proceeding to outline the metaphysic itself: the 'fundamental law', the 'primal law of beauty', the 'necessary harmony' etc.—all of which serve to corroborate and underpin his central tenet that every being, and every constituent part of every being, exists entirely in its own right, as a direct, and intrinsically valuable, manifestation of the primal law, not as an expedient, intrinsically worthless link in a mechanistic apparatus serving a purpose beyond itself.

This, then, is the credo at the heart of the Trial Lecture—and it is equally the credo at the heart of the entire corpus of his work. In his poetic writing as much as in his scientific philosophy, he holds sacred the fullness of natural, unmediated Life and its rich manifestation in the being of each individual. On rare and fleeting occasions he can celebrate it positively for its glorious presence. But mostly he must celebrate it negatively in its absence—by railing rhapsodically, sardonically at its loss, its denial, its suppression.

that every organ is adapted to a special use'; 'Teleology in this larger sense, or the doctrine that behind all the facts open to scientific enquiry—there is 'Mind and Will' as the ultimate cause of all things—does not fall within the scope of scientific method.' Büchner uses the term in its functionalist, non-metaphysical sense; indeed it is precisely the *absence* of a metaphysical dimension that Büchner criticizes in the 'teleological' approach. In the more normal sense of the word it is of course Büchner who subscribes to a (metaphysical) teleology (cf. Zons, 75).

3
Routing the Robots

BÜCHNER'S passionate antagonism to every kind of anti-life force or process is evident at every turn in his poetic work. But it is particularly clear in the way that he sets up a distinct gallery of fools and rogues, each of whom is gleefully cast in the role of Aunt Sally and made the target of a scathing barrage of derision or contempt.

That philosophy should be the target of one such barrage is scarcely surprising. Mention was made earlier of Büchner's remark in a letter to Gutzkow that his (stupefying) immersion in philosophy was giving him fresh insights into the poverty of the human mind. This letter—written in November or December 1835—then continues: 'Meinetwegen! Wenn man sich nur einbilden könnte, die Löcher in unsern Hosen seien Pallastfenster, so könnte man schon wie ein König leben; so aber friert man erbärmlich.' (ii. 450; *What the hell! If only we could delude ourselves that the holes in our trousers were palace windows, we could live like a king; as it is though, we're miserably cold.*) This brief aside is like a signpost pointing directly towards *Leonce und Lena* (which Büchner probably wrote only six months or so later, in June–July 1836[1]). The cold reality is certainly there in the peasantry with their 'Löcher in ... Jacken und Hosen' (127–8; *holes in ... jackets and trousers*). So too, above all, is the false palace of philosophy, complete with its lunatic king—a pocket emperor literally without any clothes: on his very first appearance (108–9) he is made to prance around the stage 'almost naked' ('Er läuft fast nackt im Zimmer herum'). As the curtain goes up on this manifest crackbrain, he is at once heard declaiming on the primacy of mind—the word 'denken' (*think*) occurs no fewer than four times in his first brief utterance: 'Der Mensch muß denken und ich muß für meine Unterthanen denken, denn sie denken nicht, sie denken nicht.' (*Human beings must think, and I must think for my subjects, for they never think, they never think.*) The gulf between creatural reality, and intellectual

---

[1] Cf. opening paragraphs of Ch. 11 below.

abstraction and posturing—an abiding theme of Büchner's—is conveyed here with a visual impact that seems like Jean Genet more than a century before his time. There he stands, this ridiculous King of the Realm of Bum, stripped almost naked in all his flesh-and-blood reality. But his mind churns out a definition of his being that is arrant philosophical gobbledygook, and he desperately half-begs, half-orders his robotic minions to grasp his unreal meaning: 'Die Substanz ist das "an sich", das bin ich. . . . Begriffen? An sich ist an sich, versteht ihr?' (*The essence is the 'of itself', that's what I am. . . . Understood? Of itself is of itself, do you see that?*) In *Woyzeck* Büchner will have another superior belabour another inferior with a similarly absurd tautology: 'Moral das ist wenn man moralisch ist, versteht er.' (362; *Morality is when one is moral, do you see that.*) The king covers his nakedness—but sees himself climbing not into the stuff of his clothes, but the abstractions of philosophy: 'Jetzt kommen meine Attribute, Modificationen, Affectionen und Accidenzien, wo ist mein Hemd, meine Hose?' *(Now we turn to my attributes, modifications, affections and accidents, where is my shirt and where are my trousers?)* Again and again in Büchner, the genitals and excretory organs serve as the one irrefutable mark of brute reality; and so it is here: the monarch is aghast to find his fly still open. But, of course, he sublimates the problem: what for Danton was 'das häßliche Ding' (71; *the ugly appendage*) becomes for our mind-struck monarch the repository of free will: 'Halt, pfui! der freie Wille steht davorn ganz offen.' (*Stop, how obscene! Free will is all agape down there.*) And anyway, he is easily armed against whatever obscure threats to his notions may lurk in those regions: he has only to don his cuffs, and he is instantly stiff with morality: 'Wo ist die Moral, wo sind die Manschetten?'

This comic cameo is sparklingly theatrical: it would be a poor director who didn't have his audience guffawing at the antics of the man as he 'progresses' from natural nakedness to the extravagant trappings of tinpot kingship. It is by no means gratuitous buffoonery, however. This man is dangerously unhinged; dangerously remote in his grand cerebral abstractions from any kind of warm and genuine reality, from 'das frische grüne Leben'.

One telling symptom of this is his frail hold on his own identity and existence. He has closed himself off from that essential immediacy of intuitive existence so precious to Büchner, and has committed his being instead to an artificial, mechanistic system produced by the 'secondary' processes of the mind. This grand but unreal system is threatened by even the tiniest hitch: 'Die Kategorien sind in der schändlichsten Verwirrung, es sind zwei Knöpfe zuviel zugeknöpft, die Dose steckt in der rechten Tasche. Mein ganzes System ist ruinirt.' (*My categories are in the most scandalous confusion, two buttons too many have been done up, my snuffbox has been put in the right-hand pocket. My entire system is ruined.*) 'Confusion' is the by-word of this devotee of order: 'Die Menschen machen mich confus, ich bin in der größten Verwirrung'; 'Der Mensch bringt mich in Confusion, zur Desperation. Ich bin in der größten Verwirrung'; 'Der Mensch hat mich vorhin confus gemacht' (108, 131, 133; *These people are making me muddled, I am in the greatest confusion; The fellow is making me desperately muddled, I am in the greatest confusion; That fellow muddled me up just now*). Having no longer any immediate sense of his own being, he no longer has any positive sense of his own identity:

Der Mensch muß denken. [*Steht eine Zeit lang sinnend.*] Wenn ich so laut rede, so weiß ich nicht wer es eigentlich ist, ich oder ein Anderer, das ängstigt mich. [*Nach langem Besinnen.*] Ich bin ich.—Was halten Sie davon, Präsident? (109)

Human beings must think. [*Stands a while reflecting.*] When I speak out loud like that, I never know who it really is, me or someone else, it frightens me. [*After much reflection.*] I am me.—President, what is your opinion on the matter?

His underling's reply (together with its robotic echo) is a masterpiece of subversive servility that could come straight from Lewis Carroll:

PRÄSIDENT [*gravitätisch langsam*]. Eure Majestät, vielleicht ist es so, vielleicht ist es aber auch nicht so.
DER GANZE STAATSRATH IM CHOR. Ja, vielleicht ist es so, vielleicht ist es aber auch nicht so.

PRESIDENT [*slowly and with gravity*]. Your Majesty, it may be the case, but it may equally not be the case.
THE ENTIRE COUNCIL OF STATE IN UNISON. Yes, it may be the case, but it may equally not be the case.

The king's derogation of his own identity is grave enough. But what makes him essentially monstrous behind the comic veil of harmlessness is the fact that he robs everyone else of their identity and individuality too. Being crippled by his mania for the mind and its constructs, he can hobble through life only by making his minions into his crutches, by subordinating them entirely to his own distorted purposes—a grim enactment of the anathema of functionalism, of 'Die größtmöglichste Zweckmäßigkeit'. He can manage nothing out of his own spontaneous being. He needs to be dressed by a brace of valets. He has to tie a knot in his handkerchief to remind him of his people (108–9—the entire mass of whom, no matter how hungry, ragged, or careworn, are strictly commanded to turn out 'voluntarily' to line the royal wedding-route with a suitably well-fed, well-clad, and happy demeanour; 127). Happiness for the king is a scheduled event, a long-term planning decision: 'habe ich nicht den Beschluß gefaßt, daß meine königliche Majestät sich an diesem Tag freuen ... sollte? War das nicht unser festester Entschluß?' (129; *did I not make a formal resolution that my royal majesty should this day be happy? Was this not our most solemn resolve?*) He needs his lackeys to function as his memory: he orders a valet to remind him what the knot in his handkerchief was to remind him of; he censures the President for not remembering what it was that he (the king) wanted to address the Council about (109). His courtiers are ordered to share his every emotion (though in the interests of propriety it is forbidden to weep without a handkerchief, 130). When the king mops his face on account of the heat, his Councillors must likewise mop their faces; when they walk, they must walk 'symmetrically' (109); when they speak, they speak in chorus; when the king abdicates, they have to labour on as the indispensable slaves of his mania:

Ich ... werde sogleich ungestört jetzt bloß nur noch zu denken anfangen. Mein Sohn, du überlässest mir diese Weisen [*er deutet auf den Staatsrath*], damit sie mich in meinen Bemühungen unterstützen. Kommen Sie meine Herren, wir müssen denken, ungestört denken. [*Er entfernt sich mit dem Staatsrath.*] (133)

I shall now begin at once to do nothing at all but simply think unhindered. My son, you will let me have these wise fellows [*he points to the Council of State*] so that they may sustain me in my efforts. Come gentlemen, we must think, we must think unhindered. [*He departs with the Council of State.*]

If it is anti-life philosophizing that is pilloried in the barren antics of the king in *Leonce und Lena*, it is anti-life scientizing that is pilloried in Büchner's most savagely satirical stooge: the monomaniacal Doctor in *Woyzeck*.

Doctors have been a favourite butt of stage humour for many centuries, most notably perhaps in the archetypal *Dottore* of the *commedia dell'arte*. Büchner's target, however, is a quite different kind of creature. The stock figure of traditional comedy was ridiculed because of his blundering incompetence: there was a comic disparity between the pompous pretensions of the profession, and the bungling quackery that pre-scientific medicine all too easily amounted to. Büchner's Doctor is a new breed altogether, and a far more dangerous one: a man whose patients are sacrificed not to a *lack* of science, but to an *excess* of it. Where the king was rapt in his philosophical 'system', the Doctor is rapt in his scientific 'theory'. Running amok aboard the relentless steamroller of modern experimentalism, he subordinates everything and everyone to his single aim of revolutionizing science, and thus immortalizing his name ('Es giebt eine Revolution in der Wissenschaft, ich sprenge sie in die Luft', 366; 'meine Theorie, meine neue Theorie . . . ich werde unsterblich', 371).

One of the grimly comic contrasts at the heart of the satire is the gross contradiction between the attitudes that we might expect to find in a doctor, and the attitudes that this particular monster displays. Medicine—we might reasonably suppose—is about helping suffering individuals by trying to cure their disorders and relieve their pain. For our madman, it is exactly the other way round. He is not interested in helping anyone save only himself; and the worse the disease or disorder, the more he likes it. At his first appearance on stage he is instantly referred to (in the H2 version[2]) as 'Herr Sargnagel' (371; *Mr Coffin-Nail*; cf. 370, 372)—an apt designation, for the only thing that he likes more than a thoroughly ill patient is a thoroughly dead one. When he steams across the stage at the beginning of the scene with the Hauptmann, he is on his way to a pregnant patient. Not to bring her relief, of course. She will be dead in a month, he coldly declares, and should make her dispositions accordingly (371). Far from being a regrettable loss, the death of the 'stupid cow' will gain him an 'interesting specimen' ('In 4 Wochen, dummes Thier, sie giebt ein interessant's Präparat', 371). He is full of glee at the wonderfully promising 'apoplectic constitu-

---

[2] Cf. Ch. 15 below.

tion' of the Hauptmann, and excitedly spells out to his terrified victim the various possible results of the keenly anticipated stroke: unilateral paralysis, or, with a real bit of luck, complete cerebral palsy and a consequent vegetable existence ('oder aber Sie[3] können im besten Fall geistig gelähmt werden u. nur fort vegetiren', 370). In a grotesque act of pseudo-consolation, he tells the Hauptmann what an 'interesting case' he will make; and if God in his kindness only partly paralyses his tongue, they will be able to perform the most immortal experiments: 'Übrigens kann ich Sie versichern, daß Sie einen von den interessanten Fällen abgeben u. wenn Gott will, daß Ihre Zunge zum Theil gelähmt wird, so machen wir d. unsterblichsten Experimente.' (370).

His chief victim, of course, is poor Woyzeck, whose abject poverty and underdog status he cruelly exploits by commandeering his body in exchange for a pittance. Needless to say, his concern is not to minister to Woyzeck's crying needs, but to have a convenient bodily mechanism upon which he can experiment by deliberately making it malfunction. He has subjected Woyzeck to a three-month diet of nothing but peas, and is delighted at the results (394–6): he notes with implicit satisfaction that the diet has made his victim's hair drop out; he is overjoyed ('ganz erfreut') at his paroxysm of trembling; in a harrowing inversion of the fairground scene, in which animals are displayed as quasi-humans, he displays a human as a quasi-animal, a 'Bestie' not far removed—he claims—from a donkey, and he urges his students to poke and prod this splendid specimen, and observe the wonderful irregularity of his pulse, the fascinating abnormality of his eyes: 'Meine Herrn . . . Meine Herrn . . . sehn Sie, der Mensch [cf. the Barker, 343: 'Meine Herren! Meine Herren! Sehn Sie die Creatur'], seit einem Vierteljahr ißt er nichts als Erbsen, beachten Sie die Wirkung, fühlen Sie einmal was ein ungleicher Puls, da u. die Augen . . . fühlen Sie meine Herrn fühlen Sie, [*sie betasten ihm Schläfe, Puls u. Busen*]'. Whereas earlier Woyzeck had watched the Barker drill his performing ape and horse, he himself is now degraded into a performing human when the Doctor orders him to waggle his ears as a practical demonstration of the relevant musculature. To borrow splintered phrases from the H2 fairground scene: 'Grotesk! Sehr grotesk!'; 'was ein grotesker Effect' (348).

---

[3] Here and in the ensuing quotations, Büchner's 'sie' and 'ihr' have been normalized to 'Sie' and 'Ihr'.

Above all, of course, there is Woyzeck's most magnificent malfunction, the thing that makes him such a specially 'interesting case', such a 'phenomenon' (368, 375), and which even earns him a minuscule bonus—namely his dementia, his 'most beautiful aberratio mentalis partialis, type 2, such a beautifully pronounced example' ('die schönste aberratio mentalis partialis, d. zweite Species, sehr schön ausgeprägt', 368).

But there is a savage irony here that ensures that the Doctor, as well as being a loathsome victimizer, is at the same time a laughable victim—the butt of excoriating comedy. The 'type 2 dementia' that he diagnoses with such ecstasy in his human guinea-pig is obsessionalism: Woyzeck is gripped, he declares, by an 'idée fixe' (368). But he himself is far more drastically demented in his *own* idée fixe. In his obsessive fixation on experimentation at all costs, and to the exclusion of all else, he is a comical if dangerous crackpot. There is a glorious incongruity here that runs right through the presentation of the Doctor, and serves as a counterweight to his otherwise unbearable oppressiveness. He has deliberately and systematically diminished Woyzeck's humanity; but he is himself more impoverished in his lack of humanity than his victim could ever be. He berates Woyzeck for his lack of willpower in piddling in the street, and grandiloquently trumpets the dominance of mind over nature: 'Die Natur! Hab' ich nicht nachgewiesen, daß der musculus constrictor vesicae dem Willen unterworfen ist? Die Natur! Woyzeck, der Mensch ist frei, in dem Menschen verklärt sich die Individualität zur Freiheit.' (366; *Nature! Have I not proved that the musculus constrictor vesicae is subordinate to the will? Nature! Woyzeck, man is free, in man individuality is transfigured as freedom.*) But this claim is rendered comical on several counts. For one thing, nature *has* defeated mind, or at any rate manners: just as free will gaped open in King Peter's fly, so it is the same area that has seen nature take its course in the form of Woyzeck's contract-breaking piddle ('Aber H. Doctor, wenn einem die Natur kommt'). For another thing, the Doctor/Professor's own behaviour—just like the king's—most eloquently contradicts his words: he does not behave at all like a warm-blooded free agent, but as a well-oiled, tunnel-visioned automaton driven by an inhuman obsession. What is most grotesque and preposterous of all, however, is the fact that the Doctor propounds his grandiose doctrine of individual freedom to the very individual whom he has in effect enslaved. In his verbiage he erects a temple to liberty and individuality; in his acts he denies the very existence of individuals, seeing them merely as potential specimens that are worthy of interest only insofar as they are deliciously pathological and preferably dead. The pattern is familiar: King Peter, too, spoke of free will—and allowed those around him no jot of freedom or individuality: his son must marry by royal command, his Councillors must walk and gesture like machines, his subjects are compelled to show voluntary contentment.

In their essence, King Peter and the Doctor are not funny at all: they are blinkered tyrants who indulge their obsessions wholly at the expense of others (in *Dantons Tod*, as we shall see, Robespierre is revealed—in a singularly unfunny perspective—to be just such a tyrant). Büchner renders both monarch and medico comical despite their tyranny by ridiculing them in the very exercise of their power: they treat others as their playthings, but are themselves laughably robotic puppets at the mercy of their mechanistic obsessions, whilst their careful schemes are easily upset by the spontaneous workings of nature: Woyzeck's piddle; and the real love of the real Leonce and Lena inside the seeming automata at the wedding.

The Hauptmann—a kind of Laurel to the Doctor's Hardy—is a splendid variant on this comic model of power ridiculed. Notwithstanding the very different context and economy of the *Woyzeck* fragments, this nameless bundle of humanity plays a role similar to that of King Peter: both individuals occupy the supreme power position within their respective plays—but in comic contrast to the might and mantle of their positions, both of them are puny and petrified, and utterly dwarfed by their ostensible victims. There are even verbal echoes: just as the monarch was easily thrown into confusion ('Die Menschen machen mich confus', etc.), so too is the military man: 'Er macht mich ganz confus' (362; *You're making me all confused*). Connected to this is the most revealing similarity between them: their shared sense of fear. In giving himself over to the 'secondary business' of thought and its factitious systems, the king, as we have seen, loses his grip on his identity—and it frightens him ('das ängstigt mich'). Such fear—at once existential, and born of undue thinking—is the Hauptmann's paramount characteristic, and the one that renders his authority most laughable: 'Es wird mir ganz *angst* um die Welt, wenn ich an die Ewigkeit *denke*'; 'es *schaudert* mich, wenn ich *denk*, daß sich die Welt in einem Tag herumdreht'; 'die Pferde machen mir ganz *Angst*; wenn ich *denke*, daß die armen Bestien zu Fuß gehn müssen'; 'H. Doctor ... Sie machen mir ganz *Angst*'; 'H. Doctor *erschrecken* Sie mich nicht' (360 (2 ×), 370, 371, 370; *I'm terrified for the world when I think of eternity; it gives me the shudders to think that the world revolves in a day; the horses terrify me; when I think that the poor beasts have to get around on foot; Doctor you're terrifying me; Doctor, don't frighten me*).

In his *horror vacui*, the Hauptmann is potentially much more interesting than he might appear: while the Doctor rushes along with eyes only for his single narrow goal, and the king sees little beyond his philosophical Legoland, the Hauptmann is stricken by glimpses of an abyss that in varying forms critically affects the destinies of all Büchner's central characters. What it reveals to the Hauptmann—a kind of unwilling parish-pump Spinozan—is the terror of infinitude as against the finite, of eternity as against the moment. He can express it only in a helpless King Peter-like tautology, but the gulf is all the more agonizing for that: 'ewig das ist ewig, das ist ewig, das siehst Du ein; nun ist es aber wieder nicht ewig und das ist ein Augenblick, ja, ein Augenblick' (360; *for ever is for ever, it's for ever, you can see that; but then again it isn't for ever, it's a moment, yes, a moment*). Viewed in this tortured cerebral perspective, time appears monstrous, 'ungeheuer': it is endless eternity ('Es wird mir ganz angst um die Welt, wenn ich an die Ewigkeit denke'); it is also the vast expanse of each man's existence that somehow has to be lived through: 'Woyzeck, bedenk' er, er hat noch seine schöne dreißig Jahr zu leben, dreißig Jahr! macht 360 Monate, und Tage, Stunden, Minuten! Was will er denn mit der ungeheuren Zeit all anfangen?' (360; *Woyzeck, just think, you still have a good thirty years to live, thirty years! That's 360 months, and all those days, hours, minutes! What on earth are you going to do with all this vast expanse of time?*); additionally and perversely, however, it is also a terrifying transience, the relentless clockwork revolutions of each individual's brief existence: 'Woyzeck, es schaudert mich, wenn ich denk, daß sich die Welt in einem Tag herumdreht, was n'e Zeitverschwendung, wo soll das hinaus? Woyzeck, ich kann kein Mühlrad mehr sehn, oder ich werd' melancholisch.' (360; *Woyzeck, it gives me the shudders to think that the world revolves in a day, what a squandering of time, where's it all going to end? Woyzeck, I can't bear to see a mill-wheel turning any more—it makes me melancholic*.) Hence the Haumptmann's terror at the spectre of death in the gloating prognostications of the Doctor (370), and in the melancholy vision of the overcoat hanging on its peg like a suicide's corpse: 'H. Doctor, ich bin so schwermüthig, ich hab so was schwärmerisches, ich muß immer weinen, wenn ich meinen Rock an d. Wand hängen sehe, da hängt er.' (370; *Doctor, I'm so melancholy, I have this terrible imagination, it makes me weep whenever I see my coat hanging on the wall, just hanging there.*)

The Hauptmann thus shares the kinds of existential insight that characterize all Büchner's eponymous heroes. But his response is far from heroic. Whereas Woyzeck, the apparently abject underling, leaps into the abyss with a passion both grand and futile, the Hauptmann for all his rank and power offers the comical spectacle of a truly abject coward cringing from the precipice with tight-shut eyes, and seeking refuge in artificial constructs that put him wholly on a par with those dangerous cranks, the philosophizing monarch and the scientizing medic.

These refuges are twofold. The first—a frequent target of Büchner's—is the void-bridging artifice of sheer activity: 'Beschäftigung, Woyzeck, Beschäftigung!' (360). If the Hauptmann can fill his day with a measured routine of unhurried activity, he can perhaps shut his mind to those terrifying insights that make him so 'melancholy'. But his would-be cocoon is constantly threatened by the frantic bustle of his fraught and nervy servant and the manic scientist—and so we find him both at the beginning and at the end of his two scenes desperately imploring them to steady their pace: 'Langsam, Woyzeck, langsam; ein's nach d. andern; Er macht mir ganz schwindlich'; 'Geh' jezt u. renn nicht so; langsam hübsch langsam die Straße hinunter' (360, 364: the shaving scene; *Slowly, Woyzeck, slowly; one thing after another; you make me feel quite giddy; Off you go now, and don't run like that: slowly, nice and slowly down the street*); 'H. Doctor . . . Rennen Sie nicht so . . . Sie hetzen sich ja hinter d. Tod drein. Ein guter Mensch, der sein gutes Gewissen hat, geht nicht so schnell'; 'Mir wird ganz schwindlich vor den Menschen, wie schnell' (370, 375: the street scene; *Doctor, don't run like that. You're chasing your own death, you are. A good sort of chap with a good sort of conscience just doesn't move that fast; These people make me feel quite giddy; how fast they go*).

The Hauptmann's other, and even more revealing resort is the mantle of a specious morality, the vacuity of which is perfectly expressed in the absurd circularity of its definition: 'Moral das ist wenn man moralisch ist' (362; *Morality is when one is moral*). The sheer expediency of this convenient cloak is repeatedly thrown into sharp comic relief. Thus for instance it serves to insulate him from the menace of time: 'Aber Woyzeck, die Tugend, die Tugend! Wie sollte ich dann die Zeit herumbringen? ich sag' mir immer: Du bist ein tugendhafter Mensch, [*gerührt*] ein guter Mensch, ein guter Mensch.' (362; *But virtue, Woyzeck, virtue! How else am I supposed to get through the day? I keep telling myself, 'You're a virtuous chap*, [*mawkishly*] *a good chap, a good chap.'*) It also helps to soften the terrifying prospect of death conjured up by the Doctor: at least—so he imagines—the people gathered around his corpse will say what a very good chap he was: 'sie werden sagen, er war ein guter Mensch, ein guter Mensch' (370). It even enables the Hauptmann to magic his dismal cowardice into a decided virtue: 'ein guter Mensch ... hat sein Leben lieb, ein guter Mensch hat keine courage nicht! ein Hundsfott hat courage!' (375; *good chaps know what life is worth, good chaps don't have courage! only scoundrels have courage!*)

In particular, the Hauptmann can take refuge in a devious sense of moral superiority over those around him. For one thing, he can make a virtue of his deliberately tortoise-like mode of anaesthetic activity, and thus by implication cast aspersions on the Doctor in his frantic scurryings: 'Ein guter Mensch, der sein gutes Gewissen hat, geht nicht so schnell. Ein guter Mensch.' Much more importantly, he can try to lift himself up by doing Woyzeck down. Woyzeck, after all, is beyond the pale: by fathering a bastard, he has banished himself from the realm of all decent, upright folk, and from the benedictions of that bastion of rectitude, the garrison church. The passage in which this is conveyed is a small masterpiece of acid comedy in which the Hauptmann unwittingly betrays all his spineless and detestable vacuity as he leaps from cruel belittlement to mawkish condescension, and thence to a posture of censorious moralism founded on nothing more solid than his own empty phrases and the platitudes of the local padre:

> O er ist dumm, ganz abscheulich dumm. [*gerührt*] Woyzeck, er ist ein guter Mensch, ein guter Mensch—aber [*mit Würde*] Woyzeck, er hat keine Moral! Moral das ist wenn man moralisch ist, versteht er. Es ist ein gutes Wort. Er hat ein Kind, ohne den Segen der Kirche, wie unser hochehrwürdiger H. Garnisonsprediger sagt, ohne den Segen d. Kirche, es ist nicht von mir. (362)

Oh you're so stupid, so completely and appallingly stupid. [*mawkishly*] Woyzeck, you're a good chap, a good chap—but [*with dignity*] you've got no morality! Morality is when one is moral, do you see. Such a good word. You've got a child without the blessing of the Church, as our most venerable padre puts it, without the blessing of the Church—his words, not mine.

Büchner's theatrical genius is perfectly mirrored at this juncture. At the exact mid-point of the scene—almost to the word—he first contrives a sudden climax in the Hauptmann's gratuitous, mincing, pharisaical censure of Woyzeck over his child, then uses this to trigger an electrifying change in the whole tenor and mood of the scene that throws the Hauptmann into splendid disarray and definitively exposes him as a windbag and a fraud. It is the pattern of the dialogue that alters most conspicuously. Up to this point it has been entirely dominated by the Hauptmann: Woyzeck has done nothing but punctuate his rantings with a laconic and rhythmic refrain: 'Ja wohl, Herr Hauptmann', 'Ja wohl, H. Hauptmann', 'Schlimm, Herr Hauptmann . . .', 'Ja wohl, H. Hauptmann'. All of a sudden, however, goaded into action by the stigmatizing of his child, Woyzeck unleashes a barrage of words that demolish the officer's humbug and leave him thoroughly confused and bruised ('ganz confus', 'ganz angegriffen', 362, 364).

The turning of the tables against the blustering Hauptmann that is enacted here is a most enjoyable spectacle. But it is also a most significant one for the terms in which it is carried out. All too often, this scene, and especially its second half, is represented as a powerful but straightforward blast of social criticism: *épater le bourgeois*! With its mocking exposure of the Hauptmann and his pseudo-morality, it is without doubt a powerful satire on the specious values of an oppressor class. But our excitement at the cock-shy should not blind us to the fact that Büchner is engaged in a complex critique of a serious issue: just how *are* we to see the problem of morality? A poignant question indeed when we remember that the critique is expressed through a man who soon will commit a murder most foul—in response to what he sees as a sin most foul on the part of his victim.

Woyzeck's first counterblast against the Hauptmann is in defence of his child, and he immediately begins to assert a crucial point: that morality is not 'given', and especially not god-given, but invented and imposed by men. A bastard child may be an outcast in the eyes of the lawgivers of the established Church, but in the eyes of God he is infinitely precious: 'Herr Hauptmann, der liebe Gott wird den armen Wurm nicht drum ansehn, ob das Amen drüber gesagt ist, eh' er gemacht wurde. Der Herr sprach: Lasset die Kindlein zu mir kommen.' (362; *But sir, the good Lord won't look over the poor little mite to check that a prayer was said before he was made. The Lord spake: suffer the little children to come unto me.*) What this also makes clear is that the kind of morality invoked by the Hauptmann against Woyzeck and his child is truly pharisaical: it is not an ethos bearing on the inner self, but a system of conventions, formalities, outward appearances. As such, it amounts to a mere adornment, a kind of aesthetical adjunct: 'Es muß was Schöns seyn um die Tugend, Herr Hauptmann.' (362; *Must be a lovely thing, sir, virtue.*)

One reason why Woyzeck and his kind cannot enjoy this adornment is that they are in a constant sweat keeping the wheels turning for those that can; and the point is driven home with a justly famous hyperbole: 'Unseins ist doch einmal unseelig in der und der andern Welt, ich glaub' wenn wir in Himmel kämen so müßten wir donnern helfen.' (362; *Us lot just don't have no chance in this world or the next, I reckon if we ever got to heaven we'd have to help with the thunder.*) This reason is offensive enough. But it is compounded by another one at least as offensive: this decorous morality is a luxury available only to those with the necessary cash: 'Wir arme Leut. Sehn Sie, Herr Hauptmann, Geld, Geld. Wer kein Geld hat. Da setz eimal einer seinsgleichen auf die Moral in die Welt.' (362; *Poor, that's what we are. See, it's money, sir, money. If you don't have no money. Morality don't get much of a look in when our sort gets made.*) Virtue is above all a badge of prosperity; and Woyzeck would gladly be virtuous if he had the money and material insignia of wealth: 'wenn ich ein Herr wär und hätt ein Hut und eine Uhr und eine anglaise und könnt vornehm reden, ich wollt schon tugendhaft seyn [u. hätt mich copuliren lassen in der Kirch' mit Chaise u. Pferd]'[4] (362; *if I was a gent with a hat and a watch and a nice frock-coat and could talk all posh, I'd be virtuous alright [and I'd have had meself spliced in church with a horse and carriage]*)[4].

---

[4] The square brackets are Lehmann's, and indicate that Büchner wrote the words in the manuscript, but then crossed them out.

The pivotal factor in this whole scene is of course the child—or more precisely its illegitimate begettal. Once again, just as with King Peter and the Doctor, it is the genital area that serves as the epitome of natural forces that threaten to belie all neat systems of the mind. Just because the poor cannot afford the moral trappings of polite society, they cannot be expected to suppress their natural lusty vigour: 'Man hat auch sein Fleisch und Blut.' (362). Even the Hauptmann admits to stirrings of what he terms 'love', be they ever so minimal and masturbatory: 'Fleisch u. Blut? Wenn ich am Fenster lieg, wenn's geregnet hat und den weißen Strümpfen so nachsehe wie sie über die Gassen springen,—verdammt Woyzeck,—da kommt mir die Liebe. Ich hab auch Fleisch u. Blut.' (362; *Flesh and blood? When I lie by the window when it's rained and watch those white stockings as they hop across the street—dammit Woyzeck—I feel love coming over me. I'm flesh and blood too.*) Even the grammar reinforces the sense of sexuality as a natural force unbidden by the mind: 'da kommt mir die Liebe'—and this is echoed through Woyzeck a few lines later: 'wir gemeine Leut, das hat keine Tugend, es kommt einem nur so die Natur' (*us common folk don't have no virtue, it's nature what comes over us, that's all*). And of course it is precisely the same expression that provokes the Doctor into his outburst on free will: 'Aber H. Doctor, wenn einem die Natur kommt.'

All three of the corrosive cameos discussed so far in this chapter have achieved their effect by pillorying individual figures. But needless to say, Büchner is not attacking individuals as such: the king, the Doctor and the Hauptmann are purpose-built Aunt Sallies, clockwork puppets designed to embody particular attitudes and systems of mind, and to demonstrate how contemptibly specious these are, and how grotesquely remote from the real pulse of life. Such figures are accordingly only a device; they are highly effective—especially since they serve as a butt of comedy, a kind of ritual whipping-boy—but they are not indispensable to Büchner's purpose. He can achieve a similar, if much less dramatic effect by the reverse process: instead of setting up a 'baddy' to take a pasting in the cock-shy, he can show us a 'goody' flinging the brickbats. This is well demonstrated in his treatment of a crucial anathema: contemporary art forms, and their crass divorce from the vibrant reality of life. A crucial issue indeed, considering that Büchner in his own artistic practice flew so thoroughly—and so consciously—in the face of fashion that he deprived himself of an audience for well over half a century.

The first attack is mounted quite early in *Dantons Tod* in a fiery diatribe put into the mouth of Camille Desmoulins. This diatribe is discursive rather than dramatic, but this does not jar on the audience—not least because Camille's speech serves as the follow-up to a brief but delectable piece of theatrical 'business': the fragment of dialogue between the 'First Gentleman' and 'Second Gentleman' that closes the 'Promenade' scene (itself quite a departure from conventional dramatic practice). In the case of this fleeting episode, Büchner again makes use of comic stooges: he sets up the two 'Gentlemen' in a posture of swaggering confidence, then instantly deflates them. What he does first is to float a balloon of bewonderment at the seeming marvels of the contemporary stage—and, while he's at it, of modern technology with its extraordinary discoveries and its supposedly gigantic strides along the path of human progress:

ERSTER HERR. Ich versichre Sie, eine außerordentliche Entdeckung! Alle technischen Künste bekommen dadurch eine andere Physiognomie. Die Menschheit eilt mit Riesenschritten ihrer hohen Bestimmung entgegen.
ZWEITER HERR. Haben Sie das neue Stück gesehen? Ein babylonischer Thurm! Ein Gewirr von Gewölben, Treppchen, Gängen und das Alles so leicht und kühn in die Luft gesprengt. Man schwindelt bey jedem Tritt. Ein bizarrer Kopf. (36)

FIRST GENTLEMAN. I assure you, an extraordinary discovery! It changes the whole face of the technical arts. Humanity speeds with giant strides towards its noble destiny.
SECOND GENTLEMAN. Have you seen the new play? A tower of Babel! A labyrinth of vaults and stairs and passages, and all so boldly, so lightly flung in the air. It makes you giddy just to watch. What a bizarre mind.

The imagery is perfect for a Büchner spoof. Here are two creatures vaunting the gigantic progress of technological man, the spectacular complexity of a mind-wrought edifice. But it takes only a puddle to halt their own progress. And why? Because for all the giddy confections of the theatre, the Second Gentleman is terrified that the actual ground upon which he stands is merely a shell, 'eine dünne Kruste', and that beneath it is an abyss that will readily devour him—thus he has to be helped across the 'dangerous' puddle: it is a hole through which, he believes, he could easily fall ('ich meine immer ich könnte durchfallen, wo so ein Loch ist', 36).

Camille's philippic immediately supervenes (37). It is discursively non-dramatic; wholly irrelevant to the plot; wholly irrelevant to the persona of Camille. And yet it is immensely revealing and important—one of numerous ostensible irrelevancies in *Dantons Tod* that penetrate far beyond the surface level of story-line, setting, and character, and reflect some of Büchner's most essential concerns.

It is not generally remarked that Büchner directs his tirade almost wholly against the consumers, not the concocters, of prevailing public art forms—prevailing, that is, in *Vormärz* Germany, not in revolutionary Paris. Here is this tyro of 21, exploding into creativity with his first play—and at once lambasting his potential public for perverted values that will ensure that he himself will long be crying in the wilderness. Not that there is any shortage of enthusiasm for the arts on the part of the public: they avidly patronize theatre, music, and art-exhibitions. But the arts are to them what philosophy is to King Peter, what morality and time-filling activity are to the Hauptmann: a blatant refuge from reality. They despise reality as they perceive it: pull them out of the theatre and stick them in the street, and they are disgusted by what seems to them a miserable spectacle: 'Sezt die Leute aus dem Theater auf die Gasse: ach, die erbärmliche Wirklichkeit!' (37). They see around them not God's creatures, but mere banality, and so they prefer to bury themselves in plays and poems and novels and ape the postures there displayed: 'Sie gehen in's Theater, lesen Gedichte und Romane, schneiden den Fratzen darin die Gesichter nach und sagen zu Gottes Geschöpfen: wie gewöhnlich!' They have eyes and ears for reality only insofar as it is wholly travestied: artified into stilted semblances and broken down into neat little packages in theatres, concert halls, and art galleries: 'Ich sage euch, wenn sie nicht Alles in hölzernen Copien bekommen, verzettelt in Theatern, Concerten und Kunstausstellungen, so haben sie weder Augen noch Ohren dafür.' They don't want the image of real people with all the rich variety of genuine emotion—'das Schweben und Senken im menschlichen Gemüth'—but blatant puppets that clank about the stage on iambic feet, and display a 'character' that unwinds with clockwork logic: 'Schnizt Einer eine Marionette, wo man den Strick hereinhängen sieht, an dem sie gezerrt wird und deren Gelenke bey jedem Schritt in fünffüssigen Jamben krachen, welch ein Character, welche Consequenz!' Worst of all in Büchner's view: they want *ideals*, and so they delight in puppets that *look* like real humans with coat and trousers, limbs and a face, but in fact are mechanical objects representing nothing but a single idea, emotion, or maxim: 'Nimmt Einer ein Gefühlchen, eine Sentenz, einen Begriff und zieht ihm Rock und Hosen an, macht ihm Hände und Füße, färbt ihm das Gesicht und läßt das Ding sich drei Acte hindurch herumquälen, bis es sich zulezt verheirathet oder sich todtschießt[5]—ein Ideal!'

This is all very well. It is easy to see why Büchner is so antagonistic to prevailing art forms, and the escapist proclivities that encourage them in their wholesale avoidance of anything approaching authentic reality. But we need to take the argument a stage further, and ask what alternative he proposes. What does he *mean* by 'reality', and how does he see this reality being effectively rendered in art? In the end, the only truly cogent answers to these questions will be found in his actual practice throughout his own art. But there are also various pointers to a conscious aesthetic programme—and it is these pointers that we shall now consider.

---

[5] There is a curious echo of this turn of phrase in Büchner's letter to his brother Wilhelm of 2 Sept. 1836, with its characteristic tone of self-irony (he was almost certainly struggling with both *Woyzeck* and *Leonce und Lena* at the time): 'ich [bin] gerade daran, sich einige Menschen auf dem Papier todtschlagen oder verheirathen zu lassen' (ii. 460; *I am just in the process of getting various people to marry or murder each other on paper*).

4
The Quick and the Dead

ONE of the happy side-effects of the fact that *Dantons Tod*—alone among his works—was published in Büchner's lifetime is that it provoked him into mounting a specific defence of his artistic position: a highly unorthodox one, as he well knew, not calculated to endear him either to the theatre-going public (cf. Camille's tirade), or to the political regime—or indeed to his own parents. It is to his parents that he duly writes on 5 May 1835, some two and a half months before his (bowdlerized) play actually appeared. His naked aim is to pre-empt the adverse judgement that he plainly anticipates, should a copy of the play happen by some mischance to fall into their hands (he clearly has no intention of sending them one himself): 'Im Fall es euch zu Gesicht kommt, bitte ich euch, bei eurer Beurtheilung vorerst zu bedenken, daß [etc.]' (ii. 438; *In case it comes to your notice, may I beg you, before you make your judgement, to bear in mind that [etc.]*). From the outset he offers a double defence that seeks to minimize, even to disguise, his own creative role: in writing his play, he asserts, he was simply reproducing the realities of history; and in so doing he had no alternative but to stick rigidly to the facts whatever they might be: 'Ich betrachte mein Drama wie ein geschichtliches Gemälde, das seinem Original gleichen muß'; 'ich [mußte] der Geschichte treu bleiben und die Männer der Revolution geben . . . wie sie waren' (ibid.; *I regard my play as a historical portrait that must exactly resemble its original*; *I had to be true to history and depict the men of the Revolution as they actually were*). Within days of the play's publication in middle-to-late July 1836, he feels driven to offer his parents much more detailed explanations ('Ueber mein Drama muß ich einige Worte sagen', ii. 443). And once again, his plea is that he is merely recording history exactly as it happened; indeed he has the bright idea of representing himself as being literally a historian: 'der dramatische Dichter ist in meinen Augen nichts, als ein Geschichtschreiber . . . Seine höchste Aufgabe ist, der Geschichte, wie sie sich wirklich begeben, so nahe als möglich zu kommen' (ibid.; *the dra-*

matist is in my view nothing other than a historian . . . His supreme task is to get as close as possible to history as it actually happened). The great advantage of this line of argument is that it serves to deflect the charge of 'immorality' that appears to have been levelled at him even by this very early stage ('die sogenannte Unsittlichkeit meines Buchs', ibid.): if God didn't make history suitable for the reading of young ladies, then no one can blame *him* if his drama is equally unsuitable ('da ist es mir auch nicht übel zu nehmen, wenn mein Drama ebensowenig dazu geeignet ist', ibid.). The writer, he asserts, is not a preacher of morality ('kein Lehrer der Moral', ii. 444), and it would be wrong for his (quasi-historiographical) work to be any more moral or *im*moral than history itself ('Sein Buch darf weder *sittlicher* noch *unsittlicher* sein, als die *Geschichte selbst*', ii. 443; Büchner's italics).

He envisages two particular counter-arguments, and pre-emptively dismisses both of them (ii. 444): (i) 'if you must show reality as it is, then don't choose such a nasty bit of it'; (ii) '*don't* show reality as it is: show it as it should be'. Acceptance of the first proposition, he retorts, would mean condemning the greatest masterpieces of literature ('so müßten die größten Meisterwerke der Poesie verworfen werden'); moreover, one would have to abandon history because of its immorality, go blindfold in the street because of its lewdness, and curse God for creating a world so full of debauchery:

> Wenn man *so* wollte, dürfte man keine Geschichte studiren, weil sehr viele unmoralische Dinge darin erzählt werden, müßte mit verbundenen Augen über die Gasse gehen, weil man sonst Unanständigkeiten sehen könnte, und müßte über einen Gott Zeter schreien, der eine Welt erschaffen, worauf so viele Liederlichkeiten vorfallen. (ibid.; Büchner's italics)

As for the second proposition, he has a double reply. He has no intention of trying to improve on God's world, he says, since God doubtless made it as it was meant to be. And anyway, what would be the likely outcome of such an attempt? Not 'Menschen von Fleisch und Blut' (*flesh-and-blood humans*), but 'Marionetten mit himmelblauen Nasen und affectirtem Pathos' (*marionettes with sky-blue noses and affected rhetoric*).

In his refutation of both these propositions, Büchner echoes his critique of contemporary art-forms in Camille's tirade, and he is clearly expressing his true position about what he does *not* do: he does not exclude any part of reality on account of its crudeness, and in general he does not distort it to make it suit some noble ideal. With regard to what he *does* do, however, his explanations vis-à-vis his parents are by no means so straightforward and persuasive. This is scarcely surprising in the circumstances. He stood in the deepest disfavour with his worthy father: although very much a chip off the old block in his scientific endeavours (both his father and his grandfather were doctors, indeed medicine had been in the family for generations), he was a renegade from respectability in all other respects: a fugitive from the law, a disgrace to the family, and a distinct threat to its social position (as the tribulations of the Minnigerode family following the arrest of Büchner's friend and fellow-activist Carl Minnigerode showed only too clearly).[1] Büchner accordingly writes his letter home as a black sheep who has inflicted yet another scandal on his parents, and wants to forestall animosity and censure so far as he can. The measure of his anxiety is given by his willingness to tell a blatant lie: whereas in truth Gutzkow and/or the publishers had systematically pruned the text, Büchner blithely protests to his parents that some hack had actually *added* 'various crudities' which would never have sullied his own lips ('Außerdem hat mir der Corrector einige Gemeinheiten in den Mund gelegt, die ich in meinem Leben nicht gesagt haben würde', ii. 443). This deliberate lie shows very clearly how Büchner instantly identifies 'immorality' (and not political subversiveness) as the ingredient that will prove most offensive to his age. His whole defence of the play is explicitly an answer to the charge of immorality that has apparently already been levelled at it: 'Was übrigens die sogenannte Unsittlichkeit meines Buchs angeht, so habe ich Folgendes zu antworten'; and it closes with him predicting and pre-empting hostile press reviews in similar terms: the paid hacks of the government, he says, are in business to dismiss its opponents as moronic—or immoral ('die Regierungen müssen doch durch ihre bezahlten Schreiber beweisen lassen, daß ihre Gegner Dummköpfe oder unsit-

---

[1] The strained relationship between Büchner and his father is clearly reflected in the latter's only surviving letter to his son (written just weeks before the latter's death), in which he speaks of his severe distress at all the difficulties and anguish Georg had caused the family through his 'imprudent conduct': 'mein Gemüth war noch zu tief erschüttert, durch die Unannehmlichkeiten alle, welche Du uns durch Dein unvorsichtiges Verhalten bereitet und gar viele trübe Stunden verursacht hast', ii. 500. According to Karl Emil Franzos (in the Introduction to his 1879 edition of Büchner's works), Ernst Büchner did not even allow Georg's name to be mentioned in his presence.

tliche Menschen sind', ii. 444; and sure enough, Büchner was being vilified a few months later as the purveyor of 'filth' and 'excrescences of immorality' etc.).

Büchner's defence of his play, then, or more accurately his defence of himself as its author, is a case of special pleading, even to the point of a downright lie—and we should not let ourselves be taken in by what is essentially a smokescreen.[2] This applies above all to Büchner's central argument with its two complementary components: 'to them that see only filth in my play, I say (i) that I simply hold a mirror to historical reality, and (ii) that the foulness of the mirror-image is simply the foulness of reality itself'. Both parts of this calculated argument are diversionary. Büchner's true stance is most emphatically not that of a neutral mirror-holder, a mere scribe of history ('nichts, als ein Geschichtschreiber'). And the reality that he chooses to convey is not mere vileness. Anyone reading his protestations vis-à-vis his parents without knowing *Dantons Tod* itself could easily suppose that the play must be an unremittingly black portrayal of the violent, depraved, cynical, and ungodly doings of a bunch of political gangsters ('Danton und die Banditen der Revolution', 'ihre Liederlichkeit', 'ihre Gottlosigkeit', 'blutig, liederlich ... und cynisch', ii. 443–4, 438), with all of this being conveyed by means of 'indecent expressions' echoing the 'notoriously obscene language of the time' ('unanständige Ausdrücke', 'die weltbekannte, obscöne Sprache der damaligen Zeit', ii. 444). Equally, one might infer that Büchner saw little else in history, in the public street, in the world in general, but filth of one kind or another: 'unmoralische Dinge', 'Unanständigkeiten', 'Liederlichkeiten' (ibid.). The peculiar irony here is that, in trying to forestall the censure of his own parents, Büchner was also giving grist to the mill of those later devotees of his work who see it as bleakly pessimistic or nihilistic. The truth behind the smokescreen is very different. Vile doings and circumstances are indeed depicted, both profusely and vehemently. But they are never the whole story; and they are never gratuitous or salacious. On the contrary, they are elements in a richly Brueghelish or Hogarthian tableau that is not neutrally mirrored or mimicked from life, but created afresh out of

[2] Cf. Thomas Michael Mayer, ' "Wegen mir könnt Ihr ganz ruhig sein..." Die Argumentationslist in Georg Büchners Briefen an die Eltern', in H. Gersch, T. M. Mayer, G. Oesterle (eds.), *Georg Büchner Jahrbuch*, 2/1982 (Frankfurt, 1983), 249–80.

a dynamic vision of existence at once deeply positive and ethically committed.

Some hints of this are even tucked away in the July 1835 letter to his parents. He declares the dramatist to be 'nothing but a historian'—but immediately contradicts himself by saying in the same breath that the dramatist is nevertheless *superior* to the historian in that he creates history anew; he transports us into the very life of an age instead of giving us just a bare narrative; he offers us characters instead of characterizations; a palpable presence instead of mere descriptions ('der dramatische Dichter ist in meinen Augen nichts, als ein Geschichtschreiber, steht aber *über* Letzterem dadurch, daß er uns die Geschichte zum zweiten Mal erschafft und uns gleich unmittelbar, statt eine trockne Erzählung zu geben, in das Leben einer Zeit hinein versetzt, uns statt Charakteristiken Charaktere, und statt Beschreibungen Gestalten gibt', ii. 443). The key vocabulary of 'creativity' and 'life' then typically recurs later in the same letter: writers invent and create real figures, he says; they bring bygone eras back to life ('Der Dichter ... erfindet und schafft Gestalten, er macht vergangene Zeiten wieder aufleben', ii. 444). A little later again, he mocks the Idealist writers for producing puppets instead of real flesh-and-blood people. And this takes us straight back to Büchner's onslaught in *Dantons Tod* against the mechanical puppets and stilted semblances, the 'Marionetten' and 'hölzernen Copien', so dear to contemporary patrons of the arts in their blinkered aversion to full-blooded reality. Again here, we find that the essential emphasis is on Life; on the need for art in all its forms to catch the living pulse of a vibrant, ever-changing, creative force at work in all reality. This is the very heart of his criticism of the art-public—and it is expressed with a unique intensity that marks out this brief passage as one of Büchner's most crucial statements:[3]

[3] A fundamental interpretative issue is involved here: are we ever justified in ascribing to Büchner the ideas or attitudes of his characters? It has been argued that Büchner never at any point makes his characters into mouthpieces, and that every utterance in his poetic œuvre arises solely out of the specific situation within which it occurs ('Büchner [läßt] an keiner Stelle die Sprechenden zu Sprachrohren werden ... Jede philosophische oder religiöse Äußerung ist genauestens aus der Situation motiviert'; Burghard Dedner, 'Bildsysteme und Gattungsunterschiede in *Leonce und Lena, Dantons Tod* und *Lenz*', in Dedner (ed.), *Georg Büchner: Leonce und Lena. Kritische Studienausgabe, Beiträge zu Text und Quellen* (Frankfurt, 1987), 182). But many powerful utterances in Büchner are remarkable precisely because they so conspicuously do *not* arise out of the given dynamic of plot, character, mood etc.; and Dedner is not at all convincing when he suggests that Camille's extraordinary

Sie vergessen ihren Herrgott über seinen schlechten Copisten. Von der Schöpfung, die glühend, brausend und leuchtend, um und in ihnen, sich jeden Augenblick neu gebiert, hören und sehen sie nichts. (37)
They forget their Maker for his incompetent copyists. They hear and see nothing of the glow, the hum the radiance of creation regenerating itself in and around them each second of the day.

This, for Büchner, is the ardent, living truth of reality, and this is what he means to recreate in his own art, instead of the prevailing 'stilted copies', 'puppets', 'grimacing masks' ('Fratzen') produced by a pseudo-art that is sterile like Pygmalion's statue (37), and which, while purporting to show life itself, in fact perverts nature by depicting what is lifeless—like the painter David sketching corpses in the Paris Terror, and claiming to catch on paper the 'final spasms of life' ('die letzten Zuckungen des Lebens') of the very dead victims (37).

This vision of true and false kinds of art is given its fullest expression in the famous Kaufmann episode of *Lenz*—by far the longest and most programmatic statement of Büchner's aesthetic-ethical standpoint that we possess.

In this instance, relatively little breath is wasted on the kinds of art that Büchner rejects: he simply has Lenz sketch in the position that is already familiar to us from his letters home, and from Camille's speech. Idealism is again attacked (anachronistically, given the time setting of *Lenz*) for its insufferable attempts to 'improve' reality by transfiguring it ('die Wirklichkeit verklären', 86)—attempts that produce only 'Holzpuppen' (*wooden puppets*) instead of real people (87); and it stands accused of the most obnoxious contempt for human nature: 'Dieser Idealismus ist die schmählichste Verachtung der menschlichen Natur.' (87). Through Camille's mouth he inveighed against the 'schlechten Copisten' and their 'hölzernen Copien'—those dreary copy-artists who produce nothing but caricatures; now, through Lenz's mouth, he reinforces his critique in characteristic terms: a writer should let his characters develop out of their own inner resources, he argues, rather than imposing on them some pattern copied from outside that leaves one with no sense of the surge and throb of life, muscles, pulse: 'man kann die Gestalten aus sich heraustreten lassen, ohne etwas vom Äußern hinein zu

speech is motivated simply by his lover's need to sound off in his beloved Lucile's presence ('Seinen Hymnus auf die Schöpfung trägt Camille in Anwesenheit Luciles, d. h. als Liebender, vor'; loc. cit.).

kopiren, wo einem kein Leben, keine Muskeln, kein Puls entgegen schwillt und pocht' (87).

This stress on the 'inner' as against the 'outer' is of cardinal importance. The reason that mere 'copying' is so futile is that outward appearances can be wholly deceptive; or to be more precise: we can be wholly deceived by the way we *perceive* things. This point was insistently made in the Camille passage: people have eyes and ears only for stilted copies of reality, and are blind and deaf to that creative force burning within and around them: 'wenn sie nicht Alles in hölzernen Copien bekommen . . . so haben sie weder Augen noch Ohren dafür'; 'Von der Schöpfung . . . hören und sehen sie nichts.' Now, in *Lenz*, exactly the same image is used: the writer must have the right kind of eyes and ears to hear and see what really matters: 'Man muß nur Aug und Ohren dafür haben.' (87). Only on the basis of this very special kind of perception can an artist be truly creative and satisfy the single but stringent criterion that Büchner asserts: that a work of art have the real breath of Life, a real potential for Being—so that it is then quite irrelevant how 'ugly' or 'beautiful' it may outwardly seem, provided that the created work carry emotional conviction in its sense of exuberant life: 'Ich verlange in Allem—Leben, Möglichkeit des Daseins, und dann ist's gut; wir haben dann nicht zu fragen, ob es schön, ob es häßlich ist, das Gefühl, daß Was geschaffen sey, Leben habe, stehe über diesen Beiden, und sey das einzige Kriterium in Kunstsachen.' (86). And it is only rarely, we are told, that we encounter anything that measures up to this singular standard: Shakespeare, folk-songs, and occasionally Goethe pass the test—'Alles Übrige kann man ins Feuer werfen.' (87; *Everything else can be thrown in the fire.*)

But what does all this mean in specific terms? What exactly does Büchner have in mind when he says that the true writer must have a special sensitivity, a special kind of eye and ear?

The first—and strikingly non-aesthetic—prerequisite is an absolute love of man: only through such love can one gain true insight, and see beyond the outward appearances of an individual's lowly station or seeming ugliness: 'Man muß die Menschheit lieben . . ., es darf einem keiner zu gering, keiner zu häßlich seyn, erst dann kann man sie verstehen' (87). Only on the basis of this eye-opening love of man, furthermore, is it possible to fulfil the next requirement: to leave behind one's own identity, to leave behind the entire world of outward appearances, and enter empathetically into the essential and particular being of any least individual: 'Man muß die Menschheit lieben, um in das eigenthümliche Wesen jedes einzudringen'. It is this loving empathy that then enables the writer to bring the imaginative process to completion by reproducing or re-creating in art that innermost life and vitality that he has been privileged to penetrate and experience: 'Man . . . senke sich in das Leben des Geringsten und gebe es wieder'.

A crucial element that Büchner predicates at all stages of this creative process is the power of feeling. It is a precondition in the writer himself, who could not otherwise possess that indispensable love of man that alone gives him understanding. But it is also the very thing in the actual object of empathy that the writer's special eye and ear enable him to register and respond to: no matter how prosaic people may seem on the surface, 'die Gefühlsader ist in fast allen Menschen gleich, nur ist die Hülle mehr oder weniger dicht, durch die sie brechen muß. Man muß nur Aug und Ohren dafür haben.' (ibid.; *the pulse of feeling is the same in almost all human-beings, the only difference is the thickness of the covering that it has to penetrate. One simply needs eyes to see it and ears to hear it.*) Finally, after the loving sensitivity of the writer to the innermost quality of feeling in the people portrayed, the work of art itself stands or falls by its impact on the *emotions* of its audience. Such displays of mere outward beauty as the Belvedere Apollo or Raphael's Madonnas accordingly fail the test for Lenz/Büchner: 'ich muß gestehen, ich *fühle* mich dabei sehr todt. Wenn ich in mir arbeite, kann ich auch wohl was dabei *fühlen*, aber ich thue das Beste daran.' (88, my italics; *I have to confess that things like that leave me quite cold. If I work at it within myself, I can doubtless generate some feeling, but it takes a real effort.*) The criterion is then made quite explicit: 'Der Dichter und Bildende ist mir der Liebste, der mir die Natur am Wirklichsten giebt, so daß ich über seinem Gebild fühle, Alles Übrige stört mich.' (88; *The writers and artists I like the most are those that most strongly convey to me the reality of nature, with the result that their work inspires me with feeling; everything else troubles me.*)

In trying to grasp the full meaning of all this, we need to resist a bevy of alluring sirens. Language itself can easily inveigle us—especially English language: words like 'real', 'nature', 'feeling', particularly when used in the literary context of the nineteenth century, tend to carry with them an insidious host of assumptions and associations. And we are perhaps all the more prone to enticement because Büchner's undertaking is so extraordinary, so exceptional: it is easier and altogether more comfortable if we can explain him away to ourselves by seeing him in some neatly labelled pigeonhole—'Late Romanticism', 'Late Late Sentimentalism', 'Early Realism'. But nothing could offend more fundamentally against the spirit of his work, which constantly inveighs against all the readymade labels, masks, pat assumptions and categories that offer themselves as a refuge from life. The vital realm that he envisions is beyond all labels and stereotypes, almost beyond the descriptive power of words—that is why, for him, the writer must *re-create* reality in all its vigour, and not offer mere descriptions or dry narrative ('Beschreibungen', 'eine trockne Erzählung', 443). He can put up banners bearing words like 'Schöpfung', 'Leben', 'Möglichkeit des Daseins', 'Wirklichkeit', 'das eigenthümliche Wesen jedes', 'Gefühl', and 'fühlen'; but he means a force, a presence, an innermost vitality that cannot properly be described, but only felt and lived—provided the creator has the right eyes and ears to perceive it, and the audience the right eyes and ears to receive it.

It is altogether in the spirit of this that Büchner has Lenz not only expound his argument, but also exemplify it, thus bringing it vividly to life. He lauds Dutch painters over Italian ones because, instead of offering the mere sensation of beauty ('die bloße Empfindung des Schönen', 87), they offer real, graspable substance: 'sie sind . . . die einzigen faßlichen [Maler]' (88). He then cites two particular Dutch paintings—and proceeds to create two small miracles of creative transposition from medium to medium, from painted image to verbal image. The second of these two renderings is exemplary—not only in its perfect economy of means, but because it shows Büchner's imaginative eye so clearly at work:

Eine Frau sitzt in ihrer Kammer, das Gebetbuch in der Hand. Es ist sonntäglich aufgeputzt, der Sand gestreut, so heimlich rein und warm. Die Frau hat nicht zur Kirche gekonnt, und sie verrichtet die Andacht zu Haus, das Fenster ist offen, sie sitzt danach hingewandt, und es ist als schwebten zu dem Fenster über die weite ebne Landschaft die Glockentöne von dem Dorfe herein und verhalle der Sang der nahen Gemeinde aus der Kirche her, und die Frau liest den Text nach.[4]

---

[4] A Nicolaes Maes painting matching this description hangs today in the museum at Gotha. Maes was a pupil of Rembrandt's who for part of his career was particularly fond of painting women spinning, reading the Bible, or preparing meals.

A woman sits in her room, prayer-book in hand. All is Sunday-fresh and tidy, the clean sand scattered, so pure and warm and homely. The woman couldn't go to church, and she is saying her prayers at home, the window is open, she sits turned towards it, and it is as though the sound of the village bells were floating across the wide, flat landscape into her window, and the singing of the congregation comes echoing over from the nearby church, and the woman follows the words in her prayerbook.

This is no catalogue of surface details, but the evocation of the picture's spirit. It is as though, by some alchemy, the fixed images of the paint were coming alive. What at first seems description—'Es ist sonntäglich aufgeputzt, der Sand gestreut'—is suddenly a lived presence: 'so heimlich rein und warm'. There is a sense not just of stasis ('sitzt', 'ist', 'gestreut') but of action: 'verrichtet', 'schwebten', 'liest'. There is a kind of synaesthesia whereby the visual image is resonant with sound. And the sound *moves*: across the countryside and in through the window—first in a subjunctive 'as if' mode ('als schwebten'), then as an actual event in the indicative ('verhallet'). None of these atmospheric elements are gratuitous, however: they all serve to celebrate what is clearly the essential subject of the painting in Büchner/Lenz's reading: a simple, profound Communion. The woman is on her own, yet not on her own: she is at one with her community and her God in a shared act of worship (a poignant image when we remember that Lenz himself is a doomed outsider in a similarly coherent community).

The treatment of the other Dutch painting[5] is no less revealing as a practical demonstration of Büchner/Lenz's aesthetic. It is particularly fascinating because it involves a double transposition: the biblical text of Jesus and the two disciples at Emmaus having been rendered in the fixed image of the painting, both text and painting are so to speak re-rendered and re-animated in Büchner's 'description'. For the sake of comparison, the relevant verses in Luke 24 are these (in the King James version):

13 And, behold, two of them went that same day to a village called Emmaus, which was from Jerusalem about threescore furlongs.
14 And they talked together of all these things which had happened.

---

[5] This picture of 'Christ and the Disciples at Emmaus' is almost certainly the one by Carel van Savoy that is still to be seen in Darmstadt. There is even a specific reference to the painting in the diaries of Büchner's friend Alexis Muston following a joint visit to the museum: 'Un Christ à Emmaus m'a également frappé, mais je ne me souviens pas de l'auteur'.

¹⁵ And it came to pass, that, while they communed together and reasoned, Jesus himself drew near, and went with them.
¹⁶ But their eyes were holden that they should not know him.
¹⁷ And he said unto them, What manner of communications are these that ye have one to another, as ye walk, and are sad? ...
²⁸ And they drew nigh unto the village, whither they went: and he made as though he would have gone further.
²⁹ But they constrained him, saying, Abide with us; for it is toward evening, and the day is far spent. And he went in to tarry with them.
³⁰ And it came to pass, as he sat at meat with them, he took bread, and blessed it, and brake, and gave to them.
³¹ And their eyes were opened, and they knew him; and he vanished out of their sight.
³² And they said one to another, Did not our heart burn within us, while he talked with us by the way, and while he opened to us the scriptures?

In these lines, so Büchner has Lenz declare, there resides 'the whole of nature' ('die ganze Natur'), and he goes on to demonstrate his vision of that totality—in the process transforming the steady, expansive, past-tense 'history' of the Bible into a living tableau of extraordinary intensity. The events of hours are compressed into moments, but moments of a presence that transcends time; the plump story-line is pared to its leanest essentials, and delivered not with the conjunction-rich leisure of the original with its score of 'ands', but with driving parataxis; prior to the central happening, tension is created out of nothing through an inspired, almost verbless piece of scene-painting; and afterwards the tension is 'unwound' again through a shift of mode, a reversion to the plummier, conjunctivized cadences of the biblical original:

Es ist ein trüber, dämmernder Abend, ein einförmiger rother Streifen am Horizont, halbfinster auf der Straße, da kommt ein Unbekannter zu ihnen, sie sprechen, er bricht das Brod, da erkennen sie ihn, in einfach-menschlicher Art, und die göttlich-leidenden Züge reden ihnen deutlich, und sie erschrecken, denn es ist finster geworden, und es tritt sie etwas Unbegreifliches an, aber es ist kein gespenstisches Grauen; es ist wie wenn einem ein geliebter Todter in der Dämmerung in der alten Art entgegenträte ... (88)

It is a sombre twilight evening, on the horizon a monotonous streak of red, the road half in darkness, a stranger approaches, they talk, he breaks bread, with their simple humanity they realize who he is, and the divine suffering in his features calls out to them, and they are afraid, for it has grown dark, and they are touched by something beyond understanding, but it is not some ghostly dread; it is like a dead beloved coming up to you in the twilight, just as they used to . . .

Once again, as with the other painting, what Büchner chiefly celebrates here is a profound communion. Blessed with his special eye and ear, he communicates to us an act of communication in which the blind are given back their sight ('But their eyes were holden', 'And their eyes were opened'). And how is this insight accomplished? Not through words, not through processes of the rational mind. Already in the biblical text, this is strongly emphasized. In their blindness, 'they talked together', 'they communed together and reasoned'; they are upbraided by Christ: 'What manner of communications are these that ye have one to another . . .?' In their reliance on reasoning, they are deaf to their heart and its intuitions: 'O fools, and slow of heart to believe . . .!' (verse 25); and they realize afterwards that their heart had been speaking to them, if only they had listened: 'Did not our heart burn within us, while he talked with us by the way . . .?' When they finally recognize Christ, Büchner stresses that they do so by virtue of their 'simple humanity', not their intellect ('in einfach-menschlicher Art'); and what gets through to them is not so much Christ's spoken words, but the eloquence of his Passion—'die göttlich-leidenden Züge reden ihnen deutlich'—and the eloquence of that supreme act of communion, the breaking of bread: 'er bricht das Brod, da erkennen sie ihn'.

Besides the two Dutch paintings, there is a further exemplification in the *Lenz* passage of Büchner's aesthetic credo—and it is the first and most important of them all. The pictures that he envisions here are not painted re-creations, however inspiring, but the very stuff of living, changing reality itself. The passage in question follows immediately on the reference to the 'Gefühlsader' (*pulse of feeling*) in all human beings, and with its 'I saw . . .' formulation it clearly serves to demonstrate what is meant by 'Man muß nur Aug und Ohren dafür haben':

Wie ich gestern neben am Thal hinaufging, sah ich auf einem Steine zwei Mädchen sitzen, die eine band ihre Haare auf, die andre half ihr; und das goldne Haar hing herab, und ein ernstes bleiches Gesicht, und doch so jung, und die schwarze Tracht und die andre so sorgsam bemüht. Die schönsten, innigsten Bilder der altdeutschen Schule geben kaum eine Ahnung davon ... Sie standen auf, die schöne Gruppe war zerstört; aber wie sie so hinabstiegen, zwischen den Felsen war es wieder ein anderes Bild.

This is powerful enough in itself, but the gloss that follows adds a programmatic thrust of unforgettable force:

Die schönsten Bilder, die schwellendsten Töne, gruppiren, lösen sich auf. Nur eins bleibt: eine unendliche Schönheit, die aus einer Form in die andre tritt, ewig aufgeblättert, verändert (87)

Yesterday as I walked up by the valley, I saw two girls sitting on a stone, one putting up her hair, the other helping; and her golden hair cascading down, and a pale grave face, and so very young, and her black peasant dress, and the other so helpful, so full of concern. Even the most intense, most beautiful paintings of the old German school give scarcely a hint of it ... They stood up, the beautiful tableau was gone for ever; but as they clambered down among the rocks, there was yet another picture. The most beautiful images, the most resonant harmonies, coalesce, dissolve. Only one thing abides: an infinite beauty that passes from form to form, eternally changed and revealed afresh

These two young girls, so unsentimentally touching in their fluid simplicity, are perfect exemplars of Büchner's precepts about 'Gestalten' rather than 'Beschreibungen', 'Charaktere' rather than 'Charakteristiken'. The extraordinary and compelling achievement of this evocation is that the girls seem instantly real, a 'seen', 'felt' presence of flesh and blood, not dream-puppets like the golden girls of a Hoffmann or a Stifter—and yet at the same time they *are* emblematic, they are the embodiment of an ideal (a pattern we shall encounter again and again in Büchner's portrayal of females). The vision of eternal change and renewal of course echoes the image in *Dantons Tod* of living creation incessantly regenerating itself, 'die Schöpfung, die ... sich jeden Augenblick neu gebiert'. But the paean on beauty reminds us above all of the radiant faith that Büchner was to express so programmatically in the Trial Lecture: his belief in a fundamental law of beauty that generates the highest and purest of forms out of the simplest of patterns, and creates in the process a necessary harmony ('ein Urgesetz, ein Gesetz der Schönheit, das nach den einfachsten Rissen und Linien die höchsten und reinsten Formen hervorbringt', 'die nothwendige Harmonie in den Aeußerungen eines und desselben Gesetzes').

Once we appreciate the relevance of this underlying credo, we are also able to understand more clearly what might otherwise seem a troubling element in the *Lenz* passage: Büchner's apparent acceptance of ugliness. The artist must not let himself be deterred by ugliness, we are told ('es darf einem . . . keiner zu häßlich seyn', 87); and the recipient of his art should not bother about its beauty or its ugliness provided it is exuberantly alive ('wir haben dann nicht zu fragen, ob es schön, ob es häßlich ist', 86). What he means, however, is the *outward* appearance of ugliness: that superficial face of reality that so disgusts Camille's theatre-goers once out in the street ('die erbärmliche Wirklichkeit!'); that outer barrier or 'Hülle' that all too easily masks the pulse of feeling, the 'Gefühlsader', that throbs in every individual. Just as there can be a sterile void behind the mere sensation of surface beauty—'die bloße Empfindung des Schönen' aroused by the Belvedere Apollo or the Madonnas of Raphael—so also an essential and infinite beauty can be found beyond appearances conventionally classed and despised as 'ugly', provided one has the eyes and ears to perceive it. And this is a *pure* beauty hidden behind the ugliness—not the *beauté noire* of modern decadence: Baudelaire's *charogne*, Rimbaud's decaying soldier, Kafka's pullulating maggots. It is the living manifestation of an 'Urgesetz', of a benign pattern of being whereby every least element in nature exists in its own right and for its own sake: 'Alles, was ist, ist um seiner selbst willen da.'

In the light of all this, it need hardly be stressed that Büchner's aesthetic evinced in his letters, in Camille's tirade, in the Kaufmann episode of *Lenz*, is actually much more an aesthetic: it is an integral part of his ontology, his whole ethic of existence. He advocates a particular mode of art not because it is more effective, more satisfying, more pleasing (though it is in fact all of these things), but because he believes it to be the only authentic and therefore valid one, the only way of perceiving, capturing, and conveying the inward beauty of the living world, and thereby doing it proper justice. Even then, he sees it as a difficult undertaking, and in a sense an impossible one. Do we retain the vital essence of the butterfly when we skewer it to our display board? The fluid beauty of the two young girls in the valley is beyond even the most beautiful and deeply felt paintings of the old German school, Lenz/Büchner remarks. He then imagines having the Medusa-like power to turn such a tableau into stone, and summon a gaggle of spectators: 'Man möchte manchmal ein Medusenhaupt seyn, um so eine Gruppe in

Stein verwandeln zu können, und den Leuten zurufen.' (87); but the implication is that the petrified image would at best be like Camille's Pygmalion: alive, but sterile (37). The point is made explicitly in the context of the 'unendliche Schönheit' evoked a little later, that abiding and infinite beauty that slips from form to form in a constant process of change and renewal: 'man kann sie aber freilich nicht immer festhalten und in Museen stellen und auf Noten ziehen und dann Alt und Jung herbeirufen, und die Buben und Alten darüber radotiren und sich entzücken lassen' (87; *but of course you can't always capture it and stick it in museums or put it into music, then summon all and sundry and have them prattling away, both young and old, and getting all excited*).

As we shall see, this too is by no means simply a professional difficulty confronting artists. It bears on an existential problem at the very heart of Büchner's concerns: how can the fullness and quickness of life be seized? Danton's lament to Marion is eloquent: 'Warum kann ich deine Schönheit nicht ganz in mich fassen, sie nicht ganz umschließen?' (22; *Why can't I take your beauty wholly into myself, wholly enfold it within my arms?*) Or there are the 'wild' imaginings of Lenz that seem at first sight just the mark of his gathering insanity: 'er meinte, er müsse den Sturm in sich ziehen, Alles in sich fassen, er dehnte sich aus und lag über der Erde, er wühlte sich in das All hinein' (79; *he thought he should draw the storm right into himself, take everything into himself, he stretched himself out and lay over the earth, he burrowed his way into the all*). Or there is the ecstasy of Leonce—sudden and brief—at the climax of the comedy: 'Mein ganzes Sein ist in dem einen Augenblick ... Wie frischathmend, schönheitglänzend ringt die Schöpfung sich aus dem Chaos mir entgegen.' (125; *All my being is in this single moment ... Out of chaos comes creation, bursting forth towards me, so alive and new, so radiant with beauty.*) Furthermore, Leonce's totality of being and vision of creation are not only a defeat of chaos, but a defeat of metaphorical death. Büchner, this ardent apostle of life, is incurably obsessed with death and its imagery. Danton in the first lines of the play tells Julie that he loves her like the grave ('ich liebe dich wie das Grab', 9); *Woyzeck* opens with the vision of a decapitated head; Leonce's love for Rosetta is a corpse entombed within his skull; Lena is to him an exquisite corpse ('schöne Leiche', 125) whom he biblically bids 'Arise and walk' ('Steh auf ... und wandle')—and so she does, thus giving him his ecstasy. Poor Lenz has no such luck. He too bids a corpse arise and walk ('Stehe auf und wandle!', 93); but this is a real corpse, albeit simultaneously an image of his unresurrectable love, Friederike Brion—'und die Leiche blieb kalt' (93; *and the corpse remained cold*). Why introduce this here? Because once again it relates directly to Büchner's vision of true art, which has to catch the living breath of reality, and triumph over fixity, rigor, deadness, sterility. It is surely no coincidence that of the two Dutch paintings so beautifully re-created by Lenz-Büchner, one is a picture of a man arisen from the dead—and mysteriously communicating his living presence to the heart and the spirit of his disciples.

Part II

Dantons Tod

5
A Dance of Delusions

WHEN we remember that Büchner has Camille in his tirade vituperate first and foremost against the blindness and deafness of art-patrons to anything that smacks of reality, when we also recall that for him the prime requirement of a true artist is that he should have a special insight, a special eye and ear, enabling him to penetrate to the inward reality of things, then it is all the more telling and apt that the very first word uttered in his work is 'Sieh' (*look*). What distinguishes Büchner as a writer is mirrored in his protagonists: they are alive to an order of realities that others do not recognize. Not only does Danton say 'Sieh . . .' to Julie, but Leonce says 'Sehen Sie' to his Tutor within seconds of the comedy's beginning, and Woyzeck, too, in the opening scene of the H2 draft frantically asks whether his companion sees and hears what he does: 'Siehst du . . .?', 'Hörst du's Andres? Hörst du's', 'Hörst du . . .?' (339). Nothing is more decisive for the destinies of all his protagonists than this special insight: it sets them apart from the rest—but it also destroys them (or in the case of Leonce in his happy-ending comedy, threatens to destroy him).

What is it that Danton sees at the very beginning of Büchner's creativity? It seems almost a mockery of what will be said in the Kaufmann passage in *Lenz*. There, it is a question of seeing beyond the surface ugliness to the essential beauty hidden within. Here, it is exactly the opposite: Danton sees beyond a mask of prettiness—'Sieh die hübsche Dame'—to the ugly reality it conceals. But it is not self-mockery, and no kind of self-contradiction. It is a first salvo in that sustained onslaught of which Camille's tirade is also part: an onslaught on a corrupt society dedicated to falseness and pretence. Here is a play by a famous political subversive about the famous death of a famous revolutionary; yet it opens not with affairs of state or public politics, but with private deceit and its seductive allure. The sheer disposition of the stage is expressive: Hérault-Séchelles and a gaggle of women around a card-table, immersed in their lubricious game, and then quite separate—'etwas weiter weg'—

Danton in the role of looker-on, for a moment almost a one-man Greek chorus. Instantly the card-game is shown to us through his eyes: as a masquerade, as a symbolic enactment of promiscuous duplicity. The pretty lady handles her cards with an air of demureness—'wie artig sie die Karten dreht'—but in truth she is an accomplished double-dealer who shows different suits to different people: 'cœur', her heart, to her husband, 'carreau', her cunt, to her lovers: 'ja wahrhaftig sie versteht's, man sagt sie halte ihrem Manne immer das cœur und andern Leuten das carreau hin.' Twice more in this expository opening, the card-game is put in the spotlight—and each time it is depicted as a blatant masquerade of sexuality. On the first occasion (9), one of the 'ladies' around the card-table—the same one, perhaps, that Danton referred to—bursts out with a nudge-and-a-wink complaint at the lewd suggestiveness of Hérault's fingers as he fiddles with his cards: 'es ist nicht zum Ansehn' (*it's a disgusting sight*). On the second occasion (10), the spotlight returns for Hérault to project the game entirely in terms of salacious sexuality. What is especially chilling here is that there is a kind of double masquerade. The game of cards is sexuality in disguise; but beneath the first disguise is another: the cynical pretence of genuine love and fairy-tale purity. We hear the *language* of love in various derivatives of 'lieben': 'verliebtes Abentheuer', 'Liebeserklärungen', 'Liebschaft'; and Hérault offers magical archetypes: a Queen, a Fairy, Princes transformed into spiders. But the reality is unlovely and unmagical: the 'love-adventure' is a commodity paid for in cash; the 'declarations of love' are obscene gestures; the 'love-affair' ends in a string of pregnancies. The grotesqueness of all this is further compounded by Hérault's lascivious tut-tutting as he imagines the playing-cards fucking each other with abandon as they come to fall on one another in the pack: 'Ich würde meine Tochter dergleichen nicht spielen lassen, die Herren und Damen fallen so unanständig übereinander und die Buben kommen gleich hinten nach.' (*I wouldn't let my daughter play such games, the Kings and Queens tumble on top of each other in such disgusting fashion, and the Knaves soon follow after.*)

Büchner was of course quite right to protest to his parents that any immorality in his play lay in the subject-matter and not in his portrayal of it. He was also no doubt right to argue that it is not the writer's task to teach morality ('Der Dichter ist kein Lehrer der Moral', ii. 444); certainly he himself never explicitly moralizes or sermonizes. Once again, though, we must not let ourselves be taken in by his 'scribe of history' ploy, and by the associated claim that a true drama should be neither more nor less moral than history itself ('weder sittlicher noch unsittlicher . . . als die Geschichte selbst'). In reality, his own stance is emphatically not neutral—as this opening sequence in his first play demonstrates beyond doubt: both in what he chooses to show, and in the way he chooses to show it, he evinces a profound, uncompromising morality. There is no pulpit-preaching or tub-thumping, to be sure, but something far more effective: the relentless exposure of falseness and inadequacy by reference to an implicit and almost forbiddingly stringent standard—not to say ideal—of integrity, wholeness, genuineness. Büchner points the finger and bids us see what he sees in all its garish fraudulence: 'Sieh die hübsche Dame!'

Sexuality is the keynote of this acerbic opening (quite unprecedentedly frank in modern German literature, and unmatched at least until Wedekind's *Frühlings Erwachen* over fifty years later); but it is important for us to realize that sexuality in itself is not Büchner's target here. Although it is true that sexuality as such was indeed profoundly problematic for him, as we shall see in due course, that is not the case at this particular juncture. What he harshly illuminates is the duplicity with which it is practised. This is the real focus of the anger and the anguish in Danton's opening 'chorus': that these people are living a lie. 'Truth' and 'lying' are immediately and explicitly cited—but in a tone of bitter irony, with Danton's remark that the woman 'truly' understands deception ('ja wahrhaftig sie versteht's'), and with his sardonic bon mot on the allure of lying: 'Ihr könntet einen noch in die Lüge verliebt machen.' (*You could even make a man fall in love with lies.*) The card-players are all pretending: the game itself is a cover; the smirking indignation of the 'lady' at the obscene mimicry of Hérault's fingers is a fraud; Hérault himself sports the mask of moral censure and parental concern whilst in the very act of intensifying the libidinous atmosphere ('so unanständig', 'Ich würde meine Tochter dergleichen nicht spielen lassen'). We have seen this kind of hypocritical 'morality' before: the Hauptmann wags his finger at Woyzeck—'Er hat keine Moral!'— but reveals moments later how he is overcome with 'love' when he ogles women's ankles as they skip across the puddles. And we are shown it repeatedly in *Dantons Tod*. Simon is apoplectic with righteous indignation at his daughter's prostitution, conveniently forgetting that he lives off her earnings, and that if her clients didn't take down their trousers, he himself would have none to put on (13). Marion's mother was hot on the 'fine virtue' ('schöne Tugend') of chastity, and sternly guarded her daughter from taint, but her visitors were allowed (or encouraged?) to engage in louche conversations (21). Yet another mother and her daughter appear in the 'Promenade' scene (35–6), and layer upon layer of falseness is revealed with a kind of fierce relish: (i) the mother—clearly one of those blind devotees of false ideals that Büchner/Camille will inveigh against in the following scene—has her head in a cloud of sentimental twaddle that links her daughter's virtue with the scent of flowers and the imagined 'purity' (i.e. sexlessness) of nature: 'Der Duft einer Blume, dieße natürlichen Freuden, dießer reine Genuß der Natur! [*Zu ihrer Tochter.*] Sieh, Eugenie, nur die Tugend hat Augen dafür' (36; *The scent of a flower, these natural pleasures, this pure delight in nature!* [*To her daughter.*] *See, Eugénie, only virtue has eyes to behold it.*); (ii) Eugénie and her escort mouth all the right platitudes to humour Madame, but it is sheer pretence: within moments of professing demurely to have eyes only for her dear Mama, the 'good child' Eugénie ('Gutes Kind!') is furtively devouring a passing spectacle of sexual scandal; (iii) this latter is introduced in terms that directly echo the opening of the play: 'Sehen Sie dort die hübsche Dame . . .?' (*See that pretty lady over there?*)—and we are shown yet another pretty lady engaged on yet another act of adulterous deception; (iv) once again, there is a lascivious pretence of moral condemnation: 'EUGENIE. Wie unanständig, ich hätte Lust roth zu werden.' (*EUGÉNIE. How very indecent, I quite want to blush.*)

By casting Danton right from his first utterance in the role of a man uncontrollably allergic to pretence and false appearances (a role that he will also bestow in due course on Leonce), Büchner is able to organize his entire play in terms of the exposure of masks, delusions, falsehoods—and the concomitant search for truth. The expository force of the opening scene lies chiefly in the way that it so insistently establishes this pattern. No sooner has the 'hübsche Dame' been revealed in all the lewd reality of her two-timing marriage than the focus abruptly shifts, and Danton shows his own relationship with his wife in the harshest possible light: after the triumph of lies, the desperate challenging of mutual faith and knowledge. Apparently out of the blue, but in oblique and perfect

A Dance of Delusions

response to Danton's exposure of the other woman, Julie asks an extraordinary question: 'Glaubst du an mich?' (*Do you believe in me?*), and then a few moments later she half-states, half-asks: 'Du kennst mich Danton.' (*You do know me, Danton.*) These brief lines serve as cues for a famous litany of despair, an anguished recital of isolation and individuation. What Büchner has Danton lament in his own relationship is essentially what he lamented in the 'pretty lady's': Julie is no tart, and he no cuckold, but there is nevertheless an impenetrable mask of outward appearances that prevents any true communion, any knowledge of the other's real self. Their inner selves are there alright, and reach out longingly towards each other, but in vain: both are hopelessly trapped within their own carapace, their own coarse, elephantine exterior, and condemned to utter isolation: 'Wir sind Dickhäuter, wir strecken die Hände nacheinander aus aber es ist vergebliche Mühe, wir reiben nur das grobe Leder aneinander ab,—wir sind sehr einsam.' As for Danton 'knowing' Julie: oh yes, he knows her—but his knowledge is conventional and superficial to the point of falsity, comprehending only the features of her doll-like mask: the darkness of her eyes, the curliness of her hair, the fineness of her complexion, her parrot-like cry of 'Dear Georges!', 'Dear Georges!' After the image of the thick, impenetrable hide: the image of the impenetrable casing of the skull, hiding forever the other's inner reality: 'Aber [*er deutet ihr auf Stirn und Augen*] da da, was liegt hinter dem? Geh, wir haben grobe Sinne. Einander kennen? Wir müßten uns die Schädeldecken aufbrechen und die Gedanken einander aus den Hirnfasern zerren.' (*But [pointing to her eyes and forehead] there, there! What lies behind there? Let's face it, our senses are pretty crude. Know one another? We'd have to smash our skulls and tear the thoughts from the very fibres of each other's brain.*)

This is powerful stuff, to be sure, and it has beguiled innumerable critics into taking it as gospel, as a classic statement of Büchner's supposed pessimism. We should be on our guard, however, for it is by no means as definitive as it might appear. What of the images of impenetrability, for instance—the elephantine hide and the barrier of the skull? How do they hold up against that similar yet fundamentally different barrier-image in *Lenz*: 'die Gefühlsader ist in fast allen Menschen gleich, nur ist die Hülle mehr oder weniger dicht, durch die sie brechen muß. Man muß nur Aug und Ohren dafür haben.'? The barrier is *not* impenetrable. Danton's problem is that he is beating on it at quite the wrong place. It is a gross delusion for him to suppose—with his bleakly reasoning mind—that the *mind* of Julie contains her reality. What Lenz/Büchner will call 'das eigenthümliche Wesen jedes', the 'particular being' or 'essence' of each individual (87), does not reside in 'Gedanken' impenetrably enfolded within 'Hirnfasern' locked away beneath the 'Schädeldecke' (*thoughts, brain fibres, vertex*). Danton is just like the two disciples at Emmaus who 'talked' and 'reasoned' and were 'fools' in being 'slow of heart to believe', so that they were blind to the reality staring them in the face. Only when we realize this—and it has long gone unrealized—can we appreciate the full power of this astonishing opening sequence. Two quite different, quite contrary languages speak to us here. There is the language of words and mind: Danton's cruelly anguished pronouncements representing his and Julie's relationship as one of bleak isolation and separateness. But even as these rasping words are being voiced, they are gainsaid by the mute but more telling language of the physical-emotional reality being enacted on the stage. Separateness is indeed a glaring aspect of the opening tableau of the play—but separateness as between the unit constituted by the card-players, and the unit constituted by Danton and Julie. This is not only deducible from the dialogue, but specifically called for by the initial stage direction (note especially the emphatic full-stop in the middle): 'Hérault-Séchelles, einige Damen (am Spieltisch). Danton, Julie (etwas weiter weg . . .)' (*Hérault-Séchelles, a few ladies (at a gaming table). Danton, Julie (somewhat further away . . .)*). How richly incongruous that Danton should paint his chilling word-picture of isolation and mutual inaccessibility—whilst with our own eyes we see the warm picture of his oneness with Julie. And they are at one not only by being a unit that contrasts with the card-players, but by the actual disposition of their bodies: they are not merely standing next to each other, or seated, like the card-party, around a table, but Danton is specifically 'auf einem Schemel zu den Füßen von Julie' (*on a stool at Julie's feet*)—scarcely the tableau that Büchner would have chosen if he had wanted the spatial language of the stage to underwrite and reinforce the language of Danton's words. What he offers us instead is the spectacle of a man whose brain, intent as always upon its 'secondary business', imagines one kind of reality—oblivious that his body and his heart are living out another. And having first shown these contradictory opposites through the different

A Dance of Delusions

languages of the intellectual-verbal and the emotional-physical, Büchner then has them collide on the one level of *words*. Danton speaks balefully of death-knell, coffin, grave, burial-mound—apt imagery in the opening minutes of a play whose very title harps on death. But it is only an extended if agonized conceit: Danton uses the language of death and burial—but what is expressed by these cold words is the warm, living reality of love:

DANTON. Nein Julie, ich liebe dich wie das Grab.
JULIE [*sich abwendend*]. Oh!
DANTON. Nein, höre! Die Leute sagen im Grab sey Ruhe und Grab und Ruhe seyen eins. Wenn das ist, lieg' ich in deinem Schooß schon unter der Erde. Du süßes Grab, deine Lippen sind Todtenglocken, deine Stimme ist mein Grabgeläute, deine Brust mein Grabhügel und dein Herz mein Sarg.

DANTON. No Julie, I love you like the grave.
JULIE [*turning away*]. Oh!
DANTON. No, listen! People say there's peace in the grave and that peace and the grave are one and the same. If that's the case, then I'm already buried when I lie in your lap. You sweet grave, your lips are passing-bells, your voice my death-knell, your breast my burial mound, your heart my coffin.

This is scarcely an endearing confession of love—it would take a seasoned necrophile to rejoice in the appellation 'Du süßes Grab'— but a confession of love it certainly is, however bizarre (and one that will have frequent echoes, equally bizarre, in the rest of Büchner's writing). And again there is an eloquently *physical* language here: no actor could convincingly deliver these words without expressive gestures to match—cradling his head in Julie's lap perhaps, and caressing her lips, her breast, her heart.

In this opening scene of the play, the withering insight bestowed on the protagonist is brought to bear on altogether three quite different 'beautiful illusions'. The first is the 'hübsche Dame', the society lady whose pretty face and husband-loving demeanour mask a reality of promiscuous abandon. The second is the ideal of love, which Danton fiercely demolishes as a notion, and yet which remains before our very eyes as a lived and undeniable reality. The third is of a quite different order: the brave ideals of social-political progress.

Having begun his play in a conspicuously private realm, Büchner neatly engineers the shift to the larger realm of politics and society by bringing Camille Desmoulins and Philippeau onto the stage as virtual 'messengers from the battlefield'. Just as the play will end with the murderous reality of the guillotine, so too, in its political dimension, it begins with it: the guillotine is explicitly referred to in each of the first two speeches upon the newcomers' arrival, and its relentless toll is spelt out by Philippeau: 'Heute sind wieder zwanzig Opfer gefallen' (10; *Yet another twenty victims have met their deaths today*).

Bearing in mind that the play will describe the Revolution repeatedly and very quotably as an inhuman process with an autonomous logic of its own, it is striking that in these expository references to the guillotine, it is unambiguously depicted as a deliberate instrument of policy and political will, manipulated by a specific power-group and its specific members. Hébert and his fellow extremists have not been annihilated by a blind, impersonal force of history: they have been deliberately eradicated by the Decemvirate for political reasons; either—it is suggested—because they represented a threat to the Decemvirate's own survival (a revealing and recurrent motif to which we shall return), or else because they were insufficiently 'systematic' in their extremism (10). Saint-Just and Robespierre are instantly identified as the principal villains of the piece, and again the guillotine is depicted as an instrument of policy: they would not shrink from vastly increasing even the death-toll that Marat had proposed, in order to realize their totalitarian aim of taking humanity back to its supposed primal state and moulding it anew in the mechanistic image of Rousseau:

> HÉRAULT. Sie möchten uns zu Antediluvianern machen. St. Just säh' es nicht ungern, wenn wir wieder auf allen Vieren kröchen, damit uns der Advokat von Arras [Robespierre] nach der Mechanik des Genfer Uhrmachers [Rousseau] Fallhütchen, Schulbänke und einen Herrgott erfände.
> PHILIPPEAU. Sie würden sich nicht scheuen zu dem Behuf an Marats Rechnung noch einige Nulln zu hängen. (10–11)

To the Dantonists, this political philosophy is a literal dead-end that has reduced France to a kind of gruesome and futile infantilism: 'Wie lange sollen wir noch schmutzig und blutig seyn wie neugeborne Kinder, Särge zur Wiege haben und mit Köpfen spielen?' (11; *How long are we to go on being filthy and bloody like new-born babes, with coffins for cradles and heads for playthings?*) What is desperately needed, so they declare, is *progress*—'Wir müssen vorwärts'; and progress, they believe, entails a quite different programme from that pursued by the Jacobin faction of Robespierre and Saint-Just.

One can only blink at the rapidity and effectiveness with which Büchner establishes the essential character of the play's political debate. Almost within seconds of Camille's and Philippeau's arrival with their news of the latest inflation in the extermination-rate, it begins to be made clear that what is involved is not simply a disagreement over tactics, and certainly not a mere clash of personalities, but a conflict about fundamental questions of ends and means—a conflict of divergent ideologies and value systems (11).

In essence it is a debate about the State and the individual—the first such debate in German literature in specifically political terms.[1] The basic issue is stark and simple: should individuals be a function of their State, or should the State be a function of its individuals? Büchner has the Dantonists emphatically support the latter view, and equally emphatically reject the former. In arguing for new 'Staatsgrundsätze', new principles on which the State should be based, they reject the prevailing mechanisms of prescription and control: instead of the imposition of duties, there should be the enjoyment of rights; instead of behaviour being judged according to its conformity to a moral code, it should be judged according to the well-being that it generates; instead of a punishment-system designed to enforce obedience, force should be used only where necessary for self-protection: 'In unsern Staatsgrundsätzen muß das Recht an die Stelle der Pflicht, das Wohlbefinden an die der Tugend und die Nothwehr an die der Strafe treten.' On this view, it is the absolute right of every individual to assert their own individuality and their own nature, and to enjoy life in their own way, with the sole proviso that their enjoyment must not be at someone else's expense, or hinder someone else in their own enjoyment: 'Jeder muß sich geltend machen und seine Natur durchsetzen können . . . Jeder muß in seiner Art genießen können, jedoch so, daß Keiner auf Unkosten eines Andern genießen oder ihn in seinem eigenthümlichen Genuß stören darf.' This means that instead of the State determining the visage of its citizens, their own preponderant

---

[1] Büchner's great predecessor in this crucial area is, of course, Friedrich Schiller. It is a sharp irony that Schiller's work was so comprehensively taken over and distorted by the cultural-political establishment of the early 19th c. that his unprecedented achievements in exploring the dangerous interface of polis and individual were rendered quite invisible to Büchner.

individuality must determine the visage of the State: 'Die Individualität der Mehrzahl muß sich in der Physiognomie des Staates offenbaren' (TMM 15;[2] originally included in the manuscript, but then replaced by the sentence beginning 'Jeder muß in seiner Art genießen können'). And instead of the State being a rigid straitjacket tolerating nothing but strict and universal conformity, it must be a raiment so diaphanous and delicate that it snugly accommodates the body of its people without ever impeding it in its pulsating, vigorous, sinuous vitality: 'Die Staatsform muß ein durchsichtiges Gewand seyn, das sich dicht an den Leib des Volkes schmiegt. Jedes Schwellen der Adern, jedes Spannen der Muskeln, jedes Zucken der Sehnen muß sich darin abdrücken.' No fewer than three times within a dozen lines, Büchner has the Dantonists condemn those who use their State authority to try to impose on everyone else a straitjacket of their own particular fancy. It is a question of rights: it is no concern of the State how sensible or silly, cultured or uncouth, nice or nasty, beautiful or ugly a person may happen to be—everyone has the right to be as they are: 'sie hat einmal das Recht zu seyn wie sie ist' (11). And by the same token, no one has the right to inflict their particular notions on others: 'es hat Keiner das Recht einem Andern seine eigenthümliche Narrheit aufzudringen'; 'wir sind nicht berechtigt ih[m] ein Röcklein nach Belieben zuzuschneiden'. As for the Jacobins: they have to be stopped from trying to bind a nun's veil around the deliciously naked and amiably dissolute shoulders of France: 'Wir werden den Leuten, welche über die nackten Schultern der allerliebsten Sünderin Frankreich den Nonnenschleier werfen wollen, auf die Finger schlagen.'

We are confronted here by a decisive question, in effect a kind of shibboleth that serves to identify each critic's stance on a fundamental and highly contentious issue. Where, we have to ask, does Büchner himself stand in this conflict of political philosophies? According to Viëtor, Büchner 'does not think in terms of a social system that makes it possible for the individual freely to determine his own existence as a moral entity ... For Büchner it is not a question of the individual and his rights ... The political goal for which he means to strive is the liberation of the lowest class, the

[2] References beginning TMM relate to Georg Büchner, *Danton's Tod. Ein Drama*, ed. Thomas Michael Mayer (Frankfurt, 1980). Although only billed as a provisional working edition ('Studienausgabe'), this is the most detailed and authoritative edition of the play currently available.

A Dance of Delusions 89

anonymous mass, from their state of economic subordination.'[3] Are we to accept this? Are we even to be persuaded by the explicitly Marxian view of T. M. Holmes that Büchner in this opening scene is 'depicting the liberal ideology of the moderates as the protocol of bourgeois dictatorship', an ideology 'amounting to a programme of bourgeois aggression and aggrandisement that involves an endlessly intensified exploitation of the poor', perpetrated by a 'parasitic leisured class, uninvolved in the production of the goods it consumes'?[4] But this perspective is surely quite wrong. Büchner does indeed long to see the grievously oppressed and exploited masses escape from a thraldom that is economically determined. But freedom from material need and the social oppression that goes with it is only the precondition for a more profound and more positive freedom: the freedom of every individual to live out their own true being in all its particular richness. What is the first objection that Büchner raises in the Trial Lecture to the 'functionalist' school of science?—'Sie kennt das Individuum nur als etwas, das einen Zweck außer sich erreichen soll' (ii. 291; *It knows the individual only as something that is intended to fulfil a purpose beyond itself*). The individual is sacred to Büchner, and does not exist merely to be a cog in a machine and to serve a 'purpose beyond itself': 'Alles, was ist, ist um seiner selbst willen da.' He is therefore implacably opposed to any attempt from whatever quarter—be it in science, philosophy, aesthetics, morals, politics—to subordinate individuals to systems, and functionalize them into mechanical components according to an abhorrent law of 'maximum fitness for purpose' ('die größtmöglichste Zweckmäßigkeit', ii. 292). I am in two minds (or more) about many aspects of Büchner's writing; but it seems to me clear beyond doubt that the ideals voiced through the Dantonists in the first scene of the play are Büchner's own. The anathema-words 'systematisch' and 'Mechanik' are a first, unmistakable pointer: the

---

[3] 'Er denkt nicht an eine Rechtsordnung, die es dem einzelnen ermöglicht, als moralische Person sich selbst frei zu bestimmen . . . Für Büchner handelt es sich nicht um das Individuum und seine Rechte . . . Das politische Ziel, für das er kämpfen will, ist die Befreiung der untersten Volksschicht, der anonymen Masse aus ihrer ökonomischen Abhängigkeit.' Viëtor, *Georg Büchner*, 51. Cf. Gerhard Jancke, *Georg Büchner. Genese und Aktualität seines Werkes. Einführung in das Gesamtwerk* (Kronberg/Taunus, 1975), 191; Jancke's book stands as the most radically 'Jacobin' interpretation of Büchner's work and life.

[4] T. M. Holmes, 'The Ideology of the Moderates in Büchner's "Dantons Tod" ', *German Life and Letters*, NS 27 (1973/4), 94, 98, 99, 100.

ideology of the Jacobins is repellent and reprehensible precisely because it ignores the rights of individuals and seeks to forcibly 're-construct' them according to a preconceived mechanical system. The belief that every least individual 'hat einmal das Recht zu seyn wie [er] ist' exactly parallels the belief that 'Alles, was ist, ist um seiner selbst willen da.' And it is clearly Büchner's voice that we hear in the passage's most programmatic affirmation: 'Jeder muß sich geltend machen und seine Natur durchsetzen können.' (*Everyone must be able to assert their own individuality and their own nature.*) Just as Camille is his mouthpiece later on when he calls for an art that fully reflects 'das Schweben und Senken im menschlichen Gemüth', so too Camille is his mouthpiece here when he calls for a 'Staatsform' that, in enfolding the body of the people, gives full scope and expression to every muscle, pulse, and sinew. Again, it is Büchner himself who condemns any State-imposed straitjacketing of the people—recognizing in the process that the 'State' is anyway an abstract entity, and that what is done in its name is all too often the mere caprice of fallible individuals determined to inflict on others their own particular idiosyncrasies ('seine eigenthümliche Narrheit', 'ein Röcklein nach Belieben zuschneiden').

Quite apart from the fact that the beliefs and principles voiced here are the same as those advocated by Büchner on other occasions, there is other, more textual and circumstantial evidence that plainly shows how much these things matter to him. For one thing, there is no question here—notwithstanding his expedient claim vis-à-vis his parents—of Büchner simply painting a faithful and neutral historical portrait: whereas for instance Camille's first speech (about Socrates and Alcibiades) is borrowed directly from the source material (in this case from Thiers), there is scarcely a scrap of the social-political philosophy subsequently voiced through Camille and Hérault that is not of Büchner's own invention (cf. TMM 15). Far from him merely 'portraying' or 'mimicking' historical figures, he is making use of these figures to body out his own particular preoccupations. This becomes even more apparent when one considers this passage in the context of the play's economy. In terms of plot-development, or the play's nascent 'story-line', there is no reason whatsoever for an alternative political programme to be elaborated in such detail or at such length; the pure plot of the play indeed requires no *philosophical*-political dimension at all, but merely the depiction of a practical or tactical political rift sufficient

A Dance of Delusions

to motivate the deadly outcome already blazoned in the title. In terms of character portrayal, too, there is no particular logic in this passage: Hérault and Camille do not speak in their own right here, or demonstrate their specific personas in the way that a traditional stage-figure would do: it would have made no difference if what they say had been spoken by just one of them, or by some other character altogether—Philippeau, for instance. They serve here as mouthpieces, as a kind of antiphonal chorus giving voice to something that Büchner himself is most anxious to convey—and in the process delineating some of the essential issues of the play; issues that go far beyond the limitations of history, plot, persona.

But I spoke earlier of the ideal of social-political progress being unmasked in this opening scene as a beautiful illusion. How does this make sense if Büchner himself wholeheartedly believes in the ideal? It makes sense because of the bitter problem of ends and means; because of the disastrous gulf that separates the desirable from the achievable. Büchner should know. He was frantically writing his play against the background of the abysmal fiasco of *Der Hessische Landbote*, which had brought home to him at first hand what he had long since recognized: that the political and social order cannot be overthrown by the puny efforts of a few individuals (cf. the letter-fragment of June 1833, ii. 418). We hear the voice of Georg Büchner in the grand declaration of *ends*, with its insistence on the absolute necessity of these ends being realised (the verb 'müssen' is used no fewer than eleven times within thirty-odd lines). But we also hear the voice of Georg Büchner in Danton's sardonic question as to *means*: 'Wer soll denn all die schönen Dinge ins Werk setzen?' (12; *Who's going to bring about all these wonderful things?*); and again we hear the voice of this thoroughly routed activist who lives in continual fear of arrest, has a ladder constantly in place against the garden wall,[5] and will soon be forced to flee in earnest, when Danton makes his 'prophecy' that freedom is still by no means a reality, and that all of them may yet be hurt in its fiery crucible: 'die Statue der Freiheit ist noch nicht gegossen, der Ofen glüht, wir Alle können uns noch die Finger dabey verbrennen' (12). The prophecy was to come true even more cruelly than Büchner can have imagined: within the play, the re-enactment of the historical liquidation of Danton and all around him is of course simply a

---

[5] Cf. T. M. Mayer, 'Büchner-Chronik', 394.

matter of time; but in real life, more and more people connected with the *Landbote* were to find themselves scooped up by the relentless apparatus of the security services and the law, a system of such painstaking, elephantine brutality that Büchner's co-author, Ludwig Weidig, though a man of extraordinary fortitude, was to be driven to suicide in his prison cell.[6]

If we pause for a moment to take stock of the opening scene as a whole, we can only marvel at the way in which the 21-year-old tyro pulls it off: the scene has nothing about it of the orthodox exposition of traditional drama, and yet it is an exposition all the same, and a remarkably atmospheric and incisive one. What it does is to establish three distinct spheres of action and interest, which may be thought of as fitting inside one another, like Chinese boxes. At the centre is an intensely private and personal realm: the realm of the innermost self, characterized in Danton's case by the contradictory modes of cold self-isolating cerebration and warm intuitive involvement. Then there is the social realm: the realm where the private and the public intermingle, with the 'pretty lady' as its bleakly deceptive and deceitful paradigm. Finally there is the political realm: the realm of grand designs and social ideologies, of State and government, but the realm above all of political realities, of the possession and exercise of power by specific individuals and groups. All of these spheres must be considered in due course, but let us focus first on that of politics—the largest of them, but at the same time the only one that will not recur as a central topic in Büchner's subsequent writing.

---

[6] It is a strange quirk of history that Weidig died on 23 Feb. 1837, only four days after his erstwhile collaborator.

6
Fraud, Futility, Freedom

DANTONS TOD is surely the most penetrating and most complex exploration of politics in German literature—and certainly in German drama. Büchner chooses a historical period of maximum turbulence, peopled by turbulent characters, and he makes no attempt to simplify it into neat patterns—rather the reverse in fact: the rhythm of events is unashamedly irregular instead of mechanical; the settings are wildly kaleidoscopic, with nearly as many different locations as there are scenes; the two main characters are made even more complex than they appear to have been in real life. This insistent complexity is quite deliberate: it is a vivid practical demonstration of Büchner's commitment to reality in all its richness and rawness, his refusal to kowtow to a public that despised reality and sought escape in an idealized and false world of one-dimensionality, clockwork logic, patently manipulated puppets. Büchner is no less obsessed by ideals than the writers he rejected; for him, however, these ideals make sense only in the context of the real, contingent world. This is perfectly exemplified in the opening scene of the play when Camille and the others launch into their vision of a truly free society—only to be brought back to earth with a bump by Danton's simple question as to practicalities: 'Wer soll denn all die schönen Dinge ins Werk setzen?' This question, and in particular the dire epigram on the 'statue of freedom' that rings out so effectively at the close of the scene, point at once to the essential paradox of the play: it is precisely the Dantonists' politics of freedom that guarantee their own unfreedom—and their ultimate annihilation in the name of freedom.

As this suggests, the very ideal of freedom itself is shown to be problematic. The Dantonists want to end the carnage to bring about a truly free society. But this is exactly the reason why the Jacobins insist that the carnage must continue. Earlier I described Robespierre and Saint-Just as the villains of the piece, and in due course we shall see how, in their political actions, villainy and corruption are inescapably enjoined upon them by their chosen strategy. But this does not mean that their ideals as such are discredited. Indeed the essential idealism of the Jacobins is never impugned. Though we may note the propagandist expedience of such language, we are not invited to disbelieve Robespierre when he speaks of his 'passion for freedom', or implies that he and his fellows are the true 'friends of freedom' ('meine Leidenschaft für die Freiheit', 45; 'Freiheitsfreunde', 44); and along with the propaganda there is sincerity of a kind in the Jacobin accusation that the Dantonists for their part are the 'enemies of freedom' ('die Feinde der Freiheit', 18) who have variously raped, prostituted, and violated freedom (57, 70, 58–9). There can be no doubt that, in spirit, Büchner thoroughly endorses the argument that Robespierre flings at Danton in their scene together: 'Die sociale Revolution ist noch nicht fertig... Die gute Gesellschaft ist noch nicht todt, die gesunde Volkskraft muß sich an die Stelle dießer nach allen Richtungen abgekitzelten Klasse setzen.' (26; *The social revolution is not yet complete... The world of the idle rich is not yet dead, the healthy vigour of the people must take the place of this utterly effete and played-out class.*) Büchner might have had this very passage in the back of his mind then he wrote to Gutzkow in 1836:

Ich glaube, man muß... die Bildung eines neuen geistigen Lebens im *Volk* suchen und die abgelebte moderne Gesellschaft zum Teufel gehen lassen. Zu was soll ein Ding, wie diese, zwischen Himmel und Erde herumlaufen?... Sie mag aussterben, das ist das einzig Neue, was sie noch erleben kann. (ii. 455)

I believe that we have to seek the development of a new life and spirit in the *people* and let the decrepit society of today go to the devil. What's the point of such a creature careering about on God's earth? May it die out—that's the only new experience it is capable of having.

But while Büchner wholeheartedly shares this ideal in itself, he offers a massive critique of the political philosophy and programme that the Jacobins attach to it. We have already seen that what is central and sacred in Büchner's own idealist philosophy is the right of each individual freely to live his life in all its richness and fullness. What is sacred in Jacobinism, however, is not people but *ideas*; indeed they will destroy lives without limit for the sake of an idea. Straightaway in the opening scene we are told that the Jacobins would not hesitate to bump up the annihilation rate in order to achieve their goal of restructuring humanity on the Rousseauist model. Robespierre may have a genuine 'passion for freedom', but it manifests itself as a murderous scourge. This is pointedly revealed in the chilling (and historical) paradox that Robespierre himself enunciates in the Jacobin Club: 'Die Revolutionsregirung ist der *Despotismus der Freiheit* gegen die Tyrannei.' (18, my emphasis; *The revolutionary government is the* despotism of freedom *against tyranny*.) The same paradox is even more harshly illuminated by Danton's scathing question at his trial: 'Wie lange sollen die Fußstapfen der Freiheit Gräber seyn?' (63; *How long is the march of freedom to be marked by graves?*)

Nowhere is the Jacobins' subordination of people to ideas more forcefully expressed than in Saint-Just's programmatic and triumphant *tour de force* at the close of Act II (45–6)—a speech that is also remarkable for being the longest that Büchner ever composed entirely off his own bat (Robespierre's in the Jacobin Club is longer, but almost all of it derives from historical sources). With the word 'blood' as its keynote at both start and finish, the entire speech is a brazen defence of indiscriminate slaughter in the name of ideals. Saint-Just's arguments are seductive but specious. He cites the example of nature, which annihilates humans in their thousands if they happen to get in the way of a plague, a volcanic eruption, a flood; and if that is the natural law in the realm of physics, then it must equally be the law in the realm of morals:

Ich frage nun: soll die moralische Natur in ihren Revolutionen mehr Rücksicht nehmen, als die physische? Soll eine Idee nicht eben so gut wie ein Gesetz der Physik vernichten dürfen, was sich ihr widersezt? Soll überhaupt ein Ereigniß, was die ganze Gestaltung der moralischen Natur d. h. der Menschheit umändert, nicht durch Blut gehen dürfen?

Now I ask you: should moral nature show any more consideration in her revolutions than physical nature? Shouldn't an idea, just as much as a law of physics, be entitled to destroy whatever stands in its way? Shouldn't an event that transforms the entire shape of moral nature, in other words of humanity, be entitled to do so by means of blood?

But of course 'die moralische Natur' (*moral nature*) is a sheer invention: there is no 'natural law' in the moral sphere remotely equatable with the natural laws of physics. The same kind of objection applies to Saint-Just's immediately following argument, when he first of all posits a 'World Spirit' of Hegelian complexion, then claims that he and his fellow exterminators are the instrument of this spirit within the ambit of the human mind, just as volcanoes and floods are its instrument in the realm of physics, with the result that it makes no difference whether people are killed by a natural disaster like a plague, or by the Revolution: 'Der Weltgeist bedient sich in der geistigen Sphäre unserer Arme eben so, wie er in der physischen Vulkane oder Wasserfluthen gebraucht. Was liegt daran ob sie an einer Seuche oder an der Revolution sterben?'

Büchner then has Saint-Just proffer an even more monstrous justification. Human progress is normally slow, with whole generations dying during the course of the centuries: is it not quite straightforward, he asks, that proportionately more people should expire—in other words be slaughtered—in a period where history is advancing more rapidly? ('Ist es denn nicht einfach, daß zu einer Zeit, wo der Gang der Geschichte rascher ist, auch mehr Menschen außer Athem kommen?') Here Saint-Just proceeds to exemplify his argument with reference to a specific aspect of social progress. And just as Robespierre unhesitatingly translated the cause of freedom into a new despotism, so now Saint-Just defines the cause of equality in similar terms: he spells out the principle of universal equality, and enunciates a kind of 'grammar' of deathly progress: 'Jedes Glied dießes in der Wirklichkeit angewandten Satzes hat seine Menschen getödtet.' (*In the course of this sentence becoming reality, each one of its parts has taken its toll of human life.*) Achieving equality, he adds, has taken only four years where normally it would have taken a century and seen the death of several generations—'Ist es da so zu verwundern, daß der Strom der Revolution bey jedem Absatz, bey jeder neuen Krümmung seine Leichen ausstößt?' (*Is it so surprising that at every bend and every cataract the raging torrent of the Revolution spews out a new batch of corpses?*) And now, with the principal dictum thus made flesh, a few more clauses need to be added—to which a few hundred more corpses cannot be an obstacle: 'Wir werden unserm Satze noch einige Schlüsse hinzuzufügen haben, sollen einige Hundert Leichen uns verhindern sie zu machen?'

Saint-Just's third main argument is no less spurious than the others. This time he claims justification through the God-given example of the Bible. Moses purged his people in readiness for the new state of Israel by leading them through the Red Sea and the wilderness until the generation of the corrupt was wiped out by

Fraud, Futility, Freedom 97

sheer attrition; and what the Red Sea and the wilderness did for Israel, war and the guillotine will do for France: 'Moses führte sein Volk durch das rothe Meer und in die Wüste bis die alte verdorbne Generation sich aufgerieben hatte, eh' er den neuen Staat gründete. Gesetzgeber! Wir haben weder das rothe Meer noch die Wüste aber wir haben den Krieg und die Guillotine.' The analogy is doubly false. For one thing, it is a deceit for Saint-Just to imply that he and his cronies—already depicted as agents of the 'Weltgeist'—are the hand of God, as Moses was. What is more, the exodus itself is grossly distorted. Far from Jehovah destroying any of his people, by attrition or otherwise, his whole intent was to keep them intact, while strengthening their faith and confounding their enemies; re-education, not extermination, was his strategy for renewal. The Jacobin strategy could not be more different—as is demonstrated beyond all doubt by the final and supremely brutal analogy with which Büchner brings the harangue to its climax:

Die Revolution ist wie die Töchter des Pelias; sie zerstückt die Menschheit um sie zu verjüngen. Die Menschheit wird aus dem Blutkessel wie die Erde aus den Wellen der Sündfluth mit urkräftigen Gliedern sich erheben, als wäre sie zum Erstenmale geschaffen.

The Revolution is like the daughters of Pelias; it hacks humanity to pieces to make it young again. Humanity will arise from the bloodbath as the earth arose from the waters of the Flood: with pristine vigour in all its limbs, as though created for the very first time.

As demagogic propaganda this is powerful indeed, and it provokes a storm of enthusiastic applause amongst the assembled deputies, thus helping to achieve its tactical objective of ensuring the liquidation of the Dantonists. But only a fool or a fanatic could suppose that Büchner wishes us—the real audience—to respond with anything other than a thrill of horror.[1] Not least, we know what the deputies cannot know: that Saint-Just was disastrously

---

[1] Lukács—writing enthusiastically in Moscow in the midst of Stalin's purges—was profoundly wrong in representing Saint-Just as Büchner's ideal, a 'Wunschfigur' (Lukács, 212), and in describing his great speech as a 'passionate endorsement and glorification' of revolutionism and the 'necessary' liquidation of all who obstruct the onward march of history ('Im Drama gibt Büchner auf Dantons Zweifel wiederum eine gestaltete Antwort mit der großen Konventrede von Saint-Just, in der die eherne und unmenschliche Notwendigkeit der Geschichte, die ganze Generationen, die ihr im Wege stehen, revolutionär zerstampft, . . . mit leidenschaftlichem Pathos bejaht und verherrlicht wird.'; ibid. 214).

wrong; that in the event the bloodbath of the Revolution did not by any means regenerate humanity and render it pristine (as the Pelias allusion surreptitiously intimates: though butchered and boiled with the best of intentions, Pelias unsurprisingly emerged from his daughters' cookpot as nothing more than a motley of bones). But Büchner is not demonstrating simply an unfortunate historical miscalculation on Saint-Just's part: he offers us the terrifying spectacle of the mania of mind fatally allied to unbridled power; a spectacle that uncannily anticipates by a century and more the purgative madness of Stalin, Hitler, the Khmer Rouge. The lunatic king of *Leonce und Lena* and the madcap scientist of *Woyzeck* will exploit and dehumanize their minions in the name of ideas, abstractions, systems, theories; Saint-Just is prepared to annihilate them *en masse*, and to build his system out of severed heads (cf. 52). For the sake of Freedom we must have despotism; for the sake of Equality we must have corpses; for the sake of Humanity we must tear humans limb from limb. Cartesian rationalism will be attacked in the Trial Lecture for its 'dogmatism' and its remoteness from 'dem frischen grünen Leben': could there be anything more dogmatic, more thoroughly inimical to life in all its vigour and freshness, than Saint-Just's baneful apotheosis of ideas?—'Soll eine Idee nicht eben so gut wie ein Gesetz der Physik vernichten dürfen, was sich ihr widersezt?' (*Shouldn't an idea, just as much as a law of physics, be entitled to destroy whatever stands in its way?*) We might remember, too, how Descartes's entire system of abstract philosophy ('sein ganzes System'), built as it was over a yawning chasm, depended entirely on the ultimate abstraction of God (a god of theory, like Spinoza's, not a god of lived experience). The function of this God was to bridge the abyss between supposition and knowledge, between subjective perception and objective truth ('Gott ist es, der den Abgrund zwischen Denken und Erkennen, zwischen Subject und Object ausfüllt, er ist die Brücke zwischen dem . . . Denken und der Außenwelt'; cf. above, p. 34f.). Exactly the same process is shown with Saint-Just. He claims objective validity for Jacobin ideology by equating it with the physical laws of nature; by implicitly representing its exponents as the agents of God, like Moses; above all by explicitly depicting them as instruments of a Hegelian 'Weltgeist'. But in truth the ideology of the Jacobins has no objective validity at all: it is the subjective construct of overweening minds, their own particular crackpot obsession, born of their own particular fancy ('eigenthümliche Narrheit', 'nach Belieben [zugeschnitten]'); and accordingly they have no right whatever to inflict it on others.

This means in effect that the Jacobins' entire crusade to 'morally restructure' and 'regenerate' humanity, regardless of the cost in human lives, is essentially a delusion, a grotesque confidence trick that deceives even its own perpetrators. This is already suggested in the opening scene; but the point is driven home with great force in one of the play's most crucial scenes: the confrontation between Danton and Robespierre towards the end of the first act (26–7). The dynamic of this encounter is strikingly similar to the one that Büchner will use so effectively in the second half of the shaving scene in *Woyzeck*: in each case, a posture of dogmatic, censorious morality is eloquently demolished, and its exponent driven into grave confusion.

Robespierre's position, already expounded in the Jacobin Club, is restated here in all its draconian, absolutist simplicity: 'Das Laster muß bestraft werden, die Tugend muß durch den Schrecken herrschen.' (*Vice must be punished, virtue must prevail by means of terror.*) At once, the concept of punishment is challenged: 'Ich verstehe das Wort Strafe nicht.' (*I don't understand the word 'punishment'.*) This echoes the credo of the opening scene that it should be a basic principle of the state that force must be used not to punish, but only to prevent encroachment on others' rights ('In unsern Staatsgrundsätzen muß ... die Nothwehr an die [Stelle] der Strafe treten.') Rejecting the very notion of punishment as he does, and seeing no threat to legitimate rights and interests, Danton declares the liquidation programme of the Jacobins to be plain and simple murder: 'Wo die Nothwehr aufhört fängt der Mord an, ich sehe keinen Grund, der uns länger zum Tödten zwänge.' The fundamental issue, however, is the philosophy that underlies the Jacobins' entire strategy of morally restructuring humanity: the manichaean conviction that all human behaviour can be classified in terms of the moral absolutes 'vice' and 'virtue'. Danton dismisses this sheep-and-goats perspective out of hand ('ROBESPIERRE. Du leugnest die Tugend? DANTON. Und das Laster.'), and proceeds to offer a quite different model of human behaviour—a model that unquestionably reflects Büchner's own beliefs:

Es giebt nur Epicuräer und zwar grobe und feine, Christus war der feinste; das ist der einzige Unterschied, den ich zwischen den Menschen herausbringen kann. Jeder handelt seiner Natur gemäß d. h. er thut, was ihm wohl thut.

There are only epicureans, blatant ones and subtle ones, Christ was the subtlest; that's the only difference that I can see between people. Everyone behaves according to his nature: he does whatever does him good.

The stress on nature and the natural self is of course familiar, and prefigures Woyzeck's response to the Hauptmann and the Doctor when they rant about his 'lack of virtue' and the 'badness' of the world: 'es kommt einem nur so die Natur', 'Aber H. Doctor, wenn einem die Natur kommt.' But the primacy of nature is contextualized here in a most revealing way by the reference to epicureanism, meant not in the popularized sense of 'devotion to a life of ease, pleasure, and luxury' (*OED*), but in the proper sense of Epicurus' rigorous philosophy of existence—a philosophy that is conveniently summarized for us by Büchner himself in the relevant section of his excerpts from a standard philosophical handbook of the day, Tennemann's *Geschichte der Griechischen Philosophie* (ii. 403–9).

The defining characteristic of epicureanism in its antithesis to the stance of Robespierre is that it offers a practical and flexible ethic rooted in the real needs of individuals and the society that they constitute. It has a doctrine of virtue no less pronounced than that of Robespierre's forbidding puritanism, indeed 'Die Moral ist dem Epikur der wichtigste und einzige Gegenstand der Philosophie' (ii. 403; *Morality is for Epicurus the chief and only subject of philosophy*). It sees virtue, however, not as a remote and abstract absolute, not as an end in itself, but as a practical means whereby each individual strives for the 'highest good', which is happiness (also variously defined as calmness and contentment, pleasure, absence of pain): 'Die Tugend ist ein Mittel zur Glückseeligkeit. Sie hat keinen Werth an sich, ohne Rücksicht auf ihre Folgen. Tugend und Glückseeligkeit sind unzertrennlich mit einander verbunden.' (ii. 404; *Virtue is a means to happiness. It has no value in itself, without regard to its consequences. Virtue and happiness are indissolubly linked to each other.*) Virtue is thus 'right behaviour', behaviour conducive to a creature's happiness and sense of well-being within the context of their particular needs and nature; hence the epicurean insistence in the opening scene of the play that the principle of well-being, 'Wohlbefinden', replace the principle of (puritanical) virtue, and that every individual be enabled to enjoy their life in their own particular way: 'Jeder muß in seiner Art genießen können, jedoch so, daß Keiner auf Unkosten eines Andern genießen oder ihn in seinem eigenthümlichen Genuß stören darf.' (*Everyone must be enabled to enjoy life in their own way, but no one may gain their enjoyment at another's expense, nor interfere with another's particular enjoyment.*) This demonstrates the epicurean concept of wrong. Just as there is no absolute virtue, so also there is no absolute vice or evil: wrongness is any kind of behaviour that infringes the rights of others, and thus infringes the compact joining individuals in a society: 'Unrecht ist an sich kein Uebel, es muß nur der etwaigen Folgen wegen gemieden werden. Es giebt kein anderes Merkmal des Rechts, sowohl in Gesetzen als Verträgen, als den Nutzen für das gesellige Leben.' (ii. 404; *Wrong is not an evil in itself, it must be avoided only because of its possible consequences. Right has but a single characteristic, be it in the realm of laws or of compacts: it is beneficial to the life of society.*) Wrongness is thus not a metaphysical condition, but a specifically *social* phenomenon, occasioned by a specific and correctable malfunction within the network of social compacts freely entered into by all individuals to ensure 'daß Keiner dem Andern Schaden zufüge, aber auch nicht von Andern Schaden erleide' (ii. 405; *that no one does harm to others, but equally suffers no harm from others*).

The real sting in Danton's (and Büchner's) epicureanism lies in the assertion that *everyone* is an epicurean, that *everyone* lives out their own nature by doing what does them good ('Es giebt *nur* Epicuräer ... *Jeder* handelt seiner Natur gemäß d. h. er thut, was ihm wohl thut.') For this means that Robespierre, too, is an epicurean—albeit such a super-subtle practitioner (like Christ, Büchner's hyperbolic example) that the reality is not readily apparent. Robespierre sees himself, in Danton's splendid phrase, as 'der Policeysoldat des Himmels' (*heaven's policeman*); but far from defending some heavenly citadel of purity, what he is actually doing is gratifying his own private cravings in a secret and squalid form of epicureanism whereby he can get his kicks only through a monstrous sense of moral superiority over other people:

Mit deiner Tugend Robespierre! Du hast kein Geld genommen, du hast keine Schulden gemacht, du hast bey keinem Weibe geschlafen, du hast immer einen anständigen Rock getragen und dich nie betrunken. Robespierre du bist empörend rechtschaffen. Ich würde mich schämen dreißig

Jahre lang mit der nämlichen Moralphysiognomie zwischen Himmel und Erde herumzulaufen bloß um des elenden Vergnügens willen Andre schlechter zu finden, als mich.

You and your virtue, Robespierre! You've taken no bribes, made no debts, slept with no women, always worn a nice clean coat, never got drunk. Robespierre, you are revoltingly upright. I'd be ashamed to caper about for thirty years between heaven and earth wearing the same mask of morality just for the dismal pleasure of finding other people worse than myself.

The would-be puritan is thus in truth an epicurean like everyone else—but a thoroughly perverted one, since by epicurean live-and-let-live criteria his maniacal pursuit of 'virtue' is a murderous wrong. Force would be justified if there were any threat to Robespierre's own sacred right to be himself; but there is no question of that: instead, Robespierre is infringing everyone else's natural rights by gratuitously imposing his private idiosyncrasies in the guise of transcendent values:

Jeder mag sich wehren, wenn ein Andrer ihm den Spaß verdirbt. Hast du das Recht aus der Guillotine einen Waschzuber für die unreine Wäsche anderer Leute und aus ihren abgeschlagnen Köpfen Fleckkugeln für ihre schmuzzigen Kleider zu machen, weil du immer einen sauber gebürsteten Rock trägst? Ja, du kannst dich wehren, wenn sie dir drauf spucken oder Löcher hineinreißen, aber was geht es dich an, so lang sie dich in Ruhe lassen? Wenn sie sich nicht geniren so herum zu gehn, hast du deßwegen das Recht sie in's Grabloch zu sperren? Bist du der Policeysoldat des Himmels?

Anyone can defend himself if others spoil his fun. But do you have the right to use the guillotine as a washtub for other people's dirty linen, and to use their severed heads to scour the stains from their grubby clothes, just because you always wear a clean-brushed coat? Defend yourself by all means if they spit on your clothes or tear holes in it, but what business is it of yours so long as they leave you in peace? If it doesn't bother *them* going around like that, what right do you have to clap them in coffins? Are you heaven's policeman?

The exposure of Robespierre's puritanical stance, already incisively clear by the time Danton departs the stage, is given its sharpest edge through the man himself in his ensuing monologue (28). Here, in an eloquent departure from the historical evidence, Büchner suddenly shows us a quite different Robespierre: inside the outer shell of the depersonalized, ideological automaton, we see—however briefly—a vulnerable, flesh-and-blood individual, stricken by insight into his own deceit, his own immense guilt. The crucial trigger-mechanism was Danton's earlier challenge: 'Ist denn nichts in dir, was dir nicht manchmal ganz leise, heimlich sagte, du lügst, du lügst!' (*Is there really no voice within you that hasn't sometimes quietly, secretly told you 'You're lying, you're lying'?*) To Danton he declared that his conscience was clear ('Mein Gewissen ist rein'); but as soon as he is alone, he is invaded by doubt. What *is* his true motive for eliminating Danton? Is it perhaps nothing to do with ideals, but simply a manœuvre to safeguard his own personal interests?—'Halt! Halt! Ist's das eigentlich? Sie werden sagen seine gigantische Gestalt hätte zuviel Schatten auf mich geworfen, ich hätte ihn deßwegen aus der Sonne gehen heißen. . . . Und wenn sie Recht hätten?' And what of the grand ideal of 'virtue'? He cannot shake off Danton's assertion that there is no such thing; worse, he cannot shake off the implied accusation that virtue is simply an expedient platform, the artificially raised-up heels that give his ideological posture its commanding height (and which Danton deliberately kicked from under him): 'Keine Tugend! Die Tugend ein Absatz meiner Schuhe! . . . Wie das immer wieder kommt.' Thus deprived of his normal monomaniac confidence, he is delivered up to a conscience that, far from being clear and 'pure', points the bloodiest of fingers, no matter how hard he tries to smother it: 'Warum kann ich den Gedanken nicht los werden? Er deutet mit blutigem Finger immer da, da hin! Ich mag so viel Lappen darum wickeln als ich will, das Blut schlägt immer durch.' At the same time, he is forced to acknowledge his essential fraudulence, to recognize that he is indeed—as Danton had suggested—a stamping-ground of lies: 'Ich weiß nicht, was in mir das Andere belügt.'

Some of the play's most essential issues begin to surface here: questions of freedom not as a political slogan or an abstract ideal, but in terms of real people in real situations; the cardinal questions of individual freedom of action—and individual responsibility for those actions. Before tackling these vital issues, though, let us stay a little longer within the broader political context, for we need to take account of some further major elements in the play's critique of the Jacobin politics of terror.

Paramount is the question of what has actually been achieved. The revolutionary objective, after all, is noble indeed, and could justify much. If real social freedom is being brought within grasp, or at least being brought significantly nearer, then it matters little that the logic of the Jacobin apologists is specious, or that private obsessions are being indulged; even the annihilation of a few hundred or a few thousand extra victims might conceivably be reckoned a worthwhile sacrifice. But in fact the Terror has achieved precisely nothing. Far from regenerating mankind, as Saint-Just alleges, the programme of slaughter has brought not the slightest improvement in the lot of the survivors. Festooning the streetlamps with corpses has done nothing to improve the lighting; tearing holes in the bodies of others has done nothing to repair the holes in men's trousers: 'deine Verbesserung der Straßenbeleuchtung hat in Frankreich nicht heller gemacht'; 'über all den Löchern, die wir in andrer Leute Körper machen, ist noch kein einziges in unsern Hosen zugegangen' (50, and cf. 15; 42).

Büchner demonstrates this terrible futility above all through the recurrent image of hunger, showing time and again that the policy of revolution through slaughter has not even brought food and warmth, let alone anything so grand as freedom, justice, virtue. The tone is struck in the very first street scene. Simon's daughter is a whore because she is hungry: 'Ihr Hunger hurt und bettelt' (14); every successive phase of the carnage has had the same desperately futile outcome:

Sie haben uns gesagt: schlagt die Aristocraten todt, das sind Wölfe! Wir haben die Aristocraten an die Laternen gehängt. Sie haben gesagt das Veto frißt euer Brot, wir haben das Veto todtgeschlagen. Sie haben gesagt die Girondisten hungern euch aus, wir haben die Girondisten guillotinirt. Aber sie haben die Todten ausgezogen und wir laufen wie zuvor auf nackten Beinen und frieren. (14)

They told us 'Kill the aristocrats, they're a pack of wolves!'—so we strung the aristocrats from the lamp-posts. They told us 'The king's veto is devouring your bread!'—so we destroyed the king. They told us 'The Girondists are starving you to death!'—so we guillotined the Girondists. But *they* grabbed the clothes off the corpses, and *we* are still freezing with nothing to wear.

Danton is quite right when he shouts to the public in the courtroom, 'Ihr wollt Brod und sie werfen euch Köpfe hin. Ihr durstet und sie machen euch das Blut von den Stufen der Guillotine lecken.' (63; *You want bread and they throw you heads, you thirst and they make you lick the blood from the guillotine steps.*) This excites such a flurry of applause and unrest that Danton and the rest are instantly hustled away, whereupon Büchner has the crowd outside take up the cry: 'Ja das ist wahr, Köpfe statt Brod, Blut statt Wein', 'Die Guillotine ist eine schlechte Mühle und Samson [an executioner] ein schlechter Bäckerknecht, wir wollen Brod, Brod!' (63; *Yes it's true, heads instead of bread, blood instead of wine; The guillotine is a lousy flour-mill and Samson a lousy baker-boy, we want bread, bread!*) This in turn provokes a typical piece of rhetoric from a Jacobin bystander: 'Euer Brod, das hat Danton gefressen, sein Kopf wird euch Allen wieder Brot geben, er hatte Recht.' (63; *It's Danton who's gobbled up all your bread, he was right: his head will give all of you bread again.*) But of course it is arrant nonsense to say that Danton's head will give them bread; as Dillon is given to remark at one point: 'Man füttert das Volk nicht mit Leichen' (55; *You can't feed the people on corpses*). The bloody ritual of the Terror may take their minds off their hunger, but it cannot assuage it in any real sense—a point that Büchner drives home near the end of the play in the guillotine scene itself: 'EIN WEIB MIT KINDERN. Platz! Platz! Die Kinder schreien, sie haben Hunger. Ich muß sie zusehen machen, daß sie still sind. Platz!' (73; *A WOMAN WITH CHILDREN. Let me through, let me through! The kids are so hungry they're screaming their heads off. If I get 'em watching it'll shut them up. Let me through!*)

However, the undiminished hunger and deprivation of the masses makes a nonsense of Jacobin pretensions in another, much more dramatic sense. It is not simply that the Jacobin programme of terror has made no progress whatever towards that objective of freedom whose attainment might solely justify it. It is also made clear that the entire ideology of the Jacobins is in truth a charade, an attempt to lend a rational face to profound irrationality. For the Terror is not the Jacobins' creature at all; it is not subject to any purposive 'Idea' or 'World Spirit'; it is not leading towards any considered goal. It is a wild and rapacious beast, a 'tiger' (64) that manifests the boundless rage of an urban mass deprived of every necessity. For all their grandiose blether, what the Jacobins are actually doing is riding the tiger, and hanging on with all the tenacity they can muster. Eat or be eaten: it is a matter of sheer survival.

This murderous dynamic is spelt out through Lacroix (who serves as the play's most incisive political commentator). The desperate poverty of the mass: that is the awesome engine of the Terror: 'das Volk ist materiell elend, das ist ein furchtbarer Hebel' (25). These very words will be echoed by Büchner in his 'manifesto' letter to

Gutzkow in 1836: 'Für die [große Klasse] gibt es nur zwei Hebel, materielles Elend und religiöser Fanatismus. Jede Parthei, welche diese Hebel anzusetzen versteht, wird siegen.' (ii. 455; *To mobilize the great class there are only two levers, material poverty and religious fanaticism. Any party that can successfully apply these levers is bound to triumph.*) The same conviction is manifest, too, in an earlier letter to Gutzkow: 'das Verhältniß zwischen Armen und Reichen ist das einzige revolutionäre Element in der Welt, der Hunger allein kann die Freiheitsgöttin ... werden' (ii. 441; *the relationship between the rich and the poor is the only revolutionary element in the world, hunger alone can become the goddess of freedom*). But whereas in the letters the revolutionary force of hunger and poverty is deemed capable of being harnessed to transform society and bring freedom in place of tyranny,[2] in the specific historical context of his play Büchner depicts a revolution that has gone berserk. Denied the food that they so urgently need, the masses in their raging hunger and frustration have turned into a beast with an appetite for corpses so insatiable that if the ruling junta doesn't provide them, it will devour the junta instead. This state of affairs—the hunger of the beast, and the threat this poses to the Decemvirate—is repeatedly emphasized through Lacroix with a variety of different metaphors:

Das Volk ist ein Minotaurus, der wöchentlich seine Leichen haben muß, wenn er [die Decemvirn] nicht auffressen soll. (20)
Die Sache ist einfach, man hat die Atheisten und Ultrarevolutionärs aufs Schafott geschickt; aber dem Volk ist nicht geholfen es läuft noch barfuß in den Gassen und will sich aus Aristocratenleder Schuhe machen. Der Guillotinenthermometer darf nicht fallen, noch einige Grade und der Wohlfahrtsausschuß kann sich sein Bett auf dem Revolutionsplatz suchen. (20)

---

[2] The revolutionary politics of hunger and poverty sketched in Büchner's letter are of course themselves highly problematical. In order to mobilize the indispensable energy of the masses to secure their emancipation from poverty, Büchner needs them meanwhile to *remain* poverty-stricken: to feed the peasantry, he tells Gutzkow, would be to kill off the revolution ('Mästen Sie die Bauern, und die Revolution bekommt die Apoplexie.') Indeed Büchner yearns for the masses to be afflicted by even worse poverty: their true revolutionary Messiah could only be some new Moses who first visited the seven plagues of Egypt on them, thus making them desperate enough to rebel: 'nur ein Moses, der uns die sieben ägyptischen Plagen auf den Hals schickte, könnte ein Messias werden'. Cf. Hans-Georg Werner, *Studien zu Georg Büchner* (Berlin and Weimar, 1988), 37.

[das Volk ist materiell elend, das ist ein furchtbarer Hebel.] Die Schaale des Blutes darf nicht steigen, wenn sie dem Wohlfahrtsausschuß nicht zur Laterne werden soll, [Robespierre] hat Ballast nöthig, er braucht einen schweren Kopf. (25)

The people are a minotaur that needs its weekly diet of corpses if it isn't to gobble up the Decemvirate.
It's a straightforward matter, they've sent the atheists and the ultras to the scaffold, but the people are no better off, they still rush about the streets with nothing on their feet and want to make shoes from the hide of aristocrats. The guillotine thermometer can't be allowed to fall, just a few degrees more and the Committee of Public Safety can look forward to a long sleep at the Place de la Révolution.
[the people are desperate with poverty, that exerts a terrible force.] The scale-pan of blood cannot be allowed to rise if it is not to turn into a lamp-post for the Committee of Public Safety. Robespierre needs ballast, he needs a weighty head.

Büchner is not content merely to describe this dynamic political reality from afar, as though by a chorus or messenger: he first of all shows it dramatically in action on the stage, initially in the street-scene with Simon, then in the Jacobin Club. The crazed bloodlust of the enraged citizenry in the street-scene knows no bounds: they want to make trousers out of the skin of their oppressors and lard their soup with the melted fat of their bodies; they want to slaughter anyone they can find whose jacket is not in holes, who uses a handkerchief, who can read and write, who has the ease to enjoy himself (14). Robespierre himself is carefully brought onto the stage at this point so that we can see him faced with this murderous and unquenchable rage:

ROBESPIERRE. Was giebt's da Bürger?
DRITTER BÜRGER. Was wird's geben? Die paar Tropfen Bluts vom August und September haben dem Volk die Backen nicht roth gemacht. Die Guillotine ist zu langsam. Wir brauchen einen Platzregen.
ERSTER BÜRGER. Unsere Weiber und Kinder schreien nach Brod, wir wollen sie mit Aristocratenfleisch füttern. Heh! todtgeschlagen wer kein Loch im Rock hat.
ALLE. Todtgeschlagen! todtgeschlagen! (15)
ROBESPIERRE. What is the matter citizens?
THIRD CITIZEN. What's the matter? The few drops of blood in August and September haven't reddened the cheeks of the people. The guillotine is too slow. We need a downpour.

FIRST CITIZEN. Our wives and children cry for bread, we want to feed them with the flesh of aristocrats. Death to anyone with no holes in his coat!
ALL. Death to them, death!

The message is the same at the bloodthirsty start to the following scene in the Jacobin Club, when the envoy from Lyon makes plain his demands. It is a Jacobin's task to kill, he declares; to show mercy is to murder the Revolution ('Eure Barmherzigkeit mordet die Revolution', 16). What he and his comrades want is an avalanche of corpses, enough to blot out the entire city of Lyon, enough to fill the Mediterranean so full that the English navy runs aground on bodies.

Faced with these raging pressures, Robespierre politically speaking has no alternative: if he wishes to remain on top, he must placate the beast. And so his encounter with the populace in the street-scene concludes with him promising them a 'Blutgericht' (16; *bloody reckoning*, but with the connotation also of a 'feast of blood');[3] while his great speech at the Jacobin Club confirming the continuation of the Terror ends with a blatant act of appeasement directed specifically at the Parisian masses and the provincial radicals:

Beruhige dich tugendhaftes Volk, beruhigt euch ihr Patrioten, sagt euern Brüdern zu Lyon, das Schwert des Gesetzes roste nicht in den Händen, denen ihr es anvertraut habt.—Wir werden der Republik ein großes Beispiel geben. (20)

Rest assured, you people of virtue! Rest assured, you valiant patriots! Tell your brothers in Lyon that the sword of justice shall not rust in the hands of those to whom you entrusted it.—We shall offer the Republic a great example!

And with these words, only half-way through the opening act, the Dantonists' fate is virtually sealed.

What this implies is a dynamism in the process of political events that is autonomous and unstoppable—and time and again this is reflected in the images used by those involved: 'der reißende Strom der Beispiele' (19), 'der Strom der Revolution' (46), 'die Lava der Revolution' (52, 58), 'die Sündfluth der Revolution' (70), 'die Rosse der Revolution' (28) (*the rushing torrent of examples [of liquidations]*; the Revolution as *torrent, lava, deluge, wild horses*). On the face of it, this would seem to point to the grimmest paradox of all:

[3] Cf. Fouquier-Tinville's description of the carefully mixed bunch of prisoners that Danton is to be tried with: 'Es ist ein pikantes Gericht. Das Volk braucht dergleichen.' (51; *It's a spicy dish. The people need such things.*)

not only are the men of power, the would-be architects of absolute freedom, quite incapable of freeing the masses even from their hunger, but they are themselves unfree, the slaves of a wild and senseless barbarism. Nothing, it might seem, could more eloquently demonstrate that 'hideous fatalism of history' that Büchner speaks of in his all too famous letter to Minna Jaeglé:

Ich studirte die Geschichte der Revolution. Ich fühlte mich wie zernichtet unter dem gräßlichen Fatalismus der Geschichte. Ich finde in der Menschennatur eine entsetzliche Gleichheit, in den menschlichen Verhältnissen eine unabwendbare Gewalt, Allen und Keinem verliehen. Der Einzelne nur Schaum auf der Welle, die Größe ein bloßer Zufall, die Herrschaft des Genies ein Puppenspiel, ein lächerliches Ringen gegen ein ehernes Gesetz, es zu erkennen das Höchste, es zu beherrschen unmöglich. (ii. 425–6)

I have been studying the history of the Revolution. I felt as though utterly crushed by the hideous fatalism of history. I find in human nature a terrible sameness, in human circumstances an ineluctable violence vouchsafed to all and to none. Individuals are but froth on the waves, greatness a mere coincidence, the mastery of geniuses a dance of puppets, a ridiculous struggle against an iron law that can at best be recognized, but never mastered.

But this notorious passage is surely one of the reddest herrings in German literary history—an expression of mood, a rhetorical extravaganza, that critics have been far too ready to regard as apodictic and definitive. Büchner is emphatically not a fatalist or a determinist. Even in the face of a raging maelstrom like the French Revolution, he sees astonishing scope for freedom of action—far more than we find reflected, say, in Schiller's *Maria Stuart*, a play that *Dantons Tod* uncannily parallels: Robespierre exercises his power much more freely than does his analogue Elisabeth; and whereas Maria can make good the 'grievous blood-guilt' of her past only because imprisonment and execution are forced upon her, with Danton it is quite the reverse: he deliberately turns his back on his similarly bloody and guilty past—and it is by this very act that he consciously lays himself open to imprisonment and death. How ironic and arresting that Büchner, for all his scorn of Schiller's idealism, for all his modern reputation as a supreme pessimist, should in this crucial respect be more classical than the classics, who showed their heroes—Faust, Tasso, Iphigenie, Orest, Johanna,

Maria—outfacing the hostile circumstances of their nature and/or their environment, if at all, only by dint of eleventh-hour tactics, shifts, and subterfuges that regularly test the audience's credulity. And yet this should not surprise us, given Büchner's faith in the essentially beauteous and benign order of the world; his rejection of any tendency to functionalize and devalue the individual; his belief, above all, that the apparently autonomous processes at work in history and society are created not by 'Fate', howsoever constituted, but by men, and are accordingly capable of being tactically managed by men, and—given time and judicious use of the appropriate 'Hebel'—strategically changed.

'Tactical' and 'strategic' are in fact useful labels to designate the two quite distinct kinds of freedom of action that Büchner envisages within the context of *Dantons Tod*. It is in the strategic sense that Robespierre and the Jacobins are unfree: their overwhelming instinct for survival leaves them no option: they have to kill to avoid being killed; and their professed idealist objectives of freedom, virtue, renewal of mankind are accordingly so much straw. But in tactical terms their freedom of manœuvre is very large indeed. The rhetoric of 'torrents', 'lava flows', 'minotaurs', 'wild horses' tends to obscure the fact that, whilst there is no possibility of arresting the dynamic of the Revolution, especially in its prevailing berserk state, there is enormous scope for tactical interventions that retard or accelerate the process, or deflect it in such a way that it destroys one's enemies and not oneself. Precisely this political reality is indicated by a revealing but rarely quoted image that Büchner has Robespierre voice almost in the same breath as the allusion to the 'wild horses of the Revolution': 'Wir werden das Schiff der Revolution nicht auf den seichten Berechnungen und den Schlammbänken dießer Leute stranden lassen, wir müssen die Hand abhauen, die es zu halten wagt' (28; *We shall not let the ship of the Revolution run aground on the shallow designs or filthy mudflats of these people, we must hack off the hand that ventures to stop it*). This is a particularly fascinating metaphor, because it depicts all three components in the political process: there is the 'ship of the Revolution' whose immense inertial force expresses the surging and irrational 'Wille des Volks' (15; *will of the people*); but there are also the steersmen who guide the ship (cf. Robespierre's remark 15–16: 'Aber Volk ... Deine Gesetzgeber ... werden deine Hände führen'; *But people ... Your lawgivers ... will guide your hand*); and finally there are those outside the ship that dare to impede its passage, and who are enough of a threat to necessitate energetic counter-measures.

At every significant juncture of the play, we are offered the spectacle of the Jacobins cunningly and skilfully practising the black art of power politics, constantly manipulating events to their own advantage. The scene in the Jacobin Club is a breathtaking object-lesson. On one perspective Robespierre is plainly shanghaied by history: he has no alternative but to appease the 'minotaur' with corpses. On another perspective, it is clear that what he is compelled to do happens to suit him very nicely. There is even the suggestion that he has deliberately engineered the crisis, or at least exacerbated it, by biding his time and keeping the 'minotaur' on relatively short rations, thus worsening its hunger and making the destruction of his rivals more certain:

Wir warteten nur auf den Schrei des Unwillens, der von allen Seiten ertönt, um zu sprechen. Unsere Augen waren offen, wir sahen den Feind sich rüsten und sich erheben, aber wir haben das Lärmzeichen nicht gegeben, wir ließen das Volk sich selbst bewachen, es hat nicht geschlafen, es hat an die Waffen geschlagen. Wir ließen den Feind aus seinem Hinterhalt hervorbrechen, wir ließen ihn anrücken, jezt steht er frei und ungedeckt in der Helle des Tages, jeder Streich wird ihn treffen, er ist todt, sobald ihr ihn erblickt habt. (17)

These howls of anger ringing out from every side are all we were waiting for in order to speak out. Our eyes were open, we saw the enemy gird themselves and rise, but we did not give the alarm, we let the people be their own sentinel, they have not slumbered, they have sounded the call to arms. We let the enemy emerge from their hiding-place, we let them advance, and now they stand exposed and unprotected in the full glare of day, vulnerable to any attack, you have only to fasten your eyes upon them and they are dead.

During the remainder of the speech (most of it historical), we can only marvel at Robespierre's demagogic skill in vilifying the Dantonists as soft, corrupt, self-serving parasites and traitors, while thereby setting them up as juicy targets for the carefully nurtured wrath of the masses. And at the end of the scene, the success of his rhetoric is carefully emphasized: '[*Allgemeiner Beifall.*] VIELE STIMMEN. Es lebe die Republik, es lebe Robespierre!' (20; [*General applause.*] MANY VOICES. *Long live the Republic, long live Robespierre!*)

In the subsequent phases of the Jacobins' tactical campaign, it is Saint-Just who makes the running, as is made clear when he seeks out Robespierre after the latter's confrontation with Danton. For all Saint-Just's public rhetoric later on about the 'Weltgeist' controlling the course of events, Büchner shows him here as being acutely aware of the fact that success could go either way, and that they must act fast if they are to keep the initiative; he even threatens to ride roughshod over Robespierre himself if he prevaricates: 'Wir werden den Vortheil des Angriffs verlieren. Willst du noch länger zaudern? Wir werden ohne dich handeln. Wir sind entschlossen.' (29; *We'll lose the advantage of attack. Are you going to go on vacillating? We'll act without you. Our minds are made up.*) He has a clear plan of action, involving the summoning of all the key Committees, and a precise objective: the eradication of the entire Dantonist faction, whom he has already catalogued in a 'hit-list' of names; he has even foreseen Robespierre's scruples regarding his childhood friend Camille, and comes carefully armed with the wherewithal to scatter them (29). The immediate step to be taken is a formal indictment, but for Saint-Just this is the simplest of matters: whatever his precise intentions may have been, Robespierre has set the ball rolling, it merely has to be helped on its way:

ROBESPIERRE. . . . Weg mit ihnen! Rasch! . . . Hast du die Anklage bereit?
ST. JUST. Es macht sich leicht. Du hast die Andeutungen bey den Jacobinern gemacht.
ROBESPIERRE. Ich wollte sie schrecken.
ST. JUST. Ich brauche nur durchzuführen (30)

ROBESPIERRE. . . . Away with them! Quickly! . . . Is the indictment ready?
SAINT-JUST. That's easily done. You prepared the way in your speech to the Jacobins.
ROBESPIERRE. I wanted to frighten them.
SAINT-JUST. Act on your words, that's all I need to do

We gain an insight here into the way that political processes can so easily evolve through a kind of leap-frog sequence of individual inputs: however mighty the cumulative momentum of events may be, it is brought about only by successive participants progressively building on the errors and initiatives of their predecessors: Robespierre took his cue from Legendre's suicidal outburst at the Jacobin Club (17; Lacroix, 20: 'du hast die Decemvirn zur Energie gezwungen, du hast ihnen die Hand geführt'); now Saint-Just is exploiting the initiative of Robespierre.

The Jacobins' demagogic ability to control the direction of events, already evident in the Jacobin Club, is amply confirmed in the National Convention scene that brings Act II to its tumultuous conclusion. A perfect measure of Robespierre's and Saint-Just's skill in manipulating their audience is afforded by Büchner's carefully graded stage directions. At first there is 'heftige Bewegung': a surge of unrest amongst the Deputies provoked by Legendre's energetic plea on behalf of the arrested Dantonists (43). But thereafter the Deputies are won over ever more resoundingly to the Jacobins' will: 'Beyfall', 'Allgemeyner Beyfall', 'Die Deputirten erheben sich sämmtlich zum Zeichen allgemeiner Beystimmung'; finally, at the close of Saint-Just's monumental speech, 'Langer, anhaltender Beyfall. Einige Mitglieder erheben sich im Enthusiasmus', 'Die Zuhörer und die Deputirten stimmen die Marseillaise an' (44–6; *Applause; General applause; The Deputies rise to their feet as one man in a gesture of universal approval; Long, sustained applause. Some members rise to their feet in their enthusiasm; Spectators and Deputies strike up the Marseillaise*).

The most blatant demonstration of the power of individuals to influence developments lies, of course, in the Jacobins' repeated manipulation of the judicial process. The first manœuvre occurs when none other than the court president, Herrmann, colludes with the prosecutor in rigging the jury (51). When, in due course, Danton nonetheless begins to get the upper hand in the courtroom, Herrmann simply adjourns the proceedings on the most transparent of pretexts (54). Despite these machinations, Danton still threatens to come out on top; but they are able to seize on the happy coincidence of General Dillon's madcap prison-cell plot. They know full well that the plot is sheer fantasy—but they also know that it gives them just the excuse they need to fix the trial for good and all: 'BARRÈRE. Das sind Mährchen. ST. JUST. Wir werden sie aber mit dem Mährchen in Schlaf erzählen.' (58). At this juncture we even see Saint-Just determining not only the outcome of the trial, but the special decree of the National Convention that will legitimate that outcome: 'Der Convent muß decretiren [etc.]'. The National Convention duly obliges with the requisite decree, which empowers the court to exclude the accused from the proceedings more or less at its discretion; and hey presto: within minutes of its proclamation, Danton and the rest are being forcibly bundled from the court, and are thus prevented at a stroke from exerting any further influence on that power-house of the Revolution, the hungry and enraged masses.

This brings us to Danton himself. Why is it that the Jacobins, having seized control of the 'ship of the Revolution', have to demonstrate so much expertise in the art of political manœuvring and skulduggery? It is not that the 'ship' itself is difficult to handle: as the Jacobin Club and National Convention scenes show, Robespierre and Saint-Just find it easy to give it its head, while simultaneously steering it in the direction they desire. Their problem is Danton, who not only proves exceedingly resistant to being run down and obliterated, but threatens against all the odds to scramble aboard and take over command—exhibiting in the process a quite phenomenal ability to affect the course of history.

Büchner's Danton also happens at this stage to present a particular problem to us, the reader and audience—a problem of perspective that in a stage production can be obviated only by directing and acting of an especially imaginative order. The fact is that the Danton that we (mostly) experience on the stage is profoundly, antithetically different from the Danton familiar to both friend and foe within the ambit of the play. Our Dr Jekyll is their Mr Hyde; a disparity neatly encapsulated within the text by the description of Danton at one point as 'Dieße Dogge mit Taubenflügeln!' (49; *This dove-winged mastiff!*)

'Our' Danton is unmistakably apparent from the moment the curtain rises to reveal him as a rumpled figure slumped more or less on the periphery of the action, itself conspicuously peripheral. His demeanour thereafter is eloquent. He takes no part in the card-game, no part in the discussion of political actualities and ideals. He slouches on the sidelines, summoning sufficient energy only to pour scorn on the morals of the 'pretty lady', his relationship with his wife, the aspirations of his friends. Their politicking drives him from the stage. He is a man apparently hopelessly stricken by lethargy, laziness, ennui ('Trägheit', 'Faulheit', 'Langeweile'; 38, 33, 33); a man whose inability or unwillingness to act spells doom for himself and all his friends: 'Du stürzest dich durch dein Zögern in's Verderben, du reißest alle deine Freunde mit dir.' (31).

Nothing could be more different from the Danton that looms in the memories of those around him, those who knew him before the play's beginning; a persona that reasserts itself only briefly and partially within the present of the play, and which the reader—as distinct from the theatre audience—must accordingly conjure up for himself from the indirect evidence scattered throughout the text (a jigsaw or 'mosaic' process that mimics one of the central images of the play). The 'other' Danton is the very spirit of the Revolution in its most dynamic, most violent form, its 'evil genius' in one victim's view ('Er ist der böse Genius der Revolution', 49). There is almost a mystique of energy and strength in the play—Robespierre in particular is repeatedly given to speak of the 'Kraft' of the people, of the Republic, of the 'wild horses of the Revolution' (15, 18, 19; 18; 28)—and Danton is its towering embodiment, the epitome of energy, action, dynamism. He is 'Der Mann, welcher im Jahre 1792 Frankreich durch seine Energie rettete' (43; *The man who in 1792 saved France through his energy*). He is the notorious 'Mann des September' (25): the driving force behind the Terror of September 1792 who 'fed the infant brood of the Revolution on the dismembered bodies of aristocrats' (54). It was he with his 'Energie' (54) who led the band of men whose 'Spannkraft' (17; *vigour*) ensured the capture of the Tuileries and the massacre of the Royal Guard in August 1792. There is even a superhuman, mythic aura attached to him: Robespierre speaks of his 'gigantische Gestalt' (28; *giant stature*); his captors fear his 'gewaltige Glieder' (42; *mighty limbs*); Barrère compares him to Siegfried in his apparent invulnerability (57); just before his death there is even the suggestion of a 'twilight of the gods': the sky is suddenly presented as an Olympus on the verge of extinction with its gods fading and sinking into nothingness: 'wie ein ausglühender Olymp mit verbleichenden, versinkenden Göttergestalten' (72). In his brief, phoenix-like resurrections, Danton describes himself as one of those 'gewaltige Naturen' (*mighty natures*) that even destiny cannot dispense with (53); and he describes his voice as an instrument that forged weapons out of gold, a hurricane ('Orkan') that submerged the lackeys of despotism beneath a flood of bayonets (54).

All this relates to the past; but what of the present? Faced only with 'our' Danton, it is difficult for us as reader/spectator to see much beyond his persona of a weary, reclusive roué who scarcely even has the energy to get himself dressed. Again, those within the play have a very different view. Why is Saint-Just so insistent that they must obliterate Danton and his retinue at all costs, even if they have to strangle them with their bare hands (57)? Because they fear him ('Sie tödten ihn aus Furcht', 64); they fear his immense political charisma: underneath it all he remains the 'bogyman of the Revolution' ('die Vogelscheuche der Revolution', 51), a man who is capable of seizing the Revolution by the scruff of the neck and 'raping freedom'—Jacobinese for 'dislodging us from power' ('bleibt Danton am Leben, so wird er [die Revolution] am Gewand fassen und er hat etwas in seiner Gestalt, als ob er die Freiheit nothzüchtigen könnte', 57). As we have already seen, events demonstrate that these fears are amply justified. His ultimate failure is due not so much to the machinations of the Jacobins as to the fact that he himself does too little, too late. As Büchner emphasizes through the ever perceptive Lacroix after the first courtroom scene: 'hättest du dich etwas früher so um dein Leben gequält, es wäre jezt anders' (60; *things would be different now if you had started this battle for your life a bit earlier*). And there is surely no reason to doubt this assessment. After all, even though he starts too late and is speedily silenced, his success in rocking the boat is out of all proportion to the extreme brevity and exiguousness of his counter-attacking opportunities. Nothing indicates this more clearly than the desperate counter-counter-measures to which the Jacobins are forced to resort: having already thoroughly perverted the process of the courts, they even have to bring in the full weight of a trumped-up government edict in order to stifle the mighty voice of this single and singular individual.

One crucial feature of this whole tactical battle for ascendancy and survival calls for special mention, and that is the fact that its outcome hinges at every point on the exercise of power not through force of arms, but through the force of words. *Dantons Tod* is a remarkable study in propaganda and demagoguery: the first work in German literature to highlight this ever more looming aspect of modern society and politics. Büchner knew that the key to any revolution lies in the immense power inherent in the masses, the only force potentially capable of transforming the structure and values of a society from within. But he also knew that this potential is not spontaneously self-activating or self-directing: its energy has to be tapped and channelled. As we have already seen, the only 'levers' available, in his view, for this tapping and channelling process were 'material deprivation' and 'religious fanaticism'; but anyone capable of manipulating these two levers was assured of success ('Jede Parthei, welche diese Hebel anzusetzen versteht, wird siegen.') *Der Hessische Landbote* constituted a classic attempt to realize this aim—and to realize it through propaganda. It failed abysmally. But the context of *Dantons Tod* is categorically

Fraud, Futility, Freedom 117

different: the challenge for the successive juntas in the French Revolution was not how to rouse a profoundly dormant 'tiger', but how to manage a beast that was already rampant and ravenous. Both adversaries in the power struggle of *Dantons Tod* are shown meeting the challenge in the same way: they set the tiger at each other's throats—by whipping it into a frenzy with the power of their tongues. It is no exaggeration to say that the only reason that the Jacobins win is because they command a more prominent and a more secure propaganda platform, and because they are able in the end to hustle Danton from his own meagre platform and thereby render him instantly and utterly powerless.

We have already followed the general progress of this lethal war of words, with the Jacobin Club, the National Convention, and the Revolutionary Tribunal serving as its key locations. But one can also hardly fail to be struck by the special emphasis that Büchner places on the power of words. In Danton's case this begins in the very first scene. It is Danton, says Camille, who will 'launch the attack' on the Jacobins—a *verbal* attack in the National Convention ('du wirst den Angriff im Convent machen', 11). Danton himself speaks of the Convention as the only arena offering him a chance of success ('der Convent,—das wäre noch ein Mittel', 32); and after his arrest, Legendre tries this very ploy (only to be swiftly out-manœuvred by the Jacobins): 'Er muß vor den Schranken des Convents gehört werden. Der Erfolg dießes Mittels ist sicher, was sollten sie seiner Stimme entgegensetzen?' (42; *He must be tried and heard before the Convention. It's a ploy that's bound to work: how could they counter the power of his voice?*) When Saint-Just comes to Robespierre to force him onto the offensive, it is the effect of Danton's words that he identifies as the menace: 'Er ... sprach in Epigrammen ... die Leute blieben stehn und zischelten sich in die Ohren, was er gesagt hatte' (29; *He spoke in epigrams ... people stopped and whispered what he'd said in one another's ear*). In the two courtroom scenes, Danton repeatedly stresses the might of his voice—most notably when he declares that it was his voice that forged weapons for the people from the gold of the aristocrats; his 'hurricane voice' that 'buried the lackeys of despotism beneath a flood of bayonets' (54; see also 52, 62). This very remark on the power of his voice demonstrates the point precisely, for it provokes 'loud applause', and forces Herrmann to curtail the hearing there and then—on the ironic pretext that Danton's voice is exhausted.

In the case of the other characters, too, there is a striking emphasis on the power of language. The first street-scene is a case in point. It is the sheer rhetoric of the First Citizen and Third Citizen (14) that whips the crowd into a murderous frenzy (and it is a verbal quip by the Young Man that alone saves him from a lynching). The case of Camille Desmoulins is also not without relevance: as editor of *Le Vieux Cordelier* he is the first newspaper propagandist in German literature—and it is of course his journalism that seals his fate (29–30). As for Robespierre, we several times see him in action as a demagogue; and it is fascinating to see how this man—who twice in the play is symbolically identified with the 'Tribüne', or speaker's rostrum (24, 30)—launches the campaign that will ultimately destroy his rival: 'ROBESPIERRE. Ich verlange das Wort. DIE JACOBINER. Hört, hört den Unbestechlichen! ROBESPIERRE. Wir warteten ... um zu sprechen.' (17; ROBESPIERRE. *I demand to speak.* THE JACOBINS. *Listen! Listen to Robespierre the incorruptible!* ROBESPIERRE. *We waited ... before speaking.*)

Perhaps the most arresting aspect of the play in this regard is the way that Büchner sharply highlights the primacy of language by repeatedly depicting political rhetoric not merely as a prelude or stimulus to action, but as a mode of action in itself. Robespierre's pronouncement that 'virtue must reign through terror' not only causes Lacroix 'pain in the neck', but is described by Danton as 'hewing boards for the guillotine' (24). When Saint-Just is about to go off and prepare his report to the National Convention on the prison plot, Barrère tells him 'Ja, geh St. Just und spinne deine Perioden, worin jedes Komma ein Säbelhieb und jeder Punkt ein abgeschlagner Kopf ist.' (58; *Yes go, Saint-Just, and weave your paragraphs in which every comma is a sword-thrust and every full-stop a severed head.*) We have already seen how Büchner has Saint-Just himself use the same metaphor in his great speech at the close of Act II, when he describes the proposition of universal equality as a 'sentence' ('Satz'), each constituent part of which has killed its quota of victims, and which is 'punctuated' by bloody turning-points of the Revolution; a sentence, moreover, that will have others tacked onto it at the cost of many more corpses (46). Most telling of all, however, and justly famous, is the accusing challenge that Büchner has Mercier fling in the faces of the Dantonists in prison:

Geht einmal euren Phrasen nach, bis zu dem Punkt wo sie verkörpert werden. Blickt um euch, das Alles habt ihr gesprochen, es ist eine mimische Uebersetzung eurer Worte. Dieße Elenden, ihre Henker und die Guillotine sind eure lebendig gewordnen Reden. Ihr bautet eure Systeme, wie Bajazet seine Pyramiden, aus Menschenköpfen. (52)

Just follow your rhetoric through to the point where it becomes reality. Look around you: what you see is what you've said, it is the very enactment of your words. These poor bastards here, their executioners, the guillotine: they are your speeches come to life. You built your grand systems as Bayezid built his pyramids: out of human heads.

No one could suppose that Büchner in any way approved of the outcome of the process here envisaged: Mercier is undoubtedly expressing the author's own abiding hostility to those who construct their abstract and spurious systems at the expense of others. Nobody could be in any doubt, either, that such systems are indeed spurious: the Terror is futile, the Jacobins' professed ideology of freedom, moral renewal, etc. is a monstrous deceit and delusion. But that is not the point at issue. What matters here is Büchner's clear belief, attested time and again in the play, that however remote the ideal of a free society may be, men nevertheless have extraordinary power to shape the course of events, even to the extent of riding the tiger, of steering the wild 'ship of the Revolution' in the direction they want it to go. *Dantons Tod* is most emphatically not a 'tragedy of determinism' (Hans Mayer[4]), it does not show mankind in 'inescapable subjection to the inscrutable and inflexible laws of history' (Maurice Benn[5]). Such a view implies a kind of absolutism in Büchner that is in fact anathema to him: far from having an all-or-nothing sense of freedom/unfreedom, he sees a whole spectrum of possibilities offering a middle ground of the greatest value and importance. Even in his perfect society, after all, freedom would not be absolute, but would be a benign epicurean compromise: every individual would have the right to live out their own nature in full, but not to the extent of infringing the similar freedom of others. Existing forms of society fell agonizingly short of this ideal; but even so, Büchner saw remarkable scope for men to exercise different kinds of limited freedom, and thus avoid being flotsam and jetsam tossed to and fro on the tide of social-historical developments. We

[4] Hans Mayer, *Georg Büchner und seine Zeit*, 205.   [5] Benn, 35–6.

have seen the tactical freedom and the power to influence events displayed in the battle for supremacy and survival; and we shall see that in Danton's case Büchner demonstrates another kind of freedom—much nobler and more profound, but also more paradoxical.

7
Metamorphosis and Choice

The metamorphosis of Danton is doubly challenging. It is difficult enough for us to see beyond his almost incessantly torpid, 'dove-winged' demeanour, and discern the raging 'mastiff' so unforgettably familiar to both friend and foe within the play. But even when we appreciate that this lamb-among-wolves is himself an erstwhile super-wolf, we still face the cardinal question as to why he should have undergone such a startling and lethal transformation in the first place—a problem exacerbated by the fact that the change is already complete before the curtain ever rises; by the fact that even Danton's closest associates are at least as puzzled as we are; and by the fact that Büchner never offers us any neatly packaged answers.

Büchner's alternative to the predictable, puppet-like characters so scathingly disparaged in Camille's tirade against prevailing art-forms is manifest in all its fullness in Danton: a figure of rich complexity whose protean moods reflect the 'Schweben und Senken im menschlichen Gemüth', and whose behaviour is explicable only in terms of a multiplicity of motives, insights, and miscalculations that variously relate to the different dimensions of his being, from the most public to the most intensely private.

One of the most obvious, albeit one of the least essential reasons for Danton's fatal inactivity lies in his misjudgement of the political realities of his situation, based on a mistaken belief in his own invulnerability. The true position is spelt out to him at an early stage by Lacroix: the Jacobins need his head to save their own; they could never afford to let him survive as a 'holy relic' or a 'monument' that might serve as a rallying point for opposition; immediate action is imperative if the Dantonists are to stand any chance of turning the tables (25). Danton well recognizes the general truth that the Revolution, like Saturn, has a habit of devouring its own children—'Ich weiß wohl,—die Revolution ist wie Saturn, sie frißt ihre eignen Kinder.' But in the very next breath he declares his blind conviction that the Jacobins will simply not dare to touch him: 'Doch, sie werden's nicht wagen' (25). His encounter with Robespierre galvanizes him briefly into action (27), but torpor rapidly overtakes him again, and we find him taking refuge in the same delusion: 'Und endlich—und das ist die Hauptsache: sie werden's nicht wagen . . . sie werden's nicht wagen.' (33; *And anyway—and this is the main thing—they won't dare to do it . . . they won't dare to do it.*) Even when he knows, later on, that the decision to arrest him has already been taken, he still persists in his fatal error: 'Das ist leerer Lärm, man will mich schrecken, sie werden's nicht wagen.' (39; *It's an empty threat, they're trying to frighten me, they won't dare to do it.*) This is sharply ironic in two distinct respects. Danton's overall state of passivity is due essentially to his seeing the truth too clearly: how ironic that this fatal insight should be compounded at critical junctures by a fatal blindness. Then there is the particular nature of his blindness: his conviction that the Jacobins won't have the guts to attack him. As the towering colossus of the Revolution, still possessed of his gigantic reputation and with his power-base among the people still potentially to hand ('Mein Name! das Volk!', 25), he imagines himself to be both invulnerable and indispensable: 'Sie hatten nie Muth ohne mich, sie werden keinen gegen mich haben; die Revolution ist noch nicht fertig, sie könnten mich noch nöthig haben' (25; *They had no courage without me, they won't have any against me; the revolution isn't finished, they might still need me*). But of course he is mistaken in every detail. His prestige and power-base, far from protecting him, are precisely the reason why he must be eradicated. The fact that the Revolution is unfinished will ensure not his preservation, but his destruction—a fact underlined through Robespierre just a few lines later, when he tells Danton that to cry halt to a half-finished revolution is to dig one's own grave ('wer eine Revolution zur Hälfte vollendet, gräbt sich selbst sein Grab', 26). As for the Jacobins' supposed lack of courage, this is the sharpest irony of all. They will indeed dare—having learnt their daring from none other than Danton himself: 'Wagt!' Saint-Just implores his colleagues at a crucial moment, 'Danton soll uns das Wort nicht umsonst gelehrt haben' (57; *Dare! Danton taught us the word—let's show that we've learnt it*).

Danton's arrant misreading of the political landscape is perhaps the most obvious factor in the play that contributes to his extinction, but it remains nonetheless an essentially secondary element: it reinforces his fatal inactivity, but it does not cause it. To find the true origins of his behaviour—as Büchner represents them—we have

Metamorphosis and Choice 123

to probe a little further. Why, we might ask, has the mighty Danton allowed things to come to such a desperate pass in the first place? And precisely this question is thrown at him within the text by Lacroix: 'Warum hast du es dazu kommen lassen?' (32)—a question that serves to cue his longest speech in the play so far (only his Conciergerie monologue, 66–7, will be longer). The speech is classic Büchner: with its severely paratactic grammar, it perfectly embodies his vision of a reality so rich and multiple that it can scarcely be seized and fixed in the medium of art. We are offered no neat and all-unifying counterpoint, but a kaleidoscope of discrete, disparate elements.

One such element is inevitably that of politics. Deluded though Danton is in his assessment of his individual position, he is perceptive about the political situation as a whole, identifying two decisive and complementary factors. One is the Dantonists' complete lack of a power-base. The masses might conceivably be drummed up ('Mein Name! das Volk!'), but in the meantime they have no organized support—at best they might muster an army of whores to do battle with the hags around the guillotine: 'Uebrigens, auf was sich stützen? Unsere Huren könnten es noch mit den Guillotinenbetschwestern aufnehmen, sonst weiß ich nichts.' The second factor is the really crucial one, and in essence accounts for the first: the prevailing confluence of political forces happens in all respects to strengthen the Jacobins' grip on the 'ship of the revolution': (i) the Jacobins have established virtue at the top of the revolutionary agenda—having simultaneously and very effectively branded the Dantonists as the hotbed of vice that must needs be eradicated ('die Jacobiner haben erklärt, daß die Tugend an der Tagesordnung sey'); (ii) the power-group of the *Cordeliers* are hostile to Danton because they hold him responsible for the liquidation of their leader Hébert ('die Cordeliers nennen mich Héberts Henker'); (iii) the Paris Commune are now grovelling to the Jacobins following the incarceration of their leader Chaumette ('der Gemeinderath thut Buße'); (iv) although the National Convention might possibly offer a useful avenue of action, it would be no more likely to give way than in its successful power-struggle with the Commune ('der Convent,—das wäre noch ein Mittel! aber es gäbe einen 31. Mai, sie würden nicht gutwillig weichen'; the Commune–Convention struggle began on 31 May 1793). The effect produced by all these factors is trenchantly summarized: Robespierre is the dogma of the Revolution, and as such there is no getting rid of him: 'Robespierre ist das Dogma der Revolution, es darf nicht ausgestrichen werden.' Danton's verdict is then reinforced by a further allusion to their own impotence—their inherent impotence as creatures, not creators, of the Revolution: 'Es gienge auch nicht. Wir haben nicht die Revolution, sondern die Revolution hat uns gemacht.'

Two things may be said about this political analysis of Danton's. For one thing, it is not entirely correct. As a general proposition, Danton's creatures-not-creators remark is a self-belittling distortion of the facts, made seductive only by its language: as we have seen, the Revolution is shown throughout the play to be altogether a two-way process in which the actions of the participants simultaneously influence, and are influenced by, the course of events. At the more particular level, Danton in his present state of 'dove-winged' inertia grossly underestimates his own political clout, just as surely as he underestimates the daring of his opponents: even if he himself does not appreciate it, the Jacobins certainly realize that the mighty 'hurricane' of his rhetoric could easily sweep them from the helm.

The other thing to be said about Danton's analysis is that, interesting though it may be in itself, it does not begin to answer Lacroix's question. It helps to illuminate the situation as it currently stands, but does not help us to understand how or why it arose.

One vital clue is in fact offered in Danton's immediate response to Lacroix (before his talk of politics). Why did he allow things to come to such a pass?—because in the end he was paralysed by ennui, by a kind of existential tedium: 'Warum hast du es dazu kommen lassen? / Dazu? Ja wahrhaftig, es war mir zuletzt langweilig.' And we are instantly offered an explanation of this tedium: what paralysed Danton, we are told, was his sense of being trapped in an endless and inescapable round of sameness: 'Immer im nämlichen Rock herumzulaufen und die nämlichen Falten zu ziehen! Das ist erbärmlich.' (*Traipsing around for ever in the same coat with the same creases! It's pitiful.*) This echoes the very beginning of the scene, where Büchner gave us a living demonstration of Danton's ennui at work. When last we saw him, at the end of his encounter with Robespierre in the previous scene, he seemed at last to have been jolted into action: 'Wir dürfen keinen Augenblick verlieren . . .' (27; *We haven't a moment to lose* . . .). But now we find him seized anew by torpor:

CAMILLE. Rasch Danton wir haben keine Zeit zu verlieren.
DANTON [*er kleidet sich an*]. Aber die Zeit verliert uns.
Das ist sehr langweilig immer das Hemd zuerst und dann die Hosen drüber zu ziehen und des Abends in's Bett und Morgens wieder heraus zu kriechen und einen Fuß immer so vor den andern zu setzen, da ist gar kein Absehens wie es anders werden soll. Das ist sehr traurig und daß Millionen es schon so gemacht haben und das Millionen es wieder so machen werden und, daß wir noch obendrein aus zwei Hälften bestehen, die beyde das Nämliche thun, so daß Alles doppelt geschieht. Das ist sehr traurig. (31)

CAMILLE. Quick Danton, we've no time to waste.
DANTON [*putting on his clothes*]. But time is wasting us.
It's very boring, always putting on first your shirt and then your trousers, crawling into bed at night and out again in the morning, always putting one foot in front of the other, with not the slightest prospect of anything changing. It's sad, and that millions have done so before and millions will do so again and that we consist moreover of two halves doing the selfsame thing so that everything happens twice over—it's very sad.

What we crucially need to understand about this desperate lament of Danton's is that it is indeed despair—but in the strict etymological sense of the 'action or condition of . . . *losing hope*' (*OED*). True, the despair signals itself; but what it chiefly signals is the vastness of the hope that it replaces, and of which it is the inverse expression. The twice-used word 'traurig' points the way: 'sadness' is comprehensible only as the expression of loss, of which it is simultaneously the measure. And of course we already know the implicit yardstick that makes existence as here experienced appear so unbearable in its unrelieved and empty sameness. After all, experience in itself is declared to be full of a vibrant, rich, incessantly self-renewing creativity ('die Schöpfung, die glühend, brausend und leuchtend . . . sich jeden Augenblick neu gebiert'); every least being is supposed to be replete with its own intrinsic worth and purpose ('Alles, was ist, ist um seiner selbst willen da'); there is supposed to be a 'primal law of beauty' at work in all things creating a 'necessary harmony'. I have argued before that it is Büchner's heightened sense of harmony that explains his agonized sensitivity to dissonance ('ach, wir armen schreienden Musikanten')—and it is precisely the metaphor of music that Büchner puts into Danton's mouth to explain why existence in its infinite sameness appears to him now so pitiful ('erbärmlich'): 'So ein armseeliges Instrument zu seyn, auf dem eine Saite immer nur einen Ton angiebt!' (*To be such a miserable instrument on which but a single note is sounded by a single string!*) What this implies is a huge unrealized potential: the monotone is so unbearably monotonous because there could and should be rich and resonant harmonies from the multitude of 'strings' and 'notes' that essentially belong to the human 'instrument'. There is a curious inversion here if we think for a moment of Camille's tirade only two scenes later. Büchner will have Camille rail against the public for despising reality as 'erbärmlich', and preferring and fostering a crass reductivism in the arts. But in his prevailing mood, Danton himself sees reality as 'erbärmlich', and his whole perspective is severely reductive—by Camille's, and Büchner's, own criterion. This is clear enough when we hear him depicting life as a single sound on a single string, but it is even clearer towards the end of the scene when, after first welcoming premature death, he delivers three rhetorical antitheses in succession, each disparaging existence more hyperbolically than the last: they might have imagined wearing a grand mantle, living a life of epic breadth, quaffing the essence of existence from capacious vessels; but their bodies were too puny for their would-be mantle, their minds and stamina fit not for an epic but only for an epigram, the essence of existence so vestigial as to fill not a tub but a liqueur-glass:

Es ist recht gut, daß die Lebenszeit ein wenig reducirt wird, der Rock war zu lang, unsere Glieder konnten ihn nicht ausfüllen. Das Leben wird ein Epigramm, das geht an, wer hat auch Athhem und Geist genug für ein Epos in fünfzig oder sechzig Gesängen? S' ist Zeit, daß man das bißchen Essenz nicht mehr aus Zübern sondern aus Liqueurgläschen trinkt, so bekommt man doch das Maul voll, sonst konnte man kaum einige Tropfen in dem plumpen Gefäß zusammenrinnen machen. (33)

For Danton in this despairing mood, even the agony of the Terror seems attractive as a refuge from the infinite blankness of ennui: if normal life is an empty charade in which everyone acts out a repetitive, senseless role, then a dramatic, drumroll exit before an excited guillotine audience is preferable to death from disease or old age; after all, what could better enable people to escape from their *taedium vitae* into a comforting posture of sentiment, nobility, virtue, or wit:

Die Leute befinden sich ganz wohl dabey [i.e. in the Terror]. Sie haben Unglück, kann man mehr verlangen um gerührt, edel, tugendhaft oder witzig zu seyn oder um überhaupt keine Langeweile zu haben? Ob sie nun an der Guillotine oder am Fieber oder am Alter sterben? Es ist noch vorzuziehen, sie treten mit gelenken Gliedern hinter die Coulissen und können im Abgehen noch hübsch gesticuliren und die Zuschauer klatschen hören. Das ist ganz artig und paßt für uns, wir stehen immer auf dem Theater, wenn wir auch zulezt im Ernst erstochen werden. (33)

Characteristically, Danton's despair is brought to a dramatic climax with a concentrated rhetorical flourish: 'Endlich—ich müßte schreien, das ist mir der Mühe zuviel, das Leben ist nicht die Arbeit werth, die man sich macht, es zu erhalten.' (33; *Anyway—I'd have to scream, it's all too much bother, life's not worth all the effort it costs just to keep it going.*)

No one should suppose that this is Büchner's, or even Danton's, definitive standpoint. We need not go as far as Lacroix, who dismisses Danton's expostulations as a cloud of verbiage to excuse his lethargy ('[Er] glaubt kein Wort von dem was er gesagt hat. Nichts als Faulheit!', 33). It is genuine alright—but as a transient, if costly mood that Danton will quite soon be forced to abandon: flirting with death from a distance is all very well, but once it stares him in the face he will rage against it with belated but unmistakable passion: 'Ich kann nicht sterben, nein, ich kann nicht sterben. Wir müssen schreien, sie müssen mir jeden Lebenstropfen aus den Gliedern reißen.' (61; *I cannot die, no, I cannot die. We must scream and shout, they'll have to wrench every last drop of life from my body.*) As already suggested, the real significance of Danton's despair is that it gives a measure of the hope that is lost.

The key is offered in the opening fanfare of ennui, in the giveaway sentence 'da ist gar kein Absehens wie es *anders werden* soll': the absence of any prospect of change—that is undoubtedly a major cause of Danton's fatal lethargy. Exactly this was signalled in the opening scene of the play, when Büchner had Danton counter the grand ideals of his companions with the simple but devastating question: 'Wer soll denn all die schönen Dinge ins Werk setzen?' (*Who's going to bring about all these wonderful things?*) What provoked the 'mastiff's' metamorphosis was his recognition of the truth shouted out by the play as a whole: that the systematic savagery of the Revolution has achieved precisely nothing. This failure he ascribes to two distinct but complementary factors:

(i) human beings are inherently flawed, a defect or deficiency is programmed into our make-up from the outset: 'Es wurde ein Fehler gemacht, wie wir geschaffen wurden, es fehlt uns etwas, ich habe keinen Namen dafür'; (ii) to remedy this fundamental flaw, we would need to be capable of working miracles—but we have no such powers: we are 'lousy alchemists' ('wir sind elende Alchymisten'). This is why he could stomach the battle no longer: what is the point of tearing each other's bodies apart when they are incapable even of naming or locating the inbuilt flaw, let alone remedying it: 'Ich hab es satt, wozu sollen wir Menschen miteinander kämpfen? ... es fehlt uns etwas, ich habe keinen Namen dafür, wir werden es einander nicht aus den Eingeweiden herauswühlen, was sollen wir uns drum die Leiber aufbrechen?'

We have seen elsewhere in the play how Büchner highlights the spectre of a noble idealism gone berserk: a search for freedom that is itself despotic; a campaign for humanity that is inhuman. It is this spectre that haunts Danton—and it is given poignant shape in the ironically rhetorical 'variations on a theme' voiced through Camille (a pre-echo of Danton's courtroom cry, 'Wie lange sollen die Fußstapfen der Freiheit Gräber seyn?', 63):

Pathetischer gesagt würde es heißen: wie lange soll die Menschheit im ewigen Hunger ihre eignen Glieder fressen? oder, wie lange sollen wir Schiffbrüchige auf einem Wrack in unlöschbarem Durst einander das Blut aus den Adern saugen? oder, wie lange sollen wir Algebraisten im Fleisch beym Suchen nach dem unbekannten, ewig verweigerten x unsere Rechnungen mit zerfezten Gliedern schreiben?

To put that in more stirring terms: how long is humanity in its eternal hunger to carry on devouring its own limbs? or: how long are we shipwrecked sailors in our unquenchable thirst to continue sucking the blood from each other's veins? or: how long, in our search for the unknown x that is ever denied us, are we mathematicians of the flesh to write our equations with shattered limbs?

Again, there is no reason to assume that this reflects Büchner's own position, and in particular we should not suppose that this apostle of a 'primal law of beauty' endorses the view that mankind is inherently and irremediably flawed. For him, the problem lay not in the eternal nature of man, but in the very specific conditions of the age; as Danton is given to say later on in a calmer mood, when he accepts the charge that he and his fellow Terror-ists constructed their systems out of human heads: it was the curse of the *age* that men these days fashioned all their schemes out of human flesh: 'Man arbeitet heut zu Tag Alles in Menschenfleisch. Das ist der Fluch unserer Zeit.' (52). What matters in Danton's despairing response to Lacroix's question, therefore, is not his *interpretation* of their failure to bring about change, but his recognition of the *fact* that they had failed, and in the prevailing circumstances would inevitably continue to fail. The Revolution has turned out to be nothing but a murderous cascade of botches and bungles, and Danton can stomach it no longer: 'Ich bin der Hudeleien überdrüssig' (38), 'Ich hab es satt' (32).

This brings us—at last—close to the heart of Danton's ennui. He is literally sick to death of the manifest futility of the Revolution and has accordingly turned his back on it—and this is, above all, an *ethical* response. What is involved is a specific and deliberate act of choosing—nowhere more clearly signalled than in Danton's classic (and historical) declaration 'ich will lieber guillotinirt werden, als guillotiniren lassen' (32; *I prefer to be guillotined than to guillotine others*). Death descends remorselessly upon Danton throughout this aptly entitled play; but it is a death that he has freely and consciously wished upon himself. We saw how Robespierre enjoys extraordinary 'tactical' freedom, whilst being totally unfree in his kill-or-be-killed compulsion to survive; now we see how the erstwhile 'Dogge' Danton has exercised extraordinary 'strategic' freedom by refusing to continue as a butcher—even at the cost of being butchered himself.

With this we reach what is surely the deepest well-spring of Danton's metamorphosis. Why did the raging 'mastiff' stop in his tracks and sprout improbable 'dove-wings'? Because of the irresistible inner voice of conscience. We begin to glimpse this deepest realm of Danton's psyche, as Büchner envisions and presents it, only when we see him on his own, for the first time, in the scene 'Freies Feld' (39). We are abruptly confronted here by the fact that Danton's most profound and implacable enemy is not Robespierre and the rest of the Jacobin gang, but his own intolerable memory. We already know from the previous scene that someone has offered him a place of refuge ('einen Zufluchtsort', 38), and now we see him in the very act of fleeing—but realizing all of a sudden that in trying to save his own life all he is doing is ensuring the survival of the implacable enemy within him: 'meinen Feind d. h. mein

Gedächtniß'. The play's most grimly ironic version of the kill-or-be-killed motif presents itself here: Danton must annihilate his memory to prevent it from destroying him; but he can do so only by annihilating himself; his only refuge from destruction is death:

Der Ort soll sicher seyn, ja für mein Gedächtniß, aber nicht für mich, mir giebt das Grab mehr Sicherheit, es schafft mir wenigstens *Vergessen*! Es tödtet mein Gedächtniß. Dort aber lebt mein Gedächtniß und tödtet mich. Ich oder es? Die Antwort ist leicht. [*Er erhebt sich und kehrt um.*]

The place is safe, they say; yes, safe for my memory, but not for me; I'll find more safety in the grave, at least it'll grant me oblivion! It'll destroy my memory. Go on, and my memory will live and destroy me. It or me? The answer is easy. [*He stands and turns back.*]

The 'Freies Feld' scene is an unnervingly abrupt and cerebral snapshot: we see Danton delineate his torture on the rack of memory with chilling analytical detachment, as though he were talking of someone else. But then, with spectacular bravura, Büchner conjures out of nothing a diametrically different mood and perspective. The lights go down, the lights come up—and there is Danton, not clinically musing on his plight in the daytime calm of the countryside, but suffering it with terrible immediacy in the nocturnal clamour of the city. As so often in the play, Büchner brilliantly exploits the technique of starting a scene as it were in the middle: the opening words mark the end of a waking nightmare, they are the agonized cry of a man just surfacing from a vision of hell:

Will denn das nie aufhören? Wird das Licht nie ausglühn und der Schall nie modern, will's denn nie still und dunkel werden, daß wir uns die garstigen Sünden einander nicht mehr anhören und ansehen?—September!—(40)

So is it never going to stop? Will the lights never fade and the noise never die, will it never be dark and still so we no longer hear and see our vile sins?—September!—

Only afterwards are we told what happened before: Danton's apocalyptic nightmare as he slept in his bed, his terrified awakening, his tortured vision by the window.

What is conveyed here with tremendous elliptic, poetic force is the sense of a man who presumed too much. A giant of a man who thought he could mount and tame the wild stallion of the world in its steaming headlong rush, only to find himself dragged along willy-nilly with nothing beneath him but a terrifying abyss:

Metamorphosis and Choice 131

Unter mir keuchte die Erdkugel in ihrem Schwung, ich hatte sie wie ein wildes Roß gepackt, mit riesigen Gliedern wühlt' ich in ihrer Mähne und preßt' ich ihre Rippen, das Haupt abwärts gebückt, die Haare flatternd über dem Abgrund. So ward ich geschleift. Da schrie ich in der Angst, und ich erwachte. (41)

He has managed to leap from the raging stallion, to disengage from the furious dynamic of history. But he cannot escape his implacable memory, the accusing conscience that never lets him forget the vile sins ('die garstigen Sünden') incurred through his involvement in the September massacres.[1] He goes to the window to escape his nightmare—but: 'Wie ich an's Fenster kam—durch alle Gassen schrie und zetert' es: September!' (40; *As I came to the window it howled and screamed through all the streets: September!*) No matter what he does, the very word 'September' is a corporeal and accusing presence that reaches out towards him with its 'bloody hands' (41).

As all of this makes abundantly clear, Danton's exercise of strategic freedom is far from straightforward. He has not freely freed himself from the dynamic of history, but has been forced into it by the 'enemy' within; but at the same time, this inward enemy *is* himself. What Büchner so typically shows us is a multiple being, divided both in and against itself. One part of this being is a quotidian, reflective, disingenuous self that prefers delusion to truth. This is glaringly evident in the 'Freies Feld' scene, which shows Danton desperately searching for some kind of refuge—firstly from the physical threat of the guillotine, but then from the more intimate threat of his own conscience. And sure enough, he finds delusions in which to hide: first, a conveniently comforting image of death—the falseness of which is instantly apparent to him: 'Ich kokettire mit dem Tod, es ist ganz angenehm so aus der Entfernung mit dem Lorgnon mit ihm zu liebäugeln' (39; *I'm flirting with death; it's most agreeable to make eyes at him through a lorgnette like this*

---

[1] In Sept. 1792, in the general hysteria stirred up by the threat from the Austrian and Prussian armies, the prisons of Paris were invaded and at least 1,400 inmates (more than half the capital's prison population) systematically butchered over a period of several days—an episode that 'has no equal in atrocities committed during the French Revolution by any party' (Simon Schama, *Citizens: A Chronicle of the French Revolution* (New York and London, 1989), 631). In truth, the historical Danton was not involved in the September massacres at all, and could be accused at worst of connivance: Minister of Justice at the time, he knew that the butchery was due to happen, took no action to prevent it, and then once it had begun, allegedly defended it as a 'justifiable sacrifice' (ibid., 629 ff.). Büchner's presentation of Danton in this scene is thus a typical and revealing departure from history.

from a nice safe distance); but then he finds refuge—again—in his purblind conviction that the Jacobins won't dare to touch him ('sie werden's nicht wagen'). It is in the 'September' scene, however, that we find the most splendidly specious delusion—so specious indeed that readers and critics have commonly failed to recognize that it *is* a delusion.

We have already noted how the 'September' scene advances by going backwards: after the 'presentness' of Danton's anguish at the start, we are taken progressively further back in time, as Danton recounts to Julie his experiences by the window, and the nightmare that preceded it. But then we are carried even further into the past: right back to the events that gave rise to Danton's Fury-like memory in the first place. What we need to realize from the outset is that this entire phase of the scene is an expedient act of evasion, an exercise in casuistry to ward off the 'bloody hands' that beset him in his deepest self. Couched in crisp, rhythmic stichomythia, the recital of events is a whirl of words that spins an instant and cosy cocoon of excuses:

DANTON. . . . O hilf mir Julie, mein Sinn ist stumpf. War's nicht im September Julie?
JULIE. Die Könige waren nur noch vierzig Stunden von Paris...
DANTON. Die Festungen gefallen, die Aristocraten in der Stadt...
JULIE. Die Republik war verloren.
DANTON. Ja verloren. Wir konnten den Feind nicht im Rücken lassen, wir wären Narren gewesen, zwei Feinde auf einem Brett, wir oder sie, der Stärkere stößt den Schwächeren hinunter, ist das nicht billig?
JULIE. Ja, ja.
DANTON. Wir schlugen sie, [—and now the *pièce de résistance*:] das war kein Mord, das war Krieg nach innen.
JULIE. Du hast das Vaterland gerettet.
DANTON. Ja das habe' ich. Das war Nothwehr, wir mußten.

DANTON. . . . Oh help me, Julie, my mind is numb. It was September, wasn't it?
JULIE. The kings were only forty hours from Paris...
DANTON. The fortifications overrun, the city full of aristocrats...
JULIE. The Republic was done for.
DANTON. Yes, done for. We couldn't afford to have an enemy at our backs, we'd have been fools; two enemies on a single plank, it's us or them, whoever is the stronger shoves the weaker one off, that's fair surely?
JULIE. Yes, yes.

DANTON. We beat them; that wasn't murder, it was war against the enemy within.
JULIE. You saved your fatherland.
DANTON. I did, I did. It was self-defence, we had to do it.

It ought to be difficult to mistake this for anything other than it is: a piece of self-dupery, bare-faced and casuistical. But what makes this so important is the fact that the self-dupery continues—and gives rise to one of the most famous and most misunderstood passages in all Büchner's work. It is the word 'mußten' in the extract just quoted that gives the cue:

> Das war Nothwehr, wir mußten. Der Mann am Kreuze hat sich's bequem gemacht: es muß ja Aergerniß kommen, doch wehe dem, durch welchen Aergerniß kommt.
> Es muß, das war dieß Muß. Wer will der Hand fluchen, auf die der Fluch des Muß gefallen? Wer hat das *Muß* gesprochen, wer? Was ist das, was in uns hurt, lügt, stiehlt und mordet?
> Puppen sind wir von unbekannten Gewalten am Draht gezogen; nichts, nichts wir selbst! Die Schwerter, mit denen Geister kämpfen, man sieht nur die Hände nicht, wie im Mährchen.

> It was self-defence, we had to do it. The man on the cross made things easy for himself: 'It must needs be that offences come, but woe unto him through whom they come.'
> 'It must needs be': it's this 'must' that did it. Who will curse the hand on whom the curse of 'must' has fallen? Who spoke the curse? Who? What is it in us that whores, lies, steals, murders?
> Puppets, that's all we are, made to dance on strings by unknown powers; in ourselves we are nothing, nothing! Mere swords in the hands of warring spirits, the hands themselves can't be seen, that's all, like in a fairy-tale.

What has chiefly caused this famous passage to be taken—astonishingly—at face value, is the fact that it echoes a passage in the equally famous 'Fatalismus der Geschichte' letter:

> Das *muß* ist eins von den Verdammungsworten, womit der Mensch getauft worden. Der Ausspruch: es muß ja Aergerniß kommen, aber wehe dem, durch den es kommt,—ist schauderhaft. Was ist das, was in uns lügt, mordet, stiehlt? Ich mag dem Gedanken nicht weiter nachgehen. (ii. 426)

> The word *must* is one of those with which man is damned from the moment of his birth. The dictum that 'it must needs be that offences come, but woe unto him through whom they come'—is horrible. What is it in us that lies, murders, steals? I can't bear to take the thought any further.

I have suggested before that this notorious letter should not be seen as a considered and definitive philosophical statement, but as the splendidly resonant expression of a transient despair. In the specific context of the play, however, the relevant lines are not the outpouring of any kind of despair, whether transient or otherwise, but a blatant manœuvre on Danton's part, an attempt to shift the blame onto nebulous 'spirits', and so escape the agony of his conscience and the 'bloody hands' outstretched towards him. That this is indeed the object of the exercise is confirmed by its outcome: passing the buck brings instant relief, and Danton can return to bed in peace at last: 'Jezt bin ich ruhig. / Ganz ruhig, lieb Herz? / Ja Julie, komm, zu Bette!'[2]

Ironically, this new-found peace, however spurious, is rapidly shattered: within minutes, Danton will be snatched from the would-be haven of his bed, and in effect is henceforth in forfeit of his life. Once again here, it is borne in upon us that for the principal players on the revolutionary stage, there are but two real alternatives: to commit murder, or to commit suicide; to sacrifice others, or to sacrifice oneself; to choose to be a persecutor, or choose to be a victim. We have already seen this drastic reality demonstrated in several different ways; but in fact Büchner goes to quite remarkable lengths to reinforce the point. One of his chief devices is the repeated introduction of classical references (some of them taken from his sources), which, though largely lost on a modern audience, would have been instantly meaningful to Büchner's classically educated contemporaries. In the case of those allusions exemplifying the 'kill others' alternative, what is particularly emphasized is the willingness to destroy even and especially one's nearest and dearest, preferably in the name of some supposedly greater good. We have already noted Saint-Just's exhortatory reference to Pelias, butchered and boiled by his daughters in the name of rejuvenation. Virginius, cited by Simon (13), permanently safeguarded his daughter's chastity by stabbing her to death (an event that brought in its train sundry other deaths by suicide and execution; cf. Lessing's *Emilia Galotti*).

---

[2] Maurice Benn exemplifies the more traditional view of this scene when he voices his conviction that 'one would completely misinterpret Büchner if one were to suppose that there is anything either hypocritical or self-deceptive in Danton's claim to have "*had* to do it" ' (Benn, 115). To see the passage in such terms, he adds, would be to 'blunt the edge of the tragedy'. On the contrary: Danton's agonized sense of guilt and his would-be escape into casuistry greatly intensify the sense of tragedy (if tragedy it be).

Robespierre in his betrayal of Camille is likened to Nero (70), who did away with both his wife and his mother; and having declared that in the name of 'duty' and 'freedom' he would sacrifice even his brother, his friend, himself, Robespierre is compared to Brutus—the 'Brutus, der seine Söhne opfert' (24), namely Lucius Junius Brutus, who presided personally over the trial and execution of all his sons. The other, more famous Brutus, the assassin of his friend Caesar, is also a favoured exemplar: Lacroix urges Danton to invoke the spirit of Brutus and his daggers against the 'tyranny' of the Jacobin decemvirate (31), and Robespierre in his turn exhorts all those who 'carry the dagger of Brutus beneath their coats' to oppose the 'tyranny' of the Dantonists (46). Other allusions highlight the alternative option of sacrificing oneself. Lucretia, also cited by Simon (14), stabbed herself to death to eradicate the dishonour of rape. Cato of Utica killed himself rather than submit to Caesar—this being cited by the messenger from Lyon as the only alternative to the properly Jacobin activity of killing others in the name of the Republic; whereupon someone in the assembly cries out that they too will share the 'cup of Socrates' (17). The Jacobins' tacit invitation to the Dantonists to save the executioners extra work by wiping themselves out is reflected in Lacroix's allusion to Paetus: being returned to Rome to stand trial for treason, Paetus obligingly stabbed himself to death after the example of his wife Arria, she having famously assured him with her dying gasp that it really didn't hurt: *Non dolet, Paete* (Lacroix: 'Paetus es schmerzt nicht!', 24).

Büchner's other means for giving special emphasis to this motif is to embody it repeatedly around the margins of the action, thus echoing and reinforcing the issue at the centre. Here, too, we are presented with exemplary sacrificers of others and exemplary sacrificers of self. The latter, of course, are most signally represented by Julie and Lucile, who both in effect commit suttee. As for the other category, Laflotte is a conspicuous example: he deliberately betrays his cell-mate Dillon to secure his own survival (55 f.). Barrère is another case in point: he abhors the Jacobins' government-by-guillotine, but justifies his own involvement in it by telling himself that it must be legitimate to murder others to prevent one's own murder (59 f.). The most shocking instance is clearly that involving Dumas. The scene in which he appears is in no way required by the plot: it serves exclusively to demonstrate the 'Brutus principle' in its starkest form. Dumas has denounced his own wife and secured a gruesome divorce, for the bond of bed and board is to be severed by the guillotine ('die Guillotine wird uns von Tisch und Bett trennen', 65). Büchner has him specifically cite the example of Brutus, and ask: 'Muß man denn gerade römischer Consul seyn ... um sein Liebstes dem Vaterlande zu opfern?' (65; *Do you have to be a Roman consul ... to sacrifice all you love best to your country?*)

It is a striking feature of this scene that the reader-spectator is given no opportunity to be seduced by Dumas's alleged revolutionary ardour, nor even to be neutral: by including a kind of choric 'John Citizen' in the scene, Büchner is able to categorize Dumas as a 'monster', and his attitude as 'horrible' ('ein Ungeheuer', 'entsetzlich'); at the same time, the 'infallible instinct' that Dumas extols in the Jacobins' enthusiasm for the guillotine is specifically condemned through the Citizen as the instinct of the jungle ('der Sinn des Tigers'). Essentially the same pattern applies in the Laflotte and Barrère episodes, except that in these cases the moral counter-position is vested not in a separate character, but in the kill-or-be-killed exponents themselves. Laflotte for his part is shown enduring a debate within himself, and though he has little difficulty in yielding to the dictates of survival and burying his scruples in cynical banter and casuistical quips, the scruples are nonetheless there: the gnawing conscience, the inescapable whiff of villainy ('Gewissensbisse', 'es riecht ein wenig nach Schufterei', 55). Barrère, like Laflotte, is a dedicated survivor who manages to accommodate himself to his villainy; but his scruples are sharper, his balancing act more precarious. He sees his colleagues as monsters—is he therefore not one himself ('Die Ungeheuer! ... Und ich?', 59)? He is only fitfully convinced by his self-exculpatory tale of the jailbird who, in the September prison massacres, opportunistically saved his own life by joining the killers and murdering a fellow inmate. 'Wer kann was dawider haben?', he asks (*Who can blame him?*); but his moral self probes at the arithmetic of such casuistry, and far from satisfying his conscience, he can only manage to placate and distract it:

Und durft' er einen morden, durfte er auch zwei, auch drei, auch noch mehr? wo hört das auf? Da kommen die Gerstenkörner, machen zwei einen Haufen, drei, vier, wieviel dann? Komm mein Gewissen, komm mein Hühnchen, komm bi, bi, bi, da ist Futter. (60)

But if he was justified in killing *one* man, would he have been justified in killing two? or three? or even more? Where does it end? The barley grains come one by one: how many does it take to make a heap?—two? or three? or four? Come, my conscience, come, my little chicken, chk-chk-chk: here's food for you.

These brief but pointed demonstrations of irrepressible conscience are in essence variations on a theme, and serve to confirm the centrality of that theme, the chief expression of which is Danton's 'September' torment. This raging of Danton's conscience in the 'September' scene is powerful enough when taken on its own; but it becomes all the more so when we realize that it is itself a kind of echo: a more sustained, more elaborate reprise of the turmoil already visited upon Robespierre after his Act I encounter with his enemy. The similarities are remarkable indeed: here are two deadly opponents, opposite in every way—in politics, lifestyle, temperament, attitude; and yet Büchner has them suffer the voice of conscience in almost identical ways. Both men are alone, at night, by a window, exposed to a dream-like order of truth from which normally they hide. Danton had challenged Robespierre: 'Ist denn nichts in dir, was dir nicht manchmal *ganz leise, heimlich* sagte, du lügst, du lügst!' (26); and it is these very words that are echoed when Danton describes his own affliction: 'ich sprach nicht, das dacht ich kaum, das waren nur *ganz leise heimliche* Gedanken' (40). For both men, their thoughts are a swirling, ghostly presence, 'wirr und gestaltlos' for Robespierre, 'unstät, umirrend' for Danton (28, 40; *confused and formless*; *restless, wandering*). And, for both of them, their thoughts are unbearably invasive: 'Warum kann ich den Gedanken nicht los werden?' (Robespierre; *Why can't I shake off the thought?*); 'Ich möchte nicht mehr denken, wenn das gleich so spricht. Es giebt Gedanken Julie, für die es keine Ohren geben sollte.' (Danton; *I don't want to think at all any more if I'm to go on hearing the same voice. Julie, there are thoughts that no ear should hear.*) Most striking of all, their accusing consciences take shape in the same dire image of 'bloody hands': 'Warum kann ich den Gedanken nicht los werden? Er deutet mit blutigem Finger immer da, da hin!' (28); 'Was das Wort nur will? . . . Was streckt es nach mir die blutigen Hände?' (41). In their evasions, too, these erstwhile fellow butchers are shown resorting to identical excuses. In particular, there is the plea of 'necessity': 'Ist's denn so nothwendig? Ja, ja! die Republik! Er muß weg. . . . Er muß weg.' (28); 'Du hast das Vaterland gerettet. / Ja das hab' ich. Das war Nothwehr, wir mußten.' (41)—and it is of course at this point that Danton launches into the final desperate apologia that brings him (short-lived) peace. Here, too, there are further similarities. Both men build themselves up by disparaging the crucified Christ (30, 41). Both men shift the blame elsewhere: in Danton's version, our doings are blamed on invisible 'spirits' and 'unknown powers' (41), in Robespierre's they are blamed on alien 'thoughts' and 'desires' that invade and usurp our innermost being (28). And so both men can echo each other's convenient denials of responsibility: 'Wer will uns darum schelten?' (Robespierre, 28); 'Wer will der Hand fluchen, auf die der Fluch des Muß gefallen?' (Danton, 41; *Who'll blame us for that?*; *Who will curse the hand on whom the curse of 'must' has fallen?*)

In the light of all this, it is interesting to recall Büchner's preemptive protestations to his parents in May and July 1835, just before and after the play's publication. 'Faithfulness to history', we remember, was his chief defence, coupled with a piquantly Dantonesque plea of 'compulsion':

[ich bitte] euch, bei eurer Beurtheilung vorerst zu bedenken, daß ich der Geschichte treu bleiben und die Männer der Revolution geben mußte, wie sie waren, blutig, liederlich, energisch und cynisch. Ich betrachte mein Drama wie ein geschichtliches Gemälde, das seinem Original gleichen muß. (ii. 438)

I beg you to bear in mind before you form your judgement that I had to remain true to history, and to show the men of the Revolution as they were: bloody, dissolute, dynamic, cynical. I regard my drama as a historical portrait that must resemble its original.

Against the specific charge of 'immorality' that had clearly already been levelled against the play ('die sogenannte Unsittlichkeit meines Buchs'), he again wheels out the 'historiography' argument, asserting that the playwright is in his eyes 'nothing but a scribe of history', whose supreme task is to get as close as possible to history as it actually happened, and whose play therefore 'must not be any more *moral* or *immoral* than *history itself*' ('Sein Buch darf weder *sittlicher* noch *unsittlicher* sein, als die *Geschichte selbst*', ii. 443). It is not the writer's task, he asserts, to preach morality: 'Der Dichter ist kein Lehrer der Moral' (ii. 444). And the thrust of the whole argument is summed up in his famous protestation: 'Ich kann doch aus einem Danton und den Banditen der Revolution nicht Tugend-

Metamorphosis and Choice 139

helden machen!' (ii. 443; *I can't turn a Danton and the bandits of the Revolution into paragons of virtue!*)

We have already seen in an earlier context that these letters cannot be taken simply at their face value: they were a diversionary tactic, a smokescreen designed to minimize the predictable hostility of Büchner's father. In truth, Büchner did *not* see himself as the slave of history; even in the July letter itself, half smothered by the defensive rhetoric, there are unambiguous pointers to his belief that the writer does not merely catalogue the past, but brings it alive by creating it afresh in all its richness and vitality ('der dramatische Dichter ist in meinen Augen nichts, als ein Geschichtschreiber, steht aber *über* Letzterem dadurch, daß er uns die Geschichte zum zweiten Mal erschafft und uns gleich unmittelbar, statt eine trockne Erzählung zu geben, in das Leben einer Zeit hinein versetzt', ii. 443). What we now also clearly see is that this richness and vitality entail for Büchner a strong component of moral and ethical sensibility—though this, too, tends to be obscured, not to say misrepresented, in the letters (and—no doubt partly as a result of this deliberate obfuscation—has largely been lost on critics and readers). The problem arises from Büchner's rhetoric of extremes, epitomized in that famous exclamation 'Ich kann doch aus einem Danton und den Banditen der Revolution nicht Tugendhelden machen!' Plainly he doesn't turn the revolutionaries into paragons of virtue; but, contrary to his own suggestion here, he does *not* depict them, either, as the acme of vice, as unmitigated bandits who are nothing more than 'blutig, liederlich, energisch und cynisch'. Out-and-out villains would have been no better than out-and-out paragons; they would no more be fully rounded human beings, 'Menschen von Fleisch und Blut' (ii. 444), than the one-dimensional puppets of the 'Idealdichter' so scathingly disparaged in the July letter, in Camille's tirade, in the Kaufmann passage in *Lenz*. True, there is no scope in the contingent, deathly world of the Revolution for morality to prevail or predominate—either as a political programme, be it Robespierrean puritanism or Dantonist moderation; or, more particularly, as the ethos of individuals. But the moral dimension is so crucial to Büchner's vision of the overall richness of existence that he paints it vigorously and repeatedly into his picture—in the process supplementing and even altering history, or rather the available record of history, without the blink of an eye. Far from being a slavishly punctilious scribe of history, he bends it unashamedly to his purpose—as is his sovereign creative right. There is accordingly no basis whatsoever in his sources for the pangs and agonies of conscience he variously ascribes to Robespierre, Barrère, Laflotte, and precious little for the driving torment that he depicts in Danton. Equally, the Lucile of history did not volunteer herself for execution (she was arrested for allegedly plotting to spring Camille from prison); and Julie did not commit noble suicide (Danton's real wife Sophie, still only 15 at his death, remarried three years later—and outlived Büchner himself by almost twenty years).

We can more fully appreciate the importance to Büchner of this moral dimension if we recall to mind the credo expressed in the preamble to the Trial Lecture. He utterly rejects the functionalist, Cartesian view of man (and the rest of nature) as a mere assemblage of mechanical components, each of which exists solely to ensure automatic and troublefree operation of the whole (ii. 291). True, there is no explicit mention of a moral element. But it is surely implicit in his whole rejection of the 'machine' theory, and in his contrary intuition of an *anima* ('Psyche') enspiriting living matter. What is particularly revealing is his repeated rejection of the tautology that organisms exist solely in order to exist. For the functionalist school, he remarks, 'the individual' is nothing more than an entity striving to maintain its existence vis-à-vis its environment, and an entity simultaneously obliged to fulfil a purpose beyond itself ('Sie kennt das Individuum nur als etwas, das einen Zweck außer sich erreichen soll, und nur in seiner Bestrebung, sich der Außenwelt gegenüber ... zu behaupten.') Or again: 'Jeder Organismus ist für sie eine verwickelte Maschine, mit den künstlichen Mitteln versehen, sich bis auf einen gewissen Punkt zu erhalten.' (*For them, every organism is a complex machine provided with functional devices enabling it to survive over a certain span of time.*) For those of his own 'philosophical' persuasion, on the other hand, the bodily existence of an individual is *not* brought about simply for the sake of its own mechanical survival: 'so wird für die philosophische Methode das ganze körperliche Dasein des Individuums nicht zu seiner eigenen Erhaltung aufgebracht' (ii. 292).

This throws a fascinating light on the whole kill-or-be-killed motif that Büchner figures so insistently throughout *Dantons Tod*. The murderous dynamic of the Revolution has brought about an inexorable battle for survival that allows men to live only by destroying others. On the functionalist, proto-Darwinian view, every last

Metamorphosis and Choice

participant in the battle would be a mechanism automatically and blindly striving to survive. But Büchner of course does not see it that way. Despite his historical sources, he imputes to character after character an inalienable conscience that may be duped, but cannot be eradicated. Most of the characters, especially those clinging like grim death to the reins of power, *are* dedicated to survival; but in Büchner's vision their dedication is consciously, knowingly chosen, not the product of clockwork automatism. Above all, there is Danton, the heart and guts of the play: a man who, almost wholly on account of his conscience, transforms himself from a raging mastiff into a kind of sacrificial lamb: '—ich will lieber guillotinirt werden, als guillotiniren lassen'.

One of the most interesting aspects of this theme of deliberate self-sacrifice is that it is powerfully foreshadowed in Büchner's earliest writings, his schoolwork juvenilia. Of the four extant prose items (ii. 7 ff.), no fewer than three are centrally concerned with it (and the fourth, the one-page fragment 'Ueber den Traum eines Arcadiers', is too short for us to know how it would have developed; in any event it concerns the obverse of self-sacrifice: a man who fails to rouse himself to prevent the murder of a friend). In the case of the earliest text, 'Helden-Tod der vierhundert Pforzheimer', the ranting Fichtean rhetoric does not cancel out or devalue the persistent point: that in extreme adverse circumstances the only remaining but very real freedom may be the freedom to sacrifice one's own life. We might reasonably consider the heroical antics of the *Vainqueur* crew to be comically exaggerated as they scupper their ship instead of surrendering, and sink between the waves shouting 'Long live freedom!' (ii. 9)—but the essential point is perfectly serious: 'den Franken ist ein freier Tod lieber als ein sclavisches Leben' (ii. 8; *the French sailors prefer to die in freedom than live in slavery*). For the four hundred brave volunteers of Pforzheim, too, it is a question of *choosing* freedom or slavery—'Freiheit oder Knechtschaft ist die große Wahl' (ii. 11)—even though this choice means the ultimate self-sacrifice: 'Sie hatten freie Wahl, und sie wählten den Tod.' (ii. 12). The essay 'Über den Selbstmord', explicitly a review of some newly published tract on the subject (unfortunately still lost to scholarship), deals largely with suicide as an ordinary social phenomenon, and more particularly with the controversial question of the day as to whether suicide demanded blanket condemnation as irreligious, immoral, and criminal, or should be considered open-mindedly, according to the attendant circumstances. Needless to say, Büchner's standpoint is the latter. For him, suicide is at worst the unfortunate resort of people who are ill, or weak, or have lost their bearings in life. At best, however, suicide is not merely justifiable, but is a positive moral act. It is here that Büchner first refers to exemplary instances in classical antiquity, namely Cato and Lucretia, both of whom are instanced later on in *Dantons Tod*. Cato is especially highlighted: '*Cato ist vom wahren Standpunkte aus betrachtet in jeder Hinsicht zu rechtfertigen*', and his suicide is 'eine *anerkannt sittliche* Handlung' (ii. 20, Büchner's italics; *Truly considered*, Cato *is justified in every respect*; *by* common consent *a* moral *act*).

In due course, the young Büchner (still not quite 17) develops the Cato example much more extensively in his set-piece school oration specifically defending the Roman's suicide: 'Rede zur Vertheidigung des Cato von Utika'. His summary of the crucial conflict between Cato and Caesar reads like an early, classicized draft of the collision he later depicts between Danton and Robespierre:

Kato [stand] da, wie ein Gigant unter Pygmäen... Nur *ein* Mann stand ihm gegenüber. Er war *Julius Cäsar*. Beide waren gleich an Geisteskräften, gleich an Macht und Ansehn, aber beyde ganz verschiednen Charakters.... Für zwei solcher Männer war der Erdkreis zu eng. Einer mußte fallen, und *Kato* fiel, nicht als ein Opfer der Ueberlegenheit *Cäsars*, sondern seiner verdorbenen Zeit. (II. 27–8)

Cato stood there like a giant among pygmies... He had but *one* antagonist. It was *Julius Caesar*. Both men were equal in intellect, equal in power and repute, but quite opposite in character.... The world was too small for two such men. One of them had to fall, and *Cato* fell, a victim not of *Caesar* but of his corrupt age.

For Büchner's Cato as for the *Vainqueur* crew and the Pforzheim volunteers, the cardinal issue is freedom:

Katos große Seele war ganz erfüllt von einem unendlichen Gefühle für *Vaterland* und *Freiheit*... Den Fall seines Vaterlandes hätte *Kato* überleben können, wenn er ein Asyl für die andre Göttin seines Lebens, für die *Freiheit*, gefunden hätte. *Er fand es nicht*. (ii. 29)

Cato's great spirit was entirely filled by an infinite feeling for *fatherland* and *freedom*... He could have survived the downfall of his fatherland if he had found a refuge for *freedom*, the other goddess of his life. *He found it not*.

Metamorphosis and Choice 143

And so he ends his life for the sake of freedom:

Kato ... [stieß] sich das Schwert in die Brust ... um unter Sclaven nicht leben zu müssen; denn Sclaven waren die Römer, sie mochten in goldnen oder ehernen Fesseln liegen—sie waren gefesselt. Der Römer kannte nur eine Freiheit, sie war das Gesetz, dem er sich aus freier Ueberzeugung als nothwendig fügte; diese Freiheit hatte Cäsar zerstört, Kato war Sclave, wenn er sich dem Gesetz der Willkühr beugte. Und war auch Rom der Freiheit nicht werth, so war doch die Freiheit selbst werth, daß Kato für sie lebte und starb.

Cato ... buried his sword in his breast ... in order not to have to live among slaves, for slaves the Romans were: whether in chains of gold or of iron—they were indeed *in chains*. Romans knew but *one* kind of freedom, namely that law which they *freely* accepted as *necessary*; Caesar had destroyed that freedom: *Cato* was a slave if he bent to the law of a despot. But even if Rome was not worthy of freedom, freedom itself was certainly worthy that Cato should live and die for its sake.

In this formal oration by a passionate adolescent, the two antagonists are understandably, indeed quite appropriately, drawn in extreme black and white: Cato and Caesar are virtue and villainy personified. The author of *Dantons Tod* is working in a quite different context, with radically different ideas on the presentation of character, and a particular aversion to one-dimensionality. It might therefore seem far-fetched to compare Cato and Danton. With his blood-curdling past, and his present persona as a worldweary roué, Danton may seem remote indeed from the emblematic Roman of the oration. One might even suppose that Robespierre in his uncompromising puritanical severity is more akin to Cato, especially when we recall Camille's disparaging reference to the Jacobins as 'Romans' in their rigorous killjoy systematism (11). But if we look beyond the rich 'foregrounding' of the play, and beyond the rhetorical black-and-whiteness of the oration, the common ground is readily apparent: Cato and Danton confront essentially the same predicament—and meet it in essentially the same way. For Cato: although the 'altar of freedom' may have long existed, it is now destroyed (ii. 29); for Danton, the 'statue of freedom' has not yet even taken shape ('die Statue der Freiheit ist noch nicht gegossen', 12); for both of them, freedom is a present impossibility. Both recognize that their respective societies are given over to tyranny: '*Kato* ... wußte ... daß Rom sich nicht mehr erheben könne, daß es einen Tyrannen nöthig habe' (ii. 29); 'Robespierre ist das Dogma der Revolution, es darf nicht ausgestrichen werden.' (32). Both are depicted as victims not of some universal, unchanging way of things, but of a particular phase of history: Cato is 'ein Opfer ... seiner verdorbenen Zeit', he is destroyed by 'einer so heillosen Zeit' (ii. 28); revolutionary France is likewise 'eine böse Zeit' (39), and Danton is destroyed by a wave of ideological butchery that is 'der Fluch unserer Zeit' (52). Above all, of course, there is the *response* of these two 'giants among pygmies' to the grim realities that face them. Büchner's whole aim in his oration, as its title indicates, is to defend Cato against those who see and judge his actions in a false perspective—and such an approach is even more germane to Danton. Danton is certainly no Cato in the sense that he is not remotely a beacon of purest virtue, but a man irredeemably compromised by his murderous past; and far from calmly taking a decision to end his life, and then calmly, heroically enacting it, Danton is seemingly swept to his death by a combination of inertia, despair, conscience, political misjudgement. But these differences are secondary, deriving as they do from the radically different contexts involved—the historical contexts of ancient Rome/revolutionary Paris, the literary contexts of traditional oration/revolutionary drama. The heart of the matter is the moral choice exercised by Danton no less than by Cato—and for essentially the same reason. The death evoked in the title of the play is not brought about by 'unknown powers' or sadistic gods or the 'Minotaur of the Revolution' or the 'hideous fatalism of history'; it is brought about by Danton's own Damascene conversion, by the moral and ethical process within his own being that changes him from a raging mastiff to a creature with wings of a dove, and makes him willing to be guillotined himself rather than go on guillotining others. It is true, as Robespierre suggests, that he is 'trampled underfoot' by the inexorable march of the Revolution ('Wer in einer Masse, die vorwärts drängt, stehen bleibt, leistet so gut Widerstand als trät' er ihr entgegen; er wird zertreten', 28)—but only because he *chooses* to stand still and so to offer resistance to the irresistible. Danton's metamorphosis may involve no conspicuously grand and heroical gesture like Cato's act of self-immolation; but it enshrines the idea of freedom and choice no less powerfully for that. Most significantly of all, perhaps: in both cases, freedom is symbolically warranted in the face of otherwise universal *un*freedom.

8
Masks and Faces

IT is characteristic of Georg Büchner's challenge to all our assumptions that he sets us a poser even on the title page of *Dantons Tod*, when he chooses to define his play specifically as 'Ein Drama', and thereby excites expectations which the ensuing play repeatedly and pointedly refuses to satisfy, at least in conventional terms. Drama, after all, implies action; the very word itself in Greek meant 'deed' or 'action', from a verb (δρᾶν) meaning 'do, act, perform' (*OED*). On the face of it, Büchner's chosen setting is appropriate indeed to the promise of the subtitle: nothing could offer much more scope for dramatic action than 'das erhabne Drama der Revolution' (18; *the sublime drama of the Revolution*). As for the protagonist: here is a man notorious for his colossal energy, a hurricane force that did more than most to dynamize and radicalize the French Revolution. And yet Büchner offers us a spectacle in which dramatic tension and interest are generated very largely by Danton's *refusal* to act; by his extraordinary decision, already effective before the play begins, to be so to speak actively inactive, by deliberately standing still in a moving mass, thus bringing destruction upon himself and all his comrades. It is of course this process of destruction, already signalled in the title, that constitutes the plot of the play, and which thus, on a traditional, action-centred model of drama, should constitute its dynamic. In fact, however, the plot is sporadic and slight, for the most part even vestigial: only during the phase from Danton's arrest to his forcible removal from the courtroom, that is, from the final scene of Act II to the close of Act III, is there any active imbroglio, or hint of peripeteia, brought about by Danton's access of belated energy and the Jacobins' flurry of counter-measures; for the remainder of the play—rather more than two-thirds of it—very little happens, and that spasmodically.

It is a mark of Büchner's originality and of his particular genius that he creates a drama of *in*action—and does so with tremendous dramatic energy. The imperative of 'doing' that is implied in the very term 'drama' is in fact just as amply fulfilled in *Dantons Tod* as in any other, more traditional example of the genre, but at the level of *form*, not that of content. The plot with its scattered deeds and events is secondary. The real dynamic of the play derives from Büchner's powerfully kaleidoscopic technique, whereby recurrent elements—images, obsessions, ideas, motifs—are vividly juxtaposed in a rhythmic succession of sharply differentiated combinations, contexts, and perspectives. The technique is uncannily filmic, more than half a century before technology made the possibilities of the medium available: it is as if Büchner were a master of the cutting-room, splicing together clips, snippets, and sequences from several film-versions offering different angles on a single complex reality.

To some extent this vivid technique is Büchner's answer to the empty clockwork logic that he so heartily scorned in the contemporary theatre. But it is also singularly appropriate to his particular needs, inasmuch as it enables him to express in dramatic and dynamic terms what is of itself undramatic and static. For this is indeed—in the main—a drama of paralysis, a desperate lament at the absurdity and futility in the prevailing circumstances of any attempt at constructive social action—as we have seen again and again in the play's presentation of politics. In his erstwhile 'mastiff' days, Danton was action personified, a mighty agent of a revolution intended to realize the noblest ideals. Now, however, and throughout most of the play, he is the passive embodiment of disillusion and despair, and Büchner's principal means for exploring and exposing the apparently unbridgeable gulf that separates the ideal from the real.

The characteristic form of this process is of course established in the opening scene, and with a kind of bitter gusto. We are shown a woman who seems the image of prettiness, demureness, and loving fidelity, but in truth is a dedicated liar and deceiver. The bond of faith and understanding between Danton and Julie is dismissed as meaningless. The card-game is revealed as a disguised sexual frolic. The political and social ideals of the Dantonists are warmly elaborated, only to be exposed as an impossible dream. This pattern is continued in one form or another throughout the whole play, for deception and self-deception, particularly in connection with unrealizable ideals, are glaringly exposed at almost every turn. We have already encountered numerous examples of this process; but there are some other, particularly emphatic instances that demand our attention.

Masks and Faces

One of these is the 'Promenade' scene near the beginning of Act II (34 ff.)—an episode that is especially striking for being doubly 'filmic': it is a spliced-in sequence that has nothing to do with the plot; and the sequence within itself is multiply spliced, cutting abruptly between no less than eight quite separate and fragmentary speech-events. Why introduce the scene at all if it is wholly irrelevant to the plot? Because it allows Büchner with grim élan to pillory one illusion after another. The sour background reality is sketched in through the snatches of song from the Balladeer and the Beggar: a life of toil and anguish ('Unter Kummer, unter Sorgen | Sich bemühn vom frühen Morgen'), with nothing to show for it in the end but a clutch of dirt and a scrap of moss ('Eine Handvoll Erde | Und ein wenig Moos'). At the start of the scene, the Citizen delights in the birth of his newborn son—only to obliterate the promise of this new life by submerging its precious individuality in the anonymous generality of the State ('das Einzelne muß sich dem Allgemeinen...') and by choosing names that grotesquely symbolize the future adult's robot status as cannon-fodder, workhorse, and repository of rectitude: 'Pike, Pflug, Robespierre, das sind hübsche Namen' (*Pike, Plough, Robespierre: what a lovely lot of names*). The scene cuts to the two Gentlemen and the Beggar, and the worship of work is held up to ridicule. The limelight shifts to two young women—not demure young things, but raunchy prostitutes raring to score, and revelling in crass sexual banter and *double entendre*. Demureness arrives after all, it would seem, in the person of Eugénie, wafted along by verbiage about virtue, nature, joy, and purity; but all is a mask beneath which lurks unbridled prurience. The two Gentlemen return and enthuse about technological progress and human advancement and lofty elaborate structures—yet the very ground on which they stand is feared by one of them to be but a shell through which at any moment he might fall into a nameless void.

The biting effect of this *Reigen*-like interlude is considerably intensified by the fact that Danton is introduced as an on-stage spectator and twice used—as in the opening scene of the play—as a kind of one-man Greek chorus (it could be argued that his role throughout the play is more 'choric' than 'protagonistic'). The first of his outbursts, following on the prostitutes and prefacing Eugénie, spotlights sexuality in the harshest terms:

Geht das nicht lustig?
Ich wittre was in der Athmosphäre, es ist als brüte die Sonne Unzucht aus. Möchte man nicht drunter springen, sich die Hosen vom Leibe reißen und sich über den Hintern begatten wie die Hunde auf der Gasse?

Oh what fun they're having!
It's in the air, I can smell it: as if the heat of the sun were hatching lechery. Doesn't it make you want to leap in amongst them, tear your trousers from your body, and fuck them from behind like dogs in the street?

This passage has frequently been misrepresented. Far from being—as one recent critic has preposterously claimed—a 'straightforwardly crude expression of a desire for sex in the street' voiced by Danton because he is 'emotionally caught up himself in the sexual excitement of the scene',[1] the passage is a harrowing cry of despair and revulsion, bitterly ironic in its crudity and its pretence of humour: what a cruel joke if, for all our fancy notions, brute sexuality is the vile but essential truth of our condition. Existence as a joke: this is the plangent theme of Danton's second choric utterance. With its crescendo of lengthening sentences and rapidly intensifying rhythms and resonance, together with its leaps from street to grave to heaven, this is surely one of the most unnervingly poignant cries in all Büchner's work:

Muthe mir nur nichts Ernsthaftes zu. Ich begreife nicht warum die Leute nicht auf der Gasse stehen bleiben und einander in's Gesicht lachen. Ich meine sie müßten zu den Fenstern und zu den Gräbern heraus lachen und der Himmel müsse bersten und die Erde müsse sich wälzen vor Lachen.

Don't expect me to be serious! I can't see why people don't stop in the street and laugh in each other's faces. They should laugh from their windows and laugh from their graves and the heavens should burst and the earth should convulse with helpless laughter.

The most profound anguish is expressed here through the image of laughter: why can't everyone and everything—heaven and earth, the quick and the dead—recognize, as Danton thinks he himself does, that our ideals and pretensions are a hollow mockery; that copulating dogs are the truest symbol of our reality?

[1] James, 14. Cf. Reinhold Grimm, who speaks of Danton's 'crude serenity' and 'rapture' in this scene, and describes its supposed fusion of 'universal lust and lechery and laughter' as a kind of cheerful contrast to the 'universal grief and melancholy' otherwise prevailing (Grimm, *Love, Lust and Rebellion: New Approaches to Georg Büchner* (Madison, Wis., 1985), 184, 188).

Masks and Faces 149

But people in general do *not* see what Danton sees. They act out their allotted part without realizing its falseness. In the crucial 'dressing scene' that immediately precedes 'Eine Promenade', this unconscious play-acting is specifically referred to, albeit in this instance as a kind of merciful blindness. Even the misery of the Revolution is a godsend, says Danton: by encouraging postures of pathos, nobility, virtue, or wit, it constitutes the perfect defence against the void of ennui: '[Die Leute] haben Unglück, kann man mehr verlangen um gerührt, edel, tugendhaft oder witzig zu seyn oder um überhaupt keine Langeweile zu haben?' (33). On this sardonic view, the theatricality of the guillotine is a positive blessing:

Ob [die Leute] nun an der Guillotine oder am Fieber oder am Alter sterben? Es ist noch vorzuziehen, sie treten mit gelenken Gliedern hinter die Coulissen und können im Abgehen noch hübsch gesticuliren und die Zuschauer klatschen hören. Das ist ganz artig und paßt für uns, wir stehen immer auf dem Theater, wenn wir auch zulezt im Ernst erstochen werden.

What difference does it make if they die because of the guillotine, or from disease or old age? It's better to skip into the wings with sprightly limbs and a cheery wave and the applause of the spectators still ringing in one's ears. How killingly jolly, how perfectly apt: we prance on a stage throughout our lives—even if, in the end, we are killed for real.

The motif of life as a fraud or pretence is one that recurs throughout the play, after being trumpeted in its very first utterance concerning the deceptively pretty lady and the allure of lying: 'Ihr könntet einen noch in die Lüge verliebt machen.' Immediately afterwards, there is the image of Julie as a kind of talking doll, and Hérault's description of the covert sexual game enacted by the cardplayers. We are shown the spectacle of Simon, whose posturings are rendered all the more crass by his *déformation professionnelle* as a theatrical Prompter. In Camille's diatribe, we hear how people ape the caricatures they encounter in the plays, poems, and novels that constitute their reality-ersatz ('[Sie] schneiden den Fratzen darin die Gesichter nach', 37). Not least, there is the political realm and the *mauvaise foi* of its participants, exemplified above all in Robespierre and the deaf ear he turns to the 'secret voice' within himself.

Aptly enough, however, the most intense and powerful use of the motif occurs at the ringing climax of the play, namely in the final prison scene (70 f.). The cue is a puff of rhetorical posturing on

Danton's part that is promptly deflated by Hérault as so much irrelevant blether meant merely for posterity ('Das sind Phrasen für die Nachwelt, nicht wahr Danton, uns gehn sie eigentlich nichts an.') Camille then takes up the cry by describing Danton's posturing in terms of a 'mask': 'Er zieht ein Gesicht, als solle es versteinern und von der Nachwelt als Antike ausgegraben werden.' (*He's putting on a face as if he expected it to turn into stone and be dug up by posterity as an ancient relic.*) And this sets the tone for the whole of the ensuing sequence that forms the prelude to the climax proper— the famous chorus of despair with its final blast of 'chaos' and 'nothingness'. Again and again in this last-minute spasm of anguish as death comes knocking at the door, pretence and pretension are dismissed through the imagery of masks: to pout and prink and talk all posh is a waste of effort ('Das verlohnt sich auch der Mühe Mäulchen zu machen und Roth aufzulegen und mit einem guten Accent zu sprechen'); they should strip away their masks for once ('wir sollten einmal die Masken abnehmen'); there is no need to pull any faces ('Da braucht man . . . Gesichter zu schneiden'); no need to hide their agony behind their napkin ('was haltet ihr euch die Servietten vor das Gesicht'); no need for heroical grimaces ('die heroische Fratze'); above all, there is no point in their pretending amongst themselves: they know one another too well to be fooled by any laboured postures of virtue or wit, heroism or genius ('Schneidet nur keine so tugendhafte und so witzige und so heroische und so geniale Grimassen, wir kennen uns ja einander, spart euch die Mühe.')

But behind all the masks and the false pretences, what kind of reality lies concealed? In the perspective offered here, it is bleak indeed, for we are shown a vision of humanity in which there is *no* humanity, no individuality, just a terrible sameness at once brutish and mechanical. Strip away the masks from our faces, says Camille, and we should think ourselves in a hall of mirrors, for in everyone we would see identically the same primeval, ever-recurring, indestructible 'mutton-head': 'wir sähen dann wie in einem Zimmer mit Spiegeln überall nur den einen uralten, zahllosen, unverwüstlichen Schaafskopf, nichts mehr, nichts weniger'. We may appear to differ from each other, but the differences are minimal: vice and virtue, stupidity and genius are not the distinctive, man-sized attributes we imagine them to be, but puny things coexistent in all of us: 'Die Unterschiede sind so groß nicht, wir Alle sind Schurken und Engel, Dummköpfe und Genies und zwar das Alles in Einem, die vier Dinge finden Platz genug in dem nemlichen Körper, sie sind nicht so breit, als man sich einbildet.' Worse still: the tiny differences between people that we make so much of are merely variations on a single theme—the primitive process of sleep–digestion–procreation that makes us all featureless clones of each other: 'Schlafen, Verdaun, Kinder machen das treiben Alle, die übrigen Dinge sind nur Variationen aus verschiedenen Tonarten über das nemliche Thema.'

Outward pretence and essential animality: this contrast is brought into the sharpest focus when Büchner has Danton speak up and redefine it with stark and graphic economy. Hérault having remarked that Greeks and gods cried out in their pain, whilst Romans and Stoics masked their agony with a heroical grimace, Danton retorts that all were equally epicurean, in that all were busy concocting for themselves whatever set of feelings they happened to find most comfortable: 'Die Einen waren so gut Epicuräer wie die Andern. Sie machten sich ein ganz behagliches Selbstgefühl zurecht.' This is followed by a sardonic defence of narcissistic posturing: it is no bad feeling to wrap yourself in a flowing toga and glance over your shoulder in the hope of finding an impressive shadow: 'Es ist nicht so übel seine Toga zu drapieren und sich umzusehen ob man einen langen Schatten wirft.' In his original manuscript, Büchner continued the image of the all-enveloping toga: 'Die Toga, worin ich mich wickle, ist kein so übles Pflaster. S'ist wenigstens eben so gut, als wenn ich sie von mir würfe und die nackten Wunden zeigte.' (TMM 69; *The toga I use to wrap myself in is no mean bandage. At any rate it's just as good as if I threw it off and bared my naked wounds.*) But he crossed this out and substituted something very different, and much more raw. The 'disguise' motif is retained, but only in order to concentrate the underlying reality into a single image of crass carnality: the 'ugly object', 'das häßliche Ding'—in other words the human penis; yet again here—echoing the Marion scene (23) as well as 'Eine Promenade'—humans are equated with rutting dogs. Why agonize over all these things? asks Danton; what difference does it make whether we conceal our 'Schaam', our 'shameful parts', beneath garlands of laurel, roses, or vine-leaves, or openly flaunt our 'ugly object' and let it be licked by dogs?—'Was sollen wir uns zerren? Ob wir uns nun Lorbeerblätter, Rosenkränze oder Weinlaub vor die Schaam binden, oder das häßliche Ding offen tragen und es uns von den Hunden lecken lassen?'

There is no more bitterly explicit sexual metaphor in all Büchner's œuvre than this reduction of man's reality to an ugly, naked, dog-licked penis, and it brings the scene to a kind of preliminary jangling climax. With startling boldness he then switches perspective—and does so, through Philippeau, in specifically perspectivist terms: we have only to change our vantage point, and instead of bleak confusion we see grand and godly order; and what is to us a deafening cacophony, is to another's ear (God's?) a blessed 'stream of harmonies':

Meine Freunde man braucht gerade nicht hoch über der Erde zu stehen um von all dem wirren Schwanken und Flimmern nichts mehr zu sehen und die Augen von einigen großen, göttlichen Linien erfüllt zu haben. Es giebt ein Ohr für welches das Ineinanderschreien und der Zeter, die uns betäuben, ein Strom von Harmonien sind.

Whether we take this passage seriously in terms of meaning depends in turn on our own interpretative perspective; but there can be no argument about its function: it serves to trigger the extraordinary chorus—surely the most thrilling, most exuberant hymn of despair in the German language—that brings both the scene and the play as a whole to a grand-opera climax of exultant negativity. Philippeau's antithesis of earthly confusion and cacophony, as against heavenly order and harmony, is seized on by Danton, but only in order to be defined in quite different terms. What instantly takes shape is a vision of existence as ritual, sadistic torture enacted by the denizens of heaven for the indulgence of their own perverted and insatiable appetites. And there is an unmistakable tinge of masochism in the succession of torture tableaux conjured up here by the would-be victims as they picture their predicament in response to Philippeau's 'stream of harmonies':

DANTON. Aber wir sind die armen Musicanten und unsere Körper die Instrumente. Sind die häßlichen Töne, welche auf ihnen herausgepfuscht werden nur da um höher und höher dringend und endlich leise verhallend wie ein wollüstiger Hauch in himmlischen Ohren zu sterben?
HÉRAULT. Sind wir wie Ferkel, die man für fürstliche Tafeln mit Ruthen todtpeitscht, damit ihr Fleisch schmackhafter werde?
DANTON. Sind wir Kinder, die in den glühenden Molochsarmen dießer Welt gebraten[2] und mit Lichtstrahlen gekitzelt werden, damit die Götter sich über ihr Lachen freuen?

---

[2] Moloch was a Canaanite idol to whom children were sacrificed as burnt-offerings (cf. Leviticus 19: 21; I Kings 11: 7). According to Rabbinic legend, the

Masks and Faces

CAMILLE. Ist denn der Aether mit seinen Goldaugen eine Schüssel mit Goldkarpfen, die am Tisch der seeligen Götter steht und die seeligen Götter lachen ewig und die Fische sterben ewig und die Götter erfreuen sich ewig am Farbenspiel des Todeskampfes?

DANTON. But we are the poor musicians and our bodies the instruments. The ugly sounds scratched out on them: are they just there to rise up higher and higher and gently fade and die like some voluptuous breath in heavenly ears?

HÉRAULT. Are we sucking pigs, whipped to death with rods to make their meat more tasty for a princely feast?

DANTON. Are we children roasted in the fiery arms of a Moloch world[2] and tickled to death with shafts of light so the gods can delight in our laughter?

CAMILLE. Are the heavens with their winking eyes of gold a bowl of golden carp that stands on the table of the blessed gods and the blessed gods laugh for ever and the fish die for ever and the gods delight for ever in the dancing colours of their dying agony?

This sustained rhetorical crescendo requires a crisp conclusion, and the perfect trumpet-blast is delivered in Büchner's most famous one-liner: 'Die Welt ist das Chaos. Das Nichts ist der zu gebärende Weltgott.' (*The world is chaos. Nothingness its due messiah.*)

In the face of such an absolute statement of negativity, it is not difficult to understand how Büchner acquired his long-standing reputation as 'a most decided nihilist',[3] as the purveyor of 'a pessimism deeper and darker than any to be found in the previous history of German thought with the possible exception of Schopenhauer'.[4] But the grandiloquently negative vision expressed by Danton and his fellow prisoners in this scene is by no means Büchner's definitive picture of the world, his definitive philosophy. On the contrary, it is the most insidious dance of delusions to confront us anywhere in his work. The Dantonists are *in extremis*: within minutes (in stage-time) they will all be dead; in the cold light of this reality, all their previous beliefs about the value and genuineness of life appear as so many cosy and empty pretensions which they emphatically discard. But with perfectly judicious logic, Büchner shows them trading illusion for illusion: they throw off one false mantle, but, incapable of facing the cold, they instantly don another, wrapping themselves

---

victims were burnt alive by being placed in the arms of an image of the deity, whence they fell into the flames beneath (*OED*, 'Moloch').

[3] Viëtor, *Georg Büchner*, 296.
[4] Benn, 61.

warmly in the extravagant rhetoric of despair. In the penultimate gaol scene, Büchner exposed this stratagem most neatly when he showed Danton trying, but failing, to take refuge in rhetoric:

Morgen bist du eine zerbrochne Fiedel, die Melodie darauf ist ausgespielt. Morgen bist du eine leere Bouteille, der Wein ist ausgetrunken, aber ich habe keinen Rausch davon und gehe nüchtern zu Bett. . . . Morgen bist du eine durchgerutschte Hose, du wirst in die Garderobe geworfen und die Motten werden dich fressen, du magst stinken wie du willst.
Ach, das hilft nichts. Ja wohl, s'ist so elend sterben müssen. (66)

Tomorrow you're a broken fiddle, its tune played out. Tomorrow you're an empty bottle, its wine all drunk—yet I go sober to bed, stone-cold sober. . . Tomorrow you're a pair of worn-out trousers, they'll chuck you in a cupboard and the moths will eat you, stink as you will.
It's no good: it doesn't help at all. Let's face it, it's a miserable business having to die.

The rhetoric of despair is just as much a posture, an existential subterfuge, as other, more blatant ones that are contemplated in the play, such as the smokescreen of 'compulsion' that Danton and Robespierre put up in the face of their accusing consciences, or Danton's sardonic glorification of death on the scaffold in preference to a routine death through illness or old age (33), or Camille's longing for his beloved Lucile to be safely cocooned in some convenient *idée fixe* ('Der Himmel verhelf' ihr zu einer behaglichen fixen Idee', 70).

It is in this context, perhaps, that we can most usefully discuss what is arguably the thorniest single element in the play: the Thomas Payne[5] episode at the beginning of Act III (47 ff.). No other scene is more conspicuously extraneous, more provocatively separate from the dynamic of the plot. After the storm, a lull: the fanatical enthusiasm and baying of the *Marseillaise* that formed the hectic finale both to Saint-Just's great speech and to the first half of the play, is now followed by a calm interlude—a virtuoso act of intellectual juggling at once spellbinding and baffling, performed by a three-man team whom we have never encountered before, and never encounter again (except for a few sporadic utterances from one of them, Mercier, in the rest of the scene, and again in III, iii).

---

[5] Büchner uses variant spellings of several names throughout the play—not only Payne instead of Paine, but also e.g. Barrère, Hérault-Séchelles, Philippeau instead of Barère, Hérault de Séchelles, Philippeaux.

Payne is clearly the star of this interlude, but in Chaumette he is provided with a stooge of decisive importance. Historically, Chaumette was a dedicated Rationalist and Anti-Religionist who had characteristically master-minded a *Fête de la Raison* in Notre Dame, the citadel of French Catholicism; a man, too, who liked to style himself 'Anaxagoras', after the Athenian philosopher vilified for his irreligion. But Büchner depicts him as faltering in his convictions in the dark shadow of the guillotine, and the whole impetus of this episode is generated by Chaumette's abject plea for a dose of morale-boosting medicine from the author of *The Age of Reason*. As so often, the scene begins as though in mid-conversation, and we are thus prevented from knowing precisely what Chaumette might be referring to in his opening words—but it is clear that an actor would need to convey the incipient and laughable panic of a would-be *outré* rationalist stricken by irrational fears and doubts:

CHAUMETTE [*zupft Payne am Aermel*]. Hören Sie Payne es könnte doch so seyn, vorhin überkam es mich so; ich habe heute Kopfweh, helfen Sie mir ein wenig mit Ihren Schlüssen, es ist mir ganz unheimlich zu Muth.

CHAUMETTE [*tugs at Payne's sleeve*]. Listen Payne, things *could* be that way after all, it suddenly came over me just then; my head's aching today, help me a little with your logic—there's this horrible feeling inside me.

There is something distinctly King Peter-ish about Chaumette: for him, too, rationalism appears to be a fragile construct that is meant to serve as an existential refuge, but nevertheless leaves him prey to terrible confusion. He is positively ill in his anguish ('ich habe heute Kopfweh'), and the comfort he craves is a quick fix of logic. That this portrayal is comically intended is confirmed beyond doubt when Büchner has Payne respond with telling irony: he addresses his supplicant grandly by his sobriquet of Anaxagoras the fearless philosopher, but in the same breath orders him about like a child, using the familiar 'du' form, and pretends to be, not a doctor, but a priest giving catechism to a wayward believer: 'So komm Philosoph Anaxagoras ich will dich katechisiren.' The comic frame of reference is maintained throughout. Thus Payne and his sidekick Mercier invariably address Chaumette with the same ironic mixture of apparent respect and belittling familiarity (whereas they both use 'du' to him, they use the respectful 'Sie' to each other, as he also does to them). The comments of Chaumette that punctuate the dialogue swing laughably from extreme to extreme, and are lent a delightful air of ineptness and exaggeration by their sheer brevity and, especially, by the robotic repetition that characterizes all but the last of them: 'Ey wahrhaftig, das giebt mir wieder Licht, ich danke, danke,'—'Schweigen Sie! Schweigen Sie!'—'Wahr, sehr wahr!'— 'Ich danke Ihnen verbindlichst, meine Herren' (*I see the light again now, that's the truth, thank you, thank you*; *Shut up, do shut up!*; *True, very true!*; *Gentlemen, I am most deeply obliged to you*). The whole episode culminates in the sharpest irony. Hérault first 'consoles' Chaumette with a scabrous piece of religious/sexual *double entendre* that essentially mocks his rationalist posture: 'Freue dich, du kömmst glücklich durch, du kannst ganz ruhig in Madame Momoro[6] das Meisterstück der Natur anbeten, wenigstens hat sie dir die Rosenkränze dazu in den Leisten gelassen.' (*Be happy, you're through it alright, you can go ahead and worship Madame Momoro[6] as Mother Nature's masterpiece, at least she's left you all the necessary prayer-beads in your groin.*) Then, to cap it all, Büchner has Payne suggest that in the end this desperate anti-religionist will cover himself against all eventualities by taking Extreme Unction, pointing his feet towards Mecca, and having himself circumcized: 'Er traut noch nicht, er wird sich zu guter Letzt noch die Oelung geben, die Füße nach Mecca zu legen, und sich beschneiden lassen um ja keinen Weg zu verfehlen.'

The decisive importance of this comic framework, so insistently maintained throughout (yet generally ignored by critics), is that it constitutes a kind of inbuilt stage direction defining the mood and perspective of the scene as a whole. The situation is quite different from that obtaining in the case, for instance, of Camille's outburst against the arts and their consumers in Act II, where in effect Büchner is the real speaker, addressing himself directly to the reader/spectator, and temporarily suspending the business of the play. In the Payne episode, by contrast, we see what amounts to a performance within the performance: an act of virtuoso word-juggling in which Payne, ably assisted by Mercier, runs rings around Chaumette, their one-man audience and comic stooge; and of course there is a second audience present on the stage, namely the 'other

---

[6] Sophie Momoro, a former actress and the famously beautiful wife of Antoine François Momoro (a printer–publisher prominent amongst the radical *Hébertistes*) had played the part of the Goddess of Reason in Chaumette's *Fête de la Raison* in Nov. 1793. She was guillotined with the *Hébertistes* on 24 Mar. 1794 (i.e. the executions referred to by Philippeau in his opening speech in I. i).

prisoners' ('andre Gefangne') specified in Büchner's scene-heading, and any director would clearly miss a trick if he did not show these bystanders savouring the spectacle, thus suggesting an appropriate response to the real audience.

Payne's first verbal stunt is his 'proof' that there can be no God. If we disregard the comic framework, this speech can easily seem like a piece of straight philosophical logic, as though we were eavesdropping on some learned and earnest discourse. In its real stage context, however, the 'proof' is unquestionably a spoof: Chaumette wants a dose of logic, and logic is what he gets—but in the form of a delicious *parody* of systematic rationalism. To be more precise: in its exaggerated 'either . . . or . . .', 'if . . . then . . .', 'because . . . therefore . . .', 'QED' mode, it is a pastiche of Spinoza: in his Spinoza commentary, Büchner cites passages that likewise end with 'QED' (cf. ii. 242, 243); and we find exactly the kind of passage mimicked by Payne, as when Spinoza paraphrases an argument of his opponents precisely in terms of 'if . . . then', 'either . . . or . . .', 'in the former case . . . in the latter case . . .' (ii. 244: ll. 14 ff. Cf. *Cartesius*, ii. 150: 'Entweder bin ich *durch mich oder durch etwas Anderes* und dießes *Andere* ist entweder *Gott* oder ist *nicht Gott*' (*I exist either through myself or through something else and this something else is either God or it is* not God); cf. also King Peter:'—denn entweder verheirathet sich mein Sohn, oder nicht . . . entweder, oder—ihr versteht mich doch? Ein Drittes gibt es nicht.' (109; *for my son either marries or does not marry . . . either, or—you grasp my point, do you not? There is no third alternative.*))

The notion of *quod erat demonstrandum* that closes Payne's first speech is crucial, for 'Demonstration'—proof through the rigorous, logical application of mind—is the alpha and omega of dogmatic rationalism (cf. the Trial Lecture, ii. 292: 'der Dogmatismus der Vernunftphilosophen'; but cf. also ii. 277). It was Descartes's view that, of all enquirers after truth, only mathematicians—and this means in effect logicians—had managed to *demonstrate* the truth of their knowledge, thus making it both evident and certain: ' " . . . die *Mathematiker* allein [haben] es zur Demonstration d. h. zur Gewißheit und Evidenz in der Erkenntniß gebracht . . ." ' (ii. 137). It is the fundamental premiss of Cartesianism 'daß man durch Demonstration allein zu Allem gelangen könnte' (ii. 213; *that one may attain to all things solely through the process of demonstration*). The ultimate Cartesian is Spinoza. For him, the intellect is our supreme possession ('unser höchstes Gut', ii. 268); and the only possible link between human intellect and the realm of the absolute is afforded by the process of logical demonstration: 'die Demonstration ist ihm das einzige Band zwischen dem Absoluten und der Vernunft' (ii. 269). Spinoza, as we saw much earlier, even outdoes his master by elevating the reasoning mind to the ultimate status of 'being all things and being equal to all challenges': 'der demonstrirende Verstand ist Alles und ist Allem gewachsen' (ibid.); and in consequence, Spinozism is the most logical and most perfect fulfilment of the Cartesian philosophy of 'demonstration': 'In ihm [dem Spinozismus] vollendet und schließt sich die Cartesianische Methode der Demonstration, erst in ihm gelangt sie zu ihrer völligen Consequenz.' (ii. 270–1).

The central irony in Payne's stream of Spinozan language and logic is that it is used to *counter* Spinoza's own central doctrine (shared with Descartes), namely the necessary and demonstrable existence of God. On the surface, Payne is *defending* rationalism (as a system refuting God); at a deeper level, he is *attacking* rationalism (as a system guaranteeing God). We need to remember that, for Büchner, systematic rationalism of whatever kind is necessarily remote from 'dem frischen grünen Leben', and ratiocination in general is a secondary activity ('das secundäre Geschäft des Denkens') that is wholly ignorant of our essential and immediate being (ii. 140). We should also remember that the God of Descartes and Spinoza was in Büchner's view an expedient construct of the mind designed to provide a means of escape from the 'grave of philosophy' and the 'abyss of doubt', a means of bridging the 'abyss' separating subject and object, self and world, the 'gulf' separating the finite from the infinite (ii. 153, 155, 287). In Payne's dazzling first speech, intellect and logic are used to *refute* the notion of God—but the God of Descartes and Spinoza is precisely that: a notion; and it is therefore only at the level of mind that this God can be 'proved' and 'demonstrated'—in the words of Payne's fifth speech: 'nur der Verstand kann Gott beweisen'. For Büchner, Cartesian and Spinozan logic is like a mighty engine: once aboard it, we are propelled along inescapable tracks to irresistible conclusions—but there is nothing that compels us to board it in the first place, indeed there is nothing that can *justify* us in boarding it. This point is emphatically made in the 'Spinoza' commentary, as when Büchner remarks:

Masks and Faces

Der Beweis übrigens welcher aus dem Wesen Gottes, sein Deseyn demonstrirt, stützt sich nur auf eine logische Nothwendigkeit, er sagt, wenn ich mir Gott denke muß ich ihn mir als seyend denken, aber was berechtigt mich denn, Gott zu denken? (ii. 238)

The proof, incidentally, that demonstrates the existence of God on the basis of his being rests solely on a logical necessity; it says, 'If I think God, I have to think him as existing'; but what justifies me in thinking God?

Two pages earlier, the same kind of point is made (with reference to a particular proof of Spinoza's):

Dießer Beweis läuft ziemlich auf den hinaus, daß Gott nicht anders als seyend gedacht werden könnte. Was zwingt uns aber ein Wesen zu denken, was nicht anders als seyend gedacht werden kann? Wir sind durch die Lehre von dem, was in sich oder in etwas Anderm ist freilich gezwungen auf etwas zu kommen, was nicht anders als seyend gedacht werden kann; was berechtigt uns aber deßwegen aus dießem Wesen das absolut Vollkommne, Gott, zu machen? (ii. 236)

This proof is much the same as that which says that God can only be thought as existing. But what compels us to think a being that can only be thought as existing? It is true that the doctrine of 'that which is in itself or in something else' forces us to arrive at something that can only be thought as existing; but what justifies us in therefore turning this being into absolute perfectness, i.e. God?

This paragraph is followed in turn by the only oft-quoted passage in the philosophical commentaries—oft-quoted because it trenchantly adduces Büchner's essential grounds for rejecting Cartesianism, namely the primary experience of our *mind*, and the primary experience of our *emotions*:

Wenn man auf die Definition von Gott eingeht, so muß man auch das Daseyn Gottes zugeben. Was berechtigt uns aber, dieße Definition zu machen?
Der *Verstand*?
Er kennt das Unvollkommne.
Das *Gefühl*?
Es kennt den Schmerz.

If one accedes to the definition of God, then one must also concede the existence of God. But what justifies us in making this definition?
The *mind*?
It knows unperfectness.
The emotions?
They know pain.

Pain and unperfectness: these are the two great stumbling-blocks—both of them centrally prefigured in the Payne–Mercier exchange. Of the two, pain appears the more compelling through its appeal to our emotions, but in fact unperfectness is the key problem, for we are subject to pain only because we are neither Allness nor Nothingness, but a mere Something in between, a frail, finite, imperfect 'Mittelding zwischen Gott und Nichts', as Büchner's rendering of Descartes graphically expresses it (ii. 157). God in this context is not at all the same as the God of Christianity (or of any other metaphysical religion), but an abstract term, a 'collective concept' ('Collectivbegriff', ii. 242), that stands for 'perfectness', much as the symbol ∞ stands for 'infinity'; in the definition ascribed to Payne: 'Gott, d. h. . . . das Vollkommne' (48). But for God-as-perfectness to be logically, definitively proved, the problem of *un*perfectness has to be solved: 'Schafft das Unvollkommne weg, dann allein könnt ihr Gott demonstriren, Spinoza hat es versucht.' (48; *Get rid of unperfectness, only then can you demonstrate God; that's just what Spinoza tried to do.*) In Büchner's view, Spinoza—like Descartes before him—failed in this crucial task. No matter how hard he tried, he could not bridge the fundamental gulf ('Kluft') between the finite and the infinite (ii. 287); he was faced by an 'insoluble difficulty' ('eine unauflösliche Schwierigkeit', ii. 289); he encountered an 'unfathomable question'—'die unbegreifliche Frage: wie und warum denn aus Gottes vollkommnem Wesen endliches, d. i. unvollkommnes Seyn und Denken entspringe' (ibid.; *the unfathomable question as to how and why finite, i.e. unperfect being and thinking could arise out of the perfect existence of God*).

The theatre is not a lecture hall, and Büchner is not concerned in the Payne episode to deliver an intellectual discourse. On the contrary, the comic mode of performance-within-performance enables him to dance around his targets attacking them in a whole variety of different ways. After the sparkling parodistic logic of Payne's first speech, we are treated to a piece of derisive bathos at the expense of Spinoza's pantheism, when the God supposedly present in all of us is envisaged as sharing our toothache, our clap, our nightmares. A passage of deft intellectual fencing between Payne and Mercier ensues (throwing poor Chaumette into complete confusion), but this phase is rounded off with homely common sense, as though God were a slightly misguided schoolboy: if unperfectness is all that God

Masks and Faces

can create, then he'd better stop creating altogether. The same topic is raised at the end of the episode, and this time the mockery is achieved through a tongue-in-cheek *reductio ad absurdum* from Hérault: if God is all things, then he is also his opposite—unperfect as well as perfect, etc.—in which case the opposites cancel each other out, and we end up with Nothing ('es würde sich gegenseitig heben, wir kämen zum Nichts'; cf. ii. 289: the continuation of the 'Spinoza' passage quoted above!)

Just as 'God-as-perfectness' is an arbitrary construct of the mind, so too is 'God-as-creator'; indeed in both cases Payne is specifically concerned with the ways in which we *think* God ('uns Gott denken'; 48 top, 48 middle). And the concept of 'God as creator' is scorned as a kind of blinkered anthropomorphism whereby we fashion our God in the image and in the service of our own puny needs: just because *we* feel driven incessantly to action to prove to ourselves that we really exist, why impute such a miserable urge to God? Just because *we* have an extravagant need for love, and hence for people to love and be loved by, why suppose that, after an eternity of repose, some immanent spirit should suddenly have felt moved to conjure up mankind like a diner shaping figures out of bread? And do we in any case make such suppositions only in order to turn ourselves into the progeny of gods?

Ist's nicht sehr menschlich, uns Gott nur als schaffend denken zu können? Weil wir uns immer regen und schütteln müssen um uns nur immer sagen zu können: wir sind! müssen wir Gott auch dieß elende Bedürfniß andichten? Müssen wir, wenn sich unser Geist in das Wesen einer harmonisch in sich ruhenden, ewigen Seeligkeit versenkt, gleich annehmen sie müsse die Finger ausstrecken und über Tisch Brodmännchen kneten? aus überschwenglichem Liebesbedürfniß, wie wir uns ganz geheimnißvoll in die Ohren sagen. Müssen wir das Alles, bloß um uns zu Göttersöhnen zu machen?

Another false construct of the mind that is attacked here—neither for the first nor for the last time in Büchner's work—is dogmatic moralism. What we are offered is a kind of set-piece critique. A propos of nothing, the issue is flung into the ring by Mercier in his ritual sparring-partner role ('MERCIER. Und die Moral?')—and Payne dispatches it with a swift one-two. His essential argument is that such moralism is a purely tautological abstraction: 'Erst beweist ihr Gott aus der Moral und dann die Moral aus Gott.' (*First you prove God on the basis of morality, and then morality on the basis of God.*)—a tautology irreverently defined in the original manuscript version as 'Ein schöner Cirkelschluß der sich selbst im Hintern leckt' (TMM 51; *A splendid circular argument that licks its own behind*). And the reason why such an unsound edifice of morality is objectionable is soon made clear: it leads its devotees to despise those of a different persuasion ('ihre Gegner verachten'). The political allusion is plain: it is Robespierre, the supreme moralist and self-appointed 'Policeysoldat des Himmels', who holds his opponents in such despite that he is only too willing to wipe them out in order to wipe out their 'vice'.

With the able assistance of Mercier and his stooge Chaumette, Payne through his verbal acrobatics mocks the pretensions of the overweening intellect, which is equally capable of 'proving' that God does *not* exist, and that he *does* exist ('so kann es keinen Gott geben. Quod erat demonstrandum.' / 'nur der Verstand kann Gott beweisen'); which cheerfully 'proves' God on the basis of morality whilst proving morality on the basis of God; which represents as absolute truth what is only a reflection of its own inherent frailty. But is anything left unmocked? Is there anything in the Payne episode to suggest that there are other, more reliable and more positive elements to hold on to?

Two such elements that are passingly invoked are the unerring powers of judgement represented by our common sense, and by our emotions. It is earthy common sense that Payne appeals to in his mockery of Spinoza's pantheism when he expects Mercier to concede ('Sie müssen mir zugestehen') that there is precious little heavenly majesty about an immanent deity that is prone to toothache, clap, and nightmarish imaginings. As for the emotions: the intellect may be able to 'prove' its notion of God, but—so Payne declares—our feelings revolt at the very idea ('das Gefühl empört sich dagegen').

Positive elements though common sense and emotion may seem to be, however, they are figured here as being positive only in a negative sort of way, inasmuch as they are invoked to negate the intellect and its pretensions, and not in order to suggest any other, more sound alternative. This is very much in the nature of the episode as a whole, of course: Payne's role is that of a dashing demolition-artist, whereas Lenz for instance, in the very different context of the Kaufmann passage, will likewise adduce feeling and emotion, but as the centrepiece of an elaborately constructive and positive philosophy of art and existence.

Nevertheless, there are in fact some distinctly positive indications in the Payne episode. One is particularly obvious: Payne does not content himself with dismissing dogmatic moralism out of hand, but also offers an alternative ethic that is grounded not in the abstract and the absolute, but in the natural, organic self of each individual:

> Was wollt ihr denn mit eurer Moral? Ich weiß nicht ob es an und für sich was Böses oder was Gutes giebt, und habe deßwegen doch nicht nöthig meine Handlungsweise zu ändern. Ich handle meiner Natur gemäß, was ihr angemessen, ist für mich gut und ich thue es und was ihr zuwider, ist für mich bös und ich thue es nicht und vertheidige mich dagegen, wenn es mir in den Weg kommt. Sie können, wie man so sagt, tugendhaft bleiben und sich gegen das sogenannte Laster wehren, ohne deßwegen [I]hre[7] Gegner verachten zu müssen
>
> What do you people want with your morality? I don't know whether good and evil exist in themselves, but that doesn't mean I have to change the way I behave. I act according to my nature; whatever is consistent with my nature is for me good, and I do it; whatever is contrary to my nature is for me evil, and I do not do it, and I defend myself against it if it crosses my path. You can remain virtuous, as they say, and ward off so-called vice, without for that reason feeling obliged to despise your opponents

The argument is familiar: it strongly echoes both Danton's epicurean refutation of Virtue and Vice in his confrontation with Robespierre (27), and the social ideals voiced in the opening scene of the play through Hérault (11). And in every case, the central factor is the primacy of the natural authentic self, that realm of essential being that is at once remote from, and inaccessible to, the 'secondary business' of thought and all its artificial systems: 'Ich handle meiner Natur gemäß' (Payne); 'Jeder handelt seiner Natur gemäß' (Danton); 'Jeder muß sich geltend machen und seine Natur durchsetzen können' (Hérault).

---

[7] Both Lehmann and Mayer print 'ihre' (as did the original 1835 edition); but whatever Büchner actually wrote, he must have meant the second person, not the third, which would make no sense here. Note that in speech number 375 Mayer prints 'sie' where Büchner can only have meant 'Sie' (Lehmann, 47, line 32, prints 'Sie'); and in speech 380 Mayer prints '[S]ie', specifically correcting a slip on Büchner's part (Lehmann 48, line 15: 'Sie'). In the *Woyzeck* manuscripts Büchner repeatedly writes 'sie' instead of 'Sie' (cf. Lehmann 343, line 27, and *passim*).

There is one other startlingly positive element in the Payne episode that merits attention, even though it is half hidden in a fleeting subordinate clause. The context is the attack on anthropomorphism, in the midst of which occur the words 'wenn sich unser Geist in das Wesen einer harmonisch in sich ruhenden, ewigen Seeligkeit versenkt'. If no instant translation is offered here (and one was carefully avoided when the passage as a whole was cited earlier), it is because the interpretative problems posed by Büchner's œuvre are teasingly epitomized in these words, the free-floating nature of which becomes particularly clear to anyone who tries to pin down their precise meaning for the purposes of translation. What is certain is that they are exceptionally portentous: they envision a kind of mystical experience almost beyond the realm of the sayable: the absorption of the self in a wondrous 'allness'. But how are we supposed to understand this? We hear tell of our 'Geist' immerging itself in something—but what is meant by 'Geist' (a word that has already teased us before)? It is clearly not 'mind' in the sense of 'intellect', 'Verstand'—a faculty repeatedly disparaged in this episode; nor is it that 'mind' that conjures up our false thought-pictures of God. It is used entirely positively, and must surely mean mind-as-spirit, mind-as-intuition, mind as our faculty of direct, unmediated insight and knowledge. This mind-spirit, so we read, actively submerges or 'loses' itself in 'das Wesen einer . . . ewigen Seeligkeit'— but what on earth does that mean? 'Wesen' is relatively straightforward, for it can be rendered easily, if no less vaguely, as 'essence', 'being', 'totality'. But what of 'ewigen Seeligkeit', especially as it is also defined as 'harmonisch in sich ruhend'?[8] One thing

---

[8] Büchner has Lenz speak in startlingly similar terms at a crucial point in the story (between Lenz's sermon and ensuing mystic-erotic union with the divine, and the Kaufmann passage): 'Er sprach sich selbst weiter aus, wie in Allem eine unaussprechliche Harmonie, ein Ton, eine Seeligkeit sey' (86; *He expressed more of his own beliefs, saying how in all things there was an inexpressible harmony, a resonance, a blessedness*; the words 'Geist', 'Wesen' and 'Ruhe' also all recur within this context). Clear echoes can be heard again in Lenz's evocation of his beloved Friederike: 'jeder Tritt war eine Musik, es war so eine Glückseligkeit in ihr, und das strömte in mich über, ich war immer ruhig, wenn ich sie ansah' (92; *every step was music, there was such bliss in her, and it flowed over into me. I was always at peace whenever I looked at her*). Cf. also Leonce's climactic experience—thanks to Lena—of utmost Being welling up and overflowing throughout the entire universe, a stream of bliss so absolute that even a single drop is sufficient to turn him into a sacred vessel: 'dieser eine Tropfen Seligkeit macht mich zu einem köstlichen Gefäß. Hinab heiliger Becher!' (125; cf. below, pp. 259f.)

is clear: we are dealing here with a *metaphysical* order of things. What our 'Geist' intuitively discerns and gladly surrenders itself to is a realm of timeless and perfect bliss, wholly in harmony with itself, wholly at peace with itself; a realm that perfectly 'is' and has no need of 'doing', and therefore should not be anthropomorphized into 'God', all bustle and busy fingers. One other problem remains: even the conjunction that introduces the whole proposition is not clear in its meaning. 'Wenn' is a word that covers a wide spectrum, normally defined by context and time-reference: that which has definitely already happened and continues to happen ('whenever ...'); that which definitely will, probably will, or conceivably might happen ('when ...'); that which is purely conditional or hypothetical ('if ...'). In this case, however, the meaning is not fixed by either context or time-reference. We can only suppose, without absolute certainty, that the union of Self and All evoked by Payne is conceived as neither habitual nor hypothetical, but as a very real possibility (it is clear from Büchner's manuscript that he did not envisage such willed absorption as being easy to achieve: what he originally wrote was not 'sich ... versenkt', but 'sich ... zu versenken *strebt*', TMM 51; strives *to submerge itself*).

The image here of a quasi-divine essence both liquid and harmonious into which the individual *Geist* can melt, clearly parallels the later evocation, through Philippeau, of a 'Strom von Harmonien' (*stream of harmonies*); and it anticipates the Trial Lecture with its predication of a 'necessary harmony' and its metaphor of a 'hidden stream' ('Strom in der Tiefe') that man is steadily uncovering. But this faces us with a severe problem: how are we to credit such fleeting images and evocations when we are assaulted in scene after scene by quite contrary visions? The final jail scene is the crux: Philippeau's declaration of a 'stream of harmonies' is drowned in the cascade of negativism that it provokes. Which is the truth: the 'stream of harmonies' that Philippeau asserts—or the 'vile sounds' ('die häßlichen Töne') that Danton hears (71)? Are divine sadism, chaos and nothingness truly our ultimate reality? From its very first words the play relentlessly exposes our masks and mantles and postures in all their falseness, but then what is the truth that lies behind them? Should we believe Camille when he cries out that if we ever did strip away our masks, we should find that we were immutably mutton-headed clones of each other (70–1)? Or should we rather believe him when he speaks in quite contrary vein of an ardent creative process constantly regenerating itself within and around each least individual (37)? I have argued before that the despair trumpeted throughout the play is precisely that: 'despair' in its proper sense of 'hope confounded'. In the *public* realm there is scope for nothing else: the grand revolution has turned into a berserk and futile killing-machine that does nothing even to relieve the hunger of the masses, and makes the gap between the real and the ideal seem ever more profound and unbridgeable. But although the public realm conspicuously constitutes the play's deathly continuum in terms of both action and discourse, it is by no means its only dimension: scattered throughout the play are luminous fragments of a deeply *private* world. And it is here that hope finds a last resort.

9
Vénus Noire

THE problem with the private realm in *Dantons Tod* is that it is even more steeped in paradox than the rest of the play. As we shall see in the case of Camille and Lucile, and of Danton and his two women, relationships between men and women are the solitary haven in a rotten polity. But they also help to constitute that rottenness, as we see in the very first scene of the play. Sex is the bane; and Büchner is more haunted and more obsessed by sexuality than any other writer of his period, far more even than Baudelaire with his *Vénus noire* and *Vénus blanche*, than Kleist with his Käthchen and his Penthesilea, Stifter with his Johanna and Clarissa, Hoffmann with his Julia and Hedwiga.

One indication of Büchner's obsession is the frequency with which he uses sexual imagery gratuitously, as a metaphor for the non-sexual. A particularly baroque example of this occurs in the Dillon/Laflotte scene, when Laflotte is given to speak of the imminent 'rebirth' of his doomed life in the following terms:

Man könnte das Leben ordentlich wieder lieb haben, wie sein Kind, wenn man sich's selbst gegeben. Das kommt gerade nicht oft vor, daß man so mit dem Zufall Blutschande treiben und sein eigner Vater werden kann. Vater und Kind zugleich. Ein behaglicher Oedipus! (55)

You could really grow to love your life again, like your own child, if you've created it for yourself. It doesn't happen very often that you can commit incest with coincidence and become your own father. Father and child all in one. Oedipus the cosy way!

Often it is death that is evoked in the language of sex, as when Danton in the 'Freies Feld' scene 'flirts' with Death and 'makes eyes' at him from afar: 'Ich kokettire mit dem Tod, es ist ganz angenehm so aus der Entfernung mit dem Lorgnon mit ihm zu liebäugeln.' (39). In one of the play's most surreal images, Danton wishes at one point that he could expire effortlessly like a sound in music that just dies away—'kissing itself to death with its own lips' ('wie ein Ton sich selbst aushaucht, sich mit den eignen Lippen todtküßt', 67). Our old friend the 'hübsche Dame' crops up again in the first prison scene—but here she is Lady Decay ('die hübsche Dame Verwesung'), whose cheeks the Dantonists will soon be fondling (50). Later, Danton fancies that he can already smell the stench of his own corpse, so he holds his nose and imagines his body to be a woman sweating and steaming from the dance, an old familiar to whom he can mouth sweet nothings: 'Es ist mir, als röch' ich schon. Mein lieber Leib, ich will mir die Nase zuhalten und mir einbilden du seyst ein Frauenzimmer, was vom Tanzen schwitzt und stinkt und dir Artigkeiten sagen. Wir haben uns sonst schon mehr miteinander die Zeit vertrieben.' (66). At another point, death is figured in an astonishing flurry of sexual imagery as a foul and importunate gigolo, a violent rapist, a frigid old woman:

LACROIX. . . . Nicht wahr, wenn der Tod einem so unverschämt nahe kommt und so aus dem Hals stinkt und immer zudringlicher wird?

CAMILLE. Wenn er einen noch nothzüchtigte und seinen Raub unter Ringen und Kampf aus den heißen Gliedern riß! aber so in allen Formalitäten, wie bey der Hochzeit mit einem alten Weibe, wie die Pakten aufgesetzt, wie die Zeugen gerufen, wie das Amen gesagt und wie dann die Bettdecke gehoben wird und es langsam hereinkriecht mit seinen kalten Gliedern. (60)

LACROIX. . . . It's quite something, eh, when Death comes leering up to us like this with his stinking breath and thrusts himself on us more and more rudely.

CAMILLE. If at least he would rape us and tear his prey from our limbs in the heat of a frenzied struggle! But to die like this with all these formalities, as though we were marrying some ancient crone: the contract's drawn up, the witnesses summoned, the ceremony gone through—then there's a tug at the bedcovers and in she crawls, slowly seizing us in her cold embrace.

The area that Büchner most radically sexualizes is that of politics. Sometimes this is just a question of hyperbolic metaphor. The man from Lyon castigates his city as 'dieße Hure der Könige' (16; *this whore of kings*). Saint-Just wants Danton liquidated at any price, since he will otherwise 'grab the Revolution by her clothes' like a predatory lover, and looks capable of 'raping freedom' ('bleibt Danton am Leben, so wird er [die Revolution] am Gewand fassen und er hat etwas in seiner Gestalt, als ob er die Freiheit nothzüchtigen könnte', 57). A few lines later, the same personification recurs in modified form in the fulsome rhetoric of Collot, together with a sexual allusion to Greek legend:

Vénus Noire

Die Freiheit wird die Schwächlinge, welche ihren mächtigen Schooß befruchten wollten, in ihren Umarmungen ersticken, die Majestät des Volks wird ihnen wie Jupiter der Semele unter Donner und Blitz erscheinen und sie in Asche verwandeln. (58–9)

Freedom with her tight embrace will stifle these weaklings who sought to plant their seed in her mighty womb; the majesty of the people will appear unto them amidst thunder and lightning like Jupiter unto Semele and turn them into ashes.

A similar combination of sexuality ancient and modern is offered in the final prison scene:

LACROIX. Wir hätten die Freiheit zur Hure gemacht!
DANTON. Was wäre es auch! Die Freiheit und eine Hure sind die kosmopolitischsten Dinge unter der Sonne. Sie wird sich jezt anständig im Ehebett des Advokaten von Arras prostituiren. Aber ich denke sie wird die Clytemnaestra gegen ihn spielen . . . (70)

LACROIX. We're supposed to have turned freedom into a whore!
DANTON. What difference would it make? Whores and freedom—they're the most cosmopolitan things under the sun. Freedom will now prostitute herself with due decorum in the marital bed of the lawyer from Arras. But I fancy she'll prove to be his Clytemnestra . . .

Sexuality, however, is by no means simply a graphic metaphor: it is a political issue in its own right, indeed in a sense it is *the* political issue, the pivot on which the entire power struggle turns throughout the play. This is soon thrust in our faces in the street scene with Simon (12 ff.). The curtain rises on a violent and apparently quite private family fracas, occasioned by the fact that Sanna the daughter is busily engaged off-stage in sex for money. It seems at first a matter of private morality and family honour, with Prompter Simon in his alcoholic and theatrical rage belabouring his conniving wife as the very embodiment of sin and syphilis ('du . . . Sündenapfel', 'du . . . Sublimatpille'), as a 'bed of whores' and a 'bundle of depravity' ('Du Hurenbett, in jeder Runzel deines Leibes nistet Unzucht.') After the moral posturing of Simon, the common-sense economics and ethics of his wife—and in this perspective, Sanna is no scandalous sex-fiend but a model daughter doing an honest day's work and thereby keeping her parents in food and clothing ('sie ist ein braves Mädchen und ernährt ihre Eltern', etc.). But then a critically different perspective is abruptly established, and all of a sudden we are witnessing the first eruption of that volcanic process that ultimately sweeps the Dantonists to their doom. To the 'First Citizen'—at once a representative man-in-the-street and an effective agitator—the girl is neither depraved sex-fiend nor decent breadwinner, but miserable victim: she is an *'arme* Hure' who only sells her body because she is stricken with hunger and poverty, and because there are those with the cash to pay for it—a grossly exploitative group that does no work, and whose disgusting wealth has been stolen from the masses that *do* work, who in consequence remain penniless, and economically enslaved to the very parasites that have robbed them. Sex is thus the trigger for an essentially political tirade, which in turn is the trigger for political action: there is an ever more frenzied cry for corpses, whereupon Robespierre arrives and deftly harnesses the angry masses to his own cause with the promise of carnage, and a magnificent demagogic sleight of hand that turns 'you' into an invincible 'us' united against a common enemy: 'Kommt mit zu den Jacobinern. Eure Brüder werden euch ihre Arme öffnen, wir werden ein Blutgericht über unsere Feinde halten.' (16; *Come along to the Jacobins. Your brothers will welcome you with open arms, we shall wreak bloody justice upon our enemies.*)

At this level, sexuality is political in a purely functional sense: it serves as a convenient catalyst for mobilizing and then channelling the insatiable anger of the masses. We see the same process at work after the final court scene, when the harangue that successfully realigns the wavering crowd behind Robespierre includes, amidst a whole catalogue of excesses, the charge that Danton when drunk beds their wives and their daughters ('Danton . . . schläft bey euren Weibern und Töchtern, wenn er betrunken ist', 64); and the underlying popular perception that this seeks to exploit is well demonstrated in the guillotine scene when one of the women shouts to Danton that from now on he can indulge his debauchery with the worms ('He Danton, du kannst jezt mit den Würmern Unzucht treiben', 73). But of course sexuality is far more than just an expedient tactical weapon: Büchner places it with extraordinary vehemence at the very centre of the ideological conflict.

The Dantonist position is set out in the opening scene in the course of their fundamental rejection of Jacobin ideology and its attempts to reconstruct humanity from scratch and then regulate it through the imposition of a severe puritanical straitjacket that purports to have objective validity but in truth reflects the whims of those that impose it. The 'straitjacket' metaphor is taken up again in modified

Vénus Noire

form in respect of sexuality: France is a lady most lovable in her easy virtue, and the Dantonists mean to stop those who would force her into the garb of a nun: 'Wir werden den Leuten, welche über die nackten Schultern der allerliebsten Sünderin Frankreich den Nonnenschleier werfen wollen, auf die Finger schlagen.' (11). Originally this was all Büchner wrote, but he enlarged most strikingly on this theme when he redrafted the whole passage, adding no fewer than three one-sentence paragraphs:[1]

Wir wollen nackte Götter, Bachantinnen, olympische Spiele und von melodischen Lippen: ach, die gliederlösende, böse Liebe!
Wir wollen den Römern nicht verwehren sich in die Ecke zu setzen und Rüben zu kochen aber sie sollen uns keine Gladiatorspiele mehr geben wollen.
Der göttliche Epikur und die Venus mit dem schönen Hintern müssen statt der Heiligen Marat und Chalier die Thürsteher der Republik werden.
We want naked gods, Bacchantes, Olympian games and oh! from melodious lips the sounds of wicked, limb-melting love!
We don't want to stop the Romans squatting in their corner and boiling their turnips, but we want no more of their gory gladiators.
Divine Epicurus and sweet-arsed Venus must replace Saints Marat and Chalier as guardians of the Republic.

On the face of it this might seem like a philanderers' charter, but what is involved here is not moral licentiousness but poetic licence: Camille's programme is deliberately defined in extreme hyperbolic contrast to the strictures and restrictions of the killjoy Jacobins.[2] The contrasts are threefold: (i) 'Nakedness'/'clothes': Clothes are used throughout the sequence as the principal metaphor for compulsion: the Robespierreans are out to stuff humanity into uniform

---

[1] For a description of Büchner's changes, and reproductions of some of the manuscript sheets involved, see TMM 15 ff.

[2] Mayer has pointed out that Büchner's additions to his manuscript were probably inspired by his reading of Heine's *Zur Geschichte der Religion und Philosophie in Deutschland*, which had only recently appeared (in mid-Jan. 1835). One of the two Heine passages quoted by Mayer is particularly relevant for us in its contrasting of opposites: 'Wir wollen keine Sansküloten seyn, keine frugale Bürger, keine wohlfeile Präsidenten: wir stiften eine Demokrazie gleichherrlicher, gleichheiliger, gleichbeseligter Götter. Ihr verlangt einfache Trachten, enthaltsame Sitten und ungewürzte Genüsse; wir hingegen verlangen Nektar und Ambrosia, Purpurmäntel, kostbare Wohlgerüche, Wollust und Pracht, lachenden Nymphentanz, Musik und Komödien—Seyd deßhalb nicht ungehalten, Ihr tugendhaften Republikaner! Auf Eure censorische Vorwürfe entgegnen wir Euch, was schon ein Narr des Shakespear sagte: meinst du, weil du tugendhaft bist, solle es auf dieser Erde keine angenehmen Torten und keinen süßen Sekt mehr geben?' (TMM 73, n. 3).

hats, coats, and convent veils ('Fallhütchen', 'Röcklein', 'Nonnenschleier'). One counter to this is the vision of the State as a 'diaphanous raiment' ('durchsichtiges Gewand') that in no way constricts the 'body of the people' ('den Leib des Volkes'); but a more emphatic counter is the image of nakedness. This is quite explicit in the 'naked shoulders' of France and the 'naked gods'; it is plainly implied in the image of 'sweet-arsed Venus'; and it is equally if less obviously implicit in the references to the Bacchantes and the Olympian Games, for the Bacchantes, or priestesses of Bacchus, appeared near-naked in the Roman Bacchanalia, while both judges and competitors in the Games were traditionally naked. (ii) 'Relaxed rituals'/'aggressive rituals': The allusions to Bacchanalia, Olympian Games, the communal celebration of sensual love are all in sharp contra-distinction to the forbidding and deadly gladiatorial combat preferred by the puritanical, prosaic, turnip-loving 'Romans' on the other side ('Romans' in the same spirit presumably as those who in ancient Rome put a stop to the Bacchanalian festivals). The contrast was even more distinct in the manuscript, which after 'olympische Spiele' originally also conjured up 'Rosen in den Locken, funkelnden Wein, wallende Busen'—details, however, that were subsequently deleted (TMM 15; *rose-spangled hair, sparkling wine, heaving bosoms*). (iii) 'Easy tolerance'/'draconian severity': Büchner's hyperbolic technique is very clear in this counterposing of opposites: the dead radicals Marat and Chalier are the patron saints of the Jacobin 'Church Militant' (a bust of Chalier was even enshrined on the altar of a secularized church in Paris);[3] but it is not their spirit that should prevail—the repressive spirit of endless executions—but that of Epicurus and Venus, the spirit of live-and-let-live, of love and beauty freely enjoyed.

Needless to say, the same basic contrast exists for the Jacobins, but is viewed from a diametrically different vantage point. The antithesis that presents itself to them is abstract, absolute, and ominous: it is the antinomy of Virtue and Vice. We have already seen how Robespierre in his decisive speech at the Jacobin Club makes moralism the driving force of the Revolution, and terror its instrument: 'Die Waffe der Republik ist der Schrecken, die Kraft der Republik ist die Tugend.' (18). Robespierre's trumpeting of virtue is

---

[3] See also 17, where Marat and Chalier are again apostrophized as Saints ('dieße Heiligen').

of course historical, and practically everything that he says on the subject is borrowed directly from Büchner's sources. What is *not* borrowed from the sources, however, is Robespierre's particularly heavy emphasis on Vice, his insistent representation of it as a corrupting poison, an insidious threat, a crime at once moral and political:

Aber nicht zufrieden den Arm des Volks zu entwaffnen, sucht man noch die heiligsten Quellen seiner Kraft durch das Laster zu vergiften. Dieß ist der feinste, gefährlichste und abscheulichste Angriff auf die Freiheit. Das Laster ist das Cainszeichen des Aristocratismus. In einer Republik ist es nicht nur ein moralisches sondern auch ein politisches Verbrechen; der Lasterhafte ist der politische Feind der Freiheit (19)

But not content with depriving the people of their weapons, they even seek through vice to poison the most sacred wellsprings of the people's energy. This is the subtlest, most dangerous, most heinous of all assaults on freedom. Vice is the mark of Cain stamped upon the brow of aristocrats and their imitators. In a republic it is not only a moral crime but also a political one; every devotee of vice is politically an enemy of freedom

It is true that this line of argument is to some extent tactical: Robespierre is capitalizing effectively on the popular fury demonstrated in the Simon scene, and he proceeds at once to point the finger at the Dantonists as men of disgusting luxury, debauchery, and vice ('Luxus', 'Unzucht', 'Laster', 19), men who are pleading for moderation only in order to mask their own corruptness (19–20). At a deeper level, however, Robespierre is engaged upon a fanatically puritan crusade. We have already seen how Danton lays bare his suspect motives as a self-appointed 'Policeysoldat des Himmels', a Mr Clean who believes that his own spotless garb gives him the right to turn the guillotine into a washtub for others' soiled linen, and to use their severed heads as stain-removers for their dirty clothes (27)—a 'cleansing' process of monstrous foulness that ensures that all involved remain continually 'schmutzig und blutig ... wie neugeborne Kinder' (11; *dirty and bloody like newborn children*), with even Robespierre himself incapable of shielding his conscience from the relentless and accusing tide of blood (28).

Again and again in the play Büchner reinforces the sense that the real underlying issue is not political or social, but sexual. Danton's 'clean coat' analogy is paralleled almost verbatim in Camille's comment that Robespierre's clean frock-coat is France's winding sheet

('Sollte man glauben, daß der saubere Frack des Messias das Leichenhemd Frankreichs ist...?', 30). At this most subterranean level, Danton's real crime is not his 'treason against the state', nor his 'robbing of the people', nor even his potential might as a political rival—it is his sexual potency. In the graphic words given to Lacroix at the close of the prostitute scene: 'Gute Nacht Danton, die Schenkel der Demoiselle guillotiniren dich, der mons Veneris wird dein tarpejischer Fels.' (26; *Good night, Danton; the thighs of this girl are your guillotine, her mons veneris your Tarpeian Rock*; the Tarpeian Rock was a cliff from which traitors were flung to their death in ancient Rome). The same dynamic is revealed by Robespierre himself in the very first words of his monologue following the confrontation with Danton: 'Er will die Rosse der Revolution am Bordel halten machen, wie ein Kutscher seine dressirten Gäule; sie werden Kraft genug haben, ihn zum Revolutionsplatz zu schleifen.' (28; *He wants to make the mighty horses of the Revolution stop at the brothel, like a coachman reining his docile hacks; they'll have strength enough to drag him to the Place de la Révolution.*) The clearest, most programmatic indication of all is spelt out through Barrère in an exchange that also points forward to Robespierre's own destruction: by a neat irony, his obsessive crusade against sexual aberration is itself a fatal aberration in political terms:

BARRÈRE. ... Sie werden noch aus der Guillotine ein Specificum gegen die Lustseuche machen. Sie kämpfen nicht mit den Moderirten, sie kämpfen mit dem Laster.
BILLAUD. Bis jezt geht unser Weg zusammen.
BARRÈRE. Robespierre will aus der Revolution einen Hörsaal für Moral machen und die Guillotine als Katheder brauchen.
BILLAUD. Oder als Betschemel.
COLLOT. Auf dem er aber alsdann nicht stehen, sondern liegen soll. (59)

BARRÈRE. ... They'll end up turning the guillotine into a panacea for the pox. They're not fighting the moderates, they're fighting vice.
BILLAUD. We've shared the same goals—so far.
BARRÈRE. Robespierre wants to turn the Revolution into a school for morality, with the guillotine as his lectern.
BILLAUD. Or his prayer-stool.
COLLOT. On which he shall duly place his head, not his knees.

Interpreters of Büchner have generally failed to realize that the Jacobins are not concerned in essence with social, political, and economic revolution at all, but with *moral* renewal on an absolute scale. They are out to eradicate, not social inequality, political oppression, economic privation, but the abstract canker of Evil and Wickedness. Robespierre is a man with a mission—of messianic, metaphysical proportions. It is precisely in these terms that he is first introduced to us, when the audience on and off the stage are bidden to 'Hear the Messiah who is sent to choose and to judge; he shall smite the wicked with the rigour of the sword' ('Hört den Messias, der gesandt ist zu wählen und zu richten; er wird die Bösen mit der Schärfe des Schwertes schlagen', 15). Camille speaks of 'Dießer Blutmessias Robespierre' (30; *This bloody Messiah Robespierre*); and Robespierre not only specifically accepts this appellation, but goes on to describe himself as a Christ-like 'redeemer'—one who redeems his victims not through his own blood, but through theirs (30). This sense of a metaphysical and absolute mission is reinforced in Saint-Just's great speech at the close of Act II, when he compares their task with that of Moses:

Moses führte sein Volk durch das rothe Meer und in die Wüste bis die alte verdorbne Generation sich aufgerieben hatte, eh' er den neuen Staat gründete. Gesetzgeber! Wir haben weder das rothe Meer noch die Wüste aber wir haben den Krieg und die Guillotine. (46)

Before founding his new state, Moses led his people through the Red Sea and into the wilderness until the old, corrupt generation was utterly consumed. Lawgivers! We have neither the Red Sea nor the wilderness, but we have war and the guillotine.

Saint-Just's speech—Büchner's invention almost all the way through—is unambiguously clear: the Revolution for them is an event that is reshaping the *moral* order of the world in its entirety: 'ein Ereigniß, was die ganze Gestaltung der moralischen Natur . . . umändert' (45). Any amount of death and destruction is justified by such a noble end, indeed it is necessitated by it: the bloodbath of the Revolution is like the Flood—a purifying deluge that will cleanse mankind of all its sin and revive its pristine vigour: 'Die Menschheit wird aus dem Blutkessel wie die Erde aus den Wellen der Sündfluth mit urkräftigen Gliedern sich erheben, als wäre sie zum Erstenmale geschaffen.' (46; the word 'Sündflut' is an ancient folk-etymological corruption of the proper word for the Flood, *Sintflut*, reinterpreting it as a flood that is provoked by sin, *Sünde*, and duly purges it; see also 70 (Danton): 'Die Sündfluth der Revolution').

On this view, there are only two categories within mankind: those possessed of Virtue ('Tugend'), and those corrupted by Vice ('Laster'). The sole and sacred repository of Virtue is the People: 'Armes, *tugendhaftes* Volk!' (15) as Robespierre calls them almost within seconds of his first arrival on the stage; or again, at the end of the Jacobin Club speech: 'tugendhaftes Volk' (20). Anyone given to Vice is accordingly not of the people, but belongs instead amongst that leprous, cankered band known as 'aristocrats'. Once again, the decisive criterion for this differentiation is not in any sense material, but wholly abstract; to be an 'aristocrat' is not to belong to a socioeconomic class into which one was born, but to belong to those who have departed from Virtue. Robespierre speaks accordingly not of 'the aristocracy' but of 'aristocraticism' ('Aristocratismus'), a term that encompasses all who bear the stamp of Vice that is their vile badge, their 'mark of Cain': 'Das Laster ist das Cainszeichen des Aristocratismus'. It is in this sense that the Dantonists are 'these marquesses and counts of the Revolution' ('dieße Marquis und Grafen der Revolution', 19), for they 'fornicate with erstwhile marchionesses and baronesses' ('[treiben] mit ehemaligen Marquisinnen und Baronessen Unzucht'), and 'flaunt all the vices and all the luxury of the courtiers of old' ('[machen] mit allen Lastern und allem Luxus der ehemaligen Höflinge Parade').

The Jacobins' abstract antinomy of Virtue and Vice is lent a speciously palpable reality not only by being translated into a social them-and-us dichotomy, but also by being translated into a whole range of antithetical metaphors borrowed from the familiar physical world: pristine/rotten, pure/poisoned, clean/dirty, healthy/diseased. We have already encountered many instances of these metaphors: Saint-Just's reference to Moses and the systematic attrition of the old, 'rotten' element within his people (46); Robespierre's attack on those who are 'poisoning' the most sacred wellsprings of the people (19); the allusions to Robespierre as the manic purger of others' filth (especially 26 f.). The stress on 'health' and 'disease' is especially marked. To the man from Lyon, his city is not only the 'whore' of kings, but a 'leprous' whore that can only be cleansed by being drowned in the waters of the Rhone: 'dieße Hure der Könige [kann] ihren Aussatz nur in dem Wasser der Rhone abwaschen' (16). The same image is used by Robespierre when he inveighs against the Dantonists for inheriting the 'Aussatz' of the old, dead aristocracy along with their stolen clothes: 'Weg mit einer Gesellschaft, die der todten Aristocratie die Kleider ausgezogen und ihren Aussatz geerbt hat' (28); the people, on the other hand, are of course 'healthy' in their pristine vigour: 'die gesunde Volkskraft' (26; it is notable that the contrary epithet in this specific instance is a sexual one: just as 'whoring' was linked with 'vile disease' by the man from Lyon, so here the opposite of the healthy, vigorous *Volk* is a class that is degenerate through 'over-titillation': 'die gesunde Volkskraft muß sich an die Stelle dießer nach allen Richtungen *abgekitzelten* Klasse setzen'). In the same vein, Saint-Just describes Danton and his cronies as 'sick' and requiring the ultimate 'cure' of execution (58)—a remark that prompts Barrère's sardonic comment that the Robespierreans are trying to turn the guillotine into a 'panacea for the pox' ('ein Specificum gegen die Lustseuche'), and the Revolution into a 'school for morality' ('einen Hörsaal für Moral').

At the surface level of the play, all these issues are clear-cut, the battle-lines clearly drawn: 'Greeks' versus 'Romans', Cavaliers versus Roundheads, tolerant libertarians versus fanatical moralists, Danton and the Dantonists versus Robespierre and the Robespierreans. And at this level, too, there can be no doubt that it is Robespierrean moralism that is consistently derided, condemned, and worsted: deceitful in its origins and futile in its workings, by the end of the play it faces certain extinction. The battle may be won, but the war is as good as lost: Robespierre's excessive 'virtue' condemns him to the scaffold as surely as does Danton's excessive 'vice'. At a deeper level, however, things are far more complex. At this level, the apparently irreconcilable opposites ranged against each other on the surface melt into a single position having a quite different antithesis—in the shape of a dark moralism much grimmer even than Robespierre's, and also much more disturbing, in that it involves a vision of the world as almost irredeemably corrupt.

We have noted before that although the strategies of the Moderates and the Jacobins are diametrically opposed, their aspirations and assumptions are essentially identical; not for nothing were they originally a single political grouping. The decisive assumption that they share becomes apparent when we remember that the ideals of both sides depend equally on the postulate that there is a distinct entity, the *Volk*, possessed of a 'body' that is sovereignly whole, healthy, and full of vigour: there is no essential difference between the 'gesunde Volkskraft' predicated by Robespierre (26), and the pulsing, vibrant 'Leib des Volkes' that is taken for granted by

Camille (11). For both sides there are relatively minor impediments preventing the healthy body of the *Volk* from coming fully into its own: for the Dantonists, it is simply a question of removing the restrictive and alien straitjacket imposed by the Jacobins; to the Jacobins, it is simply a question of excising the poisonous and alien canker represented by the Dantonists—and as Robespierre assures the National Convention: 'Die Zahl der Schurken ist nicht groß. Wir haben nur wenige Köpfe zu treffen und das Vaterland ist gerettet.' (45; *The number of villains is not that great. We have only to strike at very few heads and our nation is saved.*) But when, in due course, these 'minor impediments' are indeed removed, it makes not a jot of difference: mankind does not arise from the bloodbath as though reborn; the *Volk* does not slough off its poverty, unfreedom, and inequality and stand revealed in healthful, pristine vigour. It would be bad enough if this failure of regeneration were due to extrinsic impediments more numerous and more massive than those envisaged by the idealists of both complexions. But Büchner's play points again and again to a far bleaker possibility: that the problem lies not in extrinsic impediments, but in intrinsic defects of the gravest kind; that the body of the people—or at least of *this* people in their specific situation—is cankered beyond hope of recovery. And in this grim vision it is sexuality that constitutes the principal canker.

How telling, and how ironic, that it should be precisely this that guarantees the failure and destruction of Robespierre. He believes that in the Dantonists he has rounded up the few remaining 'villains' that alone 'poison' the people—not realizing that his own closest associates are themselves even more vile and poisonous, and resolved furthermore to remain so. In the supremely cynical remark of Barrère's: 'Die Welt müßte auf dem Kopf stehen, wenn die sogenannten Spitzbuben von den sogenannten rechtlichen Leuten gehängt werden sollten.' (59; *The world would need to be topsy-turvy for the so-called villains to be strung up by the so-called righteous.*) When Saint-Just departs to settle the hash of the Dantonists once and for all, he is accompanied by a cloud of rhetoric from Collot invoking the 'lava of the Revolution', the mighty and impregnable 'damsel of Freedom', the invincible 'majesty of the people'—but in their very next breath Collot and his cronies are voicing their determination not to tolerate the threat that Robespierre's crusade poses to their own licentious lifestyle. The image of 'disease' comes sharply into focus here: Barrère has every reason to feel threatened

Vénus Noire 179

by Robespierre's attempts to turn the guillotine into a 'panacea for the pox'—for he is himself stricken with syphilis in one of its gravest and most advanced forms. Collot and Billaud may adopt a bantering tone in their references to Barrère's spinal cord and its progressive wasting, already so advanced that his mistress Demahy will soon be able to 'extract it from its sheath and dangle it down his back like a pigtail' (59), but in fact they are describing the clinical condition known as *tabes dorsalis*, a classic symptom of neurosyphilis, the severest form of the 'pox' in its tertiary stage. None of this will make him mend his ways, however: as soon as his doctor has afforded him some relief, he will be returning to Clichy and the secret brothel maintained by the bigwig degenerates of the Committee of Public Safety and the Committee of General Security: 'Wann kommst du wieder nach Clichy? / Wenn der Arzt nicht mehr zu mir kommt.'[4]

What of that supreme man of virtue, 'der tugendhafte Robespierre'? True, he is beyond all reproach: he has never slept with a woman ('du hast bey keinem Weibe geschlafen', 26), and is quite free of stain or blemish. But how genuine is this virtue? We have already seen how Danton dismisses it as a lie and a posture. But there is an even more devastating suggestion in the context of a remark by Barrère that Robespierre must not hear about his syphilis, when Büchner has Billaud retort that this paragon of virtue is nothing but an 'impotent Mohammed' ('Er ist ein impotenter Mahomet', 59).[5] On this view, Robespierre's messianic and 'mohammedan' zealotry stems not from moral fortitude and rectitude, but from sexual inadequacy; his rage is not that of Virtue against Vice, but the rage of impotence against virility.[6]

---

[4] Cf. Walter Hinderer, *Büchner-Kommentar zum dichterischen Werk* (Munich, 1977), 118, note headed '*Clichy* und *Demahy*'. (In his next note, Hinderer glosses Büchner's word 'Haarstern' as meaning 'comet' but this almost certainly misses the point. When Büchner writes that Barrère's spinal cord is being shrivelled by the burning rays of the 'Haarstern' that hangs over Clichy, the word is surely a *double entendre* that implies not only 'comet', but also the pubic hair of the Clichy prostitutes. This is presumably why Ludwig Büchner bowdlerized 'Haarstern' into 'Stern' in his 1850 edition. Cf. also the Jean Paul citation under 'Haarstern' in Grimm, *Deutsches Wörterbuch*: 'dasz er leicht, wie es oft dem Hesperus am himmel geschieht, für einen haar-, bart- und schwanzstern zu nehmen ist'.)

[5] The correct reading 'Mahomet' has been established only relatively recently, replacing the mistaken readings 'Masoret' and 'Masonet'. Cf. Hinderer, loc. cit.

[6] Elizabeth Boa makes a similar but more radical suggestion. Referring to Robespierre's 'agonised monologue where he bemoans the loss of his beloved Camille', Boa remarks: 'The erotic undertone suggests that his attack on the rampantly

Exactly the same argument is applied to that supposed repository of virtue, the *Volk*: its hatred of vice is born not of virtue, but of rampant jealousy; its hatred of those who enjoy the pleasures of the flesh is like the hatred of eunuchs for virile men: 'Es haßt die Genießenden, wie ein Eunuch die Männer.' (25). In the mordant analysis of Lacroix: the *Volk* refrains from indulgence in pleasure, booze, and brothels not out of virtue, but only because its senses are dulled by labour, its pockets empty, and its breath so foul that no whore would put up with them: 'das Volk ist tugendhaft . . . weil ihm die Arbeit die Genußorgane stumpf macht, es besäuft sich nicht, weil es kein Geld hat und es geht nicht ins Bordel, weil es nach Käs und Hering aus dem Hals stinkt und die Mädel davor einen Ekel haben' (25).

Whoring itself is an obsessive motif throughout the play, not only as a metaphor (Lyon as a diseased 'whore of kings', freedom as 'prostituting herself' in the bed of Robespierre, etc.), but also as an actual practice—though this too, of course, is very largely symbolic in intent. In the case of Simon's daughter Sanna, two different explanations for her behaviour are offered: in the eyes of her mother, she is simply doing an honest job of work as the family's breadwinner, using her genitals to earn the family's keep, just as in more normal times she might use her head or her hands; in the eyes of the rabble-rousing bystander, on the other hand, she has been forced into whoring and beggary by hunger and privation. We never learn the fictive truth of the matter, since Sanna herself never appears on the stage. But there might well be a quite different explanation, judging by the prostitutes that do appear. In Marion's case, for instance, sexuality is certainly not something that is forced upon her by any extrinsic economic constraint, either as a means of earning a decent living, or as a desperate resort to avoid starvation: it is her vocation and her delight, the truest expression of her natural being (21 f.). Marion is perhaps a special case, and one to which we shall return; but even when it comes to her more ordinary colleagues, Adelaide and Rosalie, Büchner does not present them as being in any sense victims of necessity: their promiscuity gratifies them sensually as well as economically—a congruence that is neatly

heterosexual Danton may be the vengeance of a repressed homosexual'. Elizabeth Boa, 'Whores and Hetairas: Sexual Politics in the Works of Büchner and Wedekind', in K. Mills and B. Keith-Smith (eds.), *Georg Büchner—Tradition and Innovation: Fourteen Essays* (Bristol, 1990), 163.

encapsulated in Rosalie's earthy *double entendre* in the 'Promenade' scene: 'Mach fort, da kommen Soldaten, wir haben seit gestern nichts Warmes in den Leib gekriegt.' (35; *Come on, there's soldiers, we've had nothing hot in our bodies since yesterday.*) Most revealing of all is the lusty song that Büchner has them sing: when asked by one of the soldiers whether their shafting makes her sore, Rosalie tells him, No, she longs for more, more, more:

SOLDAT ... [*Er singt*]. Christinlein, lieb Christinlein mein,
　　　　　　　　　　　Thut dir der Schaden weh, Schaden weh,
　　　　　　　　　　　Schaden weh, Schaden weh?
ROSALIE [*singt*].　　Ach nein, ihr Herrn Soldaten,
　　　　　　　　　　　Ich hätt' es gerne meh, gerne meh,
　　　　　　　　　　　Gerne meh, gerne meh! (35)

This gay abandon, however, is but a garish mask that signals terrible degeneracy. A measure of this degeneracy is given in the episode following Marion's monologue (23 f.). In the opening scene of the play, Camille projected his vision of an ideal future that would revive a Golden Age of free but pure and sinless sexuality presided over by 'naked gods', 'Bacchantes', the Callipygean Venus bare and beautiful. Adelaide and Rosalie are indeed new 'priestesses of the body' ('Priesterinnen mit dem Leib')—but only in terms of a grotesque and chilling parody. They and their fellow denizens of the Palais Royal are holy nuns, Sisters of the Revelation—but revelation through the flesh: 'Nönnlein von der Offenbarung durch das Fleisch'. Metaphorically they plead in their convent 'cells' for a 'blessing'; in reality they are in their brothels soliciting a fuck. Nuns were traditionally scourged to drive out their lust, but the 'punishment' administered by Legendre ('Legendre giebt einer die Disciplin') is the vile satisfying of that lust. And just as the chastity of nuns is parodied, so too is their charity. Adelaide and Rosalie are 'two Sisters of Mercy serving in the hospital of their own bodies' ('Zwei barmherzige Schwestern, jede dient in einem Spital d. h. in ihrem eignen Körper'): they are so heavily dosed with preparations of mercury to combat their own syphilis that they are veritable 'Quecksilbergruben' (*mines of mercury*), and anyone penetrating their body is guaranteed a 'Sublimattaufe', a literal dousing in mercury sublimate, a powerful poison traditionally administered as a palliative for venereal diseases. The insidious canker of sexual disease is repeatedly evoked in the play (not least in the case of

Barrère). Simon apostrophizes his wife as 'du . . . Sublimatpille' (12). In a surreal hyperbole, one of the tumbril-drivers remarks that a woman's vagina is such a well-beaten path that his mate could drive right up it with his horse and cart—but once out again he would have to go into quarantine (68; the image of a woman's body as an 'easily travelled road' is also applied to Adelaide: 'einer so gangbaren Straße' (23)—with the added spice that the word *gangbar* applies to 'goods that are easy to sell' as well as to 'roads that are easy to travel'). Most striking of all, perhaps, is Lacroix's updating of the Adonis legend, which defines the disjunction between the lost ideal and the poisonous reality with a kind of brutal relish:

Was ist der Unterschied zwischen dem antiken und einem modernen Adonis? . . . ein moderner Adonis wird nicht von einem Eber, sondern von Säuen zerrissen, er bekommt seine Wunde nicht am Schenkel sondern in den Leisten und aus seinem Blut sprießen nicht Rosen hervor sondern schießen Quecksilberblüthen an.

What is the difference between the Adonis of antiquity and a modern Adonis? . . . a modern Adonis gets torn to pieces not by a wild boar but by rutting sows, they go for his balls[7] instead of his leg, and it isn't roses that spring from his blood but crystals of mercury.

Prostitutes and prostitution are evoked in the play not for their own sake, but as a means of demonstrating in its most blatant form a pattern of unceasing and universal copulation. The picture conjured up by Lacroix on his entrance in the Marion scene is typical. With a chilling gust of laughter he sweeps away the mood of mystical communion between Marion and Danton, and substitutes

---

[7] The straightforward dictionary translation of Büchner's word 'Leisten' would be 'groins'. But whereas the word 'groin' in modern English has relatively little sexual connotation, 'Leiste' in Büchner's day routinely connoted the pudenda. Grimm, *Deutsches Wörterbuch*, defines the word 'Scham' in its sexual sense as '*pudenda*', coyly itemized in their turn as '*verenda, inguen, pubes*'. 'Leiste' is defined by Grimm as '*inguen*', but also as 'schamseite', 'schambug'. The Latin word *inguen* (from which English 'inguinal' is derived) is itself interesting. The *Oxford Latin Dictionary* describes it as meaning 'the part of the body around the sexual organs, groin', but mentions also that it was 'used to denote the sexual organs themselves'. English usage and attitudes in the 19th c. appear to have been curiously ambiguous. Under 'groin', the *OED* gives the purely descriptive, anatomical meaning, and also a figurative meaning (categorized as 'obsolete'): 'Regarded as the seat of lust'. But the entry under 'pubes' uses 'groin' in a quite different sense when it defines *pubes* as being Latin for 'the pubic hair; the groin, private parts'. The use of 'groin' as a euphemism for the genital area still survives in such phrases as 'a kick in the groin'.

instead the comic yet vile image of a lapdog and a mastiff struggling to mate in the street outside—with an avid audience of young girls, who will all too easily be corrupted by any spectacle of brute sexuality: 'man sollte vorsichtig seyn und [die Mädel] nicht einmal in der Sonne sitzen lassen, die Mücken treiben's ihnen sonst auf den Händen, das macht Gedanken' (23; *people should be careful and not even let [the girls] sit outside in the sun, or the gnats will start doing it on the backs of their hands—it'll give them ideas*). Whatever façades we may construct, sexuality is the raw reality. Waiting in the darkness with an arresting-party outside Danton's house, Simon asks the time, and receives a characteristically louche response: it is the time of night when the pendulum-penises run out of steam beneath the bed-covers: 'es ist die Zeit, wo die Perpendikel unter den Bettdecken ausschlagen' (42). In the 'Promenade' scene, Eugénie and her escort and mother wallow in verbiage about the sound of church-bells, trees in the twilight, sparkling stars, the sweet smell of flowers, their 'pure enjoyment of Nature' ('dießer reine Genuß der Natur!', 36)—but what really interests Eugénie and her companion is the salacious spectacle of the 'pretty lady' promenading with an elderly husband who little realizes that she is pregnant not with his child, but her barber's. And it is of course with the seductive speciousness of another 'pretty lady' that the whole play begins: the 'hübsche Dame' who gives her heart to her husband and her cunt to her lovers, with a guile so captivating that such women 'could make a man fall in love with lying', in Danton's bitterly sardonic phrase ('Ihr könntet einen noch in die Lüge verliebt machen'). It is Danton, too, that is given to voice an extraordinary instance of 'mask' imagery in the second half of the Marion scene: Adelaide has a 'figleaf' masking her entire body—but that figleaf is her face: 'Ihr Gesicht sieht aus wie ein Feigenblatt, das sie sich vor den ganzen Leib hält' (23); and the figleaf-face, already a bold image in itself, surreally transmutes into an entire tree that gives refreshing shade to travellers on the broad (but diseased and dangerous) highway of her body: 'So ein Feigenbaum an einer so gangbaren Straße giebt einen erquicklichen Schatten.'

Our own travels along Büchner's labyrinthine pathways have duly brought us back to the same grim vantage point that we have repeatedly encountered before, particularly in the preceding chapter: yet again we find ourselves confronted by a vision of existence as a gaudy carnival of masks, disguising a reality of infinite sameness and infinite vileness—within which brute sexuality is a principal ingredient. Sleeping, feeding, fucking: that is the dismal totality of our lives, with everything else but a variation on the one base theme: 'Schlafen, Verdaun, Kinder machen das treiben Alle, die übrigen Dinge sind nur Variationen aus verschiedenen Tonarten über das nemliche Thema' (71). Just as all of us bear on our shoulders the same 'Schaafskopf', no matter how much we may cultivate our expressions and cosmetics and accents and masks, so too we all of us carry between our legs the same repulsive animal apparatus, 'das häßliche Ding'; and instead of wrapping it in wreaths of heroical, romantical, or bacchanalian fancy, we might as well display it for what it is: a disgusting object fit only to be licked by dogs: 'Was sollen wir uns zerren? Ob wir uns nun Lorbeerblätter, Rosenkränze oder Weinlaub vor die Schaam binden, oder das häßliche Ding offen tragen und es uns von den Hunden lecken lassen?' (71).

In this kind of mood, Danton is given to see the world as vastly more corrupt than ever Robespierre does. For Robespierre, filth and lechery ('Unzucht') are an unfortunate but eradicable blot on the national escutcheon. For Danton in his bleakest moments, and no doubt for Büchner too, sexuality is part of the 'Fluch des Muß', the curse of compulsion that seems to lie on all humanity (41). Far from being a removable stain on the face of existence, *Unzucht* is its vile essence, rampant even in broad daylight, as we are shown and told in the 'Promenade' scene, when the very heat of the sun seems to bring it to rank florescence: 'es ist als brüte die Sonne Unzucht aus' (35). With one of his most acid bon mots, Danton tells Camille on the eve of their death that he means to depart from life as though leaving not a church but a brothel—for life is a whore that indulges in *Unzucht* with the whole of the world: 'Ich will mich aus dem Leben nicht wie aus dem Betstuhl, sondern wie aus dem Bett einer barmherzigen Schwester wegschleichen. Es ist eine Hure, es treibt mit der ganzen Welt Unzucht.' (67).

This vision of universal *Unzucht* is desperate indeed; but a desperate *vision* is indeed what it is, and it is matched as always by an opposite reading of the same reality, just as Danton's image of life as a cacophony of 'ugly sounds' is matched by Philippeau's contrary image of a 'stream of harmonies'. Viewed in a particular light—the garish light of the Dantonists' imminent extinction and the larger predicament of a failed revolution—the process of existence can readily be perceived as a pointless, unchanging round of brutish depravity. But this may be just as false a perspective in its own way as that of Camille's foolish consumers of contemporary culture, who are so mesmerized by its tinpot ideals that they have 'neither eyes nor ears' for the real world in all its richness, misjudging it instead to be repellent and pitiful.

So which picture of the world is true for Büchner: the pre-execution picture of gaudy appearances masking an infinitely sordid reality, or the alternative picture of sordid appearances concealing a reality of infinite creativity? In the first seconds of his first play, Büchner has Danton wonder what lies behind the outward visage of his wife. What answer does the play as a whole suggest? Does it bear out the nightmare vision of human truth as consisting in nothing but a sheep's skull and dog-licked genitals, or the contrary vision of an 'ardent, humming, radiant process of creation regenerating itself anew within and around [us] every second of the day' (37)? The easy solution might be to say that both readings of existence are equally explicable and valid within their particular contexts, or that they simply express opposite sides of a single coin. But it is crucial for us to recognize that the two alternatives are not truly on a par: the negative in Büchner arises only out of the positive; radical despair is born of radical hope; the perception of jangling dissonance stems only from the most passionate dedication to harmony. Whatever the objective truth of existence might be (supposing that there be such a thing), every word, mood, and image in Georg Büchner, even and especially the bleakest, are generated and conditioned by his essential faith, his intuition of a world order of beauty, harmony, and absolute individual value. It so happens that he and his characters live in exceptionally bad times—'Das ist eine böse Zeit'—making agonizing dissonance, ugliness, and corruption the order of the day, at any rate in the public domain of society and politics. But there remains the purely private realm. And it is this realm or, more specifically, the realm of individual man–woman relationships, conditioned but uncorrupted by the sordid character of the age, that affords the only haven that Büchner can envisage.

10
Vénus Blanche

OF the three main female characters in *Dantons Tod*, Marion is undoubtedly the most complex and the most challenging. Indeed Büchner never created a figure in any of his works more enigmatic or more haunting. Her mystery is compounded by the fact that she cannot be located in any kind of literary context that might help to define or explain her: she is unlike any female figure in the previous history of German literature—and remained without analogue for another half a century and more until Wedekind lit upon his predecessor's example. Even within Büchner's œuvre, there is no one to compare her with (except perhaps, in a limited sense, Marie). Extraordinary though it may seem, she is largely bereft of context even within *Dantons Tod* itself: she is wholly extraneous to the plot; she is never referred to in any way either before or after her single appearance; whilst Julie and Lucile, Adelaide and Rosalie, even Sanna the non-appearing daughter of Simon, are identified by name in the dialogue, 'Marion' is an identity that exists only technically, as a printed name in the dramatis personae and the play-text (in the manuscript there was originally no name at all—just an anonymous dash). During the course of her single appearance, she is in the limelight for only a quarter of the scene; and even when she does so briefly dominate the stage, she is unnervingly extrinsic to the play's continuum of action and dialogue as she delivers the longest individual speech (as distinct from public rhetoric) that Büchner ever wrote—a dramatically non-dramatic narration about people and events quite separate from any we encounter in the rest of the play. The narration itself—unprecedented in German theatre in both matter and manner—bursts upon us without warning, and from the beginning is provocatively elliptical, like a picture-story jigsaw-puzzle in which selected episodes are magicked together before our eyes, but without any of the interconnecting pieces that would serve to set them in a frame and context. The very syntax contributes to this sense of discreteness and disjunction: by the use of stark parataxis, Büchner offers us an accumulation of fragments, not the

Vénus Blanche

integrated and progressively evolving structures of hypotaxis that characterize the language in the rest of the play.

Thanks to the information carefully planted in Lacroix's closing speech in the previous scene, we are not totally at a loss when the lights go up to reveal Danton alone with an unknown, nameless woman: he is evidently with one of the 'tarts of the Palais-Royal' referred to by Lacroix moments earlier (21); and it can only be some kind of sexual manœuvre that is implied by the woman's opening rebuff 'Nein, laß mich!' Sexuality is indeed the nub: what so rapidly takes shape in the laconic narrative is a sexual history.

The story is constructed in the form of a double helix, with the narrative focus alternating rhythmically between the two distinct but interlocking spirals, which might be defined as 'external events' and 'inner processes'. The 'external' story-line, which appears the more dominant but is in fact ancillary to the story of Marion's inner development, begins with a tableau of bourgeois sexual hypocrisy:[1] Marion's 'clever' mother dinned it into her as a child that chastity was a fine virtue, systematically censored her reading matter, and sent her from the room whenever visitors arrived and broached 'certain subjects'—whilst clearly allowing, and presumably welcoming, the discussion of such dubious topics (like Hérault-Séchelles perhaps, whose moral posture vis-à-vis his daughter rested on his own intimate acquaintance with promiscuity, 10). Ironically, the mother's attempts to cocoon her child in ignorance are foiled by the all-holy Bible, where she encounters events that only stimulate her curiosity—and this first phase of the story then culminates with a wonderfully ambiguous metaphor that evokes the brooding not only of her mind, but also of her pubescent body: 'ich brütete über mir selbst'. The next external catalyst is rapidly stated, namely the onset of spring: 'Da kam der Frühling'—and this leads in to what is surely the most concentrated and most powerful depiction of sexual awakening in German literature of any period, as this young girl in her enforced ignorance and innocence watches nature's fertility explode all around her like an alien force, and then progressively envelop and invade her, divorce her from her own body, and finally fuse her into a new and potent unity of being:

---

[1] That Büchner had a bourgeois setting in mind is clear beyond doubt, not only from the text itself, but also from details originally included in the manuscript, in particular the sentence that initially began the narrative: 'Ich bin aus guter Familie' (TMM 31).

Da kam der Frühling, es gieng überall etwas um mich vor, woran ich keinen Theil hatte. Ich gerieth in eine eigne Atmosphäre, sie erstickte mich fast, ich betrachtete meine Glieder, es war mir manchmal, als wäre ich doppelt und verschmölze dann wieder in Eins.

Then spring came. Something happened all around me from which I was separate. A strange atmosphere enveloped me, I could scarcely breathe; I looked at my body, it seemed to me sometimes as though I were double, then melted again into one.

The narrative shifts back to external events: the arrival of the handsome young man with his jolly, madcap talk; the couple's association, facilitated by the unwitting mother; their progression from the proximity of chairs to the more delectable proximity of bed; their continuing and secret bed-life. But what really matters is the attendant development within Marion herself. Already at the stage of her awakening it seemed clear that Büchner was beginning to delineate not simply the typical product of a cloistered and hypocritical bourgeois upbringing (Eugénie would more readily fill that bill), but an exceptional being, possessed of a sexuality of extraordinary depth and intensity. It is just such depth and intensity that are conveyed now in a (male) vision of woman that surely belongs amongst the play's most original and provocative achievements, as Büchner has Marion sketch the relationship with the young man, and then add: 'Aber ich wurde wie ein Meer, was Alles verschlang und sich tiefer und tiefer wühlte. Es war für mich nur ein Gegensatz da, alle Männer verschmolzen in einen Leib.' (*But I became like an ocean that devoured everything and bored its way deeper and deeper. For me all men became indistinguishable, they melted into a single body.*) Büchner's sexual imagery is startling enough at other points in the play—Adelaide's body as a much-travelled highway, for instance, or the vagina vast enough for a horse and cart; but we are carried into new realms in this vision of woman as an infinite vortex of sexuality, an insatiable Charybdis to whom all men are but manifestations of undifferentiated maleness.

This image, at almost the exact centre of the narrative, constitutes its highest peak of intensity, and also its critical turning-point in terms of external events, which now rush on to a dramatic two-stage dissolution of the sexual bond: realizing at last what he has been sucked into, the handsome young man almost murders the girl with smothering kisses and throttling embraces, leaves her be with a laugh, and departs—only to reappear as a corpse carried pale and dripping past her twilight window. There is no parallel catastrophe within Marion herself: after the process of becoming ('ich wurde...'), there is the state of being ('ich bin...'—the first present tense to occur in the passage). And this 'is-ness' is almost beyond our powers of imagination: Marion is pure and extreme sensation, oneness that connects with allness through feeling alone, an entity that can melt and merge into the streaming radiance of the setting sun: 'Den Abend saß ich am Fenster, ich bin sehr reizbar und hänge mit Allem um mich nur durch eine Empfindung zusammen, ich versank in die Wellen der Abendröthe.' Only once has her being been briefly disrupted, namely by her spasm of sorrow at the death of her first lover: 'Ich mußte weinen. Das war der einzige Bruch in meinem Wesen.' Ordinary people in the ordinary world stumble from day to day in an endless mechanical round of labour punctuated by weekly stints of praying, with an annual flicker of sentimentality each birthday and an annual stirring of thought each New Year ('Die andern Leute haben Sonn- und Werktage [etc.]')—but Marion is utterly different: 'Ich begreife nichts davon. Ich kenne keinen Absatz, keine Veränderung. Ich bin immer nur Eins. Ein ununterbrochnes Sehnen und Fassen, eine Gluth, ein Strom.' (*All that for me is beyond comprehension. I know no pause, no change. I am ever the same. A ceaseless yearning and holding, an ardent fire, a swirling stream.*)

It might appear, towards the end of the monologue, as though Marion's ultimate purpose were to serve as a mouthpiece for a critique of conventional norms and values: the depiction of ordinary life as a robotic round is soon followed, in the closing lines, by a scornful rejection of prevailing morality. People point their finger at her, and her 'clever' mother died of grief—but that is stupid ('Das ist dumm'): people may throw the respectable mantle of morals or religion over their pursuits, but *all* pursuits, whether focused on sexual embraces or the adoration of Christ, are in reality chosen for the pleasure they afford, and the keenest show of piety is but the mark and product of the keenest enjoyment: 'Es läuft auf eins hinaus, an was man seine Freude hat, an Leibern, Christusbildern, Blumen oder Kinderspielsachen, es ist das nemliche Gefühl, wer am Meisten genießt, betet am Meisten.' The argument is familiar, and goes together with Marion's remark earlier in the speech that it was simply and irresistibly in her nature to become an all-devouring vortex of sexuality: 'Meine Natur war einmal so, wer kann da drüber hinaus?' A major element in the play's discourse is clearly being touched on here—and yet it is not the essential issue at this particular juncture. Danton's response is revealing. Büchner could so easily have had him expand on the nature–pleasure argument—after all, that is exactly what he does in the encounter with Robespierre in the following scene. The fascination of Marion lies, however, not in the ethical-intellectual utterances put in her mouth, but in her presence and radiance, her immanent being, at once physical and metaphysical, graspably finite yet ungraspably infinite: 'Warum kann ich deine Schönheit nicht ganz in mich fassen, sie nicht ganz umschließen?' (*Why can't I take your beauty wholly into myself, wholly enfold it within my arms?*) This line is another of the many covert stage directions scattered through the dialogue: it clearly shows the director and actors what kind of atmosphere and aura need to be generated in the sub-scene as a whole—especially as it echoes the startling prefatory words of Lacroix, which establish beyond doubt that Danton's journey into rank carnality is a quest for ultimate beauty, a search for Venus by means of the venereal:

LEGENDRE. Wo ist Danton?
LACROIX. Was weiß ich? Er sucht eben die mediceische Venus stückweise bey allen Grisetten des palais royal zusammen, er macht Mosaik, wie er sagt; der Himmel weiß bey welchem Glied er gerade ist. Es ist ein Jammer, daß die Natur die Schönheit, wie Medea ihren Bruder, zerstückelt und sie so in Fragmenten in die Körper gesenkt hat. (20–1)
LEGENDRE. Where's Danton?
LACROIX. How should I know? He's trying to recreate the Venus de' Medici piece by piece from all the tarts of the Palais-Royal; 'making a mosaic', he calls it. God knows what part of the anatomy he's working on right now. What a crying shame that nature has smashed beauty to bits, like Medea her brother, and buried it in fragments in different bodies.

This image of Beauty exploded into fragments, and needing to be pieced together again into a mosaic, a statue of perfection recovered from unperfectness, is certainly graphic, and it sets the stage very effectively for Marion's epiphany. Nevertheless, we find ourselves propelled into a dimension for which such imagery is no longer sufficient. In these deepest realms of Büchner's vision of being—for that is where he surely takes us here—Beauty is no concrete quantity to be fixed and frozen in stone, but a living, ineffable essence. We have seen this before. An example is the reference to Pygmalion's statue: alive, but sterile, in contrast to that creative life-force constantly glowing and throbbing within us (37). More pertinent still is Lenz's evocation of the two young girls and that 'infinite beauty that passes from form to form, eternally changed and revealed afresh'—a beauty that cannot always be seized and stuck in a museum, even though one might wish to be a Medusa that could turn such a sight as the girls into stone (87). What is imaged in Marion is Beauty in a similar sense. The statue metaphor may be apt for Adelaide and Rosalie, with whom Marion is bracketed in the dramatis personae; indeed Rosalie is explicitly described at one point as a 'restored torso' of which only separate fragments are genuinely antique. But if the others are an assemblage of all too graspable parts, Marion is an infinite, ungraspable totality, whole yet boundless, that Danton can neither absorb nor enfold. The image through which this is chiefly expressed is at the furthest possible remove from the fixity of stone. It is the image of *water* and *fluidity*. We find it again and again throughout the episode: this woman is like an 'ocean' ('ein Meer'), all-devouring and ever deeper; she is a 'swirling current' ('ein Strom'); she sees her own body and the bodies of men 'melt' before her eyes; she 'sinks into the waves of the setting sun', and it is water that her lover chooses for his death. Above all, perhaps, there are the extraordinary words of Danton's that crown the episode: 'Ich möchte ein Theil des Aethers seyn, um dich in meiner Fluth zu baden, um mich auf jeder Welle deines schönen Leibes zu brechen.' This image is surreal to the point of challenging our powers of imagination: Danton would like to dissolve into the air so that he could bathe Marion in the fluidum of his being and lap against her beautiful body—but she herself is already fluid, she is 'Meer' and 'Strom', and so it would be the 'waves' of her body that Danton in his ethereal state would envelop and lap against. A more visionary interfusion of being could scarcely be conceived.[2] But it *is* a vision, a yearning wish. And with a kind of masochistic glee Büchner at once overlays it with a contrary image of brute reality and failed connection in Lacroix's coldly comic depiction of the

---

[2] The limitations of Reinhold Grimm's approach to Büchner are nowhere more evident than when he speaks of Danton 'virtually stammering out these words, nearly breathless with lust and wantonness' (Grimm, *Love, Lust and Rebellion*, 187).

mastiff and the lapdog struggling to copulate in the gutter—an image that is rapidly followed by others to yield that seemingly flippant, but disturbing tableau of lust and disease already familiar to us.

In this savage juxtaposing of ethereal interfusion and the antics of alley-dogs, we see one of the clearest reflections in the play of Büchner's deep ambivalence concerning sexuality. Marion and her fellow 'Grisetten' are identical insofar as all three exist as flesh for men; and yet they represent quite different possibilities—the 'positive' and 'negative' of an extreme polarity. Adelaide and Rosalie are the unholy 'priestesses' of *Unzucht*, venereal ministrants to the 'modern Adonis', their bodies the highway for numberless herds and cartloads of men, the stamping-ground of brutish lust and breeding-ground of foul disease. Marion, by contrast, is 'Meer', 'Strom', and 'Welle', her sexuality is whole and incorruptible, her beauty infinite, her being ungraspably mystical. Beyond this, however, another extreme polarity is delineated within Marion herself. For the fluidum of her being offers contrary outcomes: where Danton envisions a wondrous union, the erstwhile lover was drowned and devoured. And in a sense Danton's vision is a deadly illusion disguising the fact that the lover's fate is essentially his own: after all, his absorption in Marion's body and what it betokens is also suicide of a kind, insofar as he offers himself up on the 'guillotine' of her thighs, the 'Tarpeian Rock' of her mons veneris. In this perspective, Marion for all her sublimity is a Siren figure, quite different from her sister-prostitutes in their coarse catholicity—yet even more insidiously lethal.[3]

Woman and death: this obsessive linkage is one of the hallmarks of Büchner's writing—and we find it emblazoned at the outset in none other than Julie, who turns out to be at once the antithesis and complement of Marion. If in Marion we are offered an image of woman as a swirling, deadly vortex, in Julie we are offered the image of woman as the means to absolute repose—so absolute that death alone is adequate to describe it. We have already seen how Danton is given to express the sense of peace he gains from Julie in the shocking language of death and burial ('Du süßes Grab, deine Lippen sind Todtenglocken, deine Stimme ist mein Grabgeläute,

---

[3] For Grimm, on the other hand, the Marion tale is essentially a 'legend of grace and redemption allotted us in a benign universe' (ibid. 192).

deine Brust mein Grabhügel und dein Herz mein Sarg', etc.). The real impact of this conceit, however, lies in the fact that it is transmuted into a kind of reality. Once the shadow of the guillotine falls on Danton, Julie betokens the 'peace of the grave' not metaphorically, but literally: he cannot bear the thought of dying without her, for she alone could bring him peace in death:

O Julie! Wenn ich *allein* ginge! Wenn sie mich einsam ließe!
Und wenn ich ganz zerfiele, mich ganz auflöste—ich wäre eine Handvoll gemarterten Staubes, jedes meiner Atome könnte nur Ruhe finden bey ihr. (61)
O Julie! If I were to go *alone*! If she were to leave me on my own! Even if I utterly dissolved, utterly disintegrated, became but a handful of tortured dust, each atom of my being could only find peace in her.

The appropriate echo is not long in coming: only minutes later, Julie, telepathically aware of her beloved's fear, sends him the message he so desperately needs: 'sag' ihm er würde nicht allein gehn. Er versteht mich schon' (64; *tell him he won't go alone. He'll know what I mean*). Soon afterwards, the same crucial words are echoed yet again in Danton's response in his cell: 'Ich werde nicht allein gehn, ich danke dir Julie' (67; *I won't go alone, I thank you Julie*). And in due course, immediately prior to Danton's own death, we witness the supreme self-sacrifice of Julie's suicide as she takes poison and dies (72-3)—a scene of great beauty in which the fictive death of the character is heightened and poeticized through her description of the whole earth appearing to die, drowned in the gathering darkness of the evening (an uncanny echo of the death of Marion's lover).

The importance for Büchner of this sense of a devotional love transcending death is signalled by the fact that he enacts it not once but twice: first in the Danton–Julie relationship, and then again, even more powerfully, in the love between Camille and Lucile, with the spotlight once more focused particularly on the woman.

It is true that on the few occasions serving to convey the love-bond between Camille and Lucile there is never any suggestion of a disparity in their emotions: they are clearly devoted to each other with equal passion. And yet there are eloquent differences in the ways that the love of each is portrayed. To some extent the sheer economy of the play is responsible for this: wholehearted though

Camille's love undoubtedly is in itself, it is only one quite small part of his persona, for he is centrally involved (like Danton) in the complex interplay of events and personalities throughout the drama; in Lucile's case, on the other hand, her devotion is her sole *raison d'être* as a character. But Büchner goes far beyond mere functional, dramaturgical requirements in the way that he magnifies and intensifies this devotion to the exclusion of all other characteristics, making Lucile in consequence appear not as a figure from the sweaty, laborious world of contingent reality (like Simon's wife, for example), but as a radiant symbol: the personification of devotion in its absolute form.

The pattern is established from the moment we first encounter her. It is to her (and Danton) that Camille delivers his tirade against culture-consumers and their distorted sensibilities and lack of eyes to see and ears to hear. Lucile, for her part, is exemplary in being all eyes and ears—but not in the way that Camille might have envisaged. For she is not in the least interested in the *content* of his words: what captivates her is the sheer sound and spectacle of her beloved in full spate: 'Was sagst du Lucile? / Nichts, ich seh dich so gern sprechen. / Hörst mich auch? / Ey freilich. / Hab ich Recht, weißt du auch, was ich gesagt habe? / Nein wahrhaftig nicht.' (37–8; *What do you say, Lucile? / Nothing, I just like watching you speak. / Do you listen to me too? / Of course I do. / Am I right? Do you actually know what I said? / No I truly don't.*) What we are shown here is not the stereotype of the brainless beauty, but the archetype of a woman whose sense and perception of existence are critically different from men's: Camille's analytical intellect is matched by his wife's voracious sensibility, her mysterious intuition. She sees at once what he is blind to: when Danton announces the news of his impending arrest, she instantly recognizes that her beloved is doomed, and her very first words after Danton's departure are already a vision of his execution, a cry of pain, a kind of goodbye: 'Ach Camille! ... Wenn ich denke, daß sie dieß Haupt!' (38; *Oh Camille! ... This precious head: to think that they...!*) Camille produces a whole catalogue of reasons why she need not worry: he and Danton are not one flesh; Robespierre was nice to him the previous day; their differences are minor; he was Robespierre's only chum at school, and the object of his special affection ever since. But as audience we have already witnessed the sealing of his fate in the Robespierre/Saint-Just scene, and we recognize the poignant finality of Lucile's goodbye as she kisses him again and again, and then, in the starkly poetic, rhythmic soliloquy that ensues, gives voice to a flood of intuitions that prefigure the sombre progression of events, from parting, to ever greater separation, to death:

[*Singt.*]   Ach Scheiden, ach Scheiden, ach Scheiden,
              Wer hat sich das Scheiden erdacht?
Wie kommt mir gerad das in den Kopf? Das ist nicht gut, daß es den Weg so von selbst findet.
Wie er hinaus ist, war mir's als könnte er nicht mehr umkehren und müsse immer weiter weg von mir, immer weiter.
Wie das Zimmer so leer ist, die Fenster stehn offen, als hätte ein Todter drin gelegen. Ich halt' es da oben nicht aus. [*Sie geht.*]

[*Sings.*]   Who had the heart
              To make lovers part
              And part and part and part?
Why *that* of all things? For that to come into my head on its own: it's bad. As he went away, I had this feeling he could never turn back and would have to go further and further away from me—further and further.
How empty the room is; the windows agape as if a corpse had lain here. I can't bear to stay. [*Exit.*]

After this initial brief but intensive projection of Lucile in the middle of Act II, she is kept alive in the back of our minds only by the most fleeting and occasional allusions (50, 55, 63)—but she is then suddenly brought forward into the limelight again as a vital element in the 'grand finale', which in effect she not only initiates but also concludes. Her reappearance in the fourth scene of Act IV is electrifying. The tumbril has just arrived, the air is thick with the foul-mouthed banter of drivers and gawping prostitutes about brothels and gargantuan poxy cunts—and there before us, as though from a different world, is this wraith Lucile, already ethereal when last we saw her, and now transfigured by a kind of poetic, Ophelian dementia. Her derangement—already foreshadowed during her earlier appearance when she supposed she must be mad to imagine Camille on the guillotine ('gelt, ich bin wahnsinnig?', 38)— enables Büchner to unleash a stream of discrete images that are superficially crazed, but serve to define and redefine the lovers' plight with plangently expressive power: Camille is a trapped colossus with the prison wall as his iron mask; he is a bird that Lucile tries in vain to attract; he is a fairytale lover whose damsel longs for him to creep to her chamber past her sleeping guardians—but with his mantle of stone he cannot even enter the outermost gate; finally, he is Lucile's 'sweet friend', bidden to join her as she dances away in pursuit of a concept that she cannot yet grasp: the concept of death. Büchner's film-like technique of intercutting quite different images of a single theme is particularly conspicuous here—and so too is his practice of heightening the tension through a disjunction of mode and matter: nothing could demonstrate the depth of Lucile's anguish more evocatively than her reference to the whole predicament as a joke ('Spaß'), and her demented laughter at the start and close of this episode (an echo of the terrible paroxysms of laughter that Danton said should rack the heaven and the earth, the living and the dead; 36).

There are few moments in the play as moving as Lucile's final appearance marking the brief envoi or postlude after Camille and the others have gone to their deaths. In a sense she carries on exactly where she left off, seeming virtually to continue the same sentence in her dedication to reflections upon death: 'Sterben! Ich will nachdenken.' (69)—'Ich will einmal nachdenken. . . . Sterben— Sterben—' (74). But the mood is totally different. There is no laughter now, no dancing dementia at the mere prospect of death, but a kind of controlled explosion of grief at its cold reality. Saint-Just in his great speech in Act II gave a cynical 'bird's eye' view of the world as a place in which even the slightest spasm of change or progress entails the erasure of countless anonymous and insignificant human lives. At the furthest possible extreme from this is Lucile's 'worm's eye' view that sees and *feels* an absolute value in every vulnerable individual. The difference between the two contrary perspectives is graphically demonstrated in Büchner's antithetical use of river imagery. With Saint-Just, we hear of the 'raging stream of the Revolution' spewing out batches of corpses at every turn (46); with Lucile, we hear of the 'stream of Life' that ought to falter and stop when even the merest drop of its waters is needlessly spilt: 'Der Strom des Lebens müßte stocken, wenn nur der eine Tropfen verschüttet würde' (74); in the equally expressive hyperbole that immediately follows: such a fell blow as Camille's destruction should leave a gaping wound on the face of the earth: 'Die Erde müßte eine Wunde bekommen von dem Streich.' A similar idea was voiced through Camille when he feared that the Dillon conspiracy was a Jacobin ploy to procure the death of his darling Lucile (cf. 62–3):

Sieh die Erde würde nicht wagen sie zu verschütten, sie würde sich um sie wölben, der Grabdunst würde wie Thau an ihren Wimpern funkeln, Crystalle würden wie Blumen um ihre Glieder sprießen und helle Quellen in Schlaf sie murmeln. (65–6)

Lo the earth would not dare to devour her, it would rise up vaultlike all around her, the sepulchral dank would sparkle like dew upon her lashes, crystals would sprout like flowers about her limbs, pellucid springs would whisper her to sleep.

But no such thing happens. The stream of life does not stand still, nor even pause for the briefest moment—as is brought home to us in Lucile's own rhythmic litany: 'Es darf ja Alles leben, Alles, die kleine Mücke da, der Vogel. Warum denn er nicht? . . . Es regt sich Alles, die Uhren gehen, die Glocken schlagen, die Leute laufen, das Wasser rinnt und so, so Alles weiter bis da, dahin—' (74; *Everything else is allowed to go on living, everything, this tiny insect here, that bird. Why not him? . . . Everything's astir, clocks tick, bells ring, folk pass, water flows, everything continues just as before, forever and forever—*). She tries to stop the world with a single scream—and it would be a poor actress that failed to wring the emotions of her audience with this magnificently futile gesture. Its inevitable outcome, and Lucile's response, are conveyed with equal poignancy, thanks to the spareness and bleakness of Büchner's parataxis: 'Das hilft nichts, da ist noch Alles wie sonst, die Häuser, die Gasse, der Wind geht, die Wolken ziehen.—Wir müssen's wohl leiden.' (74; *It makes no difference, things are just as they were, the houses, the street; the wind blows, the clouds drift.—Perhaps we just have to bear it.*)

With rough reality taking palpable shape at this point in the three passing women who so relish the public spectacle of death (75), Lucile's resigned acceptance of impotent passivity—'Wir müssen's wohl leiden.'—seems at first to be her final word. But a much less passive mood is suggested by the words that ring out the scene: 'Mein Camille! Wo soll ich dich jezt suchen?' (75; *My Camille! Where do I look for you now?*) The answer to her question and her quest is instantly revealed as the lights go up on the final scene to reveal the guillotine, at rest after the grisly business of the day. An atmosphere of earthy matter-of-factness is conjured up through the two executioners as they busy themselves about the death-machine and then depart; but this is swept away when Lucile reappears and launches into a flight of poetic transfiguration as intense as any in the play. The key rhetorical elements here are personification, metaphor, and paradox. At first, Death stalks before us as the Grim Reaper, cutting huge, indiscriminate swathes in the serried ranks of humanity:

> Es ist ein Schnitter, der heißt Tod,
> Hat Gewalt vom höchsten Gott . . .
> Viel hunderttausend ungezählt,
> Was nur unter die Sichel fällt.[4]
>
> There is a reaper, Death by name
> Whose power from God Almighty came . . .
> Myriad without number are the lives
> That fall beneath his sweeping scythe.

But this vision of Death as the random destroyer of anonymous and numberless masses—a vision already distanced through its mediation in song—is counteracted by a much more immediate and lyrical picture of Death in warmly individualized and personalized terms. The unlikely departure-point is the guillotine itself, which Lucile transfigures into a kind of benign presence. She sees it first as an 'angel' (albeit an angel of death), and one that is not only 'in repose', but which offers Lucile a 'lap' into which she climbs like a child in search of comfort ('Ich setze mich auf deinen Schooß, du stiller Todesengel'); this sense of protectiveness is greatly increased when she goes on to apostrophize the death-machine as a 'dear cradle' that lulled her Camille to sleep like a baby, and smothered him with roses ('Du liebe Wiege, die du meinen Camille in Schlaf gelullt, ihn unter deinen Rosen erstickt hast'); finally, she apostrophizes it as a friendly 'passing-bell' that sang Camille to his grave with its sweet music ('Du Todtenglocke, die du ihn mit deiner süßen Zunge zu Grabe sangst.')

An acute sense of dramatic tension is generated by the spectacle of this woman in search of her dead beloved finding comfort in the very instrument of his destruction, and the chief emblem throughout the play of unbridled savagery; and the longer the eerie calm is sustained, particularly through the rhythmic 'du . . .' personifica-

---

[4] Together with Lucile's 'Wir müssen's wohl leiden', these lines are borrowed from *Des Knaben Wunderhorn*. Cf. Hinderer, *Büchner-Kommentar*, 128.

tions, the more the tension is heightened. It is as though in the stormy coda of a symphony we were suddenly confronted by an intensely quiet passage that can only be the prelude to an imminent and final explosion of sound. And the dramatic drumroll duly reverberates, with Lucile in effect committing suttee through her suicidal shout of 'Long live the king!' ('Es lebe der König!'), an expedient that produces its desired effect in the shape of her instant arrest, and guarantees her subsequent execution. The enigma is thus resolved: Lucile embraced the guillotine so fondly because it was her only route to reunion with Camille; to condemn herself to the same 'dear cradle' is to find her way back to him at last.

Again and again throughout the play the behaviour and responses of the characters are mocked or questioned—by the characters themselves, or else by the way that Büchner presents them: the sense of mask, pretence, and posture is almost omnipresent—even in the guillotine scene itself. However, when it comes to the self-sacrifice of Lucile and Julie—potentially the target of derision as a supremely futile heroic gesture ('Schneidet nur keine . . . so heroische . . . Grimassen', 71)—there is not the faintest trace of irony or mockery. On the contrary, these crowning acts of self-immolation are conveyed with a poetic intensity unsurpassed in the rest of the play. We are offered a perfectly inverted reprise of the beginning, with the spotlight focused in each case on women. 'Look!' we were told through Danton: look at this 'pretty lady' whose pretence of wifely love masks constant betrayal; and Julie herself was declared to be remote and unknowable behind the doll-like mask of her face. What we duly behold in the catastrophe is the exact opposite: a double celebration of absolute love, devotion, and loyalty; of human powers of bonding and communion that transcend the limitations of physical existence. This is the triumph of spirit over matter—and it is a triumph that can be achieved, in Büchner's visionary world, only through the agency of women.

The sheer poetry of these final scenes of Julie's and Lucile's is spell-binding in both intention and effect. But what if we resist the spell? What are we to make of Büchner's representation of women on a more detached, more clinical view? Seen from a severely feminist vantage point, the situation is clearly dire: consciously or unconsciously, Büchner is the exponent of an exploitative patriarchy which by means of repression (sexual) and oppression (economic and social) degrades women into the servile adjuncts and playthings of men. Lucile's seeming radiance masks 'a sado-masochistic subtext'; and Julie is no more than fodder gobbled up by a male greedy for women as consumable commodities: 'Danton consumes bits of prostitute bodies and Marion's whole body, but he consumes Julie's heart and soul.'[5] One may appreciate the sincerity of this perspective and its underlying aim of deconstructing and discrediting male constructs of the feminine, but it is nevertheless tendentious to the point of distortion. Büchner *does* perceive—and tirelessly demonstrate—the workings of a socio-cultural dynamic that threatens to destroy individuals and produce instead a mass of undifferentiated automata to be used and discarded quite indiscriminately. But *all* are victims of this process, men and women alike. And as we have seen, its momentum is so powerful that it admits of only two alternatives: submit to its logic and hope to survive, or resist its logic and certainly perish. Hence the ethos of suicide so prominent in the play. Danton heroically refuses to go on being a 'hero': he deliberately stands still in a moving mass, and chooses to be killed rather than continue killing others. Julie's suicide is likewise noble in its way, and certainly not the act of a woman consumed, or debased to the status of a commodity. And Lucile's virtual suicide at the end is not the act of an abject victim, but not least a triumphant gesture of defiance, a rejection of her earlier submissiveness ('Wir müssen's wohl leiden'), a demonstration of will and the ability to choose (in this sense it is perhaps misleading to speak of her committing suttee, insofar as that suggests an act that is socially imposed, not freely chosen). And we should not forget, too, that in both cases Büchner alters history: the real Lucile did not deliberately provoke the law, but was arrested purely on the basis of Laflotte's denunciation; whilst Danton's real wife, far from poetically poisoning herself, married again and lived happily ever after.[6]

What these departures from history amount to is a kind of idealization, and with that we find ourselves in tricky terrain, for it has to be acknowledged that Büchner's heroines are never drawn as it were from life; they are never just people who happen to be female, nor women who exist in their own right and for their own sake. Curiously enough, the peripheral females *do* have the smack of

[5] Boa, 168, 165.
[6] Furthermore, her real name was Louise; 'Julie' was perhaps chosen as an echo of Shakespeare's Juliet.

reality, no matter how brief their appearance: the 'Dame' in the opening scene, Simon's wife, Eugénie—all have an instant earthiness. The heroines, however, are not really women at all in any full-blooded sense: they are emblematic projections of the male imagination, hypostases of men's ideals and desires, fears and longings. We see this most clearly in the case of Marion, who has no existence whatsoever outside her one appearance, and whose monologue derives its force and impact from the fact that it occurs not *in vacuo*, but as an intensely personal experience of Danton's. Marion is almost a dream-figure in the sense so evocatively described through Robespierre in his nocturnal musings: 'Gedanken, Wünsche kaum geahnt, wirr und gestaltlos, die scheu sich vor des Tages Licht verkrochen, empfangen jezt Form und Gewand und stehlen sich in das stille Haus des Traums.' (28; *Thoughts and wishes, barely sensed, confused and formless, that dared not face the light of day, now take on shape and substance and steal into the silent house of dreams.*) Lucile, for her part, is a wraith-like image of perfect devotion, a kind of walking wish-fulfilment. Just as Marion in Danton's eyes embodies an infinite beauty, so too does Lucile in the eyes of Camille: 'Das Licht der Schönheit, das von ihrem süßen Leib sich ausgießt, ist unlöschbar' (65; *The radiant beauty that streams from her sweet body can never be quenched*; it is here, too, that Camille speaks of how the earth would refuse to swallow up her dead body, but 'would rise up vaultlike all around her'). Julie to some extent is in a different category: she plays a realistic wifely role in the 'September' scene; and she serves as the butt of Danton's despair in the opening moments of the play. In this same first scene, however, she begins at once to be mysticized as Danton's fount of existential peace, and it is this mystical aura that increasingly prevails in the play, to the point that, when she dies, she seems like a figure from a Pre-Raphaelite painting.

Perhaps the chief characteristic of these iconic figures is that they radiate a sense not only of ideal beauty, but also of undivided wholeness and unsullied purity. A key factor here is that they are shown to exist intuitively and emotionally: their being has not been usurped or contaminated by an overweening mind and its detritus of systems, ideas, theories. This is particularly clear in Lucile's response to Camille's tirade on the contemporary arts: she hangs on every word from her beloved's lips, but is quite oblivious to the content of what he says. Marion relates to the world around her explicitly and exclusively through feeling ('ich . . . hänge mit Allem um mich nur durch eine Empfindung zusammen'), and whereas her mother is 'clever', Büchner has Marion repeatedly emphasize that cerebral understanding is not for her ('frug ich was die Leute gewollt hätten . . .'; 'es war etwas darin, was ich nicht begriff'; 'Ich begreife nichts davon'; 'ich wußte nicht recht, was er wollte'; 'ich wußte wieder nicht was er wollte'). The other essential feature here is that, in sharp contrast to virtually all the other (peripheral but earthy) females in the play, the three spotlighted women are represented as being untouched and uncorrupted by *Unzucht*, by sexuality as something brutish, vulgar, mechanical, or cankered. They stand out as islands of purity in a sea of poison. This is most conspicuously the case with Lucile, who is endowed with an aura of sensuality that is innocent, almost angelic: she is not poxy or promiscuous, nor the mistress of her hairdresser; her 'sweet body' is not a 'gangbare Straße' but a wellspring of radiant beauty; she has a childlike air, and is specifically referred to by her husband as 'lieb Kind' (38); her physicality is evoked not in terms of clockwork copulation, but of delicate kisses that remain with Camille even in gaol, dancing like visions on his lips and then modulating into precious dreams: 'Lucile, deine Küsse phantasiren auf meinen Lippen, jeder Kuß wird ein Traum' (66). With Julie too, although she is less insistently idealized, there is again no slightest trace of sordid sexuality; and it would not be far-fetched to suppose that the comfort she brings to Danton is very like the comfort that a mother brings to an anxious child. Marion is the most extraordinary case in point. She seems to be carnality incarnate when Lacroix describes her thighs and her mons veneris as Danton's guillotine and Tarpeian Rock, or when she herself speaks of her pleasure in consorting with her lover between the bedsheets. And yet she represents a sublimation of sexuality, a pure realm of sensuous being that transcends the physical contortions of copulation so savagely travestied in Lacroix's picture of the mastiff and the lapdog struggling to mate. In contrast to her apparent peers Adelaide and Rosalie, there is no suggestion that Marion is in any way contaminated by disease or bodily corruption; and the infinite beauty that Danton perceives in her is not something that he seeks to possess by penetration, but to absorb, enfold, envelop in a sublime and mystical interfusion of being.

 The supreme significance of these idealized embodiments of Woman is perhaps most clearly epitomized in a description of Lucile that was included in the manuscript of the play, but then deleted: originally Camille was given to say not only that the radiant beauty streaming from Lucile's body was unquenchable, but also that it was 'das Vestafeuer in [?] der Natur' (TMM 64; *the Vestal Fire in [?] nature*; the word 'in' is an uncertain reading). The Vestal Fire was the sacred flame that enshrined the essential spirit of Rome: so long as the flame continued to burn, the republic was held to be proof against calamity. The unquenchable radiance of Lucile's beauty is accordingly a sacred reflection of the living spirit of nature, a kind of palladium precious beyond words. What makes this notion supremely important for Büchner is that the 'sacred flame' in such as Lucile is all that enables him and his protagonists to keep their faith and find some warmth in the oppressive darkness that increasingly weighs upon them. The situation is even worse for Büchner in the Metternichian 1830s than it had been for Hölderlin—a remarkably kindred spirit—in the Napoleonic turmoil around the turn of the century. The entire created world may be informed and enspirited by the 'primal law of Beauty' and its 'necessary harmony'; but the surface terrain, the realm of everyday social, political, cultural reality, has been commandeered by hostile processes and forces: the men who seek to reconstruct humanity according to their own caprices, and build their systems out of severed heads; the 'teleologists' with their functionalistic, reductive picture of the world that turns individuals into minimal components serving some larger process; the bearers of corruption and disease with their threat of all-engulfing *Unzucht*. The 'great mass' and 'great class' of the *Volk* has the pristine health and vigour to replace the prevailing order in all its deadly effeteness and ennui—but this fundamental renewal will occur only at some indeterminate point in the distant future. In the dark, dissonant, ugly interim, there is but a single sanctuary: only through women and the mystical communion that they afford can men overcome their cold isolation and exposure and partake of the allness of being. But even this is far from easy. And at their deepest level, all Büchner's poetic works centre on their heroes' success or failure in achieving such miraculous communion.

Part III

Leonce und Lena

11
Masquerade

OF all Büchner's works, *Leonce und Lena* has taken by far the longest time to come into its own—indeed the process is still not complete. The play was disparaged from the outset. Karl Gutzkow didn't even think it worth publishing in full, and in his partial edition of 1838 he dismissed it as a 'mere attempt at a play, dashed off in a hurry', an unstageably Romantic confection by an author who, had he lived, would have been no match for the 'pullulating playwrights' of the day, a 'modest talent' comparable only with such 'lesser lights' as Achim von Arnim and Clemenz (*sic*) Brentano.[1] More than a century later we find Hans Mayer almost spluttering with disappointment at this 'ironic-romantic trifle' with all its derivativeness and airy-fairy insubstantiality; for Mayer the play was an almost incomprehensible aberration, the product of a fleeting caprice, of a passing yen for cash and kudos; it seemed to him a mockery of all that Büchner stood for.[2] In recent years, however, new perspectives have begun to open up that allow *Leonce und Lena* to be recognized at last as neither a trifle nor an aberration, but a powerful work fully on a par with the others, and altogether of a piece with them. I would go even further and suggest that *Leonce und Lena* is perhaps Büchner's most poised—and most teasing—creation.

Part of the tease unfortunately lies in the circumstance that we possess no definitive text of the play. There is a certain spice in the fact that a play that focuses repeatedly on questions of authenticity itself only exists in unauthenticated form. Not only did the play remain unpublished at Büchner's death, but almost no autograph manuscripts have survived (of the three fragments so far discovered, just one is at all substantial, and represents only an incomplete and superseded early draft of Act I, Scene i). Instead, we have to rely on the editions by Karl Gutzkow (1838) and Ludwig Büchner (1850). As already mentioned, Gutzkow printed only part of the play; and

---
[1] Dedner (ed.), *Georg Büchner. Leonce und Lena*, 15, 87.
[2] Hans Mayer, *Georg Büchner und seine Zeit*, 298 ff.

in any case his source was not Büchner's own manuscript, but a copy written out by Minna Jaeglé (which has itself disappeared). Unlike his predecessor, Ludwig Büchner published a full-length version, possibly based largely on the same Minna Jaeglé copy, but more probably based on a different handwritten copy (made by Büchner's sister Luise), or perhaps on the original manuscript. But Ludwig Büchner and Gutzkow unfortunately shared an interventionist approach to the text, particularly with regard to passages that might have offended prevailing political or moral sensibilities, and both made cuts and changes without compunction. Thanks mainly to the scholarship of Thomas Michael Mayer, we now have a 'state-of-the- art' historical-critical edition of the play reflecting all available sources, that is, the three extant manuscripts, and the Gutzkow and Ludwig Büchner editions.[3] What we do not have— and are never likely to have—is the definitive text as Büchner almost certainly left it; indeed *Leonce und Lena* is the *least* reliable text of all—and this sorry fact needs to be kept in the back of our minds throughout the discussion that follows.

Alone among Büchner's works, *Leonce und Lena* was written more or less to order: on 16 January 1836 the publisher J. G. Cotta advertised a substantial prize for 'the best one- or two-act comedy in prose or verse'. The original deadline was 15 May 1836, but in due course it was officially changed to 1 July, and may have been unofficially extended for a couple of weeks beyond that.[4] Whatever the final deadline was, Büchner missed it by a couple of days, and his manuscript was returned to him unopened. Thomas Michael Mayer considers it highly unlikely that Büchner was free to work on the play until the beginning of June, given the intensity of his work throughout May preparing his *Mémoire sur le système nerveux du barbeau* for publication (BD 90). This would mean that his second play, like his first, was written at astonishing speed, within a period of some four to six weeks. The competition version cannot have been the same as the three-act version that has come down to us

[3] Thomas Michael Mayer's 'Kritische Studienausgabe' constitutes the principal element in the volume edited by Burghard Dedner (cf. above, Ch. 4 n. 3). Page references to this volume are identified by the prefix 'BD'.

[4] See especially Hauschild, *Georg Büchner*, 343 ff. ('Zur Entstehung und Datierung von *Leonce und Lena*'); see also BD 90 ff. ('Entstehung'), and Thomas Michael Mayer, 'Zu August Lewalds "Lustspiel-Preisaufgabe" und zu Datierung und "Vorrede" von *Leonce und Lena*', in T. M. Mayer (ed.), *Georg Büchner Jahrbuch*, 1/1981, 201–10.

(since the competition rules specified a play in one or two acts), and Büchner clearly continued working on the text throughout the remaining few months of his life. *Leonce und Lena* was not of course by any means his only interest at this time, and it helps to put the play in perspective if we appreciate the hecticness and above all the extraordinary diversity of his activities in this final period of his life: he was simultaneously creating both a comedy and a tragedy (*Woyzeck*); and besides that he was deeply immersed in philosophy and his scientific work (the latter culminating in the Trial Lecture, and his ensuing course at Zurich University on comparative anatomy).[5]

All the evaluative and interpretative problems surrounding Büchner's comedy derive essentially from the very fact of its being a comedy, or rather, from the particular way in which he chooses to make use of the genre. In a nutshell, one might say that the reader/spectator is systematically denied any clear and consistent perspective, any reliable sense of orientation. In the case of *Dantons Tod*, by contrast, we had no such problem: we were encouraged to suspend our disbelief, and to behold the doings of familiar real-life figures in an identifiable place within a specific time-frame. In *Woyzeck* too, the illusion of substantiality, of a solid 'thereness', is compellingly conveyed. In *Lenz* we are again shown a historical figure in a real-life episode in a real environment. But in *Leonce und Lena* we are offered scarcely any points of reference at all, and are never allowed to settle for long into a confident rapport with the figures conjured up on page or stage.

But however disconcertingly the focus shifts and changes at the centre of the action, it is relentlessly clear and sharp at the edges: twice in the play—once towards the beginning, then again towards the end—we can delight in the spectacle of unambiguous and biting satire through the medium of peripheral characters. We have already explored the chief instance of this in an earlier chapter: the mocking of King Peter with his mindless fixation on mind and his consequent remoteness from 'fresh, green life'; his tenuous hold on

---

[5] Cf. Büchner's letter to his brother Wilhelm on 2 Sept. 1836: 'Ich habe mich jetzt ganz auf das Studium der Naturwissenschaften und der Philosophie gelegt, und werde in Kurzem nach *Zürich* gehen ... —Dabei bin ich gerade daran, sich einige Menschen auf dem Papier todtschlagen oder verheirathen zu lassen' (ii. 460; *I have now committed myself completely to the study of sciences and philosophy, and will soon be going to* Zurich ... —*Meanwhile I am busily getting various people to murder or marry one another on paper*).

his own identity; his proneness to radical confusion; his reduction of his own being and that of his minions to a set of empty mechanical processes. The element of social and political satire is further exploited in Act III, Scene iii, in the prelude to King Peter's second appearance and the ensuing wedding ceremony. The opening stage direction suggests the semblance of a great state occasion: 'Großer Saal. Geputzte Herren und Damen, sorgfältig gruppirt' (128; *Grand state-room. Gentlemen and Ladies in full finery, carefully grouped*). But by using the Master of Ceremonies and his acolytes at the front of the stage as ironic commentators, Büchner rapidly turns the apparent grandeur into farce, in the process using a neat sleight of hand: although the tableau is essentially static, a sense of what might be called dynamic disintegration is generated and sustained through a barrage of present-tense verbs denoting *change*—and change for the worse: 'Alles geht zu Grund. Die Braten schnurren ein. Alle Glückwünsche stehen ab. Alle Vatermörder legen sich um, wie melancholische Schweinsohren. Den Bauern wachsen die Nägel und der Bart wieder. Den Soldaten gehn die Locken auf.' (128; *Everything is going to pot. The roasts are shrivelling. The congratulations are all turning stale. The stand-up collars are all drooping like melancholy pigs-ears. The nails and beards of the peasants are sprouting anew. The soldiers' curls are coming undone.*) The ritualistic artificiality of the occasion is mocked through animal comparisons: not only the starched collars drooping 'like melancholy pigs-ears', but the Twelve Virgins looking like 'exhausted angora rabbits' ('erschöpfte Seidenhasen') and the Court Poet grunting around them 'like a fretful guineapig' ('der Hofpoet grunzt um sie herum wie ein bekümmertes Meerschweinchen'). In particular, the artificiality is made laughable by Büchner's characteristic stress on all-too-natural processes and compulsions: the unstoppable growth of the peasants' nails and beards; the Twelve Virgins' longing to be horizontal rather than vertical (a *double entendre* that Gutzkow carefully omitted from his edition); the schoolboys' need to go off for a piddle. On top of this, various dignitaries are singled out for ridicule: the Court Poet, of course; but also the Officers, the Court Chaplain, especially the Court Ladies. In due course the King himself arrives on stage with his phalanx of robotic State Councillors, and this serves as the cue for a further blast of ridicule: all this would-be grandiose pomp and circumstance is taking place in a kingdom of Lilliputian proportions that can be traversed in moments by a dog seeking its master, a 'realm' about as large as a village cricket-field.

The sharpest satire, however, is unleashed in the preceding scene (Act III, Scene ii; 127–8). Here too we have a group of the King's subjects waiting for the Great Royal Occasion. But these are not insiders—they are outsiders quite literally, forced to stand about in the heat of the day; not courtiers and such in all their finery ('geputzte Herren und Damen'), but peasants in their pitiful Sunday best ('Bauern im Sonntagsputz'); not people of privilege genteelly marshalled by one of their ilk, but an underclass regimented and policed by a middle-class schoolmaster,[6] who is policed in turn by an upper-class 'Landrath' (*District Prefect*). Posturing and pretence are targeted in both scenes. But whereas pretension for the privileged is a chosen way of life in which the mask has all but supplanted the visage, the pretence required of the peasantry is a temporary condition forced upon them, and starkly at odds with their miserable reality. They are ordered to conjure up a Romantic illusion of peace and plenitude: a moonlit forest full of roaming deer and glistening strawberries; but the 'moonlight' is the shiny patches on their worn-out trousers, the 'forest' their paltry firbranches stuck out in front of them, the 'deer antlers' their tricorn hats, the 'strawberries' their drink-reddened noses. At the same time they are to make their small number falsely appear like an infinite crowd:

Streckt eure Tannenzweige grad vor euch hin, daß man meint ihr wärt ein Tannenwald und eure Nasen die Erdbeeren und eure Dreimaster die Hörner vom Wildpret und eure hirschledernen Hosen der Mondschein darin, und merkt's euch, der Hinterste läuft immer wieder vor den Vordersten, daß es aussieht als wärt ihr ins Quadrat erhoben.

In a scathingly blatant contradiction, all and sundry are *commanded* to form up *voluntarily* along the royal couple's wedding route—and moreover to convey the impression that they are cleanly dressed, well-fed, and altogether contented: 'Gebt Acht, Leute, im Programm steht: "Sämmtliche Unterthanen werden von freien Stücken, reinlich gekleidet, wohlgenährt, und mit zufriedenen Gesichtern sich längs der Landstraße aufstellen." ' They have even been given a veneer of

---

[6] The Schoolmaster has a curiously double role *vis-à-vis* his peasant charges: he is at once their oppressor, and their defender and spokesman. At the close of the scene Büchner has him identify himself completely with the peasants through his 'Wir ...' (*We* ...).

education: the 'Vivat!' that they laboriously chorus at the prompting of the Schoolmaster, who sardonically claims it to be a mark of improved intelligence—after all, it's *Latin*!—: 'So Herr Landrath. Sie sehen wie die Intelligenz im Steigen ist. Bedenken Sie, es ist *Latein*.'

It would be all too easy in a stage production to subvert this scene by playing it as a light-hearted bit of comic relief featuring a stock collection of gormless country bumpkins. Büchner's peasants are not that at all. Far from being the butt of cheery comedy, they are essentially *victims* with whom we are clearly meant to sympathize; they are members of that oppressed, exploited, degraded mass so powerfully invoked in *Der Hessische Landbote*, whose substance is systematically devoured by the parasitical minority lampooned in the very next scene. For all its relentless jokiness, the language points to a shameful reality. The Schoolmaster's first utterance is typical: ostensibly it is just a play on words; but its real message is the *suffering* of the peasants:

LANDRATH. Lieber Herr Schulmeister, wie halten sich Eure Leute?
SCHULMEISTER. Sie halten sich so gut in ihren Leiden, daß sie sich schon seit geraumer Zeit aneinander halten.

PREFECT. Well, dear Schoolmaster, how are your people holding up?
SCHOOLMASTER. They're holding up so well in their agony that they've been holding on to one another for quite some time.

The peasants are guzzling alcohol—but only because they can scarcely bear the intense heat: 'Sie gießen brav Spiritus in sich, sonst könnten sie sich in der Hitze unmöglich so lange halten.' They are forbidden to scratch behind their ears—a clear suggestion that they are infected with lice. They are to refrain from blowing their noses with their fingers—a practice symbolic of the dispossessed underclass (in the revolutionary context of *Dantons Tod*, the use of a handkerchief is enough to brand the Young Man as 'an aristocrat', and nearly costs him his life; 14). The peasants are commanded to appear 'cleanly dressed'; but their jackets and trousers are full of holes (in the same episode in *Dantons Tod* the First Citizen cries death on all those 'with no holes in their coat'). They are instructed to look 'well-fed'—but in reality they are famished: there are roasts aplenty on the royal table, as we learn moments later at the start of Act II, Scene iii; but the peasants' sole privilege is to be allowed a mere smell of them. In the comic-bitter words that Büchner gives to the Schoolmaster: 'Erkennt was man für euch thut, man hat euch grade so gestellt, daß der Wind von der Küche über euch geht und ihr auch einmal in eurem Leben einen Braten riecht.' (*Show your appreciation of all that's been done for you—you've been specially placed downwind of the kitchens so that for once in your life you catch a whiff of roast meat.*) The tone may be comic, but the tenor is reminiscent of one of the bitterest passages in *Der Hessische Landbote* (a passage undoubtedly written by Büchner, not by Weidig):

Geht einmal nach Darmstadt und seht, wie die Herren sich für euer Geld dort lustig machen, und erzählt dann euern hungernden Weibern und Kindern, daß ihr Brod an fremden Bäuchen herrlich angeschlagen sey ... und dann kriecht in eure rauchigen Hütten und bückt euch auf euren steinichten Aeckern, damit eure Kinder auch einmal hingehen können, wenn ein Erbprinz mit einer Erbprinzessin für einen andern Erbprinzen Rath schaffen will, und durch die geöffneten Glasthüren das Tischtuch sehen, wovon die Herren speisen und die Lampen riechen, aus denen man mit dem Fett der Bauern illuminirt. (ii. 44, 46)

Go to Darmstadt and see what a fine time the gentlemen have at your expense, then tell your starving wives and children what a boon your bread has been for alien bellies ... then crawl back into your smoky hovels and bend to your labour on your stony fields so that your children too can one day make the journey when some crown prince and princess are about to give succour to some other crown prince, and then through the wide-open doors they can see the table-cloth off which the gentlemen eat, and smell the lamps that are fuelled with the fat of peasants' bodies.

If a sharp satirical intent is plainly evident around the edges of the play, is it perhaps not also discernible elsewhere? To some extent the answer is Yes, for in its overall setting and action *Leonce und Lena* is unarguably a bitter-sweet burlesque on the petty despotism of *Vormärz* Germany with all its effeteness, parasitism, ritualism, vacuity, its cocooned and wholly ungenuine existence. On one level, therefore, the play works throughout—and very effectively—as a kind of satirical strip-cartoon. But it is also far more than that. We see this very clearly if we consider King Peter's anxious reflections in Act I, Scene ii: '[*Steht eine Zeit lang sinnend.*] Wenn ich so laut rede, so weiß ich nicht wer es eigentlich ist, ich oder ein Anderer, das ängstigt mich. [*Nach langem Besinnen.*] Ich bin ich.—Was halten Sie davon, Präsident?' (109; [*Stands a while thinking.*] *Whenever I speak out loud like that, I never know who it really is, me or someone else, it frightens me. [After long reflection.] I am me.—President, what is your opinion on the matter?*) From one perspective this is splendid caricature that exposes the king as a comic buffoon. But at the same time it opens a Pandora's box of ontological questions—the same anxious questions that are raised when Valerio enters in disguise towards the close of the play:

PETER. Wer seid Ihr?
VALERIO. Weiß ich's? [*Er nimmt langsam hintereinander mehrere Masken ab.*] Bin ich das? oder das? oder das? Wahrhaftig ich bekomme Angst, ich könnte mich so ganz auseinanderschälen und -blättern.
PETER [*verlegen*]. Aber—aber etwas müßt Ihr dann doch sein?
VALERIO. Wenn Eure Majestät es so befehlen. (130)

PETER. Who are you?
VALERIO. Do I really know? [*He slowly removes several masks one after the other.*] Am I this? Or this? Or this? Truly it frightens me that if I keep on removing layer after layer, I might peel myself entirely away.
PETER [*disconcerted*]. But—but surely you must be something?
VALERIO. If your Majesty so commands.

King Peter is thrown into total disarray by all this ('Der Mensch bringt mich in Confusion, zur Desperation. Ich bin in der größten Verwirrung.', 131), and we duly laugh at his discomfiture. But at the same time we are discomfited ourselves, for beyond the comic spectacle of the robot-king flailing in helpless confusion, we find ourselves faced with a genuinely disturbing question: the problem of masks, façades, outward appearances, and whether they conceal some essential inner truth—or a terrifying nothingness. The real tease is that the comic mode is itself a kind of mask, like a painted face on a melancholy clown. Whilst we laugh at the verbal and physical antics of the 'fool' Valerio, at the clownish confusion of the silly king, we also subtly share that confusion, we share the fear so 'funnily' voiced through Valerio ('ich bekomme Angst...'). Though quite differently expressed and 'packaged', the fear evoked here is in essence no different from the existential terror ascribed to Lenz towards the beginning of Büchner's story: 'es faßte ihn eine namenlose Angst in diesem Nichts, er war im Leeren' (80; *he was seized by a nameless fear in this nothingness, he was in the void*). The suggestion that there might be nothingness behind Valerio's masks is a reprise in comic mode of that hideous vision conveyed through Camille towards the end of *Dantons Tod*:

wir sollten einmal die Masken abnehmen, wir sähen dann wie in einem Zimmer mit Spiegeln überall nur den einen uralten, zahllosen, unverwüstlichen Schaafskopf, nichts mehr, nichts weniger. (70–1)

we ought to remove our masks for once: we'd think ourselves in a hall of mirrors—wherever we looked we'd see only the same ass's head, no more, no less: primeval, infinite, indestructible.

Even the very imagery of 'mirrors' is intensively resumed in the continuation of the exchange between the King and Valerio:

PETER [*verlegen*]. Aber—aber etwas müßt Ihr dann doch sein?
VALERIO. Wenn Eure Majestät es so befehlen. Aber meine Herren hängen Sie alsdann die Spiegel herum und verstecken Sie Ihre blanken Knöpfe etwas und sehen Sie mich nicht so an, daß ich mich in Ihren Augen spiegeln muß, oder ich weiß wahrhaftig nicht mehr, wer [/was] ich eigentlich bin. (130; the 'wer' is in Gutzkow's version, the 'was' in Ludwig Büchner's)
PETER [*disconcerted*]. But—but surely you must be *something*?
VALERIO. If Your Majesty so commands. But in that case, gentlemen, turn the mirrors to the wall, cover your shiny buttons, and don't look at me like that lest I see my reflection mirrored in your eyes—or I truly won't know anymore who [/what] I really am.

This suggests a disturbing duality of selves: if Valerio is commanded to convert or reduce himself into a particular 'something', then this imposed and spurious self will be quite different from the true self he sees reflected in the mirror. But then again: does the image in the mirror really reflect the true self, or merely the interpretation that we wish upon it? Is there indeed such a thing as a true self, truth of any kind, a substantive reality? Or do we have nothing but the images we ourselves invent? Nowhere in Büchner's œuvre is this frightening possibility more graphically conveyed than in his comedy, and nowhere do we find a more chilling use of mirror imagery than here, when Leonce responds to Valerio's lament that the world is a monstrously vast abode:

Nicht doch! Nicht doch! Ich wage kaum die Hände auszustrecken, wie in einem engen Spiegelzimmer, aus Furcht überall anzustoßen, daß die schönen Figuren in Scherben auf dem Boden lägen und ich vor der kahlen, nackten Wand stünde. (118)

Not at all! Not at all! I scarcely dare stretch out my hands, as though in a narrow hall of mirrors, for fear of bumping into it on every side and then finding the pretty figures shattered on the ground, and there before my eyes the bare, blank wall.

Being a character in a comedy, Leonce is immune to the existential disintegration envisioned in his words, which flit past us like a black-edged cloud in a blue-painted sky. In the very different context of *Lenz*, however, we see the terrible potential within Leonce's words lived out before our very eyes. For Lenz, the world becomes not metaphorically or hypothetically but quite literally an image of his own invention—and with that he is irrevocably mad.

Dann gerieth er zwischen Schlaf und Wachen in einen entsetzlichen Zustand; er stieß an etwas Grauenhaftes, Entsetzliches, der Wahnsinn packte ihn . . . Auch bei Tage bekam er diese Zufälle, sie waren dann noch schrecklicher . . . Es war ihm dann, als existire er allein, als bestünde die Welt nur in seiner Einbildung, als sey nichts, als er, er sey das ewig Verdammte, der Satan; . . . es war die Kluft unrettbaren Wahnsinns, eines Wahnsinns durch die Ewigkeit. (98–9)

Then between sleep and waking he fell into a terrifying state; he bumped against something hideous, horrific, madness seized hold of him . . . He suffered these attacks in the daytime too, and they were then much worse . . . He felt at such moments as if he alone existed, as if the world existed only in his imagination, as if there were nothing but him, as if he were Satan, the eternally damned; . . . it was the gaping abyss of incurable madness, a madness through all eternity.

The fact that Leonce as a comic hero can suffer no real disasters, whereas Lenz at the end is virtually destroyed, reflects merely the difference in mode; it does not of course mean that the comedy is essentially or inherently less serious than the story.[7] In truth, *Leonce und Lena* is just as serious as anything else Büchner wrote, and in some ways even more disturbing—precisely because the perspective is constantly shifting, so that we are kept on edge and can never settle into any steady state of confident involvement. The words given to Valerio, when he first appears in Act III and removes his successive masks, apply as much to the play as a whole as they do to Valerio himself at that particular juncture: *Leonce und Lena* is an inspired masquerade, and we are constantly forced to wonder whether it is truly this, or that, or the other; we can never readily differentiate between mask and reality, pretence and substance.

Our problems begin with the arresting fact that there is scarcely a single constituent element in the play that is original to Georg Büchner. Plot, setting, characters, dialogue: almost everything is put

---

[7] Cf. Dedner, 'Bildsysteme und Gattungsunterschiede', BD 193.

Masquerade 217

together out of bits and pieces gleaned from other writers and traditions. As Walter Hinderer has remarked: 'Büchner made use of numerous ideas, allusions and quotations, for instance from Shakespeare, Sterne, Musset, Goethe, Holberg, Tieck, Brentano, Jean Paul, Friedrich Schlegel, the *Night Vigils* of Bonaventura, and the tradition of the *Commedia dell'arte*.'[8] Readers who are interested in the chapter and verse of Büchner's borrowings will find Hinderer's own *Büchner-Kommentar* an invaluable starting-point, for he offers the fullest catalogue presently available, and it would be pointless to try to replicate it here. In any case, what really matters is the general fact that much of the play is borrowed from here and there, rather than the particular provenance of a particular quotation or allusion. And it is especially important for us to realize that the 'derivativeness' of *Leonce und Lena* is not a weakness in the play, but a decided strength. As Hinderer himself points out: 'literary quotation constitutes the fundamental structural principle of *Leonce und Lena*, and forms part of its strategy of communication'.[9] Far from being any kind of plagiaristic patchwork or casual pastiche, *Leonce und Lena* is a brilliant montage of true originality in which the very inauthenticity of the component parts contributes actively to the effect of the whole—by helping the play to call itself constantly into question, as it were, and thereby challenge and disconcert the reader/spectator. This process begins even on the title-page, when the reader is offered a 'Preface' that is not a preface, in the form of two quotations that are not quotations, couched as questions not statements, and in a foreign language, not in German:

Vorrede
Alfieri: 'E la fama?'
Gozzi: 'E la fame?'

It is deliciously teasing that Büchner should preface a play fashioned to a considerable extent out of unacknowledged echoes, allusions, and quotations, with acknowledged 'quotations' that their purported authors never wrote. Even when we have discovered this,

---

[8] 'Büchner verarbeitete zahlreiche Anregungen, Anspielungen und Zitate, beispielsweise aus den Werken Shakespeares, Sternes, Mussets, Goethes, Holbergs, Tiecks, Brentanos, Jean Pauls, Friedrich Schlegels, den *Nachtwachen* des Bonaventura und der Tradition der *Commedia dell'arte*'; Hinderer, *Büchner-Kommentar*, 133.
[9] 'das literarische Zitat ist in *Leonce und Lena* das entscheidende ästhetische Bauprinzip und Teil der Kommunikationsstrategie'; loc. cit.

and discovered that the Italian means 'And fame [or: reputation]?', 'And hunger?', we are still faced with a complete enigma: who is asking these questions? of whom? *about* whom? do they have any bearing on the play? what do they even really *mean*, given the absence of verbs, and the conjunction 'and' conjoining them to nothing? We can surmise (as Gutzkow did[10]) that Büchner was perhaps pointing to the possible alternative outcomes of the comedy competition: success would bring him renown, failure would leave him hungry. But this is no more than a guess, and the puzzle essentially remains. We are offered an apparently portentous piece of jigsaw puzzle, but with no pointers as to how or where we should fit it in.[11]

Another puzzle soon confronts us: where are we? The list of characters tells us, after a fashion, by identifying King Peter and Princess Lena as hailing respectively from the realms of 'Popo' and 'Pipi' ('Bum' and 'Piddle'). The child in us gives a smirk of recognition, and we seem transported onto familiar ground—and yet it is a Nowhere, a kind of un-place. In *Dantons Tod* the very title in effect locates the action, soon confirmed by a barrage of topical allusions. The first paragraph of *Lenz* takes us to a real person's house in a real village in the real Vosges. Even in *Woyzeck* the setting, though non-specific, is largely realistic; we are encouraged to imagine ourselves in a quasi-real place. The scene-headings are instructive in this respect. In *Woyzeck* the definition of place is often subtly reinforced through the use of the definite article: 'Das Innere der Bude', 'Der Casernenhof', 'Die Stadt in der Ferne', 'Die Stadt', 'Der Hof des Professors'; in only three of the forty-nine scenes making up the various sequences does Büchner use an indefinite article in his scene-headings (and all these are in H1, the earliest sequence). In *Leonce und Lena*, by contrast, indefinite articles predominate. In Act I, all four scenes are rendered indeterminate in this way: 'Ein Garten', 'Ein Zimmer', 'Ein . . . Saal', 'Ein Garten'; the first three scenes of Act II are likewise indefinitely placed; and in both Acts II and III the definite article is only ever used of locations already

---

[10] In his 1838 edition Gutzkow comments that the two sentences 'sehr naiv ausdrücken, daß er mit seiner Dichtung etwas zu verdienen hoffte' (BD 15; *very naïvely express the hope that his creation would earn him something*).

[11] Cf. Kurt Ringger, 'Georg Büchner zwischen FAMA und FAME', *Archiv für das Studium der neueren Sprachen und Literaturen*, 213 (1976), 100-4; Thomas Michael Mayer, loc. cit.; Wolfgang Proß, '*Was wird er damit machen?* oder "Spero poder sfogar la doppia brama, De saziar la mia fame, e la mia fama." ' ibid. 252–6.

known to us (thus 'Ein Wirthshaus' in II. i necessarily becomes '*Das Wirthshaus*' in II. ii—though we are now also told that the inn stands 'auf *einer* Anhöhe an *einem* Fluß'). Again, the list of characters could be said to establish a distinct ambience with its recital of 'King', 'Princess', 'Governess', 'Court Tutor', etc. But the courtly setting is never identified or localized, never tied in to any larger, real-seeming community. We move from one indeterminate and discrete space to another: three gardens, all different yet largely undefined; various open spaces; various rooms in an unplaceable royal palace, and in a nameless inn in a nameless land.

One of Büchner's most subtle yet powerful devices for conditioning our sense of the fictive space of the play is to convey it not only directly, through the scene-headings and stage directions, but also indirectly, through the medium of the characters within the fiction. At its most patent level, this affects the physical disposition of the stage, and hence the actual image that we see with our eyes. Act I, Scene iii offers much the most detailed stage-set of the play— because Büchner has Leonce determine his own environment. All that the scene-heading says is 'Ein reichgeschmückter Saal, Kerzen brennen' (109; *A richly appointed room, candles burning*); but the space is then both defined and reshaped by the Prince in readiness for his encounter with Rosetta:

Sind alle Läden geschlossen? Zündet die Kerzen an! Weg mit dem Tag! Ich will Nacht, tiefe ambrosische Nacht. Stellt die Lampen unter Krystallglocken zwischen die Oleander ... Rückt die Rosen näher ... Musik! Wo sind die Violinen? Wo ist die Rosetta? (109)

Are the shutters all shut? Light the candles! Do away with the day! I want night, deep, ambrosian night. Set the lamps beneath crystal domes amongst the oleanders ... Move the roses closer ... Music! Where are the violins? Where is Rosetta?

More commonly, however, Büchner uses the characters to conjure up an image of space purely through their words, rather than through the materiality of the set—and this allows him to play all kinds of games with our spatial perceptions.

The thrust of this can be purely comic-satiric, as in Act III, Scene iii, when the grandiose Kingdom of Bum is suddenly depicted via the servants as a ludicrous Lilliput, a realm so absurdly small that Leonce and the rest can cross the border, traverse the land, and enter the palace in a matter of seconds (129–30). A similar effect is achieved through Valerio in II. i, when he describes the journey he has made with Leonce since fleeing from Bum: 'Wir sind schon durch ein Dutzend Fürstenthümer, durch ein halbes Dutzend Großherzogthümer und durch ein paar Königreiche gelaufen und das in der größten Uebereilung in einem halben Tag' (119; *We've already passed through a dozen principalities, half a dozen grand duchies and a couple of kingdoms, and all at breakneck speed in half a day*). In Valerio's following speech there is even the absurdist vision of a land entirely devoid of substance and reality: just layers-within-layers or boxes-within-boxes, at the centre—nothing (the image strongly prefigures that of Valerio with his masks):

Teufel! Da sind wir schon wieder auf der Grenze; das ist ein Land, wie eine Zwiebel, nichts als Schaalen, oder wie ineinandergesteckte Schachteln, in der größten sind nichts als Schachteln und in der kleinsten ist gar nichts. (119)

Hell and damnation, we're back at the border! This country's like an onion: nothing but layers; or like Chinese boxes: in the biggest box are smaller boxes, in the smallest box there's nothing.

At a much deeper level, however, we can find ourselves transported into a different realm altogether through the imaginative power and eloquence that Büchner bestows on his characters. In the Rosetta scene Leonce day-dreams—and his vision becomes *our* vision. The theatrical illusion is potentiated: where otherwise we see Prince Leonce in a palace, not an actor on a stage, we now see an Ancient Roman, not Leonce (while the dancing Rosetta, appropriately lit, readily becomes the visible image of Leonce's imaginings):

LEONCE [*indeß träumend vor sich hin*]. O, eine sterbende Liebe ist schöner, als eine werdende. Ich bin ein Römer; bei dem köstlichen Mahle spielen zum Dessert die goldnen Fische in ihren Todesfarben. Wie ihr das Roth von den Wangen stirbt, wie still das Auge ausglüht, wie leis das Wogen ihrer Glieder steigt und fällt! Adio, adio meine Liebe, ich will deine Leiche lieben. (111)

LEONCE [*meanwhile dreaming to himself*]. Oh, a dying love is more beautiful than one that's growing. There, I'm a Roman: to bring the exquisite banquet to a fitting close the golden fish disport themselves in all the colours of their dying agony. Oh, how the red of her cheeks dies away, how quietly the fire in her eye goes out, how gently the lilt of her limbs first quickens, then fades! Addio, addio, my love, I shall cherish your corpse.

Masquerade

A few moments later, another imaginary space is conjured out of nothing, and as Leonce bids Rosetta see it, so we see it too, much as we 'see' the spaces and objects shaped by a mime. Rosetta in her grief tries to embrace Leonce, but he fends her off:

Gib Acht! Mein Kopf! Ich habe unsere Liebe darin beigesetzt. Sieh zu den Fenstern meiner Augen hinein. Siehst du, wie schön todt das arme Ding ist? Siehst du die zwei weißen Rosen auf seinen Wangen und die zwei rothen auf seiner Brust? Stoß mich nicht, daß ihm kein Aermchen abbricht, es wäre Schade. Ich muß meinen Kopf gerade auf den Schultern tragen, wie die Todtenfrau einen Kindersarg. (111)

Take care! My head! I've buried the corpse of my love in there. Look through the window of my eyes. Do you see how beautifully dead the poor thing is? Do you see the two white roses on her cheeks, the two red ones on her breast? Don't bump me, lest one of her little arms snaps off—such a pity if it did. I must carry my head quite straight on my shoulders, like a weeper bearing the coffin of a child.

When Rosetta has gone, Büchner has Leonce turn the inside of his head into yet another imaginary but almost palpable space:

Mein Kopf ist ein leerer Tanzsaal, einige verwelkte Rosen und zerknitterte Bänder auf dem Boden, geborstene Violinen in der Ecke, die letzen Tänzer haben die Masken abgenommen und sehen mit todmüden Augen einander an. (112)

My head is an empty dance-hall, on its floor a few wilted roses and crumpled ribbons, in a corner the remnants of broken violins, the last few dancers have removed their masks and stare at each other with dead-tired eyes.

All three of these brief but vivid conjurations serve as graphic representations of the mind and mood of Leonce himself. But at the very end of this scene Büchner has him summon up a quite different realm: there before us, quite suddenly, is a vision of Italy. Italy is to be Leonce's refuge from unwanted marriage and unwanted kingship. A cockshy of alternatives is first enacted in a comically rhythmic duet: Valerio lobs up possibility after possibility, and Leonce bats them out of sight. Let's be scholars, says Valerio, or heroes, or poets, or useful members of human society—but no, no, no, and definitely no. Then let's go to the devil. No, not to the devil—to *Italy*!

Ah Valerio, Valerio, jetzt hab' ich's! Fühlst du nicht das Wehen aus Süden? Fühlst du nicht wie der tiefblaue glühende Aether auf und ab wogt, wie das

Licht blitzt von dem goldnen, sonnigen Boden, von der heiligen Salzfluth und von den Marmor-Säulen und Leibern? Der große Pan schläft und die ehernen Gestalten träumen im Schatten über den tiefrauschenden Wellen von dem alten Zaubrer Virgil, von Tarantella und Tambourin und tiefen tollen Nächten, voll Masken, Fackeln und Guitarren. Ein Lazzaroni! Valerio! Ein Lazzaroni! Wir gehen nach Italien. (117)

Valerio, Valerio, I've got it! Can't you feel the wafting spirit of the South? Can't you feel the rhythmic pulsing of its ardent azure air? The light glinting on the golden, sun-splashed earth, the sacred sea, the ancient marble columns and bodies? The great Pan sleeps, and in the shade above the distant roar of waves the mighty figures dream of Virgil and his ancient magic, of tarantellas and tambourines, of torrid, teeming nights alive with masks, guitars, and flickering torches. Lazzaroni! Valerio! Lazzaroni! We're going to Italy!

A crucial question arises here that goes to the very heart of our understanding of the play as a whole: is this passion or persiflage? Did Büchner imagine an actor delivering these lines with real feeling, or with his tongue very obviously in his cheek? With genuine enthusiasm, or the 'comic' enthusiasm explicitly called for at the close of the preceding scene (108)? On the face of it the passage might seem to be just a light-hearted spoof, a spirited send-up of the great Romantic yearning for Italy, 'das Land, wo die Zitronen blühn'. Certainly the passage echoes that tradition with peculiar intensity: as E. Theodor Voss has shown, almost every key word or phrase occurs in identical or similar form in earlier texts—Jean Paul, Heine, Platen, Goethe, Eichendorff, Johann Heinrich Voss's translation of the *Odyssey*, Musset perhaps, E. T. A. Hoffmann perhaps.[12] But this is no pastiche. Büchner performs an extraordinary trick here: within the space of a few lines he transports us from grinning irony to a deeply felt and vivid dreamscape, then back to irony again. This is partly because the echoes of the traditional passion for Italy are evocative in themselves. But it is mainly because Büchner gives them new life and resonance in what amounts to a perfectly balanced and irresistibly seductive prose-poem. The seduction is achieved mainly through rhythmic patterning: the caesuras at first succeed each other rapidly, but are then more and more spaced out

---

[12] BD 275 ff.; and see especially the 'Synoptische Übersicht', BD 422 ff. Voss's contribution to the Dedner volume is a remarkable and monumental piece of research, and I happily acknowledge my indebtedness—E. Theodor Voss, 'Arkadien in Büchners *Leonce und Lena*', BD 275–436.

until the reader/spectator is lifted to a kind of peak at the phrase 'Der große Pan schläft'; we are then returned gently to comic terrain through a repetition in reverse of the rhythmic pattern of the first half. The near-perfectness of the balance is remarkable. 'Der große Pan schläft' declares itself as the heart of the passage through its unique concentration of stressed syllables: ᴜ – ᴜ – – (upbeat/trochee/spondee—the only spondee in the passage). It is also the exact midpoint, with twenty-two stressed syllables both preceding it and following it. Furthermore, the second-half grouping of these stressed syllables by means of the caesuras is an almost exact mirror-image of the first-half pattern, so that the tension is so to speak unwound again (the commas and full-stops represent minor and major caesuras respectively):

1,1,1,1,3.5.10 (or 5,5)—'Der große Pan schläft'—9.5.3.1,1,1,2

We are taken through a kind of space- and time-warp. After the initial 'Ah Valerio, Valerio, jetzt hab' ich's!' we expect yet another ironic, dismissive sally from Leonce—but what we get is so to speak the scent of the South, and a direct invocation of the senses: 'Fühlst du nicht das Wehen aus Süden?' If we still half-expect this to turn to mockery after all, our doubts are expelled by the repeated 'Fühlst du . . .' and the long, suspensive question it introduces with its marked poetic rhythm (mainly trochaic/dactylic). Whereas in the first 'Fühlst du' phrase the south is there, but as a kind of distant promise, in the second it is already a felt presence, its sky in all its blueness not merely passive, but alive with radiance and fluid movement. The more the second 'Fühlst du' sentence proceeds, the more we feel ourselves being spirited into a vivid but visionary, even mystical world: not only is the sky perfectly blue and alive, but the earth is golden and sun-splashed, the sea is 'holy'—and suddenly we are in the midst of marble pillars and bodies (presumably statues, also of marble); we are in the realm of antiquity and classical perfection. This radiant, golden, holy, perfect place is surely Arcadia, whose god was Pan—the Arcadia created in his poetry by that 'old magician' Virgil ('dem alten Zaubrer Virgil'). It is highly apt that rhythmically the passage reaches its zenith, and hangs for a moment in suspension, at the words 'Der große Pan schläft'—for these words also mark a mythic, symbolic suspension of *time*: when Pan, the god of Arcadia, sleeps in its mid-day heat, time stands still.[13] And in this timeless present, the slumbering 'ehernen Gestalten'—suggestive of the gods of old—dream of the past ('dem alten Zaubrer Virgil'), but also of a future reawakening, of 'Tarantella und Tambourin und tiefen tollen Nächten'. With the bustling rhythm, the repeated t-sounds, the different vocabulary, we find ourselves now magicked to yet another place and time, its air of carnival joy and abandon being further reinforced by the ensuing vision of 'Masken, Fackeln und Guitarren'. Only then does the passage return to a more flippant mood and to the fictive here-and-now with Leonce's declaration of their new supposed goal: to go off to Italy and become *lazzaroni*.[14]

We shall consider the interpretative problems of this later on. In the mean time we might note that, although Leonce and Valerio never reach the magic of Italy, they nevertheless enter a very strange realm. The first and last acts are set in and around the palace of Bum, and however vague and indeterminate that may be by comparison with Danton's Paris or Lenz's Waldbach, it is relatively precise by comparison with the setting of Act II. This zone into which Leonce and Lena separately flee, and in which they ultimately find each other, is conspicuously undefined, a kind of fourth dimension, a world beyond the looking glass. It is peopled solely by the hero and heroine and their respective acolytes: there are no Kings, Court Tutors, Court Chaplains and the like to provide even the semblance of a specific context. The landscape is limitless: it is 'Open country' (118), affording a view into a remote and vague distance ('weite Aussicht', 121). It is twilight at the beginning, full night by the end. Most strikingly, perhaps, this nameless realm provokes wildly differing responses and perspectives in the four

---

[13] See especially Voss, BD 417–18, 424–5.

[14] The word *lazzarone* (plural *lazzaroni*) was quite common in both English and German in the 19th c., to the extent that it even occurs in Büchner's school geography work (he noted in an exercise book that Naples had a population of 350,000, including '60,000 Laceroni'; Voss, BD 345). The word bore very different meanings depending on the user's outlook. To the clock-watching, productivity-minded functionalist the lazzaroni were loafers and parasites (a view clearly reflected in the *OED* definition of the word: 'One of the lowest class in Naples, who lounge about the street, living by odd jobs, or by begging'); to the Arcadian idealist, on the other hand, they were the very image of how life should be savoured and enjoyed, how it should be *lived*, not merely spent. (See esp. Voss, BD 305 ff. and *passim*.) Büchner highlights the contrast in the 'Promenade' scene of *Dantons Tod*, when the two worthy Citizens remonstrate with the Beggar and offer him work—an absurd proposition in his eyes, since it would bring him a lovely coat but a worn-out body; and in any case the sun keeps him nice and warm (35).

Masquerade

characters abroad in it—as we see in the very first exchange of the act, when Valerio describes the world as 'a monstrously spacious abode' ('ein ungeheuer weitläuftiges Gebäude', 118)—only to be countered by Leonce's contrary vision of the world as a single narrow room lined with all-too-fragile mirrors. Minutes later, yet another contrary vision is offered through Lena, in response to the Governess's complaint that the world is so repulsive ('O die Welt ist abscheulich!'): 'O sie ist schön und so weit, so unendlich weit. Ich möchte immer so fort gehen Tag und Nacht.' (120; *Oh it's beautiful and so spacious, so infinitely spacious. I'd like to carry on like this for ever, night and day.*) And of course we also have Valerio's descriptions of the country as a Lilliputian assemblage of minuscule states, as a succession of onion-like layers, of boxes-within-boxes, with nothing at the centre (119).

The remark of Lena's quoted above is immediately followed by a description of the scene as night begins to fall—a picture of perfect stillness, calm, repose:

LENA. . . . Es rührt sich nichts. Was ein rother Schein über den Wiesen spielt von den Kukuksblumen und die fernen Berge liegen auf der Erde wie ruhende Wolken.
GOUVERNANTE. . . . Es wird Abend!
LENA. Ja die Pflanzen legen ihre Fiederblättchen zum Schlaf zusammen und die Sonnenstrahlen wiegen sich an den Grashalmen wie müde Libellen. (120)

LENA. . . . Nothing stirs. The red of the cuckoo-flowers glows and dances over the meadow, and the distant mountains rest on the earth like slumbering clouds.
GOVERNESS. . . . Night's coming on!
LENA. Yes, the plants are settling their tiny leaves for sleep, the rays of sunlight nod on the blades of grass like tired dragon-flies.

Only a minute or so later, essentially the same scene is described through Leonce—but in drastically different terms. He too sees stillness—but an ominous stillness full of fear, complemented by an equally ominous maelstrom of nightmarish activity:

—Welch unheimlicher Abend. Da unten ist Alles still und da oben wechseln und ziehen die Wolken und der Sonnenschein geht und kommt wieder. Sieh, was seltsame Gestalten sich dort jagen, sieh die langen weißen Schatten mit den entsetzlich magern Beinen und Fledermausschwingen und Alles so rasch, so wirr und da unten rührt sich kein Blatt, kein Halm. Die Erde hat sich ängstlich zusammengeschmiegt, wie ein Kind und über ihre Wiege schreiten die Gespenster. (122)

—How weird the evening is. Down below, a perfect stillness; up above, the fleeting, shifting clouds, the sun appearing, disappearing. See what strange figures go hurtling after each other up there, see the long white shadows with their fearfully thin legs and batlike wings—and all such swirling turmoil, while down below nothing stirs, not a leaf, not a single blade of grass. The earth has curled into a ball of fear, like a child, and above its cradle the ghosts go marching.

We then get yet another vision from Valerio: far from seeing what Leonce bids him see, Valerio has no idea what he is on about ('Ich weiß nicht, was Ihr wollt'): to him, the dedicated boozer and guzzler, the sun looks like an inn-sign, the clouds like the name inscribed on it, the earth and the river like a wine-splashed table, while they themselves are the playing-cards that God and the devil are having a game with out of sheer boredom (122).

What are we to make of these multiple and conflicting perspectives? I suggest that we can only really understand them as a particularly daring piece of illusionism. In *Dantons Tod* Büchner offers essentially a single illusion, sustained throughout: the place is Paris, the time is late March/early April 1794; and we spontaneously credit the fiction from beginning to end. Even when extra dimensions are opened up within the play, we accommodate them easily in terms of the given psychology of the characters. When the actor in the 'September' scene stands there in make-believe night by a pretend window and delivers his agonized lines, what we see in our mind's eye is Danton in Paris baring his soul. In *Leonce und Lena*, and especially in Act II, Büchner attempts something much more complex and challenging. In an un-place outside time we see projected a succession of visions, each compelling in its presentness, but often sharply at odds with what precedes or follows it. To borrow the play's own metaphor: it is as if the mirrors in Leonce's grim vision of the world as an 'enges Spiegelzimmer' had indeed shattered, and instead of the stable, reliable illusion of old there are only contrasting images briefly projected onto the 'bare blank wall', chasing each other like the 'strange figures' that Leonce sees in the clouds racing across the twilight sky.

We find the supreme example of this in the lead-up to the play's climax (124–5). In Act II, Scene iii—the only indoor scene in Act II, and a very short one—Lena, this refugee from constriction, is now

Masquerade

fleeing the unbearable constriction of the room in the inn ('Ich kann nicht im Zimmer bleiben. Die Wände fallen auf mich.') She hears the sounds of the gathering night, and to her they are harmony and repose: 'Hörst du die Harmonieen des Abends? Wie die Grillen den Tag einsingen und die Nachtviolen ihn mit ihrem Duft einschläfern!' (124; *Do you hear the harmonies of nightfall? How the day is lulled to sleep by the song of the crickets, the scent of gillyflowers!*) Moments later, at the start of Scene iv, we see her sitting on the grass outside—but we also see Valerio, and *his* impression of the night and its noises is fundamentally different and down-to-earth:

Es ist eine schöne Sache um die Natur, sie ist aber doch nicht so schön, als wenn es keine Schnaken gäbe, die Wirthsbetten etwas reinlicher wären und die Todtenuhren nicht so in den Wänden pickten. Drin schnarchen die Menschen und draußen quaken die Frösche, drin pfeifen die Hausgrillen und draußen die Feldgrillen.

It's all very lovely, nature is; but it'd be a damned sight lovelier if there were no gnats to bite you, the beds were a bit cleaner, and the death-watch didn't keep ticking in the walls. In there—people snoring, out here—frogs croaking; house-crickets racketing inside, field-crickets racketing outside.

Leonce is brought on-stage—and a third, quite different perspective is created in seconds: we are suddenly as though in Paradise: 'O Nacht, balsamisch wie die erste, die auf das Paradies herabsank.' (*Oh night, as sweet and balmy as the first that sank on Paradise.*) The spotlight shifts back to Lena—and a poetic vision takes shape that is surely the most vivid and most disturbing in all the play:

Die Grasmücke hat im Traum gezwitschert, die Nacht schläft tiefer, ihre Wange wird bleicher und ihr Athem stiller. Der Mond ist wie ein schlafendes Kind, die goldnen Locken sind ihm im Schlaf über das liebe Gesicht heruntergefallen.—O sein Schlaf ist Tod. Wie der todte Engel auf seinem dunkeln Kissen ruht und die Sterne gleich Kerzen um ihn brennen. Armes Kind, kommen die schwarzen Männer bald dich holen? Wo ist deine Mutter? Will sie dich nicht noch einmal küssen? Ach es ist traurig, todt und so allein.

A songbird twittered in its dreams, the night slips deeper into sleep, her cheek grows paler, her breath more quiet. The moon is like a sleeping child, its golden locks have tumbled over its dear face.—Oh its sleep is death. How it lies there, a dead angel on his cushion of darkness, with stars burning like candles all around him. Poor child, are the bogymen coming to take you away? Where's your mother? Won't she give you just one last kiss? Oh the sadness of it—dead, and so alone.

The lyrical shift from dreaming, twittering songbird through peaceful sleep to death and utter isolation is poignant enough in itself—but it is all the more poignant for carrying echoes of similar passages in other works. In *Woyzeck* the grandmother's 'anti-fairytale' also tells of moon and stars and death, and also climaxes in the image of a child alone ('da sitzt es noch u. ist ganz allein', 399). Moonlight, sleep, tumbling locks of hair, sorrow and radical isolation: Lenz is figured in just such terms:

er ging auf sein einsames Zimmer. Er war allein, allein! . . . er weinte über sich, sein Haupt sank auf die Brust, er schlief ein, der Vollmond stand am Himmel, die Locken fielen ihm über die Schläfe und das Gesicht, die Thränen hingen ihm an den Wimpern und trockneten auf den Wangen, so lag er nun da allein, und Alles war ruhig und still und kalt, und der Mond schien die ganze Nacht und stand über den Bergen. (85)

he went to his solitary room. He was alone, alone! . . . he wept at himself, his head sank down on his chest, he fell asleep, the full moon stood there in the sky, his locks tumbled down over temple and face, the tears still clung to his lashes and dried on his cheeks, and so he lay there now alone, and all was calm and still and cold and the moon shone down the whole night through and stood there over the mountains.

In *Dantons Tod* Marion sees the corpse of her lover being carried past her window, and again it is a twilight vision of moonlight, pallor, locks of hair: 'Den Abend saß ich am Fenster . . . Ich sah hinunter, sie trugen ihn in einem Korb vorbey, der Mond schien auf seine bleiche Stirn, seine Locken waren feucht, er hatte sich ersäuft.' (22; *That evening I sat by the window . . . I looked down, they were carrying him by in a basket, his forehead shone pale in the moonlight, his locks were wet, he'd drowned himself.*) But much the strongest echo is to be found in Julie's suicide speech, when her own slide into death is so wonderfully imaged in her picture of the earth appearing to drown in the gathering darkness beyond her window (72–3). The extent of the similarities is almost uncanny: not only do both narratives share basically the same story-line, they also share essential details: 'schläft', 'schlafendes', 'Schlaf'/'Schlummer', 'Schlafe, schlafe'; 'Wange'/'Wangen'; 'wird bleicher'/'Stets

Masquerade

bleicher und bleicher wird sie'; 'stiller'/'so still'; 'Gesicht'/'Gesicht'; 'die goldnen Locken'/'den goldnen Locken'; 'der todte Engel'/'einer Sterbenden', 'eine Leiche'; 'küssen'/'küsse'.

Lena's speech with all its resonant echoes is no ordinary piece of theatrical monologue (and least of all comic monologue), but a kind of mantra, an incantation that spirits us into the deepest realms of Büchner's poetic imagination, and conditions us to experience the most intense and most surreal encounter between two people to occur anywhere in his work. We shall consider this encounter in more detail later on. What we need to do at this stage is to note that yet another vision immediately supervenes. After Lena has rushed away, Leonce in his supreme ecstasy is as though reborn. Just before catching sight of Lena he felt *as if* in Paradise ('O Nacht, balsamisch wie die erste, die auf das Paradies herabsank'); now he sees primal Creation take shape out of Chaos before his very eyes:

> Wie frischathmend, schönheitglänzend ringt die Schöpfung sich aus dem Chaos mir entgegen. Die Erde ist eine Schale von dunkelm Gold, wie schäumt das Licht in ihr und fluthet über ihren Rand und hellauf perlen daraus die Sterne.

> Out of chaos comes creation, bursting forth towards me, so alive and new, so radiant with beauty. The earth is a chalice of dusky gold: oh how the light within it effervesces, spills over its edge in streams, and from its sparkling bubbles all the stars appear.

The vision is powerful—particularly since it, too, reverberates with echoes of other passages in other works, as we shall see in due course. But needless to say, it cannot and does not last. Valerio performs his essential function and brings Leonce—and us—down to earth with a bump. The sacral realm is not only dispelled in a trice, but rubbished as well, and we are back in the 'real' world of no-nonsense irony and flea-ridden palliasses. Our hero, quite literally yanked out of his vision by his sidekick, now longs only for plain, prosaic sleep: '—Der Himmel bescheere mir einen recht gesunden, plumpen Schlaf.'

But then: does Büchner really mean us to believe that Leonce is truly himself only as a dismissive, self-debunking ironist? Does he mean us to believe that Leonce is *ever* truly himself, or that such a thing as a true self exists in the first place? After all, we know the jest-cum-threat delivered through Valerio in the final scene as he removes mask after mask: 'Bin ich das? oder das? oder das? Wahrhaftig ich bekomme Angst, ich könnte mich so ganz auseinanderschälen und -blättern.' In this 'slight, idyllic comedy', as Gutzkow chose to call it (BD 15), Georg Büchner explores the problem of identity and the authentic self more searchingly, more desperately than anywhere in his writing.

12
Identity and Ennui

IN *Leonce und Lena* the theme of identity is already signalled in the List of Characters, even before the play itself has begun. Of the twelve characters specifically listed, no fewer than seven are introduced not as named individuals, but as nameless functionaries: 'The Governess', 'The Court Tutor', 'The Master of Ceremonies' etc.; two have names but no specific function (Valerio and Rosetta); only the three royals have both names and titles.

The various functionaries that appear throughout the play are not only devoid of names: in general they also exhibit no individual personality or behaviour whatsoever. In effect they are robots rather than people. We see this at once in the opening scene, where the Court Tutor is sent packing by Leonce precisely because he so robotically echoes his master-cum-pupil's words; and then, when he leaves, he bows and scrapes in geometrically mechanical fashion. The pattern is strongly reinforced in the scene that follows. The king's two valets not only simply parrot him and each other, but they voice their vacuities in the convoluted language of ritual obsequiousness:

PETER. . . . Kerl, was bedeutet der Knopf, an was wollte ich mich erinnern?
ERSTER KAMMERDIENER. Als Eure Majestät diesen Knopf in Ihr Schnupftuch zu knüpfen geruhten, so wollten Sie...
PETER. Nun?
ERSTER KAMMERDIENER. Sich an Etwas erinnern.
PETER. Eine verwickelte Antwort!—Ei! Nun an was meint Er?
ZWEITER KAMMERDIENER. Eure Majestät wollten sich an Etwas erinnern, als Sie diesen Knopf in Ihr Schnupftuch zu knüpfen geruhten. (108)

PETER. . . . Fellow, what is the meaning of this knot, of what did I desire to remind myself?
FIRST VALET. When it pleased your Majesty to knot this knot in your handkerchief, you desired...
PETER. Well?
FIRST VALET. To remind yourself of something.

PETER. A complicated answer! Well, what do *you* think?
SECOND VALET. Your Majesty desired to remind yourself of something when it pleased you to knot this knot in your handkerchief.

Needless to say, Büchner is not mocking the servants here, but the system that produces them. Indeed he even makes them subtly subversive of that system: reduced to the status of machines, the servants proffer no service beyond the mechanical. This was already apparent in the Court Tutor's behaviour and the Prince's testy response, and it is clear again here: the Valets' insistently dumb servility throws King Peter into complete confusion and makes him appear even more ludicrous than before. A similar subversive effect is wonderfully demonstrated a few moments later when the King is stricken by his own identity crisis: he is duly 'touched' by his minions' perfectly obsequious and opinionless clockwork response, yet it actually denies him any reassurance, any confirmation of his claim that he is indeed himself:

PETER. . . . Ich bin ich.—Was halten Sie davon, Präsident?
PRÄSIDENT [*gravitätisch langsam*]. Eure Majestät, vielleicht ist es so, vielleicht ist es aber auch nicht so.
DER GANZE STAATSRATH IM CHOR. Ja, vielleicht ist es so, vielleicht ist es aber auch nicht so. (109)

PETER. . . . I am me.—President, what is your opinion on the matter?
PRESIDENT [*slowly and with gravity*]. Your Majesty, it may be the case, but equally it may not be the case.
THE ENTIRE COUNCIL OF STATE IN UNISON. Yes, it may be the case, but equally it may not be the case.

In his letter of 28 July 1835 defending *Dantons Tod*, Büchner castigated the Idealist school for offering only puppets instead of genuine flesh-and-blood human beings ('Marionetten mit himmelblauen Nasen und affectirtem Pathos, aber nicht Menschen von Fleisch und Blut', ii. 444). Through Lenz and Camille, too, he condemns the Idealists' 'wooden puppets' (87) and the 'clanking marionettes' of the contemporary stage (37). Why then in *Leonce und Lena* does he himself show us so many puppet-like figures bereft of flesh-and-blood vitality, figures that seem to fly in the face of that fundamental aesthetic principle so powerfully enunciated in *Lenz*: 'Ich verlange in Allem—Leben, Möglichkeit des Daseins, und dann ist's gut' (86; *I demand in everything—Life, full scope for existence, then nothing else matters*)? Did he no longer believe that there is a fullness of life in even the lowliest of individuals which the writer must enter into and then express ('Man . . . senke sich in das Leben des Geringsten und gebe es wieder', 87)? But of course he *did* still believe it—as *Woyzeck* demonstrates with tremendous force. In *Lenz* Büchner had his protagonist speak of an essential love for humanity that no real artist can do without: 'Man muß die Menschheit lieben, um in das eigenthümliche Wesen jedes einzudringen, es darf einem keiner zu gering, keiner zu häßlich seyn, erst dann kann man sie verstehen' (87; *You need to love mankind to be able to reach the essential being of each individual, you must consider no one too lowly, no one too ugly, only then can you understand them*).—And in *Leonce und Lena* we find the same essential love voiced again through the protagonist at the start of Act III: 'Weißt du auch, Valerio, daß selbst der Geringste unter den Menschen so groß ist, daß das Leben noch viel zu kurz ist, um ihn lieben zu können?' (126; *Do you realize, Valerio, that even the lowliest of people have so much within them that a whole lifetime is far too short to ever love them enough?*) The trouble is that the reductivism that Büchner castigated in the realm of the arts was matched in his view by a grim reductivism within society at large. This was already an issue in *Dantons Tod*, in the Dantonists' opposition to the Jacobins' efforts to redefine humanity according to the 'mechanics' of the 'clockmaker' Rousseau (10), to impose a 'tight little coat' of their own devising that constricted the 'body of the people' and allowed no scope for 'each throb of the arteries, each flexing of the muscles, each thrill of the sinews' (11). What we see in the puppet-like functionaries of *Leonce und Lena* are people whose individual identity has been systematically denied, people who have been turned into virtual machines—commanded to be volunteers and to exhibit contentment; to walk 'symmetrically' and to mop their brow when the King mops his; to ape the King's melancholy; to sustain him in his foolish philosophizing once he has given up the crown (127, 109, 130, 133). As Valerio tells Leonce: once he becomes king he will be able to concoct civil servants out of black frock-coats and white neckties, he will be able to take his scissors to proper human beings and cut them down to size as proper soldiers ('man kann schwarze Fräcke und weiße Halsbinden zu Staatsdienern machen', 'man kann aus ordentlichen Menschen ordentliche Soldaten ausschneiden', 116). The implicit suggestion here that monarchs behave towards their subjects like monstrous children playing with toys is strongly reinforced in the sardonic lines given to Leonce as he enters on his reign at the end of the play:

Nun Lena, siehst du jetzt, wie wir die Taschen voll haben, voll Puppen und Spielzeug? Was wollen wir damit anfangen? Wollen wir ihnen Schnurrbärte machen und ihnen Säbel anhängen? Oder wollen wir ihnen Fräcke anziehen, und sie infusorische Politik und Diplomatie treiben lassen und uns mit dem Mikroskop daneben setzen? (133)

There now, Lena, do you see how full our pockets are, full of puppets and playthings? What shall we do with them? Shall we give them a moustache and an officer's sword? Or dress them in frock-coats, stick them in the ant-hill of politics and diplomacy, and settle down with a microscope to watch them scurry?

On the evidence of these lines the high-and-mighty may seem to have unlimited, almost godlike freedom to shape their subjects however they wish—but their freedom is illusory, for they are 'shaped' themselves: they too are the products of a relentlessly functionalistic system that allows no scope whatever for the essential being, the 'eigenthümliches Wesen', of *any* individual, whether high or low. Indeed King Peter is even more robotic than his robot-servants, and when Büchner has him doubt his own identity on his very first appearance, the comedy is chilling: his valets can easily be imagined as discarding their servant garb of an evening and becoming themselves again—but King Peter is stuck in his kingly role, and any 'self' he may have had has withered away. This is precisely the fate that awaits Crown Prince Leonce—and it is his horror of such an outcome that serves to generate the entire dynamic of the play, right from Leonce's opening remarks, when Büchner has him accuse the Court Tutor in effect of trying to mould him in readiness for his pre-set role in life: 'Mein Herr, was wollen Sie von mir? Mich auf meinen Beruf vorbereiten?' (105). Escape into a different identity: this is signposted as a major theme even before the play has begun, in the quotation from *As You Like It* that heads Act I: 'O wär' ich doch ein Narr! | Mein Ehrgeiz geht auf eine bunte Jacke.' (105; *Oh that I were a fool!* | *I am ambitious for a motley coat.*); and the first sub-scene then duly climaxes in Leonce's yearning exclamation: 'O wer einmal jemand Anders sein könnte! Nur 'ne Minute lang.—' (106; *If only one could be someone else for once! Just for a single minute.—*)

Before we look at Leonce more closely, two general points are worth noting about him. The first is a plain matter of fact: Leonce is by far the most dominant presence in the play. The statistics speak for themselves: Leonce has more than one-third of the play's lines (five times as many as Lena); he is present in seven of the eleven scenes; these scenes, or the relevant portions of them, constitute fully three-quarters of the play. Only Valerio approaches him in importance as a stage presence, inasmuch as he too appears in the same seven scenes, and has over one-quarter of the lines—but he is Leonce's adjunct, and thus serves largely to reinforce his master's pre-eminent role. The second point is a matter of perspective rather than measurable fact—and it is cardinal to our understanding of the play. The question is essentially this: are we supposed to view Leonce with antipathy or sympathy? Is he meant as the contemptible butt of sustained satire, or as a protagonist fully on a par with Danton, Lenz, and Woyzeck? The former view has largely predominated, particularly in the intellectual climate prevailing after the Protest Movement of the 1960s, and rests on a seemingly compelling syllogism: Büchner regards the aristocracy with contempt and loathing; Leonce is an aristocrat; therefore Büchner necessarily depicts Leonce as contemptible and loathsome, fit only for ridicule and opprobrium. But the logic is specious, and while it is undoubtedly possible to read and (worse) to perform the play in such terms, its depth and richness are instantly lost, and we are left with a travesty. It may be the function of King Peter and other peripheral characters to serve as the butt of satire, but there is far more to Leonce than that: as we shall see, he is indeed in all respects the equal of Büchner's other protagonists; like them, he is a voice crying from the edge of the abyss, albeit in comically modulated tones.

The opening lines of the play show Leonce implicitly rejecting his 'Beruf', his pre-programmed calling as the next King of Bum; the closing lines show him assuming precisely that role. In between are three distinct stages, each occupying a single act: *Act I*: exposition of an existential crisis, culminating in flight from Bumland (briefly but intensely echoed in Scene iv by Lena's parallel crisis and flight); *Act II*: journeyings in a 'fourth dimension', climaxing in the encounter with Lena; *Act III*: return to Bumland: marriage, and accession to the throne. The disposition of these acts is striking: much the greatest amount of space is devoted to Act I and its exposition of crisis ($13\frac{1}{2}$ pages in the Lehmann edition, as compared with $7\frac{1}{2}$ and $8\frac{1}{2}$ pages for Acts II and III). This distribution becomes even more striking once we appreciate the incidence of Leonce's own lines. It is often remarked that Lena says less and less throughout the play—but a similar pattern applies to Leonce too: in Act I he speaks no less than two-thirds of his total number of lines; in Act II he speaks only a quarter; in Act III only one-tenth (by way of contrast: Valerio speaks more than one-third of his lines in each of the first two acts, and rather less than one third in Act III).

Leonce's two scenes in Act I (Scenes i and iii) are both constructed on the same triadic pattern, which might be characterized as follows: (i) prelude: dialogue with Court Tutor/Rosetta; (ii) central monologue; (iii) postlude: dialogue with Valerio (the same pattern is then tellingly echoed in the climactic scene between Leonce and Lena, II. iv). Both scenes are small masterpieces of ironic writing in which the mask of comedy is used to voice a sense of deepest ennui and melancholy. Leonce's part needs to be read (and acted) from the outset in the spirit of what Lena is given to say when first she sees him:

Er war so alt unter seinen blonden Locken. Den Frühling auf den Wangen, und den Winter im Herzen. Das ist traurig. ... Es kommt mir ein entsetzlicher Gedanke, ich glaube es gibt Menschen, die unglücklich sind, unheilbar, blos weil *sie sind*. (123, but emphasis as in Mayer edition, BD 63)
He was so old beneath his golden curls. Spring on his cheeks, and winter in his heart. It's sad. ... A terrible thought occurs to my mind: I believe there are people who are unhappy, incurable, simply because *they exist*.

Sadness and melancholy are of course explicitly voiced in the opening scene—and in a way that characteristically combines the cheerful ring of comedy and a more resonant undertone of seriousness: '—Ja es ist traurig ... / Sehr traurig, Euer Hoheit. / Daß die Wolken schon seit drei Wochen von Westen nach Osten ziehen. Es macht mich ganz melancholisch. / Eine sehr gegründete Melancholie.' (105; —*Yes, it's sad ... / Very sad, your Highness. / ... that the clouds have kept travelling from west to east for three weeks on end. It fills me with melancholy. / Such justified melancholy*.) Büchner writes a very similar exchange into *Woyzeck*, with a similar mix of surface buffoonery and underlying seriousness: 'HAUPTMANN. ... Woyzeck, ich kann kein Mühlrad mehr sehn, oder ich werd' melancholisch. WOYZECK. Ja wohl, H. Hauptmann.' (360; HAUPTMANN. ... *Woyzeck, I can't bear to see a millwheel turning any more—it makes me melancholic.* WOYZECK. *Yes, Herr Hauptmann!*) In *Dantons Tod* it is again an endless, pointless round—this time of human beings dressing and undressing themselves day after day—that fills Büchner's protagonist with paralysing sadness: 'Das ist sehr traurig ... Das ist sehr traurig' (31). This first speech of Danton's in Act II, Scene i essentially expresses the theme of boredom ('Das ist sehr langweilig ....')—and it is boredom that is chiefly expressed in Leonce's first monologue:

Es krassirt ein entsetzlicher Müßiggang.—Müßiggang ist aller Laster Anfang.—Was die Leute nicht Alles aus Langeweile treiben! Sie studiren aus Langeweile, sie beten aus Langeweile, sie verlieben, verheirathen und vermehren sich aus Langeweile und sterben endlich an der Langeweile ... Alle diese Helden, diese Genies, diese Dummköpfe, diese Heiligen, diese Sünder, diese Familienväter sind im Grunde nichts als raffinirte Müßiggänger. (106)

A terrible idleness teems on every hand.—Idleness is the fount of all the vices. The things people do out of boredom! They study out of boredom; they fall in love, get married, and reproduce out of boredom; in the end they die out of boredom ... All these heroes, these geniuses, these idiots, these saints and sinners, these worthy fathers—at bottom they are nothing but well-disguised idlers.

Beyond the comic levity of these lines, the grave echoes are unmistakable. How extraordinary, and how eloquent, that Büchner should inaugurate his comedy by echoing the climactic and most despairing scene of *Dantons Tod*, when Camille speaks of the ubiquitous and immutable 'Schaafskopf' hidden behind the plethora of human masks, and then continues:

Die Unterschiede sind so groß nicht, wir Alle sind Schurken und Engel, Dummköpfe und Genies und zwar das Alles in Einem ... Schlafen, Verdaun, Kinder machen das treiben Alle, die übrigen Dinge sind nur Variationen aus verschiedenen Tonarten über das nemliche Thema. (71)

The differences between us are not that great. We're all angels and villains, idiots and geniuses, all at the same time ... Eat, sleep, procreate: everyone does it. The rest of our doings are but variations in different keys on that single theme.

But Leonce's words are an even more direct and more poignant echo of a similarly climactic passage in *Lenz*, when the protagonist is poised on the very edge of the 'abyss of incurable madness' (99). Like Danton torpid on the floor when first we see him, and Leonce torpid on his garden bench, Lenz is torpid in his bed, quite passive and motionless ('ruhig und unbeweglich'); only at the repeated prompting of Oberlin does he speak at last:

'Ja Herr Pfarrer, sehen Sie, die Langeweile! die Langeweile! o! so langweilig . . .' Oberlin sagte ihm, er möge sich zu Gott wenden; da lachte er und sagte: 'Ja wenn ich so glücklich wäre, wie Sie, einen so behaglichen Zeitvertreib aufzufinden, ja man könnte sich die Zeit schon so ausfüllen. Alles aus Müßiggang. Denn die Meisten beten aus Langeweile; die Andern verlieben sich aus Langeweile; die Dritten sind tugendhaft, die Vierten lasterhaft und ich gar nichts, gar nichts, ich mag mich nicht einmal umbringen: es ist zu langweilig! . . .' (95–6)
'Yes, Reverend, it's boredom, you see, boredom! Oh, it's all so boring . . .' Oberlin told him he should turn to God; at that he laughed and said 'Yes, if I had the good fortune to discover a pastime as cosy as yours, I'm sure I could manage to fill the time. Everything comes of idleness. Most people pray out of boredom, others fall in love out of boredom, some turn to virtue, others to vice—and for me there is nothing, nothing at all, I can't even be bothered to kill myself: it's too boring! . . .'

One cannot avoid using the English words 'boredom', 'boring' to render 'Langeweile', 'langweilig'—but they are feeble and inadequate to the point of distorting the issue. The English verb 'to bore' is not graphic in itself; it has no known etymology and no contextualizing cognates; its dictionary definition is merely 'To weary by tedious conversation or simply by the failure to be interesting' (*OED*). 'Langeweile' and 'langweilig' by contrast are expressive words in themselves, and they point at once to the essential element of *time*, or rather the *perception* of time—to wit, time as a kind of oppressive infinitude. To experience time in such terms is to suffer it—an affliction nowhere more graphically expressed than in the buffoonish yet chilling *horror vacui* of the Hauptmann when his fragile equilibrium is threatened by the hectic rushing of his servant Woyzeck in the shaving scene. If Woyzeck shaves him too quickly, what on earth is he to do with the spare ten minutes? ('Was soll ich dann mit den zehn Minuten anfangen, die er heut zu früh fertig wird?', 360). And of course he projects the same problem onto Woyzeck himself:

Woyzeck, bedenk' er, er hat noch seine schöne dreißig Jahr zu leben, dreißig Jahr! macht 360 Monate, und Tage, Stunden, Minuten! Was will er denn mit der ungeheuren Zeit all anfangen? Theil Er sich ein, Woyzeck.

Identity and Ennui 239

Woyzeck, just think, you still have a good thirty years to live, thirty years! That's 360 months, and all those days, hours, minutes! What on earth are you going to do with all this vast expanse of time? Pace it, Woyzeck, pace it!

Both the problem of time-as-infinitude, and that of finding some means of dealing with it, are immediately identified at the beginning of the Hauptmann's next speech: 'Es wird mir ganz angst um die Welt, wenn ich an die Ewigkeit denke. Beschäftigung, Woyzeck, Beschäftigung!' (*I get really frightened for the world when I think of eternity. Activity, Woyzeck, activity!*) This connects with Lenz's bleak response to Pastor Oberlin's admonition that he turn to God, when he disparages the priest's ministry as quite literally a pastime, a 'Zeitvertreib', a mere device for filling time. But it also connects directly with the opening of the comedy: Leonce fobs off the Court Tutor on the grounds that he is so extremely busy that he scarcely knows which way to turn: 'Ich habe alle Hände voll zu thun, ich weiß mir vor Arbeit nicht zu helfen.' The Hauptmann's 'Beschäftigung, Woyzeck, Beschäftigung!' is paralleled in Leonce's questions to the hapless Tutor: '—Bin ich ein Müßiggänger? Habe ich keine Beschäftigung?' (—*Am I an idler? Am I not busy?*) His professed 'Arbeit', his 'Beschäftigung', is of course both mock and mocking, it is a parody of activity-as-'Zeitvertreib': his purported task of spitting onto a stone 365 times in succession suggests the featureless passage of days in the year; he claims to spend entire days betting with himself over the momentous question of whether he has caught an odd or even number of grains of sand on his hand—'Ich . . . kann es tagelang so treiben.'

For Leonce in this mood (as also for Lenz and Danton in their respective frames of mind), existence is a meaningless tract of time that we fill out with our fictions and pretences; it is a 'bare, blank wall' (118) covered over with mirrors that reflect back to us only the specious images that we ourselves invent. In this perspective, there can be no such thing as an authentic identity. Danton's argument vis-à-vis Robespierre was dire enough: there too, all men were said to be frauds in professing to be this or that, whilst being in truth 'Epicureans' (27). But at least the 'Epicurean' argument did entail authenticity of a kind, inasmuch as every individual, whatever their façade, was said to behave in accordance with their essential nature and their inner needs ('Jeder handelt seiner Natur gemäß d. h. er thut, was ihm wohl thut', 27). The view that Büchner bestows on Leonce at the beginning of his comedy is far grimmer. There is no suggestion here that people's pseudo-identities express their essential self; we are not covert Epicureans, but covert idlers, 'raffinirte Müßiggänger'. Our 'identity' as saint or sinner, genius or idiot, hero or paterfamilias is simply a construct devised to lend spurious shape and significance to the emptiness that is our span of life. But the bitter joke for Leonce is the fact that people don't *realize* what frauds they are: they live out of boredom, they die out of boredom—'und—und das ist der Humor davon—Alles mit den wichtigsten Gesichtern, ohne zu merken warum, und meinen Gott weiß was dabei' (106; *what's more—and that's the joke of it all—they do everything with the most earnest of faces, without realizing why, and thinking God-knows-what in the process*). Leonce's terrible malady, the essence of his corrosive ennui, is the very fact that he *knows* (so he thinks) that there are no true and meaningful modes of being, only guises. It is an insight he bitterly regrets: he longs for the blessed delusions of such people as the Court Tutor—those puppets who imagine that they are genuine beings:

Alle ... sind im Grunde nichts als raffinirte Müßiggänger.—Warum muß ich es grade wissen? Warum kann ich mir nicht wichtig werden und der armen Puppe einen Frack anziehen und einen Regenschirm in die Hand geben, daß sie sehr rechtlich und sehr nützlich und sehr moralisch würde?—Der Mann, der eben von mir ging, ich beneidete ihn, ich hätte ihn aus Neid prügeln mögen. O wer einmal jemand Anders sein könnte! Nur 'ne Minute lang.

All ... are at bottom nothing but well-disguised idlers.—Why does it have to be be *me* that knows it? Why can't I take myself seriously and dress this poor puppet body of mine in a frock-coat, stick an umbrella in its hand, and turn it into something thoroughly decent, thoroughly useful and thoroughly moral? That fellow that left me just now, I envied him, I could have beaten him black and blue out of sheer envy. Oh to be someone else for once! Just for a single minute!

Unfortunately his longings are in vain: he cannot escape his insight; he cannot wrap himself in self-delusion; he cannot take himself or anything else seriously. It is because of this that he is a 'joker full of misery' ('ein elender Spaßmacher'), as Büchner has him describe himself in an early draft of the passage just quoted (138): Leonce is a compulsive ironist, a mocker, a man who can only make fun of himself and others—but fun that essentially bespeaks despair and melancholy.

It is here that Valerio comes into his own, for he is a kind of professional scoffer and debunker who serves to potentiate the mocking element in Leonce whilst not himself being tainted by melancholy. Where Leonce is torpid in his ennui, Valerio is a bundle of energy—but negative energy: he is a kind of dynamic demolitionist. Büchner has this supposedly inferior servant come bounding onto the stage, control the dialogue from start to finish (thereby speaking well over twice as many lines as his 'master')—and with great gusto deflate pretension after pretension. Intellectual discourse is ridiculed first in a splendidly absurdist burlesque:

VALERIO [*stellt sich dicht vor den Prinzen, legt den Finger an die Nase und sieht ihn starr an*]. Ja!
LEONCE [*eben so*]. Richtig!
VALERIO. Haben Sie mich begriffen?
LEONCE. Vollkommen.
VALERIO. Nun, so wollen wir von etwas Anderm reden. (106)

VALERIO [*places himself directly in front of the Prince, puts his finger on his nose, and stares at him fixedly*]. Yes!
LEONCE [*follows suit*]. Quite right!
VALERIO. You grasp my meaning?
LEONCE. Perfectly.
VALERIO. Then let's change the subject.

Valerio then rapidly debunks 'romantic feelings' ('romantische Empfindungen'), before proceeding to travesty 'sensitivity to nature' with characteristic earthiness:

Ach Herr, was ich ein Gefühl für die Natur habe! Das Gras steht so schön, daß man ein Ochs sein möchte, um es fressen zu können, und dann wieder ein Mensch, um den Ochsen zu fressen, der solches Gras gefressen. (106–7)

Ah sir, I have such a feeling for nature! The grass is such a splendid sight I'd like to be an ox to gobble it up, then a man once again to gobble the ox that gobbled the grass.

With mock pathos Valerio pretends to lament the fact that flights of enthusiasm tend to have a miserably earthy outcome:

Es ist ein Jammer. Man kann keinen Kirchthurm herunterspringen, ohne den Hals zu brechen. Man kann keine vier Pfund Kirschen mit den Steinen essen, ohne Leibweh zu kriegen. (107)

It fair makes you weep. You can't jump off a church tower without breaking your neck. You can't eat four pounds of cherries, stones and all, without suffering from belly-ache.

The sense of an endless round of futility, first conveyed in the course of Leonce's fopping of the Court Tutor, is reinforced in Valerio's suggestion that he might sit himself in a corner and sing the same vacuous song-phrase again and again the whole night through, then carry on doing so for the rest of his days (107). The theme of identity—or rather the lack of it—is picked up again when Leonce tells Valerio to stop his song as it is enough to turn anyone into a madman. Valerio sardonically retorts that at least then one would be *something*—implying that currently they are as nothing ('Halt's Maul mit deinem Lied, man könnte darüber ein Narr werden. / So wäre man doch etwas. Ein Narr! Ein Narr!', 107).

This harks back to the Act I motto from *As You Like It*: 'O wär' ich doch ein Narr!' with its ambiguous double-reference to 'fool-as-jester' and 'fool-as-madman' (an ambiguity that is clearer in German 'Narr' than in modern English 'fool'). Leonce's near-namesake Lenz does indeed go mad—and the possibility of such a fate befalling Leonce himself is plainly signalled in the course of the play. The allusion is seemingly casual and jokey when Valerio appears from under the table after the Rosetta episode: 'VALERIO. . . . Eure Hoheit scheint mir wirklich auf dem besten Weg, ein wahrhaftiger Narr zu werden. LEONCE. Ja, beim Licht besehen, kommt es mir eigentlich eben so vor.' (112–13; *VALERIO. . . . Seems to me your Highness is well on the way to becoming a veritable lunatic [/fool]. LEONCE. Yes, all things considered, that's just how it seems to me as well.*) But there is certainly nothing casual or jokey about the vision of Leonce-as-madman at the close of Act II, Scene ii, after he has begun to respond to Lena's spell. He ends his initial transport of ecstasy with a repeat of Lena's 'ist denn der Weg so lang?' (*is the way so long?*)—and Valerio promptly takes his cue:

Nein. Der Weg zum Narrenhaus ist nicht so lang, er ist leicht zu finden . . . Ich sehe ihn schon auf einer breiten Allee dahin, an einem eiskalten Wintertag den Hut unter dem Arm, wie er sich in die langen Schatten unter die kahlen Bäume stellt und mit dem Schnupftuch fächelt.—Er ist ein Narr! (123)

No, the way to the madhouse is not so very long, it's easy to find . . . Already I can see him heading that way along a broad avenue of trees on an

Identity and Ennui 243

ice-cold day in the middle of winter, holding his hat under his arm, and stepping amongst the bare trees and their longdrawn shadows, fanning his face with his handkerchief.—He's a lunatic [/fool]!

The narrative scope of Lenz allows just such a dire vision to become the fictive reality; within the very different context of comedy with its inherent playfulness and obbligato happy ending, it remains a vision—a pointer to a terrible potentiality: there but for the grace of genre goes Leonce.

Meanwhile back in Act I, Scene i, Valerio is up to his tricks by switching identities. Leonce yearned to swap his wit for unwittingness and become someone else—now Valerio does become someone else, swapping his reason for insanity and turning himself for the nonce into Alexander the Great: 'Ein Narr! Ein Narr! Wer will mir seine Narrheit gegen meine Vernunft verhandeln? Ha, ich bin Alexander der Große!' (107). The reader/spectator readily goes along with the illusion as Valerio enacts it by seeing the sunshine as his imperial crown, and a grasshopper and sundry other creatures as Commander-in-Chief, Finance Minister, courtier, Court Physician; again here, an alternative reality is conjured out of nothing. But we are rapidly disabused. Büchner has Valerio prick his own bubble: such delusions are indeed the realm of the mad, and plain reality is very different:

Und zu diesen köstlichen Phantasieen bekommt man gute Suppe, gutes Fleisch, gutes Brod, ein gutes Bett und das Haar umsonst geschoren—im Narrenhaus nämlich—, während ich mit meiner gesunden Vernunft mich höchstens noch zur Beförderung der Reife auf einen Kirschbaum verdingen könnte (107)

And on top of these delectable delusions you get good soup, good meat, good bread, a good bed and your hair cut for nothing—in the madhouse, that is; but as for me with my unshakeable sanity: I'd be lucky to get a job in a cherry tree helping the fruit to turn ripe

Madness here is not a mode of reality, but a refuge from it; and Valerio's words are an echo of those that Büchner gave to Camille in Dantons Tod after he sees his beloved Lucile in her incipient madness: 'Der Himmel verhelf' ihr zu einer behaglichen fixen Idee. Die allgemeinen fixen Ideen, welche man die gesunde Vernunft tauft, sind unerträglich langweilig.' (70; *Heaven grant her the comfort of a cosy delusion. The conventional delusions that people call sanity are unbearably boring.*) Within the comedy, Leonce offers up a similar prayer for his own escape into blissfully blinkered delusion: 'O Gott! Die Hälfte meines Lebens soll ein Gebet sein, wenn mir nur ein Strohhalm bescheert wird, auf dem ich reite, wie auf einem prächtigen Roß, bis ich selbst auf dem Stroh liege' (122; *Oh God! I'll give half my life to prayer if I'm granted but a single straw on which to ride as though on a splendid stallion until the day I'm laid on straw myself*). Within a minute of speaking these words he encounters Lena—whether as mystical reality or straw-like delusion we shall see in due course. But back in the play's opening scene no such epiphany or blessed delusion is anywhere in prospect. Instead, we are offered another comic reminder of the stereotyped categories that alone seem available in the real world, when Leonce with mock bombast asks Valerio to define himself: 'Aber Edelster, dein Handwerk, deine Profession, dein Gewerbe, dein Stand, deine Kunst?' (107; *But tell me, most noble sir, your trade, your profession, your business, your station, your craft?*) The ironic question is matched by an equally ironic reply: 'VALERIO [*mit Würde*]. Herr, ich habe die große Beschäftigung, müßig zu gehen, ich habe eine ungemeine Fertigkeit im Nichtsthun, ich besitze eine ungeheure Ausdauer in der Faulheit [etc.]' (107; *VALERIO [with dignity]. My consuming occupation is to be thoroughly idle, I am uncommonly skilled in doing nothing. I have phenomenal endurance in the realm of laziness [etc.]*). In the light of the play's ending these lines may be seen to reflect a crucial point of intersection at which 'Müßiggang' (*idleness*) is potentially a positive as well as a negative, the measure of utopian fullness as much as of dystopian vacuity. But at this juncture we can simply take note of the fact that here, almost at the end of the opening scene, Büchner contrives an echo of its beginning: Valerio's 'ich habe die große Beschäftigung, müßig zu gehen' is an unmistakable if modifed echo of Leonce's 'Bin ich ein Müßiggänger? Habe ich keine Beschäftigung?' The problem of time, and how to fill it, is thus confirmed as a central issue.

One related and particularly telling feature of the opening scene of *Leonce und Lena* is the way that Büchner plays repeatedly on the notion of acting. Already in *Dantons Tod*, play-acting was not just passively 'there' as the given medium, but was repeatedly made part of the message—in the use of 'Simon the Prompter'; in the histrionics of the orators and the inclusion of on-stage audiences; in the many allusions to life as an act (like Danton's 'wir stehen immer auf dem Theater, wenn wir auch zulezt im Ernst erstochen werden'; cf.

above, p. 149). Life as an act: this is precisely the image that Büchner makes central to Leonce's first monologue: people profess to be this or that, but in fact all are acting a part, all are 'raffinirte Müßiggänger', idlers driven by their 'Langeweile' to take refuge in some neatly labelled role. Being blissfully unaware of what is going on, they take themselves entirely seriously, and remain happily and permanently ensconced in their assumed role. Leonce however is indeed aware, and is stricken by a seemingly absolute inability to take himself seriously, to adopt some mask or other and regard it as his authentic identity. All this is stated in clear terms in the monologue; but it is a mark of Büchner's dramatic genius that he also *enacts* it in the texture of the scene. Only when he is alone in the monologue do we see Leonce's fictive self (largely expressed in the *denial* of self); for the rest, what we see is play-acting, a succession of essentially desperate japes. This is immediately evident in the sub-scene with the Court Tutor. Having implicitly refused to allow himself to be moulded into the persona of king-to-be, Leonce instantly and with blatant irony affects that of An Extremely Busy Man. Comic effects are generally procured by the exploitation of contrasts or discrepancies—and that is certainly the case here. For one thing, there is a complete disjunction between what we hear and what we see: Leonce's 'speech-bubbles' tell us he is supremely busy, while our eyes tell us that he is in fact semi-supine on a garden bench ('halb ruhend auf einer Bank'). There is also a gross discrepancy between what is ordinarily understood by 'work', and Leonce's definition of it. Leonce's whole spiel to the Court Tutor is a string of manifest inventions: there is no pretence that he *really* means to spit 365 times on the stone, or that he has *really* spent entire days betting with himself over the number of sand-grains left on his hand. His demeanour throughout is evasively ironic; instead of showing us his face, he brandishes a mask. And in the ensuing monologue we discover why: because he believes (for the present at least) that there is no such thing as real faces, only specious masks disguising infinite ennui. The same pattern then continues in the rest of the scene: the depth of Leonce's existential crisis having been summed up in his yearning to be someone else, a 'someone else' immediately appears in the person of Valerio, who sweeps him up into a flurry of tomfoolery in which spoof follows spoof. The antics and bantering tone of the two figures are comic, but also discomfiting: coming after the monologue, they seem like a dance on the edge of a precipice.

If this seems overstated, we need only turn to Leonce's next scene (I. iii), where we find a real dance being performed on stage—a dance of the most intense poignancy that speaks by turns of surface gaiety and deathly melancholy:

LEONCE. . . . Tanze, Rosetta, tanze, daß die Zeit mit dem Takt deiner niedlichen Füße geht!
ROSETTA. Meine Füße gingen lieber aus der Zeit. [*Sie tanzt und singt.*]

> O meine müden Füße, ihr müßt tanzen
> In bunten Schuhen,
> Und möchtet lieber tief, tief
> Im Boden ruhen.
>
> O meine heißen Wangen, ihr müßt glühen
> Im wilden Kosen,
> Und möchtet lieber blühen
> Zwei *weiße* Rosen.
>
> O meine armen Augen, ihr müßt blitzen
> Im Strahl der Kerzen,
> Aber lieber schlieft ihr aus im Dunkeln
> Von euren Schmerzen. (110–11; BD 37)

LEONCE. . . . Dance, Rosetta, dance, so that time goes by to the rhythmic beat of your pretty little feet!
ROSETTA. My feet would sooner go out of time. [*She dances and sings.*]

> My poor tired feet, you have to dance
> In shoes so gay,
> And yet you'd sooner rest deep, deep
> Beneath the clay.
>
> My poor hot cheeks, you have to flare
> With passion's might,
> For all the pallor you would sooner wear
> Of roses *white*.
>
> My poor, poor eyes you have to sparkle
> In the candles' light,
> And yet to flee your pain you'd sooner sleep
> In darkest night.

In fact the entire sub-scene with Rosetta builds to a tragicomic celebration—more tragic than comic—of death and burial (to be followed in Act II by a kind of resurrection) and here again play-acting is a crucial element.

Identity and Ennui 247

This proves to be the case from the very beginning of the scene (109). Whereas the resurrectional encounter with Lena will take place in a fictively real dimension of night and dreams, Leonce here contrives an entirely artificial kind of night: the prosaic light of day is deliberately shut out ('Weg mit dem Tag!'), and an illusion of mystical, magical night ('tiefe ambrosische Nacht') is summoned up before our eyes through Leonce's manipulation of the stage-set, even to the extent of cueing-in off-stage violins ('Musik! Wo sind die Violinen? ... [... *Man hört Musik aus der Ferne.*]'). The pretence is so convincing that the reader/spectator is completely taken in: Leonce's flight of lyricism seems genuinely felt, with no trace of the earlier tone of irony and mockery, and everything seems set for a lovers' tryst in a meltingly romantic ambience. But it is indeed merely an act, as we begin to realize as soon as Rosetta appears only to be greeted by a comically parrot-like response from her beau:

ROSETTA. ... Leonce!
LEONCE. Rosetta!
ROSETTA. Leonce!
LEONCE. Rosetta! (110)

Having fopped his Tutor in Scene i, Leonce cruelly toys with his sweetheart in Scene iii—and here too, as we might expect, it is corrosive ennui that Büchner makes the driving force behind his behaviour. The motifs of 'Beschäftigung', 'Müßiggang', 'Arbeit', 'Langeweile' all recur here—especially 'Langeweile'. Instead of loving and cherishing Rosetta as we may suppose him to have done in the past, Leonce makes her in effect the scapegoat for his infinite 'Langeweile'; to his jaundiced eye she seems merely the image and embodiment of his *taedium vitae*, his sense of emptiness and absence of meaning:

ROSETTA. So liebst du mich aus Langeweile?
LEONCE. Nein, ich habe Langeweile, weil ich dich liebe. Aber ich liebe meine Langeweile wie dich. Ihr seid eins .... [*Er umfaßt sie.*] Komm liebe Langeweile, deine Küsse sind ein wollüstiges Gähnen, und deine Schritte sind ein zierlicher Hiatus. (110)

ROSETTA. So you love me out of boredom?
LEONCE. No, I'm bored because I love you. But I love my boredom as much as you. You're one and the same. ... [*He embraces her.*] Come, dear boredom, your kisses are a passionate yawn, your every step a delicate hiatus.

At the heart of Leonce's malady is a perception of time as a featureless infinitude, and this is emphasized particularly in his cuttingly ironic response to Rosetta's harmless lover's question whether he will go on loving her for ever ('Du liebst mich, Leonce? ... Und immer?'):

> Das ist ein langes Wort: immer! Wenn ich dich nun noch fünftausend Jahre und sieben Monate liebe, ist's genug? Es ist zwar viel weniger, als immer, ist aber doch eine erkleckliche Zeit, und wir können uns Zeit nehmen, uns zu lieben. (110)
>
> It's a long word: 'forever'! If I love you for another five thousand years and seven months, will that be long enough? It's admittedly much less than forever, but it's quite a long time all the same, and we can take lots of time for our loving.

Leonce's role-playing is nowhere more disturbing than in the ensuing sequence with its sudden shift from quasi-ordinary dialogue into the poetic counterpoint of Rosetta's dance and song, and Leonce's daydream vision of himself feasting in ancient Rome ('Ich bin ein Römer...'). It seems clear that Büchner did indeed mean this contrapuntally: the 'indeß' in the stage direction 'indeß träumend vor sich hin' (111; *meanwhile dreaming to himself*) implies that Rosetta and Leonce perform their routines simultaneously; and given appropriate lighting and choreography, Rosetta with her melancholy song and correspondingly melancholy dance-movements becomes the poignant embodiment or enactment of Leonce's vision. Betraying his addiction to death yet again, Büchner offers us the eerie spectacle of a death at once deeply sad and deliciously beautiful—a spectacle moreover that culminates in necrophilia, be it ever so poetical:

> O, eine sterbende Liebe ist schöner, als eine werdende. Ich bin ein Römer; bei dem köstlichen Mahle spielen zum Dessert die goldnen Fische in ihren Todesfarben. Wie ihr das Roth von den Wangen stirbt, wie still das Auge ausglüht, wie leis das Wogen ihrer Liebe steigt und fällt! Adio, adio meine Liebe, ich will deine Leiche lieben.
>
> Oh, a dying love is more beautiful than one that's growing. There, I'm a Roman: to bring the exquisite banquet to a fitting close the golden fish disport themselves in all the colours of their dying agony. Oh, how the red of her cheeks dies away, how quietly the fire in her eye goes out, how gently the lilt of her limbs first quickens, then fades! Addio, addio, my love, I shall cherish your corpse.

Identity and Ennui 249

Ostensibly it is only an abstract entity, their love, that is dying; but it is so strongly personified both within Leonce's vision, and in Rosetta as she sings and dances, that the abstraction is far transcended—all the more so since Büchner has Rosetta in her song express such vivid longing for her own death. And of course the impact of Leonce's vision becomes even stronger when we realize that it echoes the climactic despair of the final gaol scene in *Dantons Tod*, when Camille imagines the firmament of air and stars as a dish of golden carp on the table of the gods—'und die seeligen Götter lachen ewig und die Fische sterben ewig und die Götter erfreuen sich ewig am Farbenspiel des Todeskampfes' (72; cf. above, p. 153).

Leonce's dream is broken by Rosetta approaching him once again ('Rosetta nähert sich ihm wieder'), and we see him revert at once to his posture of ironic, unsympathetic detachment when he mocks her tears. Moments later we see him take refuge in yet another act, when he keeps Rosetta at bay with his elaborate pretence of having enshrined the frail corpse of their love within the vault of his skull. At one level this is a kind of joke, albeit a cruel one; but beyond the joke there is also a real poignancy, particularly because Leonce's words echo Rosetta's song: where previously she had sung of her glowing cheeks wanting to take on the pallor of death as 'two white roses', Leonce now asks her if she sees the 'two white roses' on the cheeks of their dead love.

One of the most important functions of Rosetta within this expositional phase of the play is that she is the first character to serve as a real foil to Leonce. The Tutor was too much a grovelling court robot, and too briefly present; whereas Valerio in Act I, Scene i was not in any sense a foil but rather an accomplice, a virtual echo of his master. Rosetta on the other hand serves as a kind of luminous background against which Leonce's dark profile becomes quite sharply defined. Superficially Rosetta is reminiscent of Marion in that she appears once only, is never referred to elsewhere (except later in the same scene: 115), and is left entirely unexplained. Essentially, though, she is a quite different figure, without any of Marion's tantalizing prehistory, her maelstrom nature far beyond the confines of morality, her mysterious and dangerous magnetism. Indeed Rosetta is put across as the very opposite: as an exemplum of good, honest ordinariness, an unaffected, wholesome girl with all her natural emotions and values fresh and intact. The sadness in her two songs is not the poisonous ontological melancholy of Leonce, but simple and touching grief at the loss of her love. The absolute difference between them is perfectly demonstrated in Leonce's response to her tears: 'Thränen, Rosetta? Ein feiner Epikuräismus—weinen zu können.' (*Tears, Rosetta? What subtle epicureanism—being able to cry.*) Being too blighted by his ennui to find anything worth crying about, Leonce sees Rosetta's tears—like everything else in conventional life—as merely a subtle kind of fraud. But Büchner surely does not encourage us to believe Leonce here: Rosetta's tears, and her sadness in general, move us precisely because they seem warm and genuine—and as such they show up the cankered coldness of Leonce's own melancholy, the practical effects of which are simply but graphically conveyed in Rosetta's departure:

ROSETTA [*entfernt sich traurig und langsam, sie singt im Abgehn*].

> Ich bin eine arme Waise,
> Ich fürchte mich ganz allein.
> Ach lieber Gram—
> Willst du nicht kommen mit mir heim?

ROSETTA [*leaves sadly and slowly, singing as she goes*].

> Such a poor waif am I,
> I'm frightened all on my own.
> Oh dear grief I beg you—
> Won't you take me home?

As suggested earlier, the sub-scene with Rosetta is essentially a prelude that prepares the way for the central matter of Act I, Scene iii, which is Leonce's monologue—his longest speech in the play. What we are shown here is a man who has reached the ultimate depths of his existential crisis. Once again, time looms as a ruinous problem. Future time is seen in doubly negative terms—as both horribly full, and horribly unfillable. Leonce sees life stretching ahead of him as an endless and all too predictable round of dreary sameness:

Ich stülpe mich jeden Tag vier und zwanzigmal herum, wie einen Handschuh. O ich kenne mich, ich weiß was ich in einer Viertelstunde, was ich in acht Tagen, was ich in einem Jahre denken und träumen werde. (112)

I turn myself inside out twenty-four times each day, like a glove. Oh yes, I know myself, I know what I'll be thinking and dreaming in a quarter of an hour, a week, a year.

But as a corollary of this he can envisage no future of his own making, he can see no prospect of inscribing his own particular meaning on his life, which in consequence gapes at him like a great white sheet of paper that he is meant to fill with writing, but for which he cannot find even a single letter: 'Mein Leben gähnt mich an, wie ein großer weißer Bogen Papier, den ich vollschreiben soll, aber ich bringe keinen Buchstaben heraus.' As for the present, Leonce sees it in a sustained and graphic image as merely a played-out void littered only with the dead and broken leftovers from a past of pretence and frivolity:

Mein Kopf ist ein leerer Tanzsaal, einige verwelkte Rosen und zerknitterte Bänder auf dem Boden, geborstene Violinen in der Ecke, die letzten Tänzer haben die Masken abgenommen und sehen mit todmüden Augen einander an.

My head is an empty dance-hall, on its floor a few wilted roses and crumpled ribbons, in a corner the remnants of broken violins, the last few dancers have removed their masks and stare at each other with dead-tired eyes.

The Rosetta episode, however, not only triggers an intensified restatement of Leonce's familiar ennui. It also serves Büchner as the pretext for identifying what is surely the heart of his crisis: the apparent failure not only of a particular love, but of love in its totality. And in putting this across, Büchner delivers one of the key passages not only in the comedy, but in his œuvre as a whole.

Stricken as he is with ennui, Leonce can see love only as a delusion, a kind of protracted hallucination from which one ultimately emerges to re-enter the domain of sober reason and prosaic reality:

Ein sonderbares Ding um die Liebe. Man liegt ein Jahr lang schlafwachend zu Bette, und an einem schönen Morgen wacht man auf, trinkt ein Glas Wasser, zieht seine Kleider an und fährt sich mit der Hand über die Stirn und besinnt sich—und besinnt sich. (112)

What a strange thing love is. You lie in bed half-asleep for a year, then one fine morning you wake up, drink a glass of water, put on your clothes, pass your hand across your forehead, and you come to your senses—you come to your senses.[1]

---

[1] Leonce's 'und besinnt sich—und besinnt sich' is commonly understood in the now much more normal sense of 'ponder', 'think things over' (cf. the translations in

On this jaundiced view, love is merely a narcotic, and so we find Leonce ironically wondering what 'wine' might turn up for him to get drunk on today: 'In welcher Bouteille steckt denn der Wein, an dem ich mich heute betrinken soll?' It is a measure of his despair, however, that he doubts whether he is capable any more even of getting drunk: 'Bringe ich es nicht einmal mehr so weit?' Leonce is indeed in despair here—and the reason is spelt out in the most revealing terms:

—Mein Gott, wieviel Weiber hat man nöthig, um die Scala der Liebe auf und ab zu singen? Kaum daß Eine einen Ton ausfüllt. Warum ist der Dunst über unsrer Erde ein Prisma, das den weißen Gluthstrahl der Liebe in einen Regenbogen bricht?

—My God, how many women does a man need to sing his way right up and down the scale of love? Any one woman covers scarce but a single tone. Why is the haze above our earth a prism that splits the white hot stream of love into all the colours of the rainbow?

The passage rings numerous bells. The notion of love as a single streaming 'Gluthstrahl' is reminiscent for instance of Marion's description of her being in *Dantons Tod*: 'Ich bin immer nur Eins ... eine Gluth, ein Strom'. It is reminiscent of that vital creative force evoked through Camille: 'die Schöpfung, die glühend, brausend und leuchtend ... sich jeden Augenblick neu gebiert'. Above all, the passage recalls the eloquent words given to Lacroix just prior to the Marion scene: '[Danton] sucht eben die mediceische Venus stückweise bey allen Grisetten des palais royal zusammen ... Es ist ein Jammer, daß die Natur die Schönheit ... zerstückelt und sie so in Fragmenten in die Körper gesenkt hat.' In both cases there is the crucial sense of a shattered whole: beauty smashed into fragments and dispersed into different bodies; the radiant force of love split apart into the discrete notes of the scale, the different colours of the rainbow. Leonce's predicament is grim, and typically it is expressed through an antithetical image: in stark contrast to the streaming,

the OUP and Methuen edns.: '—and [you] start to think'; '—and [one] thinks to oneself'). But the term is undoubtedly meant in the older sense of 'come to one's senses', as reflected in the relevant examples in Grimm's *Deutsches Wörterbuch*, e.g.: 'wo möglich, eh sie von dem schlage sich | in Wien besinnen und zuvor dir kommen'; 'ich bin nicht krank, ich habe kraft zu stehn ... es ist vorüber, ich besinne mich wieder' (both examples are taken from Schiller). Cf. also the residual modern usage reflected in *Duden. Das große Wörterbuch der deutschen Sprache* (Mannheim, 1977): 'er hat sich endlich besonnen (er ist zur Vernunft gekommen)'.

fiery 'Gluthstrahl' of love, Leonce sits freezing in the thinnest of air: 'Ich sitze wie unter einer Luftpumpe. Die Luft so scharf und dünn, daß mich friert, als sollte ich in Nankinghosen Schlittschuh laufen.' (*I sit as though in a vacuum-jar. The air's so sharp and thin I feel as cold as if I were ice-skating in cotton trousers.*) The levity of the ice-skating image does not alter the fact that the underlying sense of cold isolation, of remoteness from what really matters, is just as severe as anything depicted in Büchner's other protagonists (for instance the terrible 'cold resignation' of Lenz at the end of the story). The comic genre allows and indeed encourages a different presentation and outcome from the other works, but the essential crisis is just as grave, and has the same destructive potential, albeit only hinted at, as for instance in Valerio's vision of Leonce journeying to the madhouse at the end of Act II, Scene ii.

Another hint at this potential occurs in the monologue itself in Leonce's enigmatic question to his non-existent companions: '—Meine Herren, meine Herren, wißt ihr auch, was Caligula und Nero waren? Ich weiß es.' (—*Gentlemen, gentlemen, do you know what Nero and Caligula were? I know.*) Nero and Caligula were of course infamously cruel and capricious tyrants, and what Büchner is surely doing here is to point to such an element within Leonce himself. His realm is merely the comic kingdom of Bum, not ancient Rome, and the entire context within which he exists and acts is comic. But within the scope and possibilities of the genre he is indeed a kind of pocket Nero or Caligula, driven by his poisonous ennui. We see this particularly clearly in the case of Rosetta. He doesn't physically destroy her—but he does destroy her figuratively, and he becomes metaphorically a Roman ('Ich bin ein Römer') when he feasts on the beautiful spectacle of their love's dying agony (111). In Act I, Scene i, he is cruel to the Court Tutor, especially in his jibe about the poor man's legs when he performs his grovelling final bow (and of course he subsequently admits that he felt like thrashing him out of pure envy, 106). Again he is systematically cruel to the hapless President in Act I, Scene iii, energetically abetted by his stooge Valerio (114–15). They fop and fluster him without pause; and when Leonce tells him he is risking a stroke by not getting his words out ('Sie riskiren einen Schlagfluß, wenn Ihnen Ihre Rede zurücktritt'), we are easily reminded of the Doctor/Professor terrifying the Hauptmann with a similar threat: 'Ja H. Hauptmann [S]ie können eine apoplexia cerebralis kriegen [etc.]' (370).

Büchner even has Leonce explicitly reflect on his nasty treatment of the President and the other members of the State Council: 'Wie gemein ich mich zum Ritter an den armen Teufeln gemacht habe! Es steckt nun aber doch einmal ein gewisser Genuß in einer gewissen Gemeinheit.' (116; *How mean of me to lord it so over those poor devils! But there's no denying it, there's a certain pleasure to be had from a certain meanness.*) We need to be clear that Büchner puts this over not as some kind of innate defect in Leonce's personality, and certainly not as a bit of psychological local colour, but rather as a distortion wrought by the cancerous malady of ennui. We are back here with the fundamental issue of identity: in his persona as a comedy-Caligula, Leonce is emphatically not 'himself'. It is only when he is bathed and regenerated by the 'Gluthstrahl der Liebe' through the person of Lena that he recovers his true being—a transformation graphically reflected in the question he puts to Valerio at the start of Act III, a question that echoes the Nero–Caligula question in its opening phrase, and yet goes on to reveal a diametrically different perspective: 'Weißt du auch, Valerio, daß selbst der Geringste unter den Menschen so groß ist, daß das Leben noch viel zu kurz ist, um ihn lieben zu können?' (126; *Do you realize, Valerio, that even the lowliest of people have so much within them that a whole lifetime is far too short to ever love them enough?*)

13
Epiphany, Death, Transfiguration

MUCH the most revealing aspect of the 'Gluthstrahl'/'Luftpumpe' passage is that it points to the source of Leonce's ennui. As we might expect from the example of Danton, the intensity of Leonce's despair reflects above all the intensity of his hope; in Leonce as in Danton, Büchner shows us an ardent idealist still fired by a residual 'Enthusiasmus' (121), but constantly confounded by reality. A clear hint of this is given in Leonce's first speech, when Büchner has him sardonically own to an ideal that is inherently and absurdly unachievable: 'O wer sich einmal auf den Kopf sehen könnte! Das ist eins von meinen Idealen.' (105; *Oh if only one could see the top of one's head for once! It's one of my ideals.*) The motif recurs soon after Valerio's first entry, when Leonce commiserates with him over his professed longing to become an ox so that he can eat the luscious grass (etc.): 'Unglücklicher, Sie scheinen auch an Idealen zu laboriren.' (107; *Poor wretch, you too seem to be afflicted by ideals.*) In the early manuscript version of the scene, Valerio's response specifically identified the gulf between ideal and reality, albeit in comic, earthy terms: 'O Gott! ich laufe schon seit 8 Tagen einem Ideal von Rindfleisch nach, ohne es irgendwo in der Realität anzutreffen.' (139; *Oh God! I've been chasing my ideal of beef for a week without meeting it anywhere in reality.*) We have already seen how Leonce attempts to flee reality at the close of Act I, Scene iii—and escape to an ideal Arcadia full of ardour, holiness, depth, intensity. Soon afterwards, towards the beginning of Act II, Scene i, Leonce's quest is given specific shape in his reply to Valerio when the latter sarcastically voices his incomprehension at the Prince's unwillingness to become King and marry a beautiful princess:

Aber Valerio, die Ideale! Ich habe das Ideal eines Frauenzimmers in mir und muß es suchen. Sie ist unendlich schön und unendlich geistlos. Die Schönheit ist da so hülflos, so rührend, wie ein neugebornes Kind. Es ist ein köstlicher Contrast. Diese himmlisch stupiden Augen, dieser göttlich einfältige Mund, dieses schafsnasige griechische Profil, dieser geistige Tod in diesem geistigen Leib. (119)

But ideals, Valerio, ideals! I have this ideal of a woman within me and must go and seek it. She is infinitely beautiful and infinitely mindless. Her beauty is as helpless, as touching, as a newborn child. What an exquisite contrast: these eyes of heavenly stupidity, this mouth of godlike inanity, this profile so asinine and classically perfect, this deadness of mind in this spiritual body.

What are we to make of this teasing passage—one of the trickiest in this trickily ironic text? It could be argued that it is merely a spoof, a derisive send-up of male idealizations of Woman. But it speaks with a double voice—most clearly in the elaborate and explicit contrasting of 'stupide', 'einfältig', 'schafnasig'/'himmlisch', 'göttlich', 'griechisch'. In his prevailing condition of radical ennui, irony is Leonce's only refuge from the abyss (as 'morality' is the Hauptmann's, or madness Lucile's). So unrealizable do his hopes and ideals seem to be that he can only profess them in a tone of mockery, pretending not to take them seriously. But in truth idealism is central to his fictive being, as is made clear beyond question in the monologue in Act I, Scene iii: he has absolute faith that the 'weiße Gluthstrahl der Liebe' is out there in all its magnificent intensity and fullness, even though in the given world it seemingly manifests itself only in refracted, fragmented form—in the discrete colours of the spectrum, in the discrete notes of the musical scale. And before long, that faith is amply borne out in his resurrectional encounter with Lena (unless, of course, that too is a delusion . . .).

Assuming that a genuine ideal is indeed envisioned despite the irony, what does it consist in? In particular, what are we meant to understand by Leonce's projection of his ideal woman as both 'unendlich schön' and 'unendlich geistlos'? Although the latter element is sharply ironized in terms of 'stupidity', 'simple-mindedness', 'asininity', 'dieser geistige Tod', I suggest that it is essentially meant quite seriously, and that it can best be understood in terms of Büchner's familiar antipathy to cerebration and ratiocination, and his concomitant stress on the direct, unmediated apprehension of existence and truth. It is as well to remind ourselves of what Büchner was writing during the very same period in his Descartes commentary:

Der Grundcharakter aller unmittelbaren Wahrheit ist das Poniren, das Affirmiren schlechthin, durch das secundäre Geschäft des Denkens gar nicht vermittelt, wesentlich nicht einmal berührt. Die Existenz seiner und der

Epiphany, Death, Transfiguration

Dinge außer uns wird auf rein positive, unmittelbare, von der Function des Denkens unabhängige Weise erkannt.... es ist positiv dem Bewußtseyn gegeben, daß das Ich ist und dießes Seyn ist dem Denken unzugänglich (ii. 140)

The basic characteristic of all unmediated truth is postulation and affirmation pure and simple, without its being mediated in any way, or even touched in any essential respect, by the secondary activity of thought. Our own existence and that of things outside us is apprehended in a purely positive, immediate way, independently of the function of thought. ... it is positively vouchsafed to our consciousness that the self exists, and this being is inaccessible to thought

For Büchner it was women above all who were untainted by the false urge to build elaborate mental constructs, and who thus apprehended existence in the purest, that is, the most immediate and 'mind-free' fashion. It is surely this that is implied when he has Marion claim that she connects with the world around her through feeling alone ('ich ... hänge mit Allem um mich nur durch eine Empfindung zusammen', 22); and it is implied again in the presentation of Lucile as a woman who is all intuition and sensibility, unencumbered by mind (cf. above, p. 194).

The question is: how does all this work out in *Leonce und Lena*? Is Leonce's 'Ideal eines Frauenzimmers' borne out or reflected in any way in Büchner's presentation of Rosetta and Lena? In this respect, statistics tell a startling tale. We know of course that Lena is a central figure in the play: she is the Princess to Leonce's Prince; she is ranked equally with him in the title; their equal status is ritually celebrated in their royal wedding; she appears in six of the eleven scenes—only one fewer than Leonce. Rosetta by comparison is unquestionably a minor figure, appearing in only one scene, and for little more than one-third of that scene. And yet these quite different degrees of dramatic importance are not matched at all by the amount that Büchner has the two figures actually say in their respective encounters with Leonce. In Rosetta's one sub-scene with Leonce, she speaks some thirty-three lines; in Lena's three appearances with Leonce, she delivers only *eleven* lines that are either addressed directly to him, or spoken when she is aware of his presence—lines that amount in all to only forty-four words (fewer for instance than Leonce speaks in the first three sentences of his opening speech). The sheer verbality of the Leonce–Rosetta encounter is a subtle indicator of the failure of their relationship: their separateness is perfectly conveyed in their bandying of words, as though across an invisible wall. And it is surely no coincidence that Büchner has Leonce comment on Rosetta's 'cleverness' and 'sharpness of mind', and her habit of winning arguments: 'Du hast Recht wie immer. Du bist ein kluges Mädchen, und ich halte viel auf deinen Scharfsinn.' (110). For all her naturalness and spontaneity and flower-like name, Rosetta is far from being 'geistlos'. Lena for her part is certainly not presented as 'geistlos' in any negative sense: she is not in the least 'stupide', 'einfältig', 'schafnasig', or 'geistig tot'. But her transcendental effect on Leonce has nothing whatever to do with mind or verbality, but rather with an ineffable radiance. In this she is an actualization of that lost presence evoked in Lenz's recollection of Friederike Brion:

Sehn Sie... wenn sie so durch's Zimmer ging, und so halb für sich allein sang, und jeder Tritt war eine Musik, es war so eine Glückseligkeit in ihr, und das strömte in mich über, ich war immer ruhig, wenn ich sie ansah, oder sie so den Kopf an mich lehnte... (92)

You see... she just had to walk through the room, singing half to herself, and every step was music, there was such bliss in her, and it flowed over into me, I was always at peace whenever I looked at her or she leant her head against me...

It is true that Leonce's metamorphosis is triggered when he hears Lena speak. But it is not a question of his mind responding to her actual words and their content; it is an entirely non-rational, even mystical process whereby the sheer resonance of her voice instantly reaches through to his deepest self—a process already prefigured in the motto chosen for this second act: 'Wie ist mir eine Stimme doch erklungen | Im tiefsten Innern...' (118; *Oh how a voice has sounded | Deep within me...*). It is Leonce's innermost being that is suddenly, wondrously enspirited, regenerated by the very sound of Lena's voice:

—O diese Stimme: Ist denn der Weg so lang? Es reden viele Stimmen über die Erde und man meint sie sprächen von andern Dingen, aber ich hab' sie verstanden. Sie ruht auf mir wie der Geist, da er über den Wassern schwebte, eh' das Licht ward. Welch Gähren in der Tiefe, welch Werden in mir, wie sich die Stimme durch den Raum gießt. (123)

—Oh that voice: 'Is the way so long?' Many voices speak over the earth and you think they speak of other things, but this one I have understood. It rests upon me like the spirit that hung over the waters before the coming of the light. What ferment in the deepest depths, what burgeoning of life within me, oh how the voice goes coursing through the very air.

What is represented here is is a virtual rebirth, in which Leonce is first explicitly delivered of his melancholy ('Gott sei Dank, daß ich anfange mit der Melancholie niederzukommen'), and then himself starts to 'become', to achieve his true being at last ('Welch Werden in mir'). Lena as the catalyst of this mystical process does indeed correspond to Leonce's 'Ideal eines Frauenzimmers', insofar as that implies a woman that is not simply 'mindless' or 'brainless', but *free* of mind with all its specious constructs; as the above passage forcefully suggests, Lena possesses 'Geist'-as-spirit, not 'Geist'-as-mind. Not only this, but Lena also brings about the fulfilment of the seemingly impossible ideal of love conveyed in the monologue in Act I, Scene iii. Whereas Leonce was previously in a cold and lonely vacuum while the 'weiße Gluthstrahl der Liebe' streamed in some cosmic Beyond, now suddenly he is embraced and bathed by the ardent fluidum of the heavens. There are even specific echoes here of the earlier passage: 'Gluthstrahl'/'glühend'; 'Die Luft so scharf und dünn, daß mich friert'/'Die Luft ist nicht mehr so hell und kalt':

Die Luft ist nicht mehr so hell und kalt, der Himmel senkt sich glühend dicht um mich und schwere Tropfen fallen. (123)

The air is no longer so clear and cold, the heavens descend and hold me in their hot embrace and heavy droplets fall.

The absoluteness of Leonce's metamorphosis is conveyed with explosive lyrical force in his climactic monologue in Act II, Scene iv after Lena has rushed off the stage. What he experiences here is no less than a divine epiphany and holy communion. Where previously in his ennui he saw only a featureless infinitude of meaningless pretence and repetitiveness, the very opposite is now revealed to him, and he suddenly experiences a supreme intensity of life, beauty, creative 'becoming'; where previously time had seemed an oppressively empty, sprawling expanse in which no particular point in past, present, or future could possess real meaning, his entire being now seems gathered up into a single vital presentness:

Zu viel! zu viel! Mein ganzes Sein ist in dem einen Augenblick. Jetzt stirb. Mehr ist unmöglich. Wie frischathmend, schönheitglänzend ringt die Schöpfung sich aus dem Chaos mir entgegen. Die Erde ist eine Schale von dunkelm Gold, wie schäumt das Licht in ihr und fluthet über ihren Rand und hellauf perlen daraus die Sterne. Meine Lippen saugen sich daran: dieser eine Tropfen Seligkeit macht mich zu einem köstlichen Gefäß. (125) *Too much! Too much! All my being is in this single moment. Now die. More is impossible. Out of chaos comes creation, bursting forth towards me, so alive and new, so radiant with beauty. The earth is a chalice of dusky gold: oh how the light within it effervesces, spills over its edge in streams, and from its sparkling bubbles all the stars appear. My craving lips reach out to drink, and this one taste of bliss makes me a precious vessel.*

This extraordinary passage, the most intense evocation of mystical communion anywhere in Büchner's writing, is all the more powerful for the wealth of mantra-like echoes it contains. The reference to 'Schönheit', for instance, echoes the 'mediceische Venus' passage in *Dantons Tod*; the assertion in *Lenz* of 'eine unendliche Schönheit, die aus einer Form in die andre tritt, ewig aufgeblättert, verändert'; the Trial Lecture with its 'Gesetz der Schönheit'. Leonce's sense of 'Schöpfung' invokes Camille's in *Dantons Tod*. The triumph over chaos echoes and reverses the triumph *of* chaos envisioned by Danton ('Die Welt ist das Chaos', 72). Leonce's lips sucking hungrily at the cup of bliss recall Lenz's experience of mystical communion: 'Jetzt, ein anderes Seyn, göttliche, zuckende Lippen bückten sich über ihm nieder, und sogen sich an seine Lippen' (84–5; *Then suddenly, a different being: lips divine leaned down towards him, met his own and sucked at them with trembling fervour*; this passage is in turn an echo of one of Büchner's most crucial letters to Minna Jaeglé: II. 426, ll. 11–16). There is an even more direct and fascinating echo of *Lenz*: the sentence 'Die Erde ist eine Schale von dunkelm Gold, wie schäumt das Licht in ihr und fluthet über ihren Rand' is an unmistakable reprise of the description in the story's final paragraph: 'die Erde war wie ein goldner Pokal, über den schäumend die Goldwellen des Monds liefen' (101; *the earth was like a goblet of gold over which the golden waves of moonlight tumbled*). What makes this echo particularly fascinating is that it exemplifies the way that Büchner incorporates similar elements in both works, but gives them quite contrary outcomes: in the comedy Leonce himself drinks at the golden cup and is inwardly regenerated; Lenz, however, is so radically alienated that he is incapable even of perceiving it: 'Lenz starrte ruhig hinaus, keine Ahnung, kein Drang; nur wuchs eine dumpfe Angst in ihm' (101; *Lenz stared out impassively, devoid of all awareness, all impulses; nothing stirred within him but a growing turbid fear*).

Sooner or later we have to ask just how seriously—or unseriously—we are meant to take Leonce's spectacular metamorphosis. But before we do, let us take a closer look at its instigator, Lena. From the outset Büchner identifies her with nature—a decidedly Wordsworthian kind of nature, not the compulsive 'Natur' pleaded by Marion (22), nor the gross 'Natur' evoked in *Woyzeck* in connection with the excreting horse (355). We see her first in a garden, with rosemary in her hair (117), and it is almost as though she has spent her entire life 'hinter der Mauer [ihres] Gartens, zwischen . . . Myrthen und Oleandern' (120; *behind the walls of [her] garden, amongst . . . myrtles and oleander*). She measures time not by clocks but by flowers: when the Governess complains that it seems 'infinitely long' since they began their flight, she replies: 'Nicht doch, meine Liebe, die Blumen sind ja kaum welk, die ich zum Abschied brach, als wir aus dem Garten gingen' (120; *Not at all, dear heart, the goodbye flowers I picked as we left the garden have scarcely wilted*); and when the Governess mentions that night is beginning to fall, she agrees: 'Ja die Pflanzen legen ihre Fiederblättchen zum Schlaf zusammen' (120; *Yes, the plants are settling their tiny leaves for sleep*). The sounds that seem to Valerio an appalling cacophony are to Lena pure harmony ('die Harmonieen des Abends'); and for her the day is lulled to sleep by the song of the crickets and the scent of gillyflowers (124). In this same scene, she cannot bear to be cooped up inside a room and heads instead for the garden, because that is where she properly belongs: 'man hätte mich eigentlich in eine Scherbe setzen sollen. Ich brauche Thau und Nachtluft wie die Blumen' (123–4; *I should really have been planted in a flower-pot. I need dew and night air as the flowers do*). This is a quite different order of being from anything Leonce has previously known, and it is a measure of his transformation that he embraces it completely—so completely that the poisonous problem of *identity* as defined by name, social standing, profession, etc. simply no longer exists:

VALERIO. . . . Aber weiß sie auch, wer Sie sind?
LEONCE. Sie weiß nur daß sie mich liebt.
VALERIO. Und weiß Eure Hoheit auch, wer sie ist?
LEONCE. Dummkopf! Frag doch die Nelke und die Thauperle nach ihrem Namen. (126)[1]

---

[1] Cf. also Leonce's response in the manuscript fragment of this scene: 'Dummkopf! Sie ist so Blume, daß sie kaum getauft seyn kann, eine geschlossne Knospe, noch ganz

VALERIO. ... But does she know who you are?
LEONCE. She knows she loves me, that's all.
VALERIO. And does your Highness know who *she* is?
LEONCE. Blockhead! Try asking a carnation or a dewdrop its name.[1]

And of course it is precisely this order of being that Büchner has Leonce propose at the close of the play as the utopian future of the whole Kingdom of Bum: having offered his new wife various alternatives to which she only shakes her head, Leonce continues:

Aber ich weiß besser was du willst, wir lassen alle Uhren zerschlagen, alle Kalender verbieten und zählen Stunden und Monden nur nach der Blumenuhr, nur nach Blüthe und Frucht. (134)
But I know better than that what you want. We'll have all clocks destroyed and all calendars banned and measure the hours and months by the flower-clock alone, by the rhythms of blossom and fruit.

For all her quintessentially natural and flower-like being, Lena is by no means presented as an epitome of peace and serenity; indeed the plot is so arranged that her being is gravely threatened from the outset by the development already signalled in the List of Characters, namely the fact that she and the Prince of Bum are due to be married. Now this is a comedy, and we might normally expect such threats not only to come to nothing in the end, but to be worked through in the meantime in a succession of oohs and aahs and comic ups and downs. No concept of comedy, however, could prepare us for what we actually get. Lena's first scene, in particular, comes as a startling surprise, for it would not be out of place in the bleakest of tragedies. What is dramatized here is an existential crisis far more pressing and acute than Leonce's earlier in the act, and just as plangent in its expression as anything we find in *Dantons Tod* or *Woyzeck*.

No one dies in this comedy with its true-to-genre happy ending; and yet Büchner contrives to make death one of its most resonant motifs. In a sense this should not surprise us: *Leonce und Lena* is a comedy of love—and love in Büchner's writing is always inextricably interwoven with death, from the opening page of *Dantons Tod* when Danton tells Julie that he loves her 'like the grave'. Already in the Rosetta episode, death is a central motif: Rosetta herself longs

---

geschlossen...' (142; *Blockhead! She's so much a flower that she can scarce have been christened; a closed bud, still completely closed*).

Epiphany, Death, Transfiguration 263

for the peace and safety of death; Leonce delights in the death agony of their dying love; he then enshrines its corpse within his skull. And now: no sooner has Lena appeared on stage than we find her echoing Rosetta and wishing for death. Her wedding dress turns instantly into burial garb, the rosemary meant as a symbol of marriage takes on its other traditional meaning as a symbol of death:

> Sieh, ich wollte, der Rasen wüchse so über mich und die Bienen summten über mir hin; sieh, jetzt bin ich eingekleidet und habe Rosmarin im Haar. Gibt es nicht ein altes Lied:
> > Auf dem Kirchhof will ich liegen
> > Wie ein Kindlein in der Wiegen... (117)

See, if only the grass would grow up all around me and the bees go humming above my head. See now, I'm fully robed, with sprigs of rosemary in my hair. Isn't there an old song:
> In the churchyard bury me deep,
> Let me like a baby sleep...

In her second speech, Büchner has her voice a whole cluster of central motifs familiar to us since the first page of *Dantons Tod*: not only death, but love and isolation too: 'O Gott, ich könnte lieben, warum nicht? Man geht ja so einsam und tastet nach einer Hand, die einen hielte, bis die Leichenfrau die Hände auseinandernähme und sie Jedem über der Brust faltete.' (117; *Oh God, I could love someone, of course I could. We're so alone after all, and grope in the dark for a hand to clasp until we die and our hands are loosed and laid out each on our separate chests.*) The continuation of this speech then begins to take us in an unexpected direction: we are suddenly in the realm of physical torture: 'Aber warum schlägt man einen Nagel durch zwei Hände, die sich nicht suchten? Was hat meine arme Hand gethan?' (*But why drive a nail through two hands that never sought each other? What has my poor hand done to deserve it?*) If this imagery seems drastic for a comedy, and especially for a figure as ethereal as Lena, it is far exceeded by what follows. When the Governess—always a comic presence, not unlike a pantomime dame—describes Lena as both an 'angel' and a 'sacrificial lamb', this seems at first merely a conceit, a turn of phrase ('Lieber Engel, du bist doch ein wahres Opferlamm', 118). But the image acquires shocking expressive force through Lena's response: 'Ja wohl—und der Priester hebt schon das Messer.' (*Yes—and the priest is already raising his knife.*) Although the picture of the priest with knife upraised evokes pagan rituals of human sacrifice, the essential image at work here is that of Christ and the Crucifixion: already hinted at in Lena's description of the impending forced marriage (the nail driven through the victims' hands), the allusion is unmistakable in the word 'Opferlamm'—a standard term for Christ as *Agnus Dei*, the Paschal Lamb sacrificed on the cross.[2] The image is then given startling prominence in the rest of Lena's speech, in which Büchner has her move on from her own individual predicament to the plight of mankind in general, and then to the whole nature of the cosmos:

—Mein Gott, mein Gott, ist es denn wahr, daß wir uns selbst erlösen müssen mit unserm Schmerz? Ist es denn wahr, die Welt sei ein gekreuzigter Heiland, die Sonne seine Dornenkrone und die Sterne die Nägel und Speere in seinen Füßen und Lenden?

—My God, my God, is it really true that we must redeem ourselves through our own pain? Is it really true that the earth is a crucified Christ, the sun his crown of thorns, and the stars the nails in his feet and the spears in his side?

One almost has to pinch oneself to remember that these words are being spoken by the sweet heroine of a comedy on her very first appearance—all the more so when we realize that they echo one of the darkest passages in *Dantons Tod*, when Robespierre, the high priest of systematic sacrifice, reflects on the charge that he is a 'Blutmessias', a 'Messiah' saving his compatriots by drowning them in their own blood:

Ja wohl, Blutmessias, der opfert und nicht geopfert wird.—Er hat sie mit seinem Blut erlöst und ich erlöse sie mit ihrem eignen. . . . Wahrlich des Menschensohn wird in uns Allen gekreuzigt, wir ringen Alle im Gethsemanegarten im blutigen Schweiß, aber es erlöst Keiner den Andern mit seinen Wunden. (30–1)

Yes indeed: 'bloody Messiah, not sacrificed himself but sacrificing others.'—*He* redeemed them with *his* blood, I redeem them with their own. . . . Verily the son of man is crucified in us all; we all writhe in blood and sweat in the Garden of Gethsemane, but none of us redeems the others with his wounds.

Although the intensity and diversity of the death imagery in

[2] Cf. Joachim Bark, 'Bibelsprache in Büchners Dramen. Stellenkommentar und interpretatorische Hinweise', in B. Dedner and G. Oesterle (eds.), *Zweites Internationales Georg Büchner Symposium 1987* (Frankfurt, 1990), 494.

Epiphany, Death, Transfiguration

Büchner's initial projection of his heroine comes as a shock, it is not in itself surprising that her existential crisis should be figured in such terms, just as it is not inherently surprising that the dying of Leonce's love for Rosetta should be conveyed through images of death. What is spectacular is that Büchner also chooses the language of death to express its very opposite: rebirth, rejuvenation, the sudden epiphany of love and life in the climactic encounter between Leonce and Lena; and the result is one of the most daring, disturbing, and poetic passages in all his work.

His basic procedure is to use the characters' words to generate a whole succession of visions that transport both them and us ever deeper into a poetic, transcendental dimension quite unconnected with the ordinary empirical world. These separate realms, and the virtual contradiction between them, are signalled at once in the alternative 'readings' of the nocturnal scene offered through Valerio and Leonce: what Valerio registers is unclean beds, aggressive insects, a cacophony of croaks, whistles, and snores; what Leonce experiences is the balm of Paradise ('O Nacht, balsamisch wie die erste, die auf das Paradies herabsank', 124). We have already looked at the poignant vision conveyed through Lena. The night is personified into a sleeping woman whose pallor and stillness hint at death. The moon is turned into a sleeping child whose sleep is explicitly death; then into a dead angel cushioned on the blackness of the night with the stars around him like funereal candles; then finally into a very human child again, quite dead, yet still prey to vulnerability, abandonment, sorrow, isolation: 'Armes Kind, kommen die schwarzen Männer bald dich holen? Wo ist deine Mutter? Will sie dich nicht noch einmal küssen? Ach es ist traurig, todt und so allein.' (*Poor child, are the bogymen coming to take you away? Where's your mother? Won't she give you just one last kiss? Oh the sadness of it—dead, and so alone.*)

Just as Lena's words are resonant with echoes of other passages (cf. above, pp. 228f.), so also is Leonce's response. At the most critical juncture of *Lenz*, too, as here in Lena's vision, there is a dead child—which Lenz attempts in vain to bring back to life:

[Er] faßte die Hände des Kindes und sprach laut und fest: 'Stehe auf und wandle!' Aber die Wände hallten ihm nüchtern den Ton nach, daß es zu spotten schien, und die Leiche blieb kalt. Da stürzte er halb wahnsinnig nieder, dann jagte es ihn auf, hinaus in's Gebirg. (93)

Grasping the hands of the child he said loudly and firmly, 'Arise and walk!' But the words echoed back from the sober walls as though in mockery, and the corpse stayed cold. He fell to the ground, half-seized by madness, then something drove him to his feet, and away into the mountains.

Lenz's attempted resurrection of the child is echoed in the comedy with the use of the very same biblical quotation: 'Steh auf in deinem weißen Kleide und wandle hinter der Leiche durch die Nacht und singe ihr das Todtenlied.' (*Arise in your dress so white and walk through the night behind the corpse to sing its threnody.*)[3] The contrary outcomes of these two episodes epitomize the opposite trajectories of the two works: whereas Lenz goes irretrievably to pieces, for Leonce everything suddenly comes together in a supremely intense experience of wholeness, blessedness, beauty, with Chaos giving way to Creation. This is rendered credible largely through Büchner's management of the fictive circumstances. In *Lenz* the child is quite literally dead—a corpse with 'cold limbs' and 'glassy eyes' on a real table in a real room. In *Leonce und Lena* the emphasis on death is even more insistent, but it is death in purely figurative terms, within a context not of sober daylight reality, but of a nocturnal zone of dream and imagination. An extraordinary process of poetic transfiguration is accomplished here: the protagonists' deliverance from all that is deathly is conveyed and celebrated through the very imagery of death itself, with the 'new' Leonce seeing himself as an 'angel of death', and Lena as a 'beautiful corpse':

LEONCE. Steh auf in deinem weißen Kleide und wandle hinter der Leiche durch die Nacht und singe ihr das Todtenlied.
LENA. Wer spricht da?
LEONCE. Ein Traum.
LENA. Träume sind selig.
LEONCE. So träume dich selig und laß mich dein seliger Traum sein.
LENA. Der Tod ist der seligste Traum.
LEONCE. So laß mich dein Todesengel sein. Laß meine Lippen sich gleich seinen Schwingen auf deine Augen senken. [*Er küßt sie.*] Schöne Leiche,

---

[3] The biblical allusion is even clearer in the surviving manuscript fragment of the scene: 'Steh auf in deinem weißen Kleid u. schwebe durch die Nacht u. sprich zur Leiche steh auf und wandle. LENA. Die heiligen Lippen, die so sprachen, sind längst Staub.' (141–2; *Arise in your dress so white and float through the night and say to the corpse, Arise and walk.* LENA. *The holy lips that spoke those words are long since turned to dust.*)

du ruhst so lieblich auf dem schwarzen Bahrtuch der Nacht, daß die
Natur das Leben haßt und sich in den Tod verliebt. (124–5)

LEONCE. Arise in your dress so white and walk through the night behind the corpse to sing its threnody.
LENA. Who speaks?
LEONCE. A dream.
LENA. Dreams are blessed.
LEONCE. Then dream yourself blessed and let me be your blessed dream.
LENA. The most blessed dream of all is death.
LEONCE. Then let me be your angel of death, and let my lips descend like angel's wings upon your eyes. [*He kisses her.*] You beautiful corpse, you lie so sweetly on the pall of night that even nature turns her back on life, and falls in love with death.

At this point Büchner has Lena ambiguously leap to her feet and rush from the stage (using the same words spoken by Marion at the beginning of her scene: 'Nein, laß mich'), and Leonce is left to deliver the climactic monologue that we discussed earlier. Here too, of course, the motif of death recurs. For Leonce in his previous condition of ennui there was no focus or fullness or meaning, and love in particular was knowable only in fragmentary form. But through Lena he experiences such an absolute totality of being, all concentrated into a miraculous presentness of time, that nothing could ever match it in the future, and death seems the only appropriate option: 'Zu viel! zu viel! Mein ganzes Sein ist in dem einen Augenblick. Jetzt stirb. Mehr ist unmöglich.' (125; *Too much! Too much! All my being is in this single moment. Now die. More is impossible.*) Having at last tasted 'Seligkeit' (only inadequately rendered by 'bliss' or 'blessedness'), he sees himself as a 'holy vessel' whose holiness can be celebrated and safeguarded only through its instant sacrifice: 'dieser eine Tropfen Seligkeit macht mich zu einem köstlichen Gefäß. Hinab heiliger Becher! [*Er will sich in den Fluß stürzen.*]' (*this one taste of bliss makes me a precious vessel. Into the deep, holy cup!* [*He makes to throw himself into the river.*]) Needless to say, he doesn't succeed: reality unceremoniously snatches him from the brink in the person of Valerio, and the whole atmosphere of the play switches back within seconds to irony, mockery, farce—a mode that then predominates through almost the entire last act. The question now remains: what are we to make of this irony, and how does it condition our understanding of the play?

14
A Flight into Paradise?

It is Valerio that wrenches Leonce (and us too, as reader/spectator) from the realm of mystical communion, and reasserts the reality of flea-ridden beds and dreamless sleep. He is indeed the most insistently ironic, debunking voice in the play, and as such he merits particular attention.

Valerio's importance is plainly apparent: he is present in seven of the eleven scenes; he has far more lines than any other character save Leonce; he has the longest single speech in the play (131); he even speaks its final words. What makes this prominent role especially intriguing is the fact that Valerio is the only figure in the play who functions outside the conventions and patterns of the society it depicts. This is hinted at even before the play begins, in that the List of Characters leaves his status and function conspicuously undefined (Rosetta is the only other figure left undefined; but her role as 'outgoing sweetheart' rapidly becomes clear in the single sub-scene in which she appears). When the curtain rises on Act I, Scene i, Leonce and the nameless Court Tutor are already present on stage, and are instantly 'placeable'—through language, behaviour, and (implicitly) dress—as recalcitrant Prince and servile functionary. In his first monologue Leonce defines society as consisting exclusively of stereotyped masks; but Valerio doesn't fit into the pattern at all. His 'otherness' is trumpeted in the manner of his arrival: the attention of the reader/spectator is grabbed by Leonce's 'Wie der Mensch läuft! [etc.]', and Valerio then comes on stage not only at a run, but also half-drunk.[1] We are then further disconcerted by the bizarre exchange immediately instigated by the unplaceable interloper—an exchange quite different in physical and verbal language from anything in the preceding episode with the Court Tutor. There is no

---

[1] Lehmann adopts a startling editorial procedure here (106), in that he chooses to conflate the two extant versions. In Ludwig Büchner's edition (which Lehmann otherwise follows), the stage direction is 'Valerio, etwas betrunken, tritt auf', and it comes *after* Leonce's two sentences beginning 'Wie der Mensch läuft!' The position and wording of Lehmann's 'Valerio, halb trunken, kommt gelaufen' is 'borrowed' from the manuscript fragment of I. i. Cf. BD 20, 21.

A Flight into Paradise?

suggestion in Act I, Scene i that Leonce and Valerio have ever even met before. There is certainly no hint of recognition in Leonce's words when he first catches sight of the other: 'Wie der Mensch läuft! Wenn ich nur etwas unter der Sonne wüßte, was mich noch könnte laufen machen.' (106; *How the man runs! If I only knew of a single thing in the world that could still make me run.*) Non-acquaintance is suggested, too, by the mode of address: Büchner has Leonce use the formal 'Sie' in two successive speeches before switching to the familiar 'du'. The early manuscript fragment of the scene is revealing in this context: in the main text of the fragment Leonce uses only the 'du' form; but in a subsequent lengthy insert in the margin, Büchner strikingly changes the style of address to 'Sie' (cf. Mayer edition, BD 22, 24). The manuscript version is even more revealing in that it strongly implies that (at that stage of Büchner's conception of things at least) Valerio was indeed exploding into Leonce's life for the first time: when he comes dashing on, he is quite literally on the run—as a deserter from some war, with the police in hot pursuit. As Büchner has him say: 'nur mein Laufen hat im Lauf dießes Krieges mein Leben vor einem Lauf gerettet, der ein Loch in dasselbe machen wollte' (140; *in the course of this war only my running has saved my life from a gun-barrel that wanted to make a hole in it*).

Valerio's function as a kind of professional *non*-functionary is of course highlighted with considerable ceremony towards the close of Act I, Scene i, when Leonce poses his ironic question as to Valerio's 'work ... profession ... trade ... station ... craft'; this cues a splendid cascade of mock grandiloquence, all showing that Valerio's sole pursuit is idleness: 'Herr, ich habe die große Beschäftigung, müßig zu gehen [etc.]' (107; cf. above, p. 244). As mentioned earlier, these words are a clear echo of Leonce's to the Court Tutor near the beginning of the scene: '—Bin ich ein Müßiggänger? Habe ich keine Beschäftigung?' Valerio is no 'raffinirter Müßiggänger' a *covert* idler masquerading as a terribly busy hero/genius/idiot/saint/sinner/paterfamilias (106): he is quite openly and dedicatedly idle. As such he is the perfect accompaniment to Leonce in his ennui-driven negativism: as the sidekick in their comic duo, he serves both to reinforce and to amplify that particular aspect of the protagonist's persona—especially in the expositional phase of the play, where it constitutes a key datum. It is in this context, incidentally, that we can best understand Valerio's habit of firing off volleys of often rather silly puns. In their vacuity and flippancy these can easily seem a weakness in the play—until we realize that they are not meant at face value, but represent a kind of pirouetting of the negative. The point is hinted at à propos of one such pun in Act I, Scene iii, when Leonce remarks to Valerio: 'Mensch, du bist nichts als ein schlechtes Wortspiel. Du hast weder Vater noch Mutter, sondern die fünf Vokale haben dich miteinander erzeugt.' (115; *Heavens, man, you're nothing but a bad pun. You've neither father nor mother, you were begotten by all five vowels together.*) Valerio's puns are a last resort of mind, of sheer wit; a kind of graffiti scrawled onto emptiness. As such they relate directly to Leonce's own ontological crisis—as is suggested through Valerio's riposte: 'Und Sie Prinz, sind ein Buch ohne Buchstaben, mit nichts als Gedankenstrichen' (*And you, Prince, are a book without letters, full of nothing but dashes*); the echo of Leonce's lament in his second monologue is clear: 'Mein Leben gähnt mich an, wie ein großer weißer Bogen Papier, den ich vollschreiben soll, aber ich bringe keinen Buchstaben heraus.' (112; *My life gapes at me like a great white sheet of paper that I'm supposed to fill with writing, but I can't manage even a single letter.*)

Büchner follows Valerio's definition of himself in Act I, Scene i with an arresting and teasing passage, a half-ironic, half-serious paean in which Leonce clasps Valerio to his bosom as a kindred spirit, as the embodiment of an ideal:

LEONCE [*mit komischem Enthusiasmus*]. Komm an meine Brust! Bist du einer von den Göttlichen, welche mühelos mit reiner Stirne durch den Schweiß und Staub über die Heerstraße des Lebens wandeln, und mit glänzenden Sohlen und blühenden Leibern gleich seligen Göttern in den Olympus treten? Komm! Komm! (108)

LEONCE [*with comic enthusiasm*]. Come to my breast! Are you one of those spirits divine that glide without effort and unbesmirched through the dust and sweat of the teeming highway of life, then enter Olympus like blessèd gods with shining feet and blooming bodies? Come to me! Come!

Valerio is of course very far from being an ethereal, Olympian divinity. On the contrary, he is earthiness personified; a being whose existential horizon extends only as far as his gut and his gullet. Food (or the lack of it) was a central motif in *Dantons Tod*; it is important in *Woyzeck* (the diet of peas); and food and drink figure large in *Leonce und Lena* through the person of Valerio. He is half-drunk when we first set eyes on him; he immediately threatens the birds and the bees by robbing them of their sustenance ('schnaufen Sie nicht so stark, oder die Bienen und Schmetterlinge müssen verhungern über den ungeheuren Prisen, die Sie aus den Blumen ziehen', 106); he then talks of scoffing the grass as an ox, then scoffing the ox that scoffed the grass. Both these latter gut-processes specifically parody ideal notions of 'romantic emotions' and 'feeling for nature'; and when Leonce explicitly talks of 'ideals', the Valerio of the manuscript version parodistically translates this into the language of food ('O Gott! ich laufe schon seit 8 Tagen einem Ideal von Rindfleisch nach, ohne es irgendwo in der Realität anzutreffen', 139; cf. above, p. 255). When he appears from underneath the table in Act I, Scene iii he is busy guzzling stolen wine and chomping at a stolen hunk of meat—not decorously, of course, but with Rabelaisian, animal zest: 'Das schmatzt.... Mach fort, grunze nicht so mit deinem Rüssel, und klappre mit deinen Hauern nicht so' (113; *How he smacks his chops! ... Get on with it, and don't grunt so with that snout of yours, don't gnash your fangs like that.*) This is even billed as a kind of temptation for Leonce—the svelte aristocrat lured by a rude primitivism: 'Der Kerl verursacht mir ganz idyllische Empfindungen; ich könnte wieder mit dem Einfachsten anfangen, ich könnte Käs essen, Bier trinken, Tabak rauchen.' (113; *The fellow's inspiring the most idyllic sensations in me; I could start over again with the simplest of things: eat cheese, drink beer, smoke tobacco.*)

The earthy, anti-idealist philosophy of life represented in Valerio is spelt out as such towards the beginning of Act II when Büchner has him fling down his pack, exhausted by the day's journeyings towards the remote idyll of Italy:

Sehen Sie Prinz ich werde philosophisch, ein Bild des menschlichen Lebens. Ich schleppe diesen Pack mit wunden Füßen durch Frost und Sonnenbrand, weil ich Abends ein reines Hemd anziehen will und wenn endlich der Abend kommt, so ist meine Stirn gefurcht, meine Wange hohl, mein Auge dunkel und ich habe grade noch Zeit, mein Hemd anzuziehen, als Todtenhemd. Hätte ich nun nicht gescheidter gethan, ich hätte mein Bündel vom Stecken gehoben und es in der ersten besten Kneipe verkauft, und hätte mich dafür betrunken und im Schatten geschlafen, bis es Abend geworden wäre, und hätte nicht geschwitzt und mir keine Leichdörner gelaufen? (119–20)

There you are, Prince, I am becoming philosophical, a picture of human life. I hump this pack with bleeding feet through frost and scorching sun, because I like a clean shirt of an evening; and when at last the evening comes, I have sunken eyes, a furrowed brow, and hollow cheeks, and just enough time to pull on my shirt—to use as my shroud. Wouldn't I have been wiser to undo my bundle from its stick, flog it at the next best inn, get drunk on the proceeds, and sleep in the shade until evening came, thus not getting sweaty and not getting corns?

To Valerio, the inn that they are approaching means only one thing: grub and booze: 'welch ein köstlicher Duft, welche Weindüfte und Bratengerüche!' (120; *what a delectable smell, what sweet aromas of wine and roast meat!*) Leonce shows no such reaction; indeed he does not share this characteristic perspective of Valerio's at all. This becomes more evident in the following scene. As Leonce surveys the benign picture presented by the inn with its rustic trappings and venerable patrons, he is seized by existential angst ('Ich bekomme manchmal eine Angst um mich', 121). Valerio's response is typical: he offers him a glass, and tells him: 'Nimm diese Glocke, diese Taucherglocke und senke dich in das Meer des Weines' (*Take this bell, this diver's bell, and immerse yourself in an ocean of wine*). It is the same a few moments later, when Leonce speaks of his problems in using up his obstinate residue of enthusiasm: alcohol, suggests Valerio, is the ideal refuge from all such problems:

Ergo bibamus. Diese Flasche ist keine Geliebte, keine Idee, sie macht keine Geburtsschmerzen, sie wird nicht langweilig, wird nicht treulos, sie bleibt eins vom ersten Tropfen bis zum letzten. Du brichst das Siegel und alle Träume, die in ihr schlummern, sprühen dir entgegen. (121)

Ergo bibamus! This bottle is not a lover, it is not an idea, it causes no birth-pains, never gets boring, never unfaithful, remains consistently the same from first drop to last. You break its seal, and all the dreams that slumber within it burst forth to greet you.

'Diese Flasche ist keine Geliebte', says Valerio approvingly—but a 'Geliebte' is precisely what Leonce is about to find at the inn; he does not escape into an 'ocean of wine' nor give himself over to alcoholic 'dreams'; above all, he does not sell off his bundle and abandon his quest. What we see reflected here is an important change in the relationship between the two figures: whereas in Act I they are fully at one with each other, a marked divergence becomes evident in Act II. This is neatly signalled in the sharp contrast between their first appearance at the start of Act II, and their first appearance together towards the beginning of the play: in I. i it is Valerio who comes bounding onto the stage full of energy, while

A Flight into Paradise? 273

Leonce has scarcely the spirit to move a muscle ('Wenn ich nur etwas unter der Sonne wüßte, was mich noch könnte laufen machen.'); in II. i, on the other hand, Valerio comes on stage panting with exhaustion ('keuchend'), while Leonce by implication is not flagging at all. Furthermore, they are instantly in harmony in I. i ('Ja! / Richtig! / Haben Sie mich begriffen? / Vollkommen')—but in II. i they instantly disagree ('die Welt ist doch ein ungeheuer weitläuftiges Gebäude. / Nicht doch! Nicht doch! Ich wage kaum die Hände auszustrecken . . .'). In fact, the divergence is already suggested at the close of I. iii, when Valerio's 'So wollen wir zum Teufel gehen' is countered by Leonce's 'Wir gehen nach Italien.' This marks the beginning of Leonce's quest, and the activation of his residual 'Enthusiasmus' ('enthusiasm' in the then-prevalent sense of divine or quasi-divine possession, of ardent faith in sacred ideals). With this, he takes Valerio into a realm where he is indeed lost, 'verloren'—as Büchner has him say in his second utterance in Act II (119); a dedicated philistine, Valerio cannot begin to understand why Leonce was not content to stay put, and become King and marry a beautiful princess (119). The change is even reflected in the pattern of the dialogue: whereas in Act I their speeches follow on from each other in a virtually unbroken flow, in Act II their dialogue is frequently discontinuous. Thus for instance Valerio's 'Ich bin verloren' does not connect directly with Leonce's preceding remark; Leonce's 'Ideal eines Frauenzimmers' speech is followed by an entirely unconnected remark ('Teufel! Da sind wir schon wieder auf der Grenze', 119); Valerio's opening questions about booze in II. ii are answered by another question on a different level and a different topic ('Siehst du die alten Bäume, die Hecken, die Blumen?', 121). In effect, the two figures now speak disparate languages, and exist in disparate worlds—a divergence perfectly exemplified in II. ii, when Leonce's vision of the gathering night in terms of words like 'unheimlich', 'entsetzlich', 'wirr', 'ängstlich' is met by an uncomprehending response from Valerio: 'Ich weiß nicht, was Ihr wollt, mir ist ganz behaglich zu Muth.' (122; *I don't know what you're on about, I'm in the cosiest of moods.*)

Dramaturgically this divergence is highly significant. Whereas in Act I Valerio is so to speak an amplificatory echo of the ironic, all-mocking protagonist, from the beginning of Act II he becomes in effect a foil, serving by means of contrast to highlight the new direction represented by Leonce's quest. This in turn has crucial implications for our interpretation of the text. It is surely clear that Valerio's voice is not that of sound, trustworthy reasonableness (like, say, Philinte's voice in Molière's *Le Misanthrope*); it is the voice of prosaic, unimaginative reality. For Valerio, the summit of idealism is a juicy hunk of beef, the only dream-zone that of the bottle, the harmony of the evening a mere cacophony. When Leonce is suddenly enspirited by Lena's magical voice in II. ii, we are surely not meant to accept Valerio's interpretation that Leonce is simply going mad (123). The issue becomes particularly acute in Act II, Scene iv, when Valerio intervenes to prevent Leonce from committing suicide, and dismisses his transport of ecstasy, his sense of an absolute fullness of being, as mere 'Lieutenantsromantik', as so much callow, romantical claptrap. It is true that Büchner shows Leonce himself being rapidly won over to Valerio's viewpoint, and reverting to his previous posture of flippant irony: 'Mensch, du hast mich um den schönsten Selbstmord gebracht. Ich werde in meinem Leben keinen so vorzüglichen Augenblick mehr dazu finden und das Wetter ist so vortrefflich. Jetzt bin ich schon aus der Stimmung.' (125; *Good heavens, man, you've deprived me of the most beautiful suicide. Never in my life shall I find such a splendidly suitable opportunity, and the weather is so ideal. I'm already quite out of the mood.*) But there is no trace of irony in Leonce's words in the following scene (III. i): Valerio may have frustrated his death-wish, but his love has blossomed so completely that he and his nameless, ineffable beloved are already resolved to marry.

In all of this Büchner is drawing on the kind of creative procedure brought to such perfection a decade or two earlier by E. T. A. Hoffmann (whose *Prinzessin Brambilla* is undoubtedly one of the many models behind the overall conception of the play—and who is specifically referred to in one of Büchner's most poignant letters to Minna Jaeglé: ii. 424). For Büchner as for Hoffmann (and countless other kindred spirits in the period), the prosaic, philistine perspective was undeniably dominant. The poetic ideals of wholeness and fullness, infinite beauty and harmony, the complete realization of human potential: these ideals were supremely valid in themselves, and cried out to be proclaimed ever and again. But in no conceivable future could they prevail against the dominant, indeed increasingly dominant order of philistine functionalism. It would accordingly be false and implausible ever to depict the ideal as though it *were* the prevailing reality. Hoffmann's *Der goldne Topf* is exemplary in this respect: the various stages in Anselmus's progression towards the poetic realm are powerfully conveyed—then always ironically relativized as being perhaps mere dreams, fits of madness, alcoholic imaginings, etc. When he is finally united with Serpentina and translated to 'Atlantis', we are not allowed to follow him there: we and the narrator remain firmly stuck in the quotidian reality of Dresden, and are vouchsafed only a *vision* of Anselmus's poetic bliss in a realm accessible to us only through our imagination. Büchner accomplishes just such a sleight of hand in *Leonce und Lena*. Throughout Leonce's phase of ennui-driven negativism in Act I, Valerio is his faithful accomplice and echo. Once he departs on his idealist quest in the 'fourth dimension' of Act II, and duly encounters Lena and experiences a kind of mystical rebirth, he essentially diverges from Valerio, who thereupon becomes the voice of earthbound reality serving to relativize the poetic dimension without ever destroying or even diminishing it. As reader/spectator we experience a succession of vivid present moments, all inherently convincing on their own terms; any of them may be called into question by its successor, but without for that being nullified or invalidated.

The process is particularly fascinating—and challenging—in the final act. We return here from the nameless Beyond of Act II to the approximation of reality represented by the Kingdom of Bum; and Büchner neatly solves the problem of the poetical 'voice' and its potential incongruity and implausibility within the given context by so to speak switching it off throughout most of the Act: Lena speaks only seven words in Act III; and Leonce not only says relatively little (just 10 per cent of his total number of lines in the play): what he does say is confined to the very beginning and the very end of the act. Indeed throughout fully two thirds of Act III, the eponymous hero and heroine are either absent from the stage, or else present but mute (and masked). This portion of the play is made up of three distinct elements: the two satirical episodes discussed earlier (the peasant scene, and the palace scene prior to the arrival of the masked quartet), and the farcical telescoped nuptials with their extended prelude, consisting mainly of Valerio's lengthy speech—the longest in the play.

Valerio's speech has two exactly equal sections: an ontological first half, and a (largely) satirical second half. The first part plays serious games with the problem of being and identity cued at the outset of the sub-scene by King Peter's question 'Wer seid Ihr?', and duly developed through Valerio's stunt of removing successive masks while asking 'Bin ich das? oder das? oder das?', and expressing the fear that he might peel himself entirely away (130; cf. above, p. 214). A neat and telling device here is Büchner's repeated inclusion of the words 'wahrhaftig' and 'eigentlich' to point up the question of what is 'truly' and 'really' the case (a question that is all the more piquant given the fact that both we and the on-stage audience are faced by a deliberate and sustained masquerade, whilst even the masked principals themselves have no idea of each other's true identity): 'Wahrhaftig ich bekomme Angst', 'ich weiß wahrhaftig nicht mehr, wer ich eigentlich bin', 'eigentlich wollte ich', 'wenn ich eigentlich selbst recht wüßte, wer ich wäre', 'eigentlich nichts als Walzen und Windschläuche', 'man könnte sie eigentlich zu Mitgliedern der menschlichen Gesellschaft machen'. Valerio having already rendered his own identity problematic in his preliminary exchanges with King Peter (who is thereby driven to 'Confusion', 'Desperation' and 'der größten Verwirrung'), he gleefully confuses the issue even further by spouting the longest sentence of the play, and confronting his on- and off-stage audiences with a mystificatory labyrinth of subordinate clauses: he had 'really' wanted to introduce himself as the third and most peculiar of the 'world-famous automata', so he claims—

wenn ich eigentlich selbst recht wüßte, wer ich wäre, worüber man übrigens sich nicht wundern dürfte, da ich selbst gar nichts von dem weiß, was ich rede, ja auch nicht einmal weiß, daß ich es nicht weiß, so daß es höchst wahrscheinlich ist, daß man mich nur so reden *läßt*, und es eigentlich nichts als Walzen und Windschläuche sind, die das Alles sagen.

if only I myself really knew who I am, although no one by the way should be surprised that I don't, since I myself know nothing of what I say, indeed don't even know that I don't know, so that it's highly probable that I am simply being *made* to talk like this, and that it is actually nothing but cylinders and airbags producing all these words.

What with Valerio's 'Walzen und Windschläuche', and his description of the two 'automata' as being nothing but an artificial mechanism made of clockwork and pasteboard ('Nichts als Kunst und Mechanismus, nichts als Pappendeckel und Uhrfedern'), we are easily reminded of Büchner's agonized letter of early March 1834, when he tells Minna how everyone had seemed to him dead and

A Flight into Paradise?

puppet-like, with glassy eyes, waxen cheeks, jerking limbs, and an internal 'Maschinerie' complete with 'Wälzchen und Stiftchen' (ii. 424). An even more direct parallel may be found in *Woyzeck*: Valerio's mock-formal introduction of his two 'exhibits' is strikingly similar to the way Büchner has the fairground Barker introduce *his* exhibits: 'Sehen Sie hier meine Herren und Damen, zwei Personen beiderlei Geschlechts . . . Nichts als Kunst und Mechanismus . . .' / 'Meine Herren! Meine Herren! Sehn [S]ie die Creatur, wie sie Gott gemacht, nix, gar nix. Sehen Sie jezt die Kunst . . .' (343; *See here, ladies and gentlemen, two persons of opposite sex . . . All artifice and mechanics . . . / Gentlemen, gentlemen! See here the creature as God made it: nothing, just nothing. Now here's civilization for you . . .*). And yet of course the whole context is different: this is playful comedy, and while our minds are challenged and teased, our emotions are not enlisted on behalf of pitiable, suffering, or threatened characters; we know full well that the two 'world-famous automata' are *not* just 'Kunst und Mechanismus . . . Pappendeckel und Uhrfedern', but full-blooded lovers (played by full-blooded actors), just as we know that Valerio in fictive reality has no problems whatever with his own identity. We are thus offered an inherently bleak perspective on human existence, but through the medium of a cheerful and enjoyable dance of words. This is yet another example of Büchner's genius for simultaneously conveying quite contrary messages: he shows us a grim vision of man as puppet, as Descartes's *homme machine* complete with 'Schrauben, Stifte und Walzen' (ii. 179; *screws, prongs and cylinders*)—but he does so in a spirit full of warmth and vitality, full of that sense of 'Leben, Möglichkeit des Daseins' extolled in *Lenz*.

Büchner shifts the focus from the ontological to the satirical at the exact midpoint of the speech, with Valerio's assertion that his two mechanical robots could readily be turned into members of human society: 'man könnte sie eigentlich zu Mitgliedern der menschlichen Gesellschaft machen'. The same phrase was used earlier in the play (near the end of Act I): having unsuccessfully suggested that they become scholars/heroes/poetic geniuses, Valerio proposes that they become 'nützliche Mitglieder der menschlichen Gesellschaft'—but this earns the sharpest riposte of all from Leonce: 'Lieber möchte ich meine Demission als Mensch geben.' (116; *I'd sooner resign as a human being.*) The clear implication is that there is nothing very human about human society. Already in the play's opening scene

Leonce represented society as consisting of so many roles, all of them false constructs serving to disguise the true driving force of ubiquitous ennui: he saw his own physical self as merely a 'Puppe', a featureless doll or puppet, that only needed to be kitted out in the appropriate garb of tail-coat and brolly in order to become 'sehr rechtlich und sehr nützlich und sehr moralisch' (106; *thoroughly upright, thoroughly useful and thoroughly moral*). Büchner now has Valerio lampoon such categories with splendid cartoonist bravura by portraying them as ridiculously specious and superficial: the two 'robots'—and by implication the robotic members of conventional upper-class society—are respectively 'very aristocratic', 'very moral', and 'very cultured' because they speak posh German, because they eat and sleep by the clock, and because the lady knows all the latest operas, while the gentleman sports cuffs; moreover, says Valerio, their impeccable digestion proves that they have a clear conscience, while their refined moral sensibility is demonstrated by the lady's seemly ignorance of any word for 'trousers', and the sheer impossibility of the gentleman ever walking *up*stairs behind a woman, or *down*stairs in front of one. In the closing two sentences of the speech an ontological element is reintroduced in the representation of love as merely another mechanical process; but the satirical thrust is maintained in the mocking of polite society and its ritualistic but effete gestures:

der Mechanismus der Liebe fängt an sich zu äußern, der Herr hat der Dame schon einige Mal den Shawl getragen, die Dame hat schon einige Mal die Augen verdreht und gen Himmel geblickt. Beide haben schon mehrmals geflüstert: Glaube, Liebe, Hoffnung!

the mechanism of love is beginning to operate, the gentleman has already carried the lady's shawl a few times, the lady has already rolled her eyes and gazed heavenwards a few times. On several occasions both have whispered 'Faith, love, hope!'

It is a prime and quite challenging feature of Büchner's comedy that its plot is minimal, and unadorned by peripeteia; it is an almost drama-less drama. Act III is particularly cheeky, in that its 'action' consists largely of people hanging about waiting for some action (first the exhausted peasants, then the exhausted courtiers, etc.). Valerio's long speech is typical in this respect: the protagonists may have arrived on stage at long last, but the speech delays the action yet further. Once the speech is finished, however, the play abruptly

A Flight into Paradise? 279

changes pace from extreme slow motion to extreme fast-forward: the masked couple are wedded in comic haste by the sorely confused Court Chaplain, and within a matter of seconds their identities are revealed, King Peter abdicates, Leonce dismisses the assembled company, and he and Valerio project their future. The question is: what are we supposed to make of this deliciously slick but teasing dénouement?

The predominant feature of the play's conclusion is that it offers at one and the same time both satisfying closure and perplexing openness. In terms of action and aesthetics, everything is beautifully rounded off: the marriage signalled in the List of Characters is duly accomplished; King Peter hands power to Leonce and conveniently exists with his retinue; and the mass of secondary figures are neatly cleared from the stage to leave the spotlight fully on the protagonists and their respective acolytes. The final coda is especially pleasing in its measuredness and balance: Leonce's closing speech has a rhythmic succession of word-pairs ('Puppen und Spielzeug', 'Schnurrbärte . . . und . . . Säbel', 'Politik und Diplomatie', 'Stunden und Monden', 'Blüthe und Frucht', 'Ischia und Capri', 'Rosen und Veilchen', 'Orangen und Lorbeern'); the whole play closes with sonorous triads from Valerio ('Makkaroni, Melonen und Feigen', 'musikalische Kehlen, klassische Leiber und eine kommode Religion'). What is particularly satisfying is the antiphonal effect that Büchner achieves by making Valerio's final speech a kind of echo of Leonce's final paragraph: they are similar in length; both have two sections; the corresponding sections are similarly introduced ('Aber ich . . .'/'Und ich . . .'; 'Und dann umstellen wir . . .'/'und dann legen wir . . .'); both sections of both speeches are triadically patterned (LEONCE: 'wir lassen alle Uhren . . . alle Kalender . . . und zählen Stunden und Monden . . .'; 'daß es keinen Winter . . . und wir uns im Sommer . . . und wir das ganze Jahr . . .'; VALERIO: 'daß wer sich Schwielen . . . daß wer sich krank . . . daß Jeder der sich rühmt . . .'; finally the two groups of noun-triads mentioned above). Aesthetically, then, the closure of *Leonce und Lena* is as complete and euphonious as any could be. Intellectually, however, the position is quite different.

For one thing, the revelation of Leonce's and Lena's true identity serves as the cue for a barrage of different interpretations and perspectives. Leonce and Lena themselves both claim to have been 'deceived' ('Ich bin betrogen. / Ich bin betrogen.'); but then one of them speaks of 'chance', the other of 'providence' ('O Zufall! / O Vorsehung!') The others' responses merely reflect their own bent: Valerio finds it all hugely funny ('Ich muß lachen, ich muß lachen'— a precise echo of Lacroix's words when he shatters the intense mood of the Danton–Marion scene, 22); the tunnel-visioned Governess sees it as the fulfilment of her fairytale dream of encountering a Wandering Prince ('Ein irrender Königssohn! Jetzt sterb' ich ruhig'; cf. 120); the King—comically robotic, as ever—switches so to speak into Emotion Mode ('Meine Kinder ich bin gerührt, ich weiß mich vor Rührung kaum zu lassen.') Far from offering the reader/spectator clear guidance, all of this is decidedly mystificatory; and our perplexity is only deepened once Leonce begins to speak. Büchner gives him three successive speeches, all of more or less the same length. The first is particularly disconcerting. Leonce initially strikes a conventionally regal pose, signalled by his use of the formal term 'meine Gemahlin' to describe his new wife; he then switches to Valerio-like ironic flippancy by playing games with words ('Stellung'–'stellen'; 'gestanden'–'Standhaftigkeit'); in the third and final sentence Büchner has him in effect deconstruct the whole dramatic fiction by suddenly speaking as an actor to his fellow actors, and categorizing the play as merely a 'Spaß'—a joke, a farce, an inconsequential bit of fun:

Gehn Sie jetzt nach Hause, aber vergessen Sie Ihre Reden, Predigten und Verse nicht, denn morgen fangen wir in aller Ruhe und Gemüthlichkeit den Spaß noch einmal von vorn an. Auf Wiedersehn!

Go home now, but don't forget your speeches, sermons, and verses, for tomorrow we shall calmly and cosily begin the entire farce all over again. Goodbye for now!

The second of Leonce's speeches again gives us no clear lead: it is a series of questions without answers; and its tone is ironic throughout. Turning to the problem of the future, it merely proposes a string of possible alternatives, none of them serious. Satire returns for a moment here: as King and Queen, so Leonce implies, he and Lena are like overgrown children with pockets full of puppets and playthings ('Nun Lena, siehst du jetzt, wie wir die Taschen voll haben, voll Puppen und Spielzeug?'); and in a reprise of Valerio's Act I joke (116), Leonce wonders whether they should amuse themselves by turning their puppet-subjects into soldiers, politicians, or diplomats. Alternatively, so he seems to suggest, they

A Flight into Paradise?

might dedicate themselves to aestheticism—to street-music and theatricals.

It is Leonce's final speech, however, together with its echo-effect sequel from Valerio, that constitutes the biggest tease of all. On the face of it this is surprising, in that Leonce no longer seems at all flippant, skittish or tongue-in-cheek: he seems to be genuinely sketching a vision for the future:

Aber ich weiß besser was du willst, wir lassen alle Uhren zerschlagen, alle Kalender verbieten und zählen Stunden und Monden nur nach der Blumenuhr, nur nach Blüthe und Frucht. Und dann umstellen wir das Ländchen mit Brennspiegeln, daß es keinen Winter mehr gibt und wir uns im Sommer bis Ischia und Capri hinaufdestilliren, und wir das ganze Jahr zwischen Rosen und Veilchen, zwischen Orangen und Lorbeern stecken.

But I know better than that what you want. We'll have all clocks destroyed and all calendars banned and measure the hours and months by the flower-clock alone, by the rhythms of blossom and fruit. And then we'll surround our little kingdom with burning-glasses so that winter will be gone for ever and in summer it will be just like Ischia and Capri, and all through the year we shall wander among roses and violets, oranges and bay.

Although—in contrast to the previous two speeches of Leonce's—the language here is not ironic, and certainly not mocking or sardonic, it nevertheless remains true to genre in being unmistakably playful: it conjures up a utopian vision whilst making its utopianism, its imaginariness, perfectly plain. Büchner reinforces this sense of playfulness by giving the last word to Valerio, the play's equivalent of the Shakespearian Fool, the traditional German Hanswurst, the Arlecchino of the *Commedia dell'arte:* no audience could resist a smile as this amiable reprobate announces his spectacular socio-political programme that would convert the Kingdom of Bum into a land of Cockaigne, that 'imaginary country' that is 'the abode of luxury and idleness' (OED), the true home of the *lazzarone*:

Und ich werde Staatsminister und es wird ein Dekret erlassen, daß wer sich Schwielen in die Hände schafft unter Kuratel gestellt wird, daß wer sich krank arbeitet kriminalistisch strafbar ist, daß Jeder der sich rühmt sein Brod im Schweiße seines Angesichts zu essen, für verrückt und der menschlichen Gesellschaft gefährlich erklärt wird und dann legen wir uns in den Schatten und bitten Gott um Makkaroni, Melonen und Feigen, um musikalische Kehlen, klassische Leiber und eine kommode Religion!

And I shall be Chief Minister, and a decree will be issued that anyone getting their hands calloused will be taken into care, anyone working themselves sick shall be punishable at law, anyone boasting of earning their bread by the sweat of their brow shall be declared insane and a danger to society. And then we shall all stretch out in the shade and ask God for macaroni, melons, and figs, for melodious voices, classical bodies, and a comfortable religion.

What kind of utopia is envisaged in this double envoi from the new King and his improbable Chief Minister? Sir Thomas More's original Utopia or 'No-Place' (the literal meaning of the Greek components in More's invented word) was 'an imaginary island, depicted ... as enjoying a perfect social, legal and political system' (*OED*). The island status of this model Nowhere is constitutive: Utopia is necessarily distinct from any known and actual reality. It is thus perhaps no coincidence that Büchner has Leonce imagine his transmogrified kingdom as a quasi-island ('daß ... wir uns im Sommer bis Ischia und Capri hinaufdestillieren'). By the same token, there is no pretence that the real German lands are to be transformed: the fictive King Leonce is omnipotent solely within the imaginary and minuscule land of Bum (itself already a kind of No-Place)—and the Grand Plan envisages turning the kingdom into a virtual island, an Arcadian enclave with its palisade of 'Brennspiegeln', entirely separate and insulated from the unregenerate polities all around it, within which, by implication, the same clocks and calendars and wintry conditions, the same punishing work routines and scarcity of food, will continue as ever to prevail. Büchner's restraint goes further still. The writer, after all, is omnipotent within the realm of his fictions, and the emphatically make-believe tenor of *Leonce und Lena* would readily have enabled Büchner—had he so wished—to show the New Arcadia, the New Cockaigne, not merely as a prospect for the future beyond the end of the play, but as a lived reality in the fictive present. Like Hoffmann with his 'Atlantis' in *Der goldne Topf*, however, he doesn't do so because he refuses to disguise the fact that in the given historical-political circumstances a new order of society can be only a potentiality, a dream to be aspired to. It is just the same with the vision of Italy at the close of Act I: it remains a vision: Leonce and Valerio never actually get there. And their journey itself is not milk and honey: Valerio at any rate puffs and pants (118), and ends up with corns on his feet and a sweaty body (120); he is in truth very far from being one of the divine spirits that supposedly enter Olympus untouched by the 'sweat and dust' of promiscuous reality (108).

It is of course only in his comedy that Büchner can stage a blissful outcome, albeit prospective rather than actual. The conventions of the genre allow him to develop an opposite trajectory to that presented in the other works: whereas *Dantons Tod*, *Lenz*, and *Woyzeck* show a gathering disintegration, disorientation, destruction, the process celebrated in *Leonce und Lena* is exactly the reverse. There are some fascinating manifestations of this—not least the fact that the positive vision at the *end* of *Leonce und Lena* is an echo of the similar vision near the *beginning* of *Dantons Tod* (11). The social-political programme conveyed through Camille and Hérault in Act I, Scene i, of *Dantons Tod* is of course differently articulated, as befits the very different mood, context, and genre of the earlier play; but the essential parallelism is clear nonetheless. There is even a specific verbal echo: Valerio's prayer for 'musikalische Kehlen' is plainly reminiscent of Camille's longing for 'melodische Lippen'. Valerio's 'klassische Leiber', too, are obliquely reminiscent of Camille's 'nackte Götter, Bacchantinnen'; indeed the whole tenor of the comedy's vision of Arcadia and Cockaigne is anticipated in Camille's glorification of 'Greek' ease as against 'Roman' (i.e. Jacobin) severity. The crucial point of similarity, however, may be seen in the motif of 'clocks': Leonce's intention of abolishing the tyranny of clocks and calendars (and therewith the principal source of ennui) is directly anticipated in Hérault's rejection of the Jacobin aspiration to remodel mankind 'nach der Mechanik des Genfer Uhrmachers' (10; *according to the mechanics of the Genevan clockmaker*). Within the specific historical framework of *Dantons Tod*, the ideals voiced through Hérault and Camille are of course quite unachievable, as is emphasized above all by Danton's caustic question: 'Wer soll denn all die schönen Dinge ins Werk setzen?' (12; *Who's going to bring about all these wonderful things?*) In the make-believe land of Bum, by contrast, Danton's question is easily answered: the omnipotent new King and his unlikely Chief Minister can wreak whatever changes they wish in the golden future beyond the close of the play. But can anything be achieved *within* the ambit of the comedy? Indeed it can—not in the public domain, but solely in the private realm of love.

Love is a crucial element in all Büchner's works, but he gives it a uniquely important role in his comedy. Two particular features distinguish it in *Leonce und Lena*: only here does it constitute the very heart of the plot; and only here do we see the genesis of a love-relationship rather than its collapse or destruction (or the effects thereof). It is true that the Rosetta episode features the demise of a relationship, and in explicit death-and-burial terms. But it is essentially a prelude: it brings Leonce's existential crisis to a head; and it shows the problem of love to be central to that crisis.

We have already traced the explosion of love between the two protagonists in Act II, but one aspect of Büchner's presentation needs particular emphasis. What he almost exclusively shows us is the man's responses, not the woman's. Lena says conspicuously little in the play as a whole, and almost nothing once she has fled the stage in II. iv; Leonce, by contrast, is given to voice his reactions at considerable length. Indeed Lena's love has to be taken virtually on trust, for the text offers only two explicit pointers: *Leonce's* assertion in III. i that she loves him ('Sie weiß nur daß sie mich liebt', 126); and the mute though eloquent gesture indicated in the play's final stage direction: 'Lena lehnt sich an ihn . . .' (133–4: *Lena leans herself against him . . .*; the same expressive gesture is figured in *Lenz*—cf. above, p. 258). On the face of it this suggests that the play is heavily biased in favour of the male viewpoint; in an essential sense, however, the very opposite is true. It is revealing in this context to consider Lena's poignant lament towards the close of her first scene (I. iv):

Pfui! Siehst du, ich schäme mich.—Morgen ist aller Duft und Glanz von mir gestreift. Bin ich denn wie die arme, hülflose Quelle, die jedes Bild, das sich über sie bückt, in ihrem stillen Grund abspiegeln muß? Die Blumen öffnen und schließen, wie sie wollen, ihre Kelche der Morgensonne und dem Abendwind. Ist denn die Tochter eines Königs weniger, als eine Blume? (117–18)

Oh fie, what shame I feel!—Tomorrow all my bloom and fragrance will be gone. Am I then like the poor, helpless stream that must needs mirror in its silent depths whatever image chooses to appear above it? Even the flowers open and shut as they wish to the morning sun and the evening breeze. Is the daughter of a king then less than a flower?

It is immediately after this that we are offered the image of Lena as a 'sacrificial lamb', with the knife supposedly already poised for her slaughter. The actual outcome is of course very different. Not only is she not figuratively annihilated, but her more specific fears are

A Flight into Paradise?

likewise never borne out: far from her suffering the fate of the 'poor, helpless stream' and having some alien man's image forced upon her, it is her own innermost spirit that enters into Leonce and gives him new life, and which he duly makes the essence of the wondrous new order envisioned at the close, with its 'Blumenuhr' in place of mechanical, spiritless clocks and calendars. Thus we see at the very heart of *Leonce und Lena* what we saw around the edges of *Dantons Tod*: for Georg Büchner it is women alone that seem to embody true being and true values.

I mentioned earlier that the revelation of the couple's true identity in III. iii cues a disconcerting barrage of different reactions amongst the characters on the stage; most of these were then quoted, but not the first and most arresting of them: Leonce's instant interpretation that in seeking to flee the horrors of an arranged marriage, they had wandered into Paradise: 'Ei Lena, ich glaube das war die Flucht *in das Paradies*.' (133, but emphasis as in Mayer, BD 84). This offers perhaps the most revealing perspective onto the central events of the play and their symbolic significance. Only a few moments before, a similar allusion—at once facetious and serious—was conveyed through Valerio after the final 'Amen' sealing the couple's marriage: 'so wäre denn das Männlein und das Fräulein erschaffen und alle Thiere des Paradieses stehen um sie' (132; *thus you might say are man and woman first created, and all the animals of Paradise stand around them*). Earlier still, the climactic encounter between hero and heroine in II. iv was prefaced by yet another reference to Paradise in Leonce's loaded description of the balmy night: 'O Nacht, balsamisch wie die erste, die auf das Paradies herabsank.' (124). In his other works Büchner repeatedly shows us his principal characters finding refuge and solace in love—but only so to speak on the fringes of the action, or else at some remote point in the past or the future. Only in *Leonce und Lena* does he place love at the centre, and celebrate it as a paradisal and *present* totality, albeit instantly relativized, and conducing to a perfect form of society-at-large only in the future that lies eternally beyond the close of the play. How extraordinary, then, that throughout much of the time that he was working on his comedy, he was also working on *Woyzeck*: in one play—a couple blissfully conjoined through their 'flight into Paradise'; in the other—the brutal disintegration of a couple in a kind of hell.

Part IV
Woyzeck

15
The Manuscripts

AT first sight it seems barely credible that Georg Büchner could have worked simultaneously on two such radically different projects as *Leonce und Lena* and *Woyzeck*; on closer inspection, it is difficult to resist the conclusion that their extreme differentness is deliberate, and that they belong together like the contrary poles of a magnet. Such a polarity is indeed hinted at by Büchner himself in his somewhat arch letter of 2 September 1836 to his younger brother Wilhelm, when he mentions that he has not only given himself over to the study of philosophy and the sciences in readiness for his forthcoming teaching post at Zurich, but is also 'busily getting some people to murder or marry each other on paper' ('—Dabei bin ich gerade daran, sich einige Menschen auf dem Papier todtschlagen oder verheirathen zu lassen', ii. 460). The range of direct opposites is certainly startling, extending as they do to every essential aspect of the two plays: comedy/tragedy; traditional three-act structure/quasi-filmic succession of often fragment-like scenes; royal prince as hero/abject underdog as hero; Leonce's torpor/Woyzeck's drivenness; fey, ethereal Lena/earthy, lusty Marie; formation of a union ('sich verheirathen')/disintegration of a union ('sich todtschlagen'); progression from society to a Beyond, then back to society/progression from a Beyond to society, then back to the Beyond. The polarities are so fundamental, so systematic, that the plays may well be best appreciated in performance by being staged back-to-back on the same bill, with the same actors/actresses playing the same complementary roles.

In speaking of *Woyzeck* in terms of stage performance, however, we bump up against the problem that there is in truth no such entity. Any theatre production billed as *Woyzeck*, any seemingly complete version of the text between the covers of a book, can unfortunately never be anything more than a construct, a best-guess composite put together out of the incomplete manuscripts that Büchner left at his death; even the very title is not Büchner's own.

For a variety of reasons, the manuscripts present enormous problems: Büchner often wrote in such a hectic fashion that his handwriting is generally difficult to read, and sometimes indecipherable even to the most skilled of palaeographers; he didn't bother to number either his pages or his scenes, and in consequence it is often impossible to establish the order of scenes with certainty; his paper and inks were of poor quality, and have not lasted well; in addition, the manuscripts have suffered extensively from the eager attentions of successive editors (most notoriously, the nineteenth-century editor Karl Emil Franzos used chemicals on the manuscripts which made the faded writing clearer for a time, but then left it even more faded than before, and in some cases physically displaced fragments of letters and punctuation marks; the discolouration of the paper caused by Franzos's well-meant but damaging ministrations can be easily seen on the facsimiles referred to below). The problems of the manuscripts loomed so large in the eyes of both Karl Gutzkow and Ludwig Büchner that they simply omitted *Woyzeck* altogether from their respective editions of Büchner's works (though it seems certain that both men were put off by the content and tenor of the manuscripts as much as by the difficulties of deciphering them). As a result, no printed version appeared at all until Franzos included *Wozzeck* in his 1879 edition—the garbled name being characteristic of a garbled text that Franzos moreover chose to 'improve' with numerous arbitrary alterations and additions of his own invention. Over the past few decades the herculean efforts of scholars—especially in the area of palaeography—have greatly improved the situation, to the point where it is unlikely ever to become significantly clearer or more definitive unless further manuscript material comes to light (an unlikely eventuality), and there is now complete or broad agreement amongst manuscript scholars regarding all major problems. A particularly momentous advance occurred in 1981 in the form of Gerhard Schmid's state-of-the-art edition of *Woyzeck*, which not only offers transcriptions of the manuscripts and a formidable critical apparatus, but also contains large-format facsimiles of the entire corpus of manuscript material (indeed the facsimiles are said to be clearer than the originals).[1]

Although the manuscript situation is convoluted, not to say confusing, we cannot really proceed without taking some account of

---

[1] Georg Büchner, *Woyzeck. Faksimileausgabe der Handschriften*, ed. Gerhard Schmid (Wiesbaden, 1981; contents: 'Faksimile. Transkription. Kommentar. Lesartenverzeichnis').

The Manuscripts

it—hence the following summary (based largely on the evidence and arguments presented by Gerhard Schmid).

There are altogether three extant manuscripts: a folio-sized set; a single quarto-sized sheet; and a quarto-sized set.

Folio Set

1. This consists of five folio-sized 'booklets', made by folding half a standard sheet of paper to yield two leaves, i.e. four pages (Schmid thinks it probable that Büchner routinely bought his paper supplies in this format, that is, as pre-folded folio-sized 'booklets').
2. It is generally agreed that these five booklets belong together.
3. It is widely agreed that Büchner wrote successively on all four pages of a booklet before going on to the next (i.e. the booklets were not interleaved).
4. It is widely agreed that the manuscript contains *two* quite separate scene-groups, with twenty-one scenes in one, and nine in the other; following the practice introduced by Werner Lehmann, these scene-groups are now commonly referred to as 'H1' and 'H2'.
5. It is widely agreed that the order of scenes in H1 and H2 is as shown in Lehmann's edition (145–65).
6. It is generally agreed that, amongst the extant manuscripts, H1 represents Büchner's earliest work on his projected play.

Single Quarto Sheet

1. The sheet contains two scenes, one of which (the Professor/Doctor scene) carries over from one page to the next, and so was unquestionably written before the other, much shorter one (the scene in which Woyzeck is rejected by his child).
2. Although it has become standard practice to lump the two scenes together under Lehmann's designation 'H3', this is strictly speaking a misnomer, in that the two scenes are dramatically unconnected with each other, and were clearly penned at different times.
3. It is widely agreed that the earlier scene (H3, 1) was written *after* the completion of H1, and *before* the composition of H2, 6 (the 'pissing scene' between Woyzeck and the Doctor).

Schmid believes that Büchner wrote H3, 1 as a try-out after completing H2, 5, and then discarded it in favour of the scene we know as H2, 6; Lehmann on the other hand believes that H3, 1 was written as an *additional* Woyzeck–Doctor scene *after* H2, 6, and perhaps even after H4, 8 (the corresponding scene in the latest manuscript). Typically, this question is an important one that can never be definitively resolved.

Quarto Set

1. There are six separate bits of paper in all, each folded to yield a quarto-sized 'booklet' of two leaves (four pages).
2. It is generally agreed that these booklets belong together.
3. It is widely agreed that the booklets were originally interleaved in pairs, each pair thus constituting a 'double- booklet' of four leaves (eight pages), and that Büchner wrote successively on all eight pages before moving on to the next such double-booklet (Büchner made the double-booklets himself by taking a standard four-page folio-sized booklet (as used for H1/H2), folding it in half, and then cutting along the top edge; the matching cut-marks are easily distinguishable on some of the facsimiles in Schmid's edition).
4. The manuscript contains seventeen scenes, generally agreed to constitute a single group, now commonly referred to in Lehmann's terminology as 'H4'.
5. It is generally agreed that H4 was written after H2.
6. It is widely agreed that the order of scenes is as shown in Lehmann's edition (168–81).

The question arises as to whether it is possible that Büchner wrote additional *Woyzeck* material that has since been lost or destroyed. The possibility certainly cannot be ruled out. For instance, there are yawning gaps in the H1 manuscript in terms of both plot and personae, and it is altogether conceivable that Büchner drafted other material that has simply disappeared. One particularly suspicious circumstance is the way that the H4 scene-group ends. H1 finishes some distance down the first page of the third folio booklet, and H2 finishes some way down the first page of the fifth. H4 on the other hand ends in mid-action very near the bottom of the eighth and last page of the third double-booklet: it is entirely possible that Büchner carried on writing in a further double-booklet that subsequently

The Manuscripts

disappeared—though of course this is pure speculation. What does seem unlikely, however, is that he embarked on a completely new manuscript, a putative 'H5' constituting perhaps a definitive draft of the play: all the evidence of the extant manuscripts strongly suggests that he was still working on the H4 version when he so unexpectedly died in February 1837 (cf. Gerhard Schmid's facsimile edition: *Kommentar*, p. 54). But speculate as we may, in the end we only have what we have: a corpus of authentic but more or less raw manuscripts, happily now accessible to us in Schmid's facsimiles; and sundry printed versions representing their editors' best endeavours in deciphering the text and ordering the scenes. (For convenience' sake, Lehmann's edition will continue as the main reference text throughout these chapters, but Schmid's readings will be drawn on wherever appropriate; see below, note 4).

A fundamental question remains to be answered: how do the various scene-groups in the manuscripts relate to each other? Are they successive stages in a single developmental process, or do they perhaps reflect quite different conceptions of the play on Büchner's part? There are some sharply divergent views on this issue, not least because it is inextricably linked in some scholars' minds with the problem of scene-order. Wilfried Buch, for instance, sees four quite separate 'Fassungen' or versions: an initial 'murder-version' (H1, 11–20); then a 'jealousy- version' (H1, 1–10, and H1, 21); then a 'grotesque version' (H2); and finally a version centred on 'suffering' (H4 and H3).[2] Werner Lehmann by contrast defines H1 and H2 as 'scene-groups' ('Szenengruppen') both belonging to the same 'first version' ('Erste Fassung'), while H4 is categorized as Büchner's 'provisional final draft' ('Vorläufige Reinschrift'). Gerhard Schmid's position is different again. He sees the three main scene-groups (H1, H2, H4) as stages in a single organic process, and thus defines them as successive 'draft stages': 'Erste/Zweite/Letzte Entwurfsstufe'. To some extent the differences are terminological rather than substantive, and indeed both Lehmann and Schmid share essentially the same view, which is also my own and that of the majority of Büchner scholars—namely that the various manuscripts reflect neither a static vision nor a radically shifting one, but instead represent phases of a single compositional process.

Before we go any further, an overview of these phases is necessary:

[2] Wilfried Buch, *Woyzeck. Fassungen und Wandlungen* (Dortmund, 1970), 11 ff.

H1

H1 is generally held to comprise twenty-one scenes (but see below, note 5). One cannot avoid using the word 'scene', but it is potentially misleading inasmuch as it suggests a finished unit within a sequence of such units. H1 is unmistakably a preliminary draft, and its successive scenes or scene-particles might best be compared to the pencil sketches and cartoons roughed out by a painter when planning a canvas. Some of the scenes are very sketchy indeed. In the case of H1, 9, for instance, the heading announces two characters ('Der Officier. Louis'), but only one appears, and speaks only a single line, devoid of any referential context. In one case (H1, 2), Büchner leaves a blank space on the manuscript which he almost certainly meant to fill in later on. In H1, 11, he tries out several different versions of a piece of dialogue, one after the other. Any given 'scene' may have been written simply as a try-out that might or might not prove useful later on; H1, 7 and H1, 13, for instance, could possibly have been meant as different try-outs for the same scene. It is notable in this context that Büchner subsequently drew a line through several of the scenes in H1—either because he had reworked them in H4 (H1, 4–7), or else perhaps because he had decided to jettison them (H1, 9; H1, 10).[3]

Dramatis personae. In H1 the main characters are named 'Louis' and 'Magreth' (also 'Margreth'); the surname 'Woyzeck' occurs only when Louis passingly refers to Magreth as 'die Woyzecke' (H1, 6)—an appellation that incidentally defines her as his wife, be it *de jure* or *de facto*; there is no reference to their having a child. There is no Drum-Major: Magreth consorts with a plain NCO ('Der Unterofficier'). Louis refers to 'Meim Officier' in H1, 8, and the heading of the following scene is 'Der Officier. Louis'—but no Officer actually appears either here or anywhere else. There is no 'Doctor' or 'Professor' (though the heading to H1, 21 includes the word 'Arzt'). One highly problematic character occurs in H1: a 'Barbier' (*Barber*), who speaks most of the lines in H1, 10, is figured again in the heading to H1, 21, and is then featured in a kind of thumb-nail sketch scribbled in at the very end of the H1 sequence

---

[3] H1, 3 is also ostensibly crossed out, but it is widely agreed that this was unintentional, and was caused by Büchner crossing out H1, 4 too vigorously (the manuscript shows this clearly; see Schmid, *Faksimile*, 2).

('BARBIER. Dogmatischer Atheist. Lang, hager, feig, schlecht [?], Wissenschftl.', 405;[4] BARBER. *Dogmatic atheist. Tall, gaunt, cowardly, bad[?], scientist*). It has often been argued that the 'Barbier' and Louis are one and the same figure, but there are no real grounds for this claim, and most Büchner scholars reject it. The following points are of note here:

1. The speeches of the 'Barbier' in H1, 10 include the second-longest in the whole of H1 (only the Barker's speech in H1, 2 is longer—by a very small margin).
2. His speeches in H1, 10 are quite different in language, tone, content, and length from any of the lines given elsewhere to Louis.
3. Various fragments of the 'Barbier's' speeches are recycled in H2/H4 via other characters (mainly the 'Handwerksburschen' (*Journeymen*), but also the Hauptmann and the Drum-Major); none of them are recycled in speeches by Woyzeck.
4. The characterization of the 'Barbier' at the foot of H1 does not fit Woyzeck as represented in any of the drafts: Woyzeck is neither a 'dogmatic atheist' nor a 'scientist', nor is he 'cowardly'.
5. Büchner put a line through H1, 10 in the manuscript—either because of the partial recycling mentioned above, or else (as Schmid believes) because he was discarding the scene as a whole, and therewith the figure of the 'Barbier'; certainly the scene bears no relation to the dramatic development in the rest of H1, and it does not tie in with developments in either H2 or H4.

---

[4] Lehmann gives *Woyzeck* in three different forms: he prints H1/H2/H3/H4 both *consecutively* and *synoptically*; and he also prints a composite version ('Lese- und Bühnenfassung'). In these chapters reference will routinely be made to the synoptic version, as this is the only one in which Lehmann gives the full text as he reads it, complete with Büchner's deletions and insertions, and with uncertain readings duly identified; any significantly different readings by Schmid will be referred to where appropriate, and identified by the prefix 'GS'. Quotations will normally *include* letters, words and punctuation marks filled in by Lehmann (e.g. Lehmann's 'Woyzeck' where Büchner wrote only 'Wzk.'); but they will normally *exclude* (a) matter deleted in the manuscripts; (b) matter that in Lehmann's view was left in by mistake when it should have been deleted; and (c) all Lehmann's editorial symbols and typographical differentiations (as these would inevitably prove confusing). In the present case, it might be noted that the word 'schlecht' is printed as an uncertain reading by Lehmann; Schmid prints '+ +', indicating a word that he considers indecipherable.

6. The most that could be said is that H1, 10 (together with the character-sketch scribbled at the close of H1) contains the merest germ of the scientist/human guinea-pig episode that Büchner develops so brilliantly in H2/H4.

Dramatic economy. H1 shows two striking features in this regard: (i) The scenes are highly action-oriented: there is no exposition or quasi-exposition, and no elaboration of character; and there are very few scenes that do not contribute directly to the story-line (H1, 1 and 2; H1, 10); (ii) The action portrayed in these scenes begins as it were in the middle.

Even without any knowledge of what happens in H2 and H4, it is clear from the most cursory reading of H1 that it represents in effect the second half of a drama. Except for H1, 10 (the 'Barbier' scene), the entire text from H1, 4 through to the end is devoted to the story of Magreth's murder: the build-up to the murder; the murder itself; the aftermath. The essential prehistory, namely the story of Magreth's infidelity, is projected only in the briefest and most allusive of terms: (i) In the closing lines of H1, 2—and then chiefly in a sentence added as an afterthought in the margin of the manuscript (the exclamation from the 'Unterofficier': 'Das ist ein Weibsbild guckt siebe Paar lederne Hose durch', 355; *What a woman see her way clean through seven pair of leather breeches*). (ii) In the two sentences of Magreth's that constitute the entirety of H1, 3: 'Der andre hat ihm befohlen und er hat gehn müssen. Ha! Ein Mann vor einem Andern.' (359; *That other feller gave him an order and he had to go. Cor! One man out in front of another.*) Even this is not certain, as the incident that Magreth refers to is not included in the text, and was probably meant to be written in later in the space left at the foot of H1, 2 (cf. 355, line 30).[5] (iii) In the opening line of H1, 5. This constitutes the only reference in H1 to Magreth physically consorting with a man—and it consists solely in Louis's outburst as he looks through the window of the inn: 'Er—Sie! Teufel!' (379;

---

[5] Although Magreth's two sentences are always treated as a separate scene, it is highly questionable whether this was Büchner's intention. If so, then it would be the only scene in the entire manuscript corpus without its own separate scene-heading. It is much more likely that he meant it as the tailpiece of H1, 2, following on from—and referring to—the new matter to be added later in the space left blank at the foot of the previous page (cf. Schmid, *Faksimile*, 1–2).

Him—her! Hellfire!; compare the corresponding scene in H4, where Büchner includes an explicit stage direction: 'Woyzeck stellt sich an's Fenster. Marie u. d. Tambourmajor tanzen vorbey, ohne ihn zu bemerken', 380; *Woyzeck positions himself at the window. Marie and the Drum-Major dance by without noticing him*).

H2

H2 comprises nine scenes in all. One of these (H2, 3, the fairground scene) reworks material from H1; all the others are new. The most striking difference as compared with H1 is that most of the scenes are much longer (H2 with its nine scenes occupies nearly as much book-space as H1 with its twenty-one). Nonetheless, Büchner was clearly still making sketches, however detailed and elaborate, and not setting out to produce definitive scenes in a definitive order: H2, 9 with its single line of dialogue is the merest germ of a scene (subsequently developed to great effect in H4, 16); H2, 5 is conspicuously sketchy with its false start, its brevity, its division into two by means of a horizontal pen-line (clear in the facsimile, but not reproduced in Lehmann's edition); H2, 3 is also plainly sketch-like, particularly in its second half; in H2, 7, Büchner tries out at least two, and probably three, different openings to the scene, and much of the subsequent dialogue is elliptical and clearly provisional. Nearly all the scenes were subsequently reworked in some form in H4 (though conspicuously *not* in the same order), and most accordingly have a line drawn through them. One significant exception is H2, 7, the scene between the Doctor and the Hauptmann: although he extensively reworked it in H4, 9, Büchner did not put a line through H2, 7; this constitutes important evidence about his intentions in the later scene (see below, p. 301).

Dramatis personae. The main characters are now identified mostly as 'Woyzeck' and 'Louise' (in H2, 5, H2, 8 and H2, 9, Büchner suddenly switches to 'Franz' and 'Louisel', having presumably forgotten his practice in previous scenes—which accordingly had perhaps been written somewhat earlier). The couple now have a child. The Drum-Major, the Hauptmann, and the Doctor all make their appearance. (The name 'Magreth' is retained in H2, but is now applied to a different character: Louise's neighbour in H2, 2.)

Dramatic economy. At first sight, H2 appears to dovetail neatly with H1 by covering precisely that phase in the overall action that the earlier draft scarcely touched on: whereas H1 depicted the murder story, H2 now depicts its necessary prehistory, to wit the infidelity story (Louise's instant sexual attraction to the strutting Drum-Major, H2, 2; his own strongly sexual response to her, H2, 5; the Hauptmann's baiting of Woyzeck about Louise's cavortings, H2, 7; Woyzeck's angry confrontation with Louise, H2, 8; her potential guilty conscience, H2, 9). One can see why Lehmann defined H1 and H2 as belonging to one and the same draft. This linkage is highly dubious, however, inasmuch as H2 is virtually the opposite of H1 in pattern and dynamic. Whereas H1 consists in a cascade of short-to-extremely-short scenes all furthering the action, but occasionally interspersed with apparently actionless interludes quite extraneous to the plot, H2 consists almost entirely of such 'interludes'. But they are 'interludes' only from a plot-centred viewpoint; on a larger view, they constitute the very essence of Büchner's emerging drama, which increasingly generates a kind of deep-level action or dramatic process that is infinitely more resonant and powerful than any surface enactment of the story-line. The beginnings of this are already evident in the 'interludes' of H1: the speeches of the Barker and the Grandmother are quite irrelevant to the plot, and yet they serve to locate the action in an intensely atmospheric and 'loaded' context. This is spectacularly the case in the opening scene of H2: it contributes nothing to the plot, and is not in any conventional sense expositional. And yet, faced by a Woyzeck scarcely recognizable by comparison with Louis in H1, we are instantly caught up in his vision of a menacing realm beyond appearances—a realm that on one level seems to be the delusion of a lunatic, while simultaneously coming across as real and disturbing (an ambiguity sharply highlighted through the medium of Andres and his half-dismissive, half-frightened response).

H3

As mentioned earlier, H3 comprises two unconnected scenes, clearly written on different occasions.

H3, 1 ('*Der Hof des Professors*'; The Professor's Courtyard). This scene presents two particular problems. One of these has already been discussed, namely the question of when the scene was written, and the associated question of whether it was in effect superseded by the Woyzeck/Doctor scene in H2 (and H4), or was meant as an *additional* encounter between the two figures. There can be no certain answer. In practical terms, the scene is a splendid piece of theatre that merits inclusion in any stage production—the only question then being where exactly to place it. The second problem in H3,1 arises from Büchner's use of the two titles 'Professor' and 'Doctor': did he have just one figure in mind, whom he first designated 'Professor' before then switching to 'Doctor'? Or did he mean two separate figures? Or was he perhaps playing around with two different conceptions of a single figure? The evidence is mixed:

1. The manuscript is relatively neat and considered-looking, and gives the clear impression that Büchner wrote the whole scene at one go, which would suggest that he switched from 'Professor' to 'Doctor' quite deliberately.
2. If 'Professor' and 'Doctor' meant one person, then practically speaking it would be well nigh impossible for him to be up in the attic one moment, and down in the courtyard the next; but practical considerations are not a strong argument, especially in a provisional draft.
3. The 'Professor' spouts on philosophy, and the 'Doctor' on biology. But the Doctor in H2, 6/H4, 8, who is unambiguously a medical experimentalist, likewise holds forth on matters of philosophy ('freedom of the individual' etc., 366, 367); and of course Büchner himself was to teach Comparative Anatomy from within the Faculty of Philosophy at Zurich, and also planned to give a course in Philosophy.
4. If the 'Professor' and the 'Doctor' were meant as separate individuals, then Büchner would surely have had them acknowledge one another's presence in some way; there would perhaps also be an explanation of how the Doctor came to be in the Professor's private courtyard.

It seems to me to be marginally more likely that Büchner had a single figure in mind; but there can be no definitive answer.

H3, 2 ('*Der Idiot. Das Kind. Woyzeck.*'). The scene is clearly intended to come very late in the play: the child's double rejection of his father only makes sense on the basis that the murder has already taken place; and the Idiot's refrain about Woyzeck having 'fallen in the water' places the scene *after* Woyzeck's retrieval of the knife from the pool, and his attempts to wash away the bloodstains (H1, 21). No one knows how Büchner intended to finish his play; but this scene tends to prove that he did not mean Woyzeck to die by drowning—an outcome arbitrarily added by Franzos in his 1879 edition, and copied by numerous subsequent editors.

H4

H4 contains altogether seventeen scenes—sixteen of them written out, and one (H4, 3, the fairground scene) consisting solely of a heading. Of these, eleven derive from H1 and H2, and six are new. H4 is much the longest of the drafts (13½ pages in Lehmann, compared with 10½ for H1, and a little over 9½ for H2). The manuscript has several distinctive features suggesting that Büchner regarded it as a relatively 'settled' text:

1. It bears none of the doodles and little drawings (mostly of heads and faces) that characterize the H1/H2 manuscript.
2. Throughout nearly all the manuscript Büchner carefully provided himself with neat, broad margins by folding the outside edges of the leaves of each booklet towards the centre in order to produce a crease mark (these creases are easily visible on many of Schmid's facsimiles).
3. From H4, 6 onwards, all the scenes except two are begun at the top of the page, even when space is available on the previous page, and in many cases it seems clear from the different handwriting that the scene-headings were written in in advance. This suggests that Büchner not only had a clearly planned scene-sequence in mind, but also knew how much space the relevant scenes would occupy.

Nonetheless, H4 is far from being a fair copy (in the sense of a copying-up of already finalized material); it is still very much a working draft in which the creative process is repeatedly apparent in crossings-out, insertions, and rapid, scrawly writing. This is particularly well demonstrated by the first of the three eight-page booklets: the first two scenes—both of them reworkings of H2 scenes—are quite evenly and steadily written; the fairground scene then consists solely of a heading with one and a half pages left blank, showing clearly that Büchner had not yet finalized it in his mind; and the next two scenes—both of them new—are full of deletions, additions, and feverish changes in the ductus of the writing. As regards the fairground scene, one can scarcely even speculate about Büchner's intentions, given that he himself had obviously not yet decided how to proceed. He already seems to have had trouble with it in H2: H2, 3 is markedly different from the corresponding two scenes in H1, and in the end simply peters out following a lengthy deletion (348). Bearing in mind that H1, 2 ends with 'Magreth' and the Unterofficier coming together thanks to the business with the watch, and that H4, 4 begins with Marie all excited about the earrings evidently given to her by her new beau, one can reasonably suppose that Büchner meant to show the beginnings of their liaison, but wasn't yet sure how to handle it. The only other problematic scene is H4, 9 ('Hauptmann, Doctor'). Although the scene as it stands ends with the two characters saying goodbye to each other, it is almost certain that Büchner intended to return to this scene and add to it. The physical evidence for this is strong: he left a large blank space (almost a whole page—considerably more than we find after any other scene); and he didn't put a line through the corresponding scene in H2 to show that he had finished with it. Dramaturgically, too, the scene is weak as it stands, in that it bears no relationship to the plot or the main characters at all. In the predecessor scene, of course (H2, 7), Büchner delivered the tense episode in which Woyzeck suddenly appears, and is cruelly baited by the Hauptmann about Marie's infidelity. Büchner's problem in H4, 9 was that he had already decided to transpose the confrontation scene between Woyzeck and Marie from *after* the baiting scene to a position *before* the equivalent scene in H4; as a result, the baiting episode no longer made sense, and he presumably had difficulties finding a new way of ending the scene and reintegrating it into the main action.

Dramatis personae. The only new figure in H4 is the money-grubbing Jew (an unhappy instance of the routine anti-Semitism of the period).

Dramatic economy. H4 carries the action right through from the beginning (and H4, 1 was unquestionably meant as the beginning) to the very threshold of the murder sequence, Woyzeck having acquired his weapon, and given away his few possessions. By adding new scenes, and by reworking and in some cases repositioning old ones, Büchner with his genius creates a unique and perfectly balanced interplay of extreme simplicity and ordinariness in the plot, and extreme intensity and richness in its multiple resonances. *Woyzeck* may be the incomplete relict of a very young man; but it stands as one of the most original, most influential works in the whole repertoire of modern drama.

16
Natur and *Kunst*

WHAT are we to make of this extraordinary work, unfinished as it is? What are the driving concerns, issues, obsessions that underlie the texts, and condition their particular shape and thrust? After *Dantons Tod* and *Leonce und Lena* (not to mention *Lenz*), we should not expect *Woyzeck* to offer answers, and indeed it does not: *Woyzeck* is a problem-play *par excellence*. This may well be one reason why Büchner had not completed it by the time he died. After all, he wrote *Dantons Tod*—a far longer play—at phenomenal speed, and the (lost) competition version of *Leonce und Lena* was likewise begun and finished within a matter of weeks. *Woyzeck*, on the other hand, clearly preoccupied him for many months, and the fact that he still never managed to finish it is surely because he had taken on the biggest challenge of his creative life, and found himself struggling to give shape to the most profound and complex questions.

One particular nettle needs to be grasped at once: although the opposite is commonly held to be true, *Woyzeck* was clearly not intended to be a 'social drama'—that is to say, a play principally aimed at exposing or documenting the iniquities of the given socio-economic system, as epitomized in the suffering of exemplary victims. One pointer to this is the fact that Büchner makes his Woyzeck relatively much better off in terms of both money and social status than the historical Woyzeck. In the period immediately prior to the murder, the real Woyzeck was jobless, homeless, and in such absolute penury that he could not afford even the meanest doss-house, and was living rough.[1] By comparison, Büchner's Woyzeck is relatively secure: he has a regular job, and another job on the side; a

---
[1] Cf. Alfons Glück, 'Der historische Woyzeck', in Anon. (ed.), *Georg Büchner 1813–1837*, 314–24. But cf. also Alfons Glück, 'Der "ökonomische Tod": Armut und Arbeit in Georg Büchner *Woyzeck*', in T. M. Mayer (ed.), *Georg Büchner Jahrbuch*, 4/1984, 167–226: in this article, Glück maintains that the central focus of *Woyzeck* is indeed the prevailing system of social 'exploitation, suppression and alienation' (167).

family of sorts; a place to sleep; and a little spare cash, however paltry. He is an exemplar of the underclass—but not of social deprivation in its extreme form; his circumstances would be enviable even to the down-and-outs of today in the cities of Europe or America. This is not to say that there is no element of social criticism in the texts: there undeniably is—but it is never more than a secondary issue. In H1, indeed, it is not an issue at all: Büchner never once shines a spotlight on socio-economic factors, and they are scarcely even mentioned in passing. The cash-nexus is fleetingly referred to in the 'Barbier's' cryptic remark that 'he is science', and that his 'scientific-ness' earns him half a gulden per week ('Ich bin die Wissenschaft. Ich bekomm für mei Wissenschaftlichkeit alle Woche ein halbe Gulden', 387; this presumably prefigures the Doctor/Woyzeck contract in H2/H4). The only other reference to money is even more fleeting, namely the reference to venal sex in one of the songs in the inn in H1, 17 ('... Behalt dei Thaler u. schlaf allein', 403; ... *Keep your money and sleep alone*). The Grandmother's tale is all about 'a poor child' ('ein arm Kind', 397); but although the child is doubtless to be imagined as economically poor (on the model of countless characters in fairytale lore), the epithet is clearly meant here in the sense of 'pitiable', for the story is patently about the nature of existence, not the nature of society.[2] In H2, economic details are woven slightly more often into the fabric of the text, but they are still not frequent, nor are they given any particular prominence. Poverty is implicitly conveyed when Büchner has Woyzeck tell Louise that they can go to the fair that evening as he has saved a bit of money ('Heut Abend auf die Mess. Ich hab wieder was gespart', 343); and of course poverty and economic exploitation are strongly implied by the monstrous arrangement whereby Woyzeck lets himself be systematically abused and degraded by the Doctor for the sake of a miserable pittance (367). Only twice in H2 does Büchner have his characters refer specifically to their poverty: Louise laments the lot of 'us poor folk' ('Ach wir armen Leut', 343); and Woyzeck utters his poignant cry when the Hauptmann taunts

---

[2] It is striking that although Büchner almost certainly drew on the fairytale 'Die Sterntaler' (*The Star Talers*), he retained none of its specific insistence on poverty: 'Once upon a time there was a little girl, her mother and father had died, and she was so poor that she had no little house to live in and no little bed to sleep in, and all she had left was the clothes on her body and a crust in her hand that some kind soul had given her.' Cf. Hinderer, *Büchner-Kommentar*, 234.

him about Louise: 'ich bin ein arm Teufel,—und hab sonst nichts auf der Welt' (375; *I'm a poor devil—and I've nothing else in the world*).

Things are markedly different in H4. Here, Büchner not only specifically thematizes poverty, but also projects it in class terms: at relevant moments, Woyzeck and Marie are no longer presented as individuals who happen to be poor, but as exemplars of a whole stratum of society—a grossly disadvantaged and quite literally 'working' class. Büchner does not refashion old H1/H2 scenes in such as a way as to include this new social-critical dimension (indeed in his reworking of H2, 2 he cuts out both Louise's 'Ach wir armen Leut', and Woyzeck's reference to his saved-up money). Instead, he incorporates the new dimension in brand-new episodes: the earrings scene, and the shaving scene (H4, 4; H4, 5). The class element is unmistakable in the remark that Büchner has Woyzeck make in response to his child's sweating brow—with the phrase 'wir arme Leut' now acquiring a far sharper edge than it had when Louise spoke it in H2, 2: 'Die hellen Tropfen steh'n ihm auf der Stirn; Alles Arbeit unter d. Sonn, sogar Schweiß im Schlaf. Wir arme Leut!' (358/360; *His forehead's all shiny with sweat; nothing in the world but work, even in your sleep you sweats. That's us poor for you!*) The class basis of poverty is equally strongly highlighted earlier in this new scene in the speech that Büchner gives to Marie, particularly through the use of the collective term 'Unsereins' (*our sort*); and what we also see here (and nowhere else in the text) is a defiant assertion that, however large the gulf between the poor and the rich, in their essential humanness they remain the same (though ironically it is precisely this 'humanness' that is already in the process of ensuring Marie's own doom):

Unseins hat nur ein Eckchen in der Welt und ein Stückchen Spiegel und doch hab' ich einen so rothen Mund als die großen Madamen mit ihren Spiegeln von oben bis unten und ihren schönen Herrn, die ihnen die Hand küssen, ich bin nur ein arm Weibsbild. (358)

Our sort don't have much, a bare little corner and a broken bit of mirror—but my mouth's just as red as them grand madames' with their full-length mirrors and their fancy gents what kiss their hands; I'm just a poor woman, that's all.

The same kind of argument is propounded minutes later in the shaving scene, only much more vehemently and programmatically.

The cue, of course, is the Hauptmann's mealy-mouthed accusation that Woyzeck, as the father of a bastard child, is devoid of 'morals':

> Wir arme Leut. Sehn sie, Herr Hauptmann, Geld, Geld. Wer kein Geld hat. Da setz eimal einer seinsgleichen auf die Moral in die Welt. Man hat auch sein Fleisch und Blut. Unseins ist doch einmal unseelig in der und der andern Welt, ich glaub' wenn wir in Himmel kämen so müßten wir donnern helfen. (362)

> We're poor folk, we are. Money, you see, sir, money. If you don't have no money. Morality don't get much of a look in when our sort gets made. We're flesh and blood too. Our sort just don't have no chance in this world or the next; I reckon if we ever got to heaven we'd have to help with the thunder.

The class argument is put even more sharply and specifically in response to the Hauptmann's lament at Woyzeck's lack of 'Tugend' (*virtue*):

> Ja Herr Hauptmann, die Tugend! ich hab's noch nicht so aus. Sehn Sie, wir gemeine Leut, das hat keine Tugend, es kommt einem nur so die Natur, aber wenn ich ein Herr wär und hätt ein Hut u. eine Uhr und eine anglaise und könnt vornehm reden, ich wollt schon tugendhaft seyn. Es muß was Schöns seyn um die Tugend, Herr Hauptmann. Aber ich bin ein armer Kerl. (362)

> Yes, sir, virtue! I'm not that far meself. Us common folk, y'see, we don't have no virtue, it's nature what drives us; but if I was a gent with a hat and a watch and a nice smart coat and could talk all posh, I'd be virtuous alright. Must be a fine thing, sir, virtue. But poor, that's what I am.

This is social criticism writ large, and it is all the more trenchant for being voiced by an underdog, who not only stands up to his pompous windbag of a master but also leaves him thoroughly deflated and confused, to the delight of the reader/spectator. It is easy to see why so many commentators have regarded it as the central issue and purpose of the work, especially given the fact that for many years this scene was routinely placed at the beginning of edition after edition, following the practice initiated by Franzos in his garbled edition of 1879, and seemingly validated by the distinguished scholar Fritz Bergemann in the numerous popular editions first launched by the publishers Insel in 1958. Franzos and Bergemann no doubt believed that that was where the scene best 'fitted', but what they did was nonetheless an act of editorial barbarism, perpetrated in the face of the incontrovertible evidence of the manuscript: the ordering of scenes in H4 may in some cases be arguable, but there is no possibility whatever that the shaving scene came first—not least because it starts part-way down the page, following the last few lines of H4, 4. Indeed the true position of H4, 5 within the scene-order of the manuscript is highly significant, for it locates Woyzeck's expostulations on poverty and morality within a far larger context than that of mere social criticism.

By using the word 'mere' I do not mean to disparage the element of social criticism within the work, but to put it in its due perspective. By placing the shaving scene first, Franzos and Bergemann wantonly and enduringly distorted the overall perspective by not only wrenching the scene from its proper context, but arbitrarily re-functionalizing it as the dramatic exposition, which in consequence sets the play going in the wrong direction and with the wrong atmosphere. There can be little doubt that at one level Woyzeck is indeed serving as Büchner's mouthpiece with his sudden and highly effective blasts of rhetoric against the iniquities of the class-system and the speciousness of the Hauptmann's supposed 'morality' (cf. above, pp. 50 ff.). But we can interpret them as straightforward, unambiguous statements of Büchner's own social-political stance only by taking them in isolation. Within their particular dramatic context they are far less clear-cut; in fact they turn out to be part of the most profound and problematic concerns of the play. This is just as well, for if Woyzeck's words represented the ultimate truth of the play, or the premiss upon which it was founded, then we would be dealing not with a sustained and poignant tragedy, but with a *pièce à thèse* embodying an all too simple syllogism: morality is a luxury beyond the means of the poor, who in consequence are driven solely by their nature; Marie and Woyzeck belong to the poor; therefore morality is beyond them, and they are driven solely by their nature. Woyzeck uses this argument vis-à-vis the Hauptmann to explain or excuse the fact that he has a bastard child: 'wir gemeine Leut, das hat keine Tugend, es kommt einem nur so die Natur'. Three scenes later, he uses exactly the same argument—again in relation to the doings of his penis—when the Doctor berates him for pissing in the street: 'Aber H. Doctor, wenn einem die Natur kommt.' (366; Büchner clearly sets up the 'Natur'–'Natur' echo in H4 quite deliberately: at the relevant point in the H2 predecessor-scene, Büchner had Woyzeck use different and much vaguer terms: 'Aber H. Doctor wenn man nit anders kann?', 367;

But Doctor, if you just can't help it?) But what do we find in the intervening two scenes? In the first of them we see Marie and the Drum-Major in a louche tête-à-tête prickling with sexuality. In the second we see Woyzeck face to face with Marie—not in this case adducing the imperatives of nature as a counter to accusations of immorality and the like, but making such accusations himself, and making them in the most drastic terms of 'mortal sin': 'Eine Sünde so dick und so breit. (Es stinkt daß man die Engelchen zum Himmel hinaus rauche könnt.) . . . Adieu, Marie, du bist schön wie die Sünde—. Kann die Todsünde so schön seyn?' (364; *A sin so big and so fat. (It stinks enough to smoke the angels out of heaven.) . . . Goodbye, Marie, you're beautiful as sin. Can mortal sin be so beautiful?*) In Woyzeck's contradictory responses to the Doctor and the Hauptmann on the one hand, and to Marie on the other, we glimpse the essential skein of fundamental issues that Büchner tries ever more keenly to unravel and illumine throughout the successive drafts: questions of civilization as against nature; moral choice as against animal compulsion; responsibility and accountability; crime and punishment; sin and retribution.

It is in just such terms that Büchner launches the entire project in the opening scenes of H1: before homing in on the doings of individual human beings within their particular society, he conjures up a context that challenges the very idea of humanity, society, civilization. The tone is struck in the first words from the 'Marktschreier' (*Barker*): 'Meine Herren! Meine Herren! Sehn sie die Creatur, wie sie Gott gemacht, nix, gar nix. Sehen Sie jezt die Kunst, geht aufrecht hat Rock und Hosen, hat ein Säbel!' (343; *Gentlemen! Gentlemen! See here the creature as God made it: nothing, just nothing. Now here's civilization for you: walks upright, wears jacket and trousers, has a sword!*) It is not clear what exactly Büchner had in mind here, but it obviously entails animals, perhaps a couple of monkeys, one in its natural state, the other tamed, and togged up like a soldier. But in any case the thrust of the words is clear: 'Kunst', that entire man-made contrivance that is culture, society, civilization, is perhaps merely an overlay that might disguise our essential creatureliness and nothingness, but can never change or overcome it. The challenging of our normal assumptions is then greatly intensified in the second scene through the device of the performing horse, which serves as a visible parody of human pretensions. Twice the horse is said by the Barker to 'put human society to shame' ('Beschäm die menschlich Societät! ... So beschäm die société.', 355)—but for very different reasons on the two occasions. In the first case it is the horse's alleged intellectual brilliance that does the trick: it may stand on four legs and have a dangling 'Schwanz' (a *double entendre* implying both 'tail' and 'penis'), but with its 'Talent' and its 'viehische Vernünftigkeit' (*brutish braininess*) it is a member of every learned society, and a professor to boot. In short, it is no mere specimen of dumb animality, but rates as an individual, a personality, a true human being: 'Ja das ist kei viehdummes Individuum, das ist eine Person. Ei Mensch ...'. For all its apparent humanness, however, it remains an 'animal human', indeed 'a beast': 'Ei Mensch, ei thierisch Mensch und doch ei Vieh, ei bête.' The point is driven home by the most graphic means: a stage direction requires the horse-cum-human to 'behave improperly', in other words to defecate or urinate in public ('das Pferd führt sich ungebührlich auf'). This is where the horse is said for the second time to 'put society to shame'—by demonstrating not its super-developed intelligence, but its abiding naturalness: 'So beschäm die société. Sehn sie das Vieh ist noch Natur, unideale [Schmid: unverdorbe] Natur!' (*There, put society to shame. See, the animal is still all nature, unideal [Schmid: unspoilt] nature!*) The whole episode turns out to have a moral, which is duly delivered— and carries us with shocking suddenness from piss and shit to ultimate questions of ontology: 'Lern Sie bey ihm. Fragen sie den Arzt, es ist höchst schädlich. Das hat geheiße: Mensch sey natürlich. Du bist geschaffe Staub, Sand, Dreck. Willst du mehr seyn, als Staub, Sand, Dreck?' (*Learn from him. Ask the doctor, it's extremely bad for you. There's the moral: man, be natural. You're made of dust, sand, dirt. Do you claim to be more than dust, sand, dirt?*) The central importance of this proposition is reflected in the fact that Büchner tries it out again later in H1, through the medium of the 'Barbier': 'Was ist der Mensch? Knochen! Staub, Sand, Dreck. Was ist die Natur? Staub, Sand, Dreck. Aber die dummen Menschen, die dummen Menschen. ... Was ist das? Bein, Arm, Fleisch, Knochen, Adern? Was ist das? Dreck? Was steckt's im Dreck?' (387; *What is man? Bones! Dust, sand, dirt. What is nature? Dust, sand, dirt. But stupid humans, stupid humans. ... What is this? Leg, arm, flesh, bones, veins? What is it? Dirt? Why's it stuck in dirt?* Büchner's handwriting is particularly problematic here; see also Schmid's readings, and his list of variants.)

Such, then, was the original departure point of *Woyzeck*: the proposition that there is perhaps nothing real beyond the grim materiality of nature and its functional processes; that all else is perhaps mere delusion and absurd pretension. Büchner raised a similar perspective in the climactic final gaol scene of *Dantons Tod*: eating, sleeping, and procreating as the only essential reality; the infinitely replicated and immutable 'Schaafskopf' as the vapid truth behind our speciously individualized masks; our ugly genitals as the true mark of our animality—'das häßliche Ding' that we might just as well not bother to disguise, but instead leave exposed for dogs to lick.

In this context it is notable that Büchner makes mention of the animal world with astonishing frequency in *Woyzeck*. The majority of cases are only passing references, but they nonetheless serve to locate the central story within a kind of menagerie of animal activity: horse, canary, monkey, dog, ass, hare, hedgehog, mole, cat, toad, lice, sundry pondlife and other small organisms, spider, wasp, cow, hornet, mouse, worm, gnat, crab, butcher-bird, beetle. In many cases, however, the animal reference is much more specific and pointed. The fairground scenes present the most elaborate example of this, not least in the H2 version, where Büchner includes a sardonic comment on the 'advance' of civilization: 'Sehn Sie die Fortschritte d. Civilisation. Alles schreitet fort, ein Pferd, ein Aff, ein Canaillevogel! Der Aff ist schon ein Soldat, s'ist noch nit viel, unterst Stuf von menschliche Geschlecht!' (348; *Observe the progress of civilization. Everything's progressing, a horse, a monkey, a canary! The monkey's already a soldier, though that's not much— bottom-most species of human kind!*) This has a particular edge to it because—like the fairground scenes generally—it merges the realms of the animal and the human; and in the process it also serves to spotlight the way Woyzeck is automatically perceived by those around him: as a soldier he rates as the lowest form of human life, more or less on a par with the performing monkey. Elsewhere, too, the lowly perception of him by other characters is expressed through animal associations. Thus the Jew from whom he buys the knife dismisses him contemptuously as a 'dog' ('Der Hund', 388). When he urinates in the street—thus repeating the 'natural' but 'improper' behaviour of the horse—the Doctor likewise compares him to a dog ('er hat auf die Straß gepißt, an die Wand gepißt wie ein Hund', 366; cf. also 367). In the cat-throwing scene the Doctor not only calls him an 'animal' ('Bestie'), but also describes him to the students as displaying regressive features that link him to the ass ('So meine Herrn, das sind so Uebergänge zum Esel', 396). Animal imagery is also used in relation to Marie and the Drum-Major—but imagery of a very different kind. Interestingly, it occurs scarcely at all in the earlier drafts: only in H2 do we find a hint of animality, when Büchner has the Drum-Major instantly see 'Louisel' as a virtual brood-mare perfectly suited to the mass propagation of him and his kind: 'Teufel zum Fortpflanzen von Kürassierregimenter u. zur Zucht von Tambourmajors!' (356). In H4, however, we find a whole train of such images. Perhaps the most forceful instance is H4, 6, the only scene in which we see Marie and the Drum-Major alone together. If Büchner had been intent on writing a 'social drama' reflecting the irresistible impact of socio-economic circumstances, then this scene would surely have taken a very different shape. As it is we see an encounter not between exemplars of a particular society, but between an emblematic male and an emblematic female who see each other in purely creatural terms. For Marie, the Drum-Major is not a potential meal-ticket: he is an 'ox' and a 'lion' in human form: 'MARIE [*ihn ansehend, mit Ausdruck.*] Geh' einmal vor Dich hin.—Ueber die Brust wie ein Rind [Schmid: Stier] u. ein Bart wie ein Löw .. So ist keiner .. Ich bin stolz vor allen Weibern.' (364; MARIE *[with intensity as she gazes at him]. Just walk up and down, go on.—Chest like an ox, and a beard like a lion .. There's not another man like you .. I'm the proudest woman in the world.*) As for the Drum-Major's response to Marie: Büchner recycles the H2, 5 'brood-mare' image ('Sapperment, wir wollen eine Zucht von Tambour-Majors anlegen. He?'); but he also has him see Marie as a 'wild animal' ('Wild Thier').

The Marie/Drum-Major encounter in H4 constitutes a new scene, so that there are no comparators in the earlier drafts; but there are some revealing changes and additions in scenes that do have predecessors. H4, 2 is a notable case in point. In the equivalent H2 scene, Büchner had Louise and her neighbour respond to the Drum-Major as follows: 'MAGRETH. Ein schöner Mann! LOUISE. Wie e Baum.' (341; MAGRETH. *Handsome man, that!* LOUISE. *Like a tree.*); in H4, though, the dialogue is altered to yield a quite new perspective: 'MAGRETH. Was ein Mann, wie ein Baum. MARIE. Er steht auf seinen Füßen wie ein Löw.' (340; MAGRETH. *What a man, like a tree.* MARIE. *Stands there like a lion.*) Even more striking, perhaps, are the changes introduced into Woyzeck's responses. In H1, 6 'Louis' hears the subterranean voices telling him to stab 'the Woyzeck woman': 'Stich, Stich, Stich die Woyzecke todt, Stich, stich die Woyzecke todt!' (383); in H4, 12, however, 'die Woyzecke' is replaced by 'die Zickwolfin': '—stich, stich die Zickwolfin todt? stich, stich die Zickwolfin todt' (382). Büchner even invents a new word here (or borrows it from some unknown source), and no one knows for certain exactly what 'Zickwolfin' is supposed to mean. But the '-wolfin' part is plain enough: Marie is being projected as a 'she-wolf'; and it is more than likely that 'Zick-' is meant as a shortened form of 'Zicke', a variant of 'Ziege' (*goat*), and a word still used today as a pejorative term for a woman (analogous to English 'bitch!')—so that Magreth is implied to be so to speak doubly animal-like. The immediately preceding inn scene (H4, 11) offers the most revealing changes of all. When Woyzeck looks through the window and sees the couple dancing past, his reaction in the original H1, 5 version is simply this: 'LOUIS [*lauscht am Fenster*] Er—Sie! Teufel! [*er setzt sich zitternd nieder*] [*Er späht, tritt an's Fenster*] Wie das geht! Ja wälzt Euch übernander! Und Sie: immer, zu—immer zu.' (379; LOUIS [listens at the window]. *Him—her! Hellfire!* [he sits down, trembling] [He looks, steps to the window] *Such a frenzy! Yes, keep at it, writhe around on top of each other! And her: 'go on, go on'*.) In H4, Woyzeck's reaction is not only far more intense and sustained—it is also critically different in its orientation:

WOYZECK [*erstickt*] Immer zu!—immer zu! [*fährt heftig auf u. sinkt zurück auf die Bank*] immer zu immer zu, [*schlägt die Hände in einander*] dreht Euch, wälzt Euch. Warum bläßt Gott nicht die Sonn aus, daß Alles in Unzucht sich übernanderwälzt, Mann und Weib, Mensch u. Vieh. Thut's am hellen Tag, thut's einem auf den Händen, wie die Mücken. [etc.] (380)

WOYZECK [*choking*] Go on!—go on! [*starts up violently then sinks back onto the bench*] Go on! go on! [*Claps his hands together.*] Whirl and writhe! Why don't God blow out the sun when he sees the whole world writhing together in lechery, men and women, man and beast. They're doing it in broad daylight, on the backs of your hands, like gnats. [etc.]

What gives this passage particular resonance is the fact that it contains strong echoes of *Dantons Tod*: Danton's 'es ist als brüte die Sonne Unzucht aus' in the 'Promenade' scene; Lacroix's 'die Mücken treiben's ihnen sonst auf den Händen' in the Marion scene (see above, pp. 182 f.); there is also a clear echo of *Der Hessische*

Landbote, in which the lords and ladies of court and aristocracy are said to 'sich ... in ihrer Geilheit übereinander wälzen' (ii. 44; *writhe together ... in their lasciviousness*). As these resonances tend to confirm, we are not confronted here simply by the spectacle of a man in the grip of insane delusions. What we witness is a critical conjuncture: the point at which the central questions of nature and morality most powerfully intersect.

17
A Question of Seeing

THE question of what exactly Woyzeck sees/imagines as he watches the dancers at the inn, and what we as readers or spectators are meant to see/imagine, is itself a crucial one, for 'seeing' is one of the key motifs in the work. Büchner's presentation of the episode is typical: the actual events take place off-stage, beyond the open windows called for in the stage directions, and except for fleeting, kaleidoscopic glimpses we register the goings-on not directly but indirectly, as mediated through Woyzeck from his voyeurish vantage point by one of the windows ('Woyzeck stellt sich an's Fenster').

This is a situational topos already familiar to us from *Dantons Tod*, in which some of the play's most poetic and powerful visions are brought about by having a character stand by a window and 'see' things that we ourselves do not see (Robespierre, 28–9; Danton, 40; Julie, 72–3; cf. Lucile, 68–9; see also Lenz, 80). References to 'eyes' and 'seeing' abound throughout the *Woyzeck* drafts, but only very rarely is it a question of the physical perception of a physical reality—and nearly all such instances involve the Doctor, who is a comic figure precisely on account of his tunnel-visioned fixation on the observable, measurable data of the physical world. His indignation when we first encounter him is because of what he has concretely seen: 'Ich hab's gesehn Woyzeck; er hat auf die Straß gepißt, an die Wand gepißt wie ein Hund ... Ich hab's gesehn, mit dießen Augen gesehn' (366; *I saw it Woyzeck, you pissed in the street, pissed against the wall like a dog ... I saw it, saw it with my very own eyes*). And why did he happen to see it? Because he was conducting a ludicrous exercise in supposedly scientific observation: 'Ich hab's gesehn, mit dießen Augen gesehn, ich steckt grade die Nase zum Fenster hinaus u. ließ die Sonnstrahlen hineinfallen, um das Niesen zu beobachten' (*I saw it, saw it with my very own eyes, I was just poking my nose through the window letting the sun shine into it so that I could observe the phenomenon of sneezing*; see also the corresponding passage in the H2 draft, 367). 'Seeing' is once again emphasized at the start of H3, 1, this time with a splendidly scurrilous descent from the sublime to the ridiculous when Büchner has the Professor address his students from his attic window: 'Meine Herrn, ich bin auf dem Dach, wie David, als er die Bathseba sah; aber ich sehe nichts als die culs de Paris der Mädchenpension im Garten trocknen.' (394; *Gentlemen, I am on the roof like David when he beheld Bathsheba; but all I behold are the bustles drying in the girls' school garden.*) A little later in H3, 1 we are shown the Doctor delightedly noticing a new species of louse, and immediately whipping out his magnifying-glass (H2, 6 also refers to a 'Mikroskop', 369); but the comedy turns decidedly black when the Doctor shifts the focus to another, more interesting object of interest, namely Woyzeck, the human guinea-pig that he has rendered so excitingly dysfunctional: 'Meine Herrn, Sie können dafür was anders sehen, sehn sie, der Mensch, seit einem Vierteljahr ißt er nichts als Erbsen, beachten sie die Wirkung, fühlen sie einmal was ein ungleicher Puls, da u. die Augen.' (394; *Gentlemen, you can see something else instead, this human specimen here, d'you see, hasn't eaten anything but peas for three months, observe the effects, just feel how irregular the pulse is, here, and notice the eyes.*)

In the great majority of cases in *Woyzeck* the motif of 'seeing' relates not to the object but to the subject. What matters is not the thing beheld, but the perspective of the beholders, and/or the meanings that they ascribe to the things they see. This is true even of the Doctor: what *he* sees with his eagle eye and his ever-ready magnifying-glass and microscope is this or that partial aspect of this or that physical specimen; what *we* see is a character whose very dedication to 'seeing' makes him blind to everything that really matters. The Hauptmann is another interesting case in point, though the very opposite of the Doctor, in that Büchner makes him highly disposed to seeing the world around him in symbolic terms. This is particularly conspicuous when he tells how the sight of a mill-wheel makes him feel melancholic, or how the sight of his coat hanging corpse-like on the wall makes him cry ('ich kann kein Mühlrad mehr sehn, oder ich werd' melancholisch', 360; 'ich muß immer weinen, wenn ich meinen Rock an d. Wand hängen sehe, da hängt er', 370). It is clear, too, when he recounts his version of 'love'—a masturbatory fantasy triggered by the mere sight of sock-clad ankles exposed for once as their female owners hop over puddles ('Wenn ich am Fenster lieg, wenn's geregnet hat und den weißen Strümpfen so nachsehe wie sie über die Gassen springen,—

verdammt Woyzeck,—da kommt mir die Liebe', 362). Indeed the Hauptmann's symbolic reading of the world is emphasized again and again: in his anxiety at Woyzeck's hectic pace, and likewise the Doctor's (360, 364; 370); in the fear inspired in him by the sight of horses (370); in his sense of vertigo as he watches Woyzeck and the Doctor rush off down the street (375).

Another facet of the motif is demonstrated in the fairground scenes, in which the on-stage audience—and by extension we ourselves as readers/spectators—are repeatedly bidden to look at the Barker's exhibits: the verb 'sehen' is used no fewer than six times in his two speeches in H1, 1 and H1, 2. But of course the performing animals are not on display for their own sake, but only as a device serving to convey a message: namely the extraneous meanings projected onto them by the Barker, which in turn help to establish a conceptual framework for the play. This functionality of the 'seeing' motif is evident in the Barker's very first words in H1, 1, with their sharp contrasting of 'Natur' and 'Kunst' ('Meine Herren! Meine Herren! Sehn sie die Creatur, wie sie Gott gemacht, nix, gar nix. Sehen Sie jezt die Kunst...', 343); and it is even plainer in the sardonic formulation in H2, 3: 'Sehn Sie die Fortschritte d. Civilisation. Alles schreitet fort, ein Pferd, ein Aff, ein Canaillevogel!' (348).

Important though it is in these various episodes, the motif of 'eyes' and 'seeing' only comes fully into its own in the context of the two protagonists. In the case of Marie (/Magreth/Louisel), it is partly a question of how she is perceived by others. In this respect, the response of the Unterofficier at the beginning of H2, 5 is revealing: 'Halt, jezt. Siehst du sie! Was n' Weibsbild.' (352; *Hold it. D'you see her! What a woman.*) The word 'Weibsbild' is eloquent: the Unterofficier doesn't see an individual human being, nor even an individual woman: what he sees is Woman, the very picture ('-bild') of female sexuality—and the sexual element is immediately made clear in the ensuing remark of the Drum-Major's: 'Teufel zum Fortpflanzen von Kürassierregimenter u. zur Zucht von Tambourmajors!' (cf. H4, 6: 364). What is even more striking, though, is the emphasis on her own eyes, as distinct from how she appears in the eyes of others. This is exemplified in the continuation of the same passage in H2, 5, where Büchner not only spotlights her eyes and their 'blackness' through the Unterofficier, but follows this up with a telling comment from the Drum-Major: 'Als ob man in ein Ziehbrunn oder zu eim Schornstein hinabguckt.' (356; *Like looking down a well or a chimney*.) In this instance, her eyes are the mark of her unfathomability; in H1, 2, however, they are the measure of something very different, namely her phenomenal sexual acuity: 'Das ist ein Weibsbild guckt siebe Paar lederne Hose durch' (355; *What a woman see her way clean through seven pair of leather breeches*). In H2, this succinct and supremely graphic image is transferred to the new, quasi-expositional second scene, where it is given even greater force by being made the climax to an intensely expressive run of dialogue. In this passage (quoted here in its H4 version), Marie's persona is projected for the first time—and the projection centres on 'eyes' and 'seeing', even in the opening two lines, albeit only implicitly. The Drum-Major marches past at the head of his band, with Marie and her neighbour avidly watching:

MAGRETH. Was ein Mann, wie ein Baum.
MARIE. Er steht auf seinen Füßen wie ein Löw.
[*Tambourmajor grüßt.*]
MAGRETH. Ey, was freundliche Auge, Frau Nachbarin, so was is man an ihr nit gewöhnt.
MARIE. [*singt*]   Soldaten das sind schöne Bursch
MAGRETH. Ihre Auge glänze ja noch.
MARIE. Und wenn! Trag sie ihre Auge zum Jud und laß sie sie putzen, vielleicht glänze sie noch, daß man sie für zwei Knöpf verkaufe könnt.
MAGRETH. Was Sie? Sie? Frau Jungfer, ich bin eine honette Person, aber sie, sie guckt 7 Paar lederne Hose durch. (340)

MAGRETH. What a man, like a tree.
MARIE. Stands there like a lion.
[*Drum-Major salutes.*]
MAGRETH. Ooh, neighbour, what a friendly sparkle in your eye, that's a novelty coming from you.
MARIE. [*sings*]   Soldiers they're such handsome lads.
MAGRETH. Yer eyes are still all shiny.
MARIE. What if they are! Take your own to the yid and get 'em polished, perhaps they'd shine too and someone could flog 'em for a couple of buttons.
MAGRETH. That from you? From you? Well missus, or is it 'miss', I'm a decent woman, I am, but you, you see clean through seven pair of leather breeches.

Through these few lines, the essential persona of the 'heroine' is both generated and communicated: before all else, Marie is sexuality personified. And not passive but proactive sexuality: with her super-acute eye for what lies hidden within men's trousers, she is potentially more predator than prey, more dominatrix than dominated. This is duly made manifest in the single scene in which Büchner shows Marie and the Drum-Major together (H4, 6): it is Marie who holds the whip hand—almost literally. And once again here, 'eyes' and 'seeing' are at the heart of the fiction: making the Drum-Major parade himself like a prize bull at a cattle market, Marie with her eyes both discerns and devours his animal potency: 'MARIE [*ihn ansehend, mit Ausdruck.*] Geh' einmal vor Dich hin.— Ueber die Brust wie ein Rind u. ein Bart wie ein Löw . . So ist keiner' (cf. above, p. 311). He tries to grab the initiative by taking her in his arms, but she repulses him—not with physical strength, but with the 'diabolical' force of her eyes: '[*er umfaßt sie*] MARIE. [*verstimmt*] Laß mich! TAMBOURMAJOR. Wild Thier. MARIE. [*heftig*] Rühr mich an! TAMBOUR. Sieht Dir der Teufel aus d. Augen?' (364; [*he puts his arms around her]* MARIE. *[crossly] Let go of me!* DRUM-MAJOR. *Wild animal!* MARIE *[vehemently] Just touch me!* DRUM-MAJOR. *Is that the devil in your eye?*) Even as a child—so Büchner has it in H2— Louisel/Marie had the same powerful eyes: Woyzeck in his jealous rage makes to attack her, but she tells him: 'Rühr mich an Franz! . . . Mei Vater hat mich nicht angreifen gewagt, wie ich 10 Jahr alt war, wenn ich ihn ansah.' (377; *Just touch me, Franz! . . . One look from me when I was ten years old and my father daredn't go for me.*) It is at precisely this point that Büchner writes one of the most famous lines in all the *Woyzeck* manuscripts: 'Weib! . . . Jeder Mensch ist ein Abgrund, es schwindelt einem, wenn man hinabsieht.' (*Woman! . . . Everyone's an abyss, it makes you giddy looking down.*) The line is too neatly aphoristic to sound right in Woyzeck's mouth, and Büchner wisely discarded it in H4; but this mismatch apart, the image is eloquent indeed: throughout the *Woyzeck* drafts we find ourselves being confronted with a vertiginous abyss, with impenetrable depths as symbolized in the well-like, chimney-like blackness of the heroine's eyes.

In the case of Woyzeck, the 'seeing' motif is just as prominent as it is with Marie, but it has an altogether different import. This is already apparent in the kind of image that is conveyed through others' perceptions of him, which serve at one level as virtual stage directions helping to define the specific *Gestus* of the role: 'Du siehst so verstört'; 'Was siehst du so sonderbar'; 'du siehst so verrückt aus'; 'Woyzeck er sieht immer so verhetzt aus'; 'Du siehst immer so

A Question of Seeing 319

verhetzt aus' (343, 377 (2 ×), 360, 364; *You look so distraught*; *Why do you look so strange, you look so crazy*; *Woyzeck you always look so worked up*; *You always look so worked up*). The chief difference, however, lies in the fact that Woyzeck sees things—and hears things—that no one else does.

In his earliest draft, Büchner relates this 'seeing' and 'hearing' solely to the murder, indeed he makes it the key element in the dramatic build-up to the murder itself. He introduces it first in H1, 5, the scene where 'Louis' sees the unnamed couple cavorting in the inn: 'Blut? Warum wird es mir so roth vor den Augen! Es ist mir als wälzten sie sich in einem Meer von Blut, all mitnander! Ha rothes Meer.' (381; *Blood? Why's everything turning so red in front of my eyes! Looks to me like they was writhing around in a sea of blood, the whole lot of them together! Oh red, red sea.*) Having seen things in H1, 5, Louis is shown hearing things in H1, 6, and thus the murder-story begins to take shape: he hears fiddles and fifes echoing the 'Immer zu! Immer zu!' of the previous scene, and hears a subterranean voice commanding him to kill: 'Stich, Stich, Stich die Woyzecke todt . . . !' (383). In H1, 7, the seeing and hearing are duly conjoined in a passage that is almost laborious in its welter of narrative detail:

Ich hab kei Ruh, ich hör's immer, wie's geigt u. springt, immer zu! immer zu! Und dann wann ich die Augen zumach, da blizt es mir immer, es ist ei großes breit Messer und das liegt auf eim Tisch am Fenster und ist in einer eng dunkel Gaß und ein alter Mann sizt dahinter. Und das Messer ist mir immer zwischen den Augen. (383)

I can't get no peace, I hear it all the time, the fiddling and the leaping: go on! go on! And then when I shut me eyes I keep seeing this flashing, it's a great big knife and it's lying on a table by the window and it's in a dark narrow alley and an old man's sitting behind the table. And the knife's always there between my eyes.

The motif is repeated in H1, 11 and H1, 13, in the one case solely as vision (389), and in the other case mainly as sound (391); then finally, after the murder is done, the motif is so to speak rounded off in H1, 19 when Woyzeck returns to recover the weapon, and is met by ultimate silence: 'Was hör ich? Es rührt sich was. Still. Da in der Nähe. Magreth? Ha Magreth! Still. Alles still!' (405; *What can I hear? Something's moving. Quiet. Here somewhere. Magreth? Oh Magreth! Quiet! Everything's quiet.*)

Of the relevant scenes, H1, 5, H1, 6 and H1, 7 are all reworked in the H4 draft, and the corresponding H4 scenes accordingly give us a fascinating insight into the way Büchner's conception developed in the meantime. In H4, 11 we find that Woyzeck's 'sea of blood' vision, so prominent in H1, 5, is not retained in any form at all; while in H4, 13 none of the narrative detailing of H1, 7 is retained—indeed the scene is a kind of intensified conflation of both H1, 7 and H1, 13 (though H1, 13 is curiously not crossed out in the manuscript). Only H4, 12 preserves all the key elements of its predecessor—but here too we find significant differences, not least Büchner's characteristic shift to an even more spare, more incisively rhythmical style. What he originally wrote in his H1 draft of the scene was this:

LOUIS. Immer! zu!—Immer zu!—Hisch! hasch, so gehn die Geigen und die Pfeifen.—Immer zu! immer zu! Was spricht da? Da unten aus dem Boden hervor, ganz leise, was, was? [*er bückt sich nieder*] Stich, Stich, Stich die Woyzecke todt, Stich, stich die Woyzecke todt! und immer lauter und jezt brüllt es, als wär der Himmel ein Rachen, stich stich die Woyzecke todt! stich die Woyzecke todt. Immer zu! Immer zu! (383/GS 3)

LOUIS. Go on!—Go on!—whish-whoosh go the fiddles and the fifes.—Go on! go on! What's that speaking there? Down there from under the ground, dead quietly, what, what? [*he bends down*] Stab, stab, stab the Woyzeck woman dead, stab, stab the Woyzeck woman dead! and louder and louder and now it's roaring as if the whole sky was a throat, stab, stab the Woyzeck woman dead, stab, stab the Woyzeck woman dead. Go on! Go on!

But Büchner immediately slimmed this down by crossing out everything from 'und immer lauter' (*and louder and louder*), and adding instead 'Was! das zischt und wimmert und donnert.' (GS 3; *What! Such hissing and whimpering and thundering.*) In H4 he takes this process much further, stripping away all non-essentials and lending the scene extra urgency by making it even more gaunt, more staccato, more insistently patterned in twos:

WOYZECK. Immer zu! immer zu! Still Musik! [*reckt sich gegen den Boden*] Ha was, was sagt ihr? Lauter, lauter,—stich, stich die Zickwolfin todt? stich, stich die Zickwolfin todt. Soll ich? Muß ich? Hör ich's da auch, sagt's der Wind auch? Hör ich's immer, immer zu, stich todt, todt. (382)

WOYZECK. Go on! Go on! Quiet, music! [*strains his ear towards the ground*] Ah, what's that, what's that you say? Louder, louder—stab, stab the wolf-bitch dead? stab, stab the wolf-bitch dead. Should I? Must I? Can I

A *Question of Seeing* 321

hear it there too, does the wind say it too? Will I go on and on hearing it, stab her dead, dead.

Whilst the seeing and hearing motif is restricted in H1 to the murder-story, it acquires a new and much larger dimension in the later drafts as Büchner sets about creating the expositional and developmental phases of his drama. The opening scenes of H2 and H4 are indeed entirely devoted to establishing this new dimension (with the later version again more compellingly spare and elliptical than its predecessor): here, Woyzeck is suddenly a visionary, a man who sees, hears, senses a kind of meta-reality beyond the ordinary appearance of things—a world of death and infinite menace. A streak across the grass is for him the mark of some fiendish nocturnal ritual of decapitation perpetrated by the Freemasons (ever responsible in the folk imagination of the period for devilish goings-on), and any outsider who stumbles upon it is doomed to die:

Ja Andres; den Streif da über das Gras hin, da rollt Abends der Kopf, es hob ihn einmal einer auf, er meint' es wär' ein Igel. Drei Tag und drei Nächt und er lag auf den Hobelspänen [*leise*] Andres, das waren die Freimaurer, ich hab's, die Freimaurer, still! (338)

To this new Woyzeck, there is a threatening presence lurking behind him, lurking beneath him in the pullulating hollowness of the earth: 'Still! Es geht was! . . . Es geht hinter mir, unter mir [*stampft auf d. Boden*] hohl, hörst du? Alles hohl da unten. Die Freimaurer!'—a presence moreover that follows him, so he tells Marie, right to the edge of the town (342). He gazes into the distance, and what he sees and hears is an Apocalyptic vision of raging heavenly fire and a roaring as though of mighty trumpets—a vision so dire that they must avert their eyes and hide: '[*starrt in die Gegend.*] Andres! Wie hell! Ein Feuer fährt um den Himmel und ein Getös herunter wie Posaunen. Wie's heraufzieht! Fort. Sieh nicht hinter dich. [*reißt ihn in's Gebüsch*]'. In H4, 2, this sense of apocalyptic doom is greatly heightened by the direct quotation from Genesis that Büchner puts in Woyzeck's mouth: 'Marie, es war wieder was, viel, steht nicht geschrieben, und sieh da ging ein Rauch vom Land, wie der Rauch vom Ofen?' (342, and cf. Genesis 19: 28; *Marie, it happened again, lots of things; is it not written: and behold, there rose up smoke from the land like smoke from a furnace?*)

There is one further new and major context in H2 and H4 in which Woyzeck is represented as a visionary, namely the scene in which the Doctor berates him for pissing in the street. This is a particularly effective episode because Büchner juxtaposes two contrary modes of seeing: the Doctor's confident fixation on surface data, and Woyzeck's groping intuition of a world *beyond* the surface. In H2, 6, the element of groping is quite literal as Woyzeck struggles to define his sense of an irresistible but obscure order or dimension of nature:

Wenn die Welt so finster wird, daß man mit den Händen an ihr herumtappen muß ... Das ist, so wenn etwas ist und doch nicht ist. Wenn alles dunkel ist und nur noch ein rother Schein im Westen, wie von einer Esse. Wenn [*schreitet im Zimmer auf und ab*] (369)

When the world grows so dark that you have to grope at it with your hands. It's like when something is, yet isn't. When everything's dark, nothing left except a red glimmer in the west, as though from a hearth. When [*strides up and down the room*]

In H4, 8—once again in a reworking that is more succinct and more trenchant than its prototype—Woyzeck's perplexity is more directly, more graphically conveyed:

Sehn sie H. Doctor, manchmal hat einer so n'en Character, so n'e Structur.—Aber mit der Natur ist's was anders, sehn sie mit der Natur [*er kracht mit den Fingern*] das ist so was, wie soll ich doch sagen, z. B. (368)

You see Doctor, sometimes people have a sort of character, a sort of structure. But it's different with nature, you see with nature [*he snaps his fingers*] it's kind of, how can I put it, for instance...

The apocalyptic atmosphere of the opening scene briefly returns as Büchner has Woyzeck attempt to articulate his experience of a meta-reality, of nature-within-nature, what he enigmatically terms 'die doppelte Natur':

H. Doctor haben sie schon was von d. doppelten Natur gesehn? Wenn die Sonn in Mittag steht u. es ist als ging d. Welt in Feuer auf hat schon eine fürchterliche Stimme zu mir geredt!

Doctor, have you ever caught a glimpse of double-nature? When the midday sun stands high in the sky and it seems as if the world is bursting into flames, a terrible voice has spoken to me!

Finally he advances an explanation of sorts, namely his folklore-ish guess as to how the secrets of the realm beyond might be deciphered:

'Die Schwämme H. Doctor. Da, da steckts. Haben Sie schon gesehn in was fur Figuren die Schwämme auf d. Boden wachsen? Wer das lesen könnt.' (*The mushrooms, Doctor. It's all there in the mushrooms. Have you seen what patterns they make on the ground? Oh to be able to read what they say.*)[1] The response of the Doctor to all this is clear and emphatic: in his eyes, Woyzeck is quite simply but quite splendidly mad, and can be slotted into a ready-made and precisely labelled pigeon-hole: 'Woyzeck, er hat eine aberratio.... Woyzeck er hat die schönste aberratio mentalis partialis, d. zweite Species, sehr schön ausgeprägt.... Zweite Species, fixe Idee, mit allgemein vernünftigem Zustand' (368; *Woyzeck, you've got an aberratio.... Woyzeck you have the most beautiful aberratio mentalis partialis, category two, such a beautifully clear example.... Category two, obsessional but otherwise generally rational*). Are we, too, meant to believe this? Are we to believe the Doctor's verdict (in H2, 6) that Woyzeck is heading for the lunatic asylum ('Woyzeck! er kommt ins Narrenhaus', 369)? Surely not. The Doctor's analysis stands discredited by the very fact that it is he who utters it, since he himself is comic precisely because of his own *idée fixe*, his robotic obsession with experiments and data. On the other hand there are also the views put in the mouths of other figures in the work. Andres—whose sole dramatic function is to serve as a foil to Woyzeck—repeatedly calls him a 'Narr', a term embracing both foolishness and *folie* (H1: 379, 383; H4: 378); and he raises the spectre of madness in the very first scene of H2, in the face of Woyzeck's frightened and frightening talk of the earth beneath their feet quaking from the monstrous doings of invisible Freemasons: 'Seyd Ihr toll!' (339). Other normative explanations are offered through Andres: in H1, 11 he assumes that Woyzeck must be drunk ('Er ist besoffen', 389); or he may be suffering from nightmares ('Drückt dich der Alp?', 391); alternatively, Woyzeck must be ill: 'Franz, du kommst in's Lazareth. Armer Du mußt Schnaps trinke u. Pulver drin das tödt das Fieber.' (392, and see also 382 and 391; *Hospital, Franz, that's what you need. Poor sod, you should drink some schnaps with a powder in it, it'll kill the fever.*) The same suggestion is offered through Marie when Woyzeck confronts her in H4, 7 following her encounter with the Drum-Major:

[1] Cf. Henri Poschmann, ' "Wer das lesen könnt". Zur Sprache natürlicher Zeichen in *Woyzeck*', in B. Dedner and G. Oesterle (eds.), *Zweites Internationales Georg Büchner Symposium* 1987, 441–52.

'Franz, du red'st im Fieber' (366; *Franz, that's the fever talking*). More commonly, though, she too sees him as mad, or close to madness. In H2, 2 and the corresponding scene H4, 2, his apocalyptic talk makes her think he is on the verge of cracking up: 'Der Mann schnappt noch über' (343; cf. also 342). In the jealousy scene in H2 she tells him he looks as mad as a cow pursued by hornets ('du siehst so verrückt aus wie n'e Kuh, die die Hornisse jagen[2]', 377); in the corresponding scene in H4 Büchner has her say that he is raving mad ('Du bist hirnwüthig Franz', 364).

The question as to Woyzeck's sanity or insanity is, of course, no invention of Büchner's: it was central to the historical case on which *Woyzeck* is very largely based; indeed it is the only reason why the case became such a *cause célèbre* in the first place.

On the evening of 2 June 1821,[3] the 41-year-old Johann Christian Woyzeck stabbed to death his sometime paramour Johanna Christiane Woost. He was rapidly arrested, and made a full confession. Although on the face of it an open-and-shut case, it nonetheless dragged on for a long time: not until 27 August 1824 was Woyzeck publicly decapitated (the first person to be executed in Leipzig for several decades[4]). Soon after his arrest, and on the basis of suggestions in the newspapers that Woyzeck was 'afflicted by periodic madness', his defence lawyer requested a full forensic-medical examination of the accused's mental condition (491, 499), and a report was duly prepared and submitted to the court by Dr Johann Christian August Clarus, an eminent Leipzig professor and *Hofrat*. Clarus deemed Woyzeck to be fully accountable for his actions, and he was duly convicted and sentenced to death. However, he was granted a last-minute stay of execution in November 1822, on the grounds that a further deposition had been made claiming that

[2] Büchner wrote the abbreviation 'jag', which Lehmann completes as 'jagt' instead of 'jagen'—as though cows were in the habit of chasing hornets. (Lehmann is not alone in this: all previous editors also print 'jagt'; cf. Thomas Michael Mayer, 'Zu einigen neueren Tendenzen in der Büchner-Forschung. Ein kritischer Literaturbericht (Teil II: Editionen)', in H. L. Arnold (ed.), *Georg Büchner III*, special number of *Text + Kritik* (Munich, 1981), 289–90).

[3] The date appears as 21 June in Clarus's report (490), but this was a printing error. Cf. Reinhard Pabst, 'Zwei unbekannte Berichte über die Hinrichtung Johann Christian Woyzecks', in T. M. Mayer (ed.), *Georg Büchner Jahrbuch*, 7/1988–9 (Tübingen, 1991), 341–2. (Alfons Glück, 314, compounds the confusion by giving 3 June as the date of the murder, but this is incorrect: the true date is indeed 2 June.)

[4] Cf. Clarus, 488 n.; Pabst, 338. Woyzeck's was not only the first execution in Leipzig for many years, it was also almost certainly the last to be staged there in public (ibid. 346 n. 12).

Woyzeck's mind was indeed disturbed (493, 499).[5] Clarus again repeatedly examined and questioned the prisoner, and concluded his second, laboriously detailed report by once again declaring that Woyzeck was *not* suffering from a disturbed mind. This finally sealed his fate, and in due course his head was struck off in the presence of a crowd so immense that whole roofs had had to be removed in order to provide extra viewing space.[6]

The central focus of Clarus's forensic interest was Woyzeck's claim to have suffered numerous supernatural or paranormal experiences—most of which are unmistakably the models for the experiences acted out by Büchner's protagonist: noises from beneath the ground, and fiery visions in the sky, both experienced in open countryside some distance from a town (511); a sense of persecution at the hands of cabbalistic Freemasons (496, 519); disembodied voices (492, 498, 499, etc.); such voices telling him 'Stich die Frau Woostin todt!' (501, 515); an apparently telepathic mind-picture of 'die Woostin' dancing with another man, accompanied by the sensation of dance-music beating out the words 'Immer drauf, immer drauf!' (514).

Clarus's verdict on these things is unambiguous, and his own summary of his conclusions is worth quoting in full:

Aus den im Vorhergehenden dargestellten Thatsachen und erörterten Gründen schließe ich: daß *Woyzecks* angebliche Erscheinungen und übrigen ungewöhnlichen Beggenisse als *Sinnestäuschungen,* welche durch Unordnungen des Blutumlaufes erregt und durch seinen Aberglauben und Vorurtheile zu Vorstellungen von einer objektiven und übersinnlichen Veranlassung gesteigert worden sind, betrachtet werden müssen, und daß ein Grund, um anzunehmen, daß derselbe zu irgend einer Zeit in seinem Leben und namentlich unmittelbar *vor, bei* und *nach* der von ihm verübten Mordthat sich im Zustande einer Seelenstörung befunden, oder dabei nach einem nothwendigen, blinden und instinktartigen Antriebe und überhaupt anders, als nach gewöhnlichen leidenschaftlichen Anreizungen gehandelt habe, *nicht* vorhanden sey. (534)

On the basis of the facts set out above, and for the reasons there discussed, I conclude as follows: that *Woyzeck's* alleged visions and other unusual

---

[5] See also Pabst, 342–3 n.9.
[6] Ibid. 347. Cf. also Glück, 322. For an extensive documentation of the entire case, see Ursula Walter, 'Der Fall Woyzeck. Eine Quellen-Dokumentation (Repertorium und vorläufiger Bericht)', in T. M. Mayer (ed.), *Georg Büchner Jahrbuch,* 7/1988–9, 351–80.

experiences must be regarded as *hallucinations,* triggered by circulatory disorders, and aggrandized through his superstition and prejudices into notions of an objective and supernatural agency; and that there is *no* reason to suppose that the said Woyzeck did at any time in his life, and more particularly *before, during,* and *after* perpetrating the murder, suffer from a disturbed mind, or that he acted pursuant to an imperative, blind, and instinctual compulsion, or indeed in any way other than pursuant to the ordinary promptings of passion.

In the course of his second report Clarus systematically explains away every single one of Woyzeck's seemingly occult experiences (see 519 ff.), arguing that in every case he either misinterpreted some phenomenon in the external, objective world, or else suffered a purely subjective delusion (519). What occasioned Woyzeck's experiences was in Clarus's emphatic view neither a supernatural agency in the world at large, nor any pathological dementia within Woyzeck himself, but a combination of moral depravity and a specific physical disorder, viz. 'congestion of the blood' (see 488, 491: 'moralische Verwilderung'; 517, 520: 'Congestionen des Blutes').

It is tempting to enter into a detailed analysis of Clarus's reports, for although he was extremely conscientious, painstaking and—by his own lights—honourable, in effect he perpetrated a fraud, producing a spectacular piece of sophistry in which scientific expertise is entirely subordinated to the perceived interests of society and the rule of law. Clarus specifically claims at one point to be acting 'according to the principles of rational medicine' ('nach Grundsätzen der rationellen Heilkunde', 520), but his real agenda is quite different: he sees himself as a stalwart defender of prevailing values, holding the line against new, progressivist voices tending to 'debase' forensic medicine into a 'cover for all and every crime' ('die gerichtliche Medicin ... zum Deckmantel aller und jeder Verbrechen herabwürdigen', 524).[7] This essentially socio-political and

---

[7] Cf. Georg Reuchlein, *Das Problem der Zurechnungsfähigkeit bei E. T. A. Hoffmann und Georg Büchner. Zum Verhältnis von Literatur, Psychiatrie und Justiz im frühen 19. Jahrhundert* (Frankfurt, Berne, and New York, 1985); see esp. ch. 5: 'Georg Büchners *Woyzeck* und das Problem der Zurechnungsfähigkeit: das Drama als Auseinandersetzung mit Grundlagen, Prinzipien und Urteilen der restaurativen Justiz und Gerichtsmedizin', 45–76. Cf. also Alfons Glück, 'Woyzeck—Clarus—Büchner (Umrisse)', in B. Dedner and G. Oesterle (eds.), *Zweites Internationales Georg Büchner Symposium* 1987, 425–40.

deeply conservative agenda is transparently evident when Clarus writes:

ich [fühle] mich gedrungen im Allgemeinen zu bemerken, . . . daß, wenn auf der einen Seite der Eifer einzelner Schriftsteller und medicinischer Collegien Entschuldigungsgründe für Handlungen aufzufinden, die im Sturme eines von ungewöhnlichen Veranlassungen bewegten Gemüths, oder im Drange eines instinktartigen, von den Banden der Natur umstrickten Willens begangen worden, höchst achtungswerth ist, dennoch auf der andern Seite auch die Verwirrung und der Nachtheil berücksichtiget werden muß, der aus der unvorsichtigen Anwendung dieser Lehre entstehen würde, wenn man fortfahren sollte, wie man bereits angefangen hat, [für] einen Mordtrieb, eine Feuerslust, eine Rauflust, einen Stehltrieb und am Ende für jedes Verbrechen einen besondern Trieb oder einen instinktartigen Zwang, eine *Nothwendigkeit* des Handelns, anzunehmen, hierdurch aber die Wirkung der Gesetze zu lähmen und die gerichtliche Medicin um ihr wohlverdientes Ansehen zu bringen. (527–8)

I feel compelled to remark . . . that while on the one hand we may greatly esteem the zeal of sundry writers and medical bodies in discovering excuses for acts committed in the turmoil occasioned in a person's emotions by exceptional events, or under the duress of an instinctual will ensnared by the bonds of nature, yet on the other hand we must take full account of the disarray and detriment that would arise from the incautious application of this doctrine if one were to continue—as one has already begun to do—to impute to every urge to murder or steal, every passion for fighting or fire-raising, and ultimately to every single crime, a specific drive or instinctual compulsion, an *imperative logic* determining the individual's actions, thereby however destroying the effectiveness of the law and robbing forensic medicine of its well-deserved repute.

Given this agenda, Woyzeck was to all intents and purposes doomed before Clarus ever set eyes on him: barring only the grossest evidence to the contrary, Clarus was pre-programmed to arrive at two concomitant findings: (i) that the prisoner exhibited no signs whatever of pathological derangement ('[ich fand] nichts, was auf die Gegenwart irgend eines krankhaften Zustandes des Gemüths, auf Wahnsinn, Tollheit oder Melancholie und deren verschiedene Formen, Grade und Complicationen zu schließen berechtigen könnte', 505); (ii) that he had suffered neither the loss nor the least diminution of his freedom of will, his ability freely to determine his own actions ('Freiheit des Willens', 'Willensfreiheit', 'freier Vernunftgebrauch', 518, 524, 525). In Clarus's eyes the situation was essentially very simple: it was common-or-garden jealousy that afflicted Woyzeck, and led to a deliberate, premeditated act of vengeance (533 f.)—for which he deserved to pay the ultimate penalty, thereby also serving as a salutary warning to others. For students of the history and philosophy of medicine, particularly in its inescapable interface with social policy, Clarus's reports are a rich resource that would indeed merit close examination. What matters for us, however, is the fact that they afforded Georg Büchner the makings of the most original and enigmatic dramatic figure that he ever created. And we need to realize that the 'real' historical Woyzeck is himself an enigma, indeed he scarcely exists at all as an objective entity: what we see in the Clarus reports—as Büchner saw also—is not Woyzeck as he actually was, or understood himself to be, but *images* refracted through the complex prism of Clarus's convictions and purposes; and these images fluctuate wildly as Clarus seeks to substantiate the different aspects of his argument. It seems more than likely that these fluctuations, and the elusiveness that they result in, fired Büchner's creative imagination at least as much as the murder-story itself, and the milieu in which it occurred. In *Woyzeck* Büchner is exploring the unknowable, the giddying abyss, a chasm as black as chimney or well. And it is perhaps the most superbly ironic conceit of the work that Büchner's explorer is Woyzeck: the enigmatic sounded out by an enigma.

This brings us back to Büchner's Woyzeck and the question of whether his visions etc. are to be understood as genuine mystical experiences, symptoms of insanity, or—as Clarus expediently maintained in the case of the real-life murderer—mere delusions. It is instructive here to cast a glance at *Lenz*. There can be no doubt whatever that Lenz himself is presented as incipiently mad at the start of the story, and wholly, irretrievably mad by the end. It thus seems yet more evidence of insanity when—after the highly charged sequence of the sermon and its nocturnal aftermath—Lenz recounts a 'supernatural' visitation:

Am folgenden Morgen kam er herunter, er erzählte Oberlin ganz ruhig, wie ihm die Nacht seine Mutter erschienen sey; sie sey in einem weißen Kleide aus der dunkeln Kirchhofmauer hervorgetreten . . . sie sey dann in eine Ecke gesunken . . . sie sey gewiß todt (85)

The next morning he came down, he told Oberlin quite calmly how his mother had appeared to him during the night: she had stepped out of the dark wall of the churchyard, dressed all in white . . . then she had sunk down in a corner . . . she was surely dead

The archetypally solid and stable Oberlin is a foil to Lenz throughout the story, and so we might reasonably expect Büchner to use him here to point up the crazedness of Lenz's vision. But what we get instead is a virtual validation of it:

> Oberlin versetzte ihm nun, wie er bei dem Tod seines Vaters allein auf dem Felde gewesen sey, und er dann eine Stimme gehört habe, so daß er wußte, daß sein Vater todt sey, und wie er heimgekommen, sey es so gewesen.

Oberlin then told him how at the time of his father's death he had been alone in the fields and had heard a voice and knew at once that his father was dead, and so it proved when he returned home.

Büchner has Oberlin continue in the same vein: he speaks of girls able to divine water and metals under the earth, of men who battle with spirits on mountain-tops; he recounts a further mystical experience of his own:

> er sagte ihm auch, wie er einmal im Gebirg durch das Schauen in ein leeres tiefes Bergwasser in eine Art von Somnambulismus versetzt worden sey. Lenz sagte, daß der Geist des Wassers über ihn gekommen sey, daß er dann etwas von seinem eigenthümlichen Seyn empfunden hätte.

he told him how once in the mountains he had been put into a kind of somnambulist trance by gazing into the fathomless void of a mountain pool. Lenz said that the spirit of the water had come over him and that in consequence he had experienced something of his essential being.

These mystical visions and visitations are not questioned or impugned in the narrative in any way; on the contrary, they are strongly implied to be both genuine and—in the context of the close-to-nature community of the Vosges—entirely normal. And then, less than two pages later, we are presented with Lenz/Büchner's famous aesthetic programme, whereby the artist, too, must be a visionary, perceiving the truth behind the outer shell: 'die Gefühlsader ist in fast allen Menschen gleich, nur ist die Hülle mehr oder weniger dicht, durch die sie brechen muß. Man muß nur Aug und Ohren dafür haben' (87). The would-be realist and idealist writers by implication have no such eye or ear (ibid.); nor—so we hear through Camille in *Dantons Tod*—do the consumers of the contemporary arts in general, who are blind and deaf to anything true and genuine, blind and deaf to the creational force pulsating without pause within and around them ('wenn sie nichts Alles in hölzernen Copien bekommen... so haben sie weder Augen noch Ohren dafür'; 'Von der Schöpfung, die glühend, brausend und leuchtend, um und in ihnen, sich jeden Augenblick neu gebiert, hören und sehen sie nichts.')

In the light of such passages, and many others in similar vein, there can be no doubt at all that Georg Büchner entertained the most vivid sense of a realm—or realms—*beyond* the physical or outward appearance of things. This was already signalled in the first moments of his first work, when he had Danton speak not only of the secret cavortings of the 'pretty lady', but also of Julie's inner truth hidden beyond the deceptive materiality of her eyes and hair, her skin and skull. In this opening scene of *Dantons Tod* Büchner shows us a protagonist lamenting his inability to penetrate the façade ('Geh, wir haben grobe Sinne. Einander kennen? Wir müßten uns die Schädeldecken aufbrechen und die Gedanken einander aus den Hirnfasern zerren.') In the opening scene of *Woyzeck*, however, he shows us the very opposite: a protagonist who barely notices the façade at all, seeing and hearing instead a menacing realm within it, beneath it; we are confronted at once with a *visionary*—a visionary more extreme and disturbing than any other in Büchner's œuvre.

It is fascinating to see how Büchner refines and intensifies this image when he reworks his H2 original to create H4, 1. His tendency towards a kind of elliptical minimalism is perfectly demonstrated in his treatment of Woyzeck's first speech, for he reuses the original, but reduces it to bare essentials:

H2	H4
Ja Andres, das ist er—der Platz ist verflucht. Siehst du den leuchtenden Streif, da über das Gras hin, wo die Schwämme so nachwachsen? da rollt Abends der Kopf, es hob ihn eimal einer auf, er meint' es sey ein Igel, 3 Tage und 3 Nächte, er wurde zwerch, und er war todt. [*leise*] Das waren die Freimaurer, ich hab es haus. (339)	Ja Andres; den Streif da über das Gras hin, da rollt Abends der Kopf, es hob ihn einmal einer auf, er meint' es wär' ein Igel. Drei Tag und drei Nächt und er lag auf den Hobelspänen [*leise*] Andres, das waren die Freimaurer, ich hab's, die Freimaurer, still! (338)

A Question of Seeing 331

This is certainly a case where less means more, for the H4 version has much greater impact—an effect enhanced by the circumstance that it is now positioned first, in place of the song from Andres that began H2, 1. The additional impact derives from several interacting factors. One such is the altered rhythm. The original has a conversational, almost casual rhythm, but the H4 version is insistently *marcato* and out-of-the-ordinary. This is most obviously the case in the severely concertina-ed first half; but it is also evident, for instance, in the contraction of '3 Tage und 3 Nächte' to 'drei Tag und drei Nächt'. Closely linked to this is the altered syntax: H4 is not only rigorously paratactic, but also disconcertingly elliptical. In H2 the 'Ja Andres' is contextualised by the two clauses that follow it, but in H4, especially given Büchner's use of a semicolon, it is strangely disembodied. In H2, 'den Streif' is the object of 'Siehst du'; in H4 its accusative case makes the absence of a verb all the more conspicuous. Another related factor is Büchner's excision of adjectives: of the four in H2, not one survives into H4. Again here, less means more: the removal of explicit description makes the passage even more haunting and disturbing than before.

What I think we see reflected in these minimalist procedures is a determination on Büchner's part to achieve a kind of *Verfremdungseffekt*, or 'distantiation effect'; to carry us beyond the bounds of the familiar towards an encounter with the Other, whatever that might prove to be. The same purpose is served by the locale: whereas *Dantons Tod* and *Leonce und Lena* both begin in relatively domesticated and structured settings, *Woyzeck* begins in a kind of unplace, a featureless, unsettling Somewhere, with the world of normality visible only in the remote distance ('Freies Feld. Die Stadt in der Ferne.') The time of day plays its part as well: we are confronted at once with a twilight world ('Es wird finster', 339)—the very opposite of the sunshine that greets us at the beginning of *Leonce und Lena* (in this respect, too, the plays are the reverse of each other: day–night–day in one, night–day–night in the other). But much the most important factor preventing any cosy sense of rapport or complicity is the laconic projection of Woyzeck himself. From the outset—especially in the rejigged and 'minimalized' H4 version—we face an enigma. Instead of defining his protagonist (as he so effectively does with Leonce in the opening sub-scene and ensuing monologue of his comedy), Büchner makes it impossible for us to get an unambiguous perspective onto Woyzeck and his vision of the world. All the features of the text conspire to produce an ambivalent response: on one level we see an apparent madman spouting apparent delusions; on another level we see a potent dramatic presence conjuring a potent illusion of meta-reality. Woyzeck is the perfect instrument for such purposes. A key factor here is the paradox that, in choosing Woyzeck as his protagonist, Büchner dares to put marginality at the centre. Danton and Leonce were central figures not only within the dramatic economy of their respective plays, but also within the society that those plays depicted. Woyzeck on the other hand exists on the outer fringe of his society, and has no particular place or station even there—in sharp contrast to the great majority of the other characters both high and low, who are identified specifically by their social rank or role, which in turn connotes for each persona both a clear framework of being, and a sense of belonging: 'The Drum-Major', 'The Officer', 'The Doctor', 'The Professor', not to mention 'The Barker', 'The NCO', 'The Grandmother', 'The Innkeeper', and numerous others. This dislocated fringe existence of the protagonist is graphically conveyed in the overall spatial dynamic of the work, which both begins and ends in nameless zones beyond the pale. It is expressed, too, in the way that Woyzeck seems to have no private, personal space—unlike Marie, for instance, who is depicted as having a home of her own, a real niche in the world, be it ever so paltry ('nur ein Eckchen in der Welt', 358). A complementary and very powerful signal is that Woyzeck is repeatedly shown rushing and running, and generally hurrying from place to place. The phrase 'Ich muß fort' (*I have to go*), together with variants on it, becomes almost a leitmotif: 'Wir müssen fort' (H2, 1 and H4, 1, spoken by Andres); 'Ich muß fort (H2, 2, H4, 2; H4, 4); 'Ich muß fort . . . ich muß fort' (H1, 4); 'Ich muß hinaus . . . Ich muß fort . . . Ich muß hinaus' (H4, 10). The pattern is reinforced by Büchner's stage directions: 'geht mit breiten Schritten ab, erst langsam dann immer schneller'; 'läuft weg'; 'er läuft hinaus'; 'er läuft weg' (375, 401, 403, 405). This unsettling unsettledness of Woyzeck's whole being is highlighted with particular force through the medium of the Hauptmann. It is the theme of both the beginning and the end of the shaving scene: 'Langsam, Woyzeck, langsam; ein's nach d. andern; Er macht mir ganz schwindlich'; 'Geh' jezt u. renn nicht so; langsam hübsch langsam die Straße hinunter' (360, 364; *Slowly, Woyzeck, slowly; one thing after another; you make me feel quite giddy; Off you go now, and don't run like that; slowly, nice and slowly down the street*). There is an even stronger emphasis when Woyzeck appears on stage in the middle of the Hauptmann–Doctor scene (H2, 7):

He Woyzeck, was hetzt er sich so an uns vorbey? Bleib er doch Woyzeck, er läuft ja wie ein offnes Rasirmesser durch die Welt, man schneidt sich an ihm, er läuft als hätt er ein Regiment Kosack zu rasirn u. würd gehenkt über dem letzten Haar nach einer Viertelstunde (373/GS 15)

Hey Woyzeck, what are you doing tearing past us like that? Just hold it Woyzeck; you rush through the world like an open razor, you'll cut us to ribbons; you run as if you had a regiment of Cossacks to shave and were due to be hanged in a quarter of an hour as you get to the very last hair

This passage shows beyond doubt that Woyzeck's hectic restlessness is essentially ontological. We are not shown simply a victim of the prevailing social system being harried from pillar to post by sundry exploiters. His drivenness arises from within his own being, his own tortured sense of existence—as is particularly clear in the term 'er hetzt sich': the driving force is within Woyzeck himself. Büchner's use of this term in H2 is quite striking, for he takes it up again in a variant form in the shaving scene (H4, 5), where Woyzeck is twice described as looking 'immer so verhetzt'. 'Verhetzen' (to incite, to stir up) is a transitive verb, and 'verhetzt' would normally imply that the person or persons so described have been activated by someone else. In these specific contexts, however, Woyzeck's 'Verhetztsein' is plainly portrayed as coming from within himself. The first such instance is relatively bland, telling us as much about the Hauptmann as it does about Woyzeck: 'Woyzeck er sieht immer so verhetzt aus. Ein guter Mensch thut das nicht, ein guter Mensch, der sein gutes Gewissen hat.' (360; *Woyzeck you always look so worked up. Good chaps don't—good chaps with a clear conscience.*) The second instance, on the other hand, is very revealing, for it points to the source of Woyzeck's unceasing agitation: he *thinks* too much: 'Du bist ein guter Mensch, ein guter Mensch. Aber Du denkst zuviel, das zehrt, Du siehst immer so verhetzt aus.' (362/4; *You're a good chap, a good chap. But you think too much, it eats away at you, you always look so worked up.*)

'Excessive thinking' may seem a curious criticism to level at the likes of Woyzeck: it is all too easy to jump to the conclusion that since he is an uneducated prole from the bottom of the social pile, he must also be stupid—'dumm', as the Hauptmann calls him, 'ganz abscheulich dumm' (362). But such a conclusion would be wrong in both the general and the particular. It flies in the face of Büchner's fundamental belief in the vast if untapped potential within the 'great mass'. More specifically and more importantly, it fails to recognize that within the given context of this drama, Woyzeck has by far the most restless, most searching mind of all the characters: he not only sees and hears things that others cannot, but also seeks desperately to understand them. *This* is the reason why he is 'immer so verhetzt'—a phrase that points beyond the time-span of the work, and helps to define his agitation as a permanent state of being, not a temporary flurry. The same thing is indicated through the Doctor's remark in H4, 8 when Woyzeck is vainly struggling to define what he sees as the differentness of nature: 'Woyzeck, er philosophirt wieder' (368; *Woyzeck you're philosophizing again!*) It is likewise implied by Marie's response to Woyzeck's hectic, portentous utterances when he briefly appears at her window in H4, 2: 'Er schnappt noch über mit den Gedanken.' (342; *He'll go berserk with those thoughts of his.*) In the corresponding scene in H2, Woyzeck's frenetic and potentially mind-blowing quest is starkly spelt out (perhaps *too* starkly, which might explain why Büchner didn't reuse these lines in the more cryptic H4 version):

WOYZECK. Pst! still! Ich hab's aus! Die Freimaurer! Es war ein fürchterliches Getös am Himmel und Alles in Gluth! Ich bin viel auf der Spur! sehr viel!
LOUISE. Narr!
WOYZECK. Meinst? Sieh um Dich! Alles starr fest finster, was regt sich dahinter. Etwas, was wir nicht fasse begreife still, was uns von Sinnen bringt, aber ich hab's aus. Ich muß fort! (343/GS 11)

WOYZECK. Pst! quiet! I've got it! The Freemasons! There was a terrible roaring in the sky and everything aglow! I'm onto things! Lots of things!
LOUISE. Fool!
WOYZECK. Think so? Look around you! Everything rigid solid dark, behind it something's moving. Something we don't grasp understand, quiet, something that sends us mad, but I've got it! I have to go!

18
Emblems and Archetypes

IN bestowing an implacable intelligence on his protagonist, Büchner makes him in this respect strikingly similar to his predecessors, Danton and Leonce. At the same time, two attendant factors make him typologically quite different: Woyzeck's intelligence is coupled with extreme marginality; and his perceptions fill him not with torpid ennui, but restless agitation. These two factors are intimately related—and as such are central to the extraordinary power and originality of Büchner's last work. By dint of existing on the margin of society, Woyzeck is denied all access to the ready-made social, moral, intellectual perspectives available to those at its centre. We see this graphically in the pissing scene, when Woyzeck struggles in vain to articulate his ardent perceptions of nature ('sehn sie mit der Natur [*er kracht mit den Fingern*] das ist so was, wie soll ich doch sagen, z. B.', 368), whereas the Doctor has an entire taxonomy instantly to hand ('Woyzeck er hat die schönste aberratio mentalis partialis, d. zweite Species, sehr schön ausgeprägt', etc.). In the shaving scene, the problem is mordantly defined through Woyzeck himself as he counters the Hauptmann's professions of 'virtue':

Ja Herr Hauptmann, die Tugend! . . . Sehn Sie, wir gemeine Leut, das hat keine Tugend, es kommt einem nur so die Natur, aber wenn ich ein Herr wär und hätt ein Hut u. eine Uhr und eine anglaise und könnt vornehm reden, ich wollt schon tugendhaft seyn. Es muß was Schöns seyn um die Tugend, Herr Hauptmann. Aber ich bin ein armer Kerl. (362)

Yes sir, virtue! . . . Us common folk, y'see, we don't have no virtue, it's nature what drives us; but if I was a gent with a hat and a watch and a nice smart coat and could talk all posh, I'd be virtuous alright. Must be a fine thing, sir, virtue. But I'm poor, that's what I am.

What we see very clearly in these lines is morality as mask; as a venal accoutrement, not an inner state. Such notions are central to the earlier plays, and are given strong billing towards the close of both, in Valerio's presentation of his two 'world-famous automata' (131), and in Camille's desperate cry that all their prinking and preening and affected accents are a waste of effort in the face of death: it is time for them at last to strip away their masks ('wir sollten einmal die Masken abnehmen . . . Schneidet nur keine so tugendhafte und so witzige und so heroische und so geniale Grimassen', 70–1). One of the defining and most crucial characteristics of Woyzeck, however, is that he has no such masks in the first place, no ready perspectives, no specious intellectual or ethical constructs in which he might find refuge. For the first time in Büchner's œuvre, we find a protagonist who exemplifies existence in the raw, shorn of all embellishments and hiding places. And in this, the figure of Woyzeck perfectly reflects the essentialist tenor of the work as a whole, which we have already seen demonstrated in Büchner's use of an ever more spare, even elliptical style. A further major aspect of this is that through his choice of Woyzeck and his marginal, minimal history, Büchner frees himself from the contingent clutter and compulsions of History, the semi-automatism of characters enacting their fixed and familiar historical/social role. He is not concerned with the plight of a famous revolutionary in a famous revolution, nor with the difficulties of a Crown Prince all too aware of his Prince-ness; instead, he confronts essential problems of human existence. This is signalled not least by the vocabulary: the word 'Mensch' and its derivatives occur in the *Woyzeck* drafts almost three times as often as they do in *Dantons Tod*, and more than twice as often as in *Leonce und Lena* (78 occurrences in *Woyzeck*, 29 in *Dantons Tod*, 34 in *Leonce und Lena*[1]); indeed the whole work can readily be seen as a kind of *Ecce homo!*—'sehn sie, der Mensch', as Büchner has the Doctor bid his students (394).

A key element in this essentialist perspective is that the personae are presented not naturalistically, as quirky individuals caught up in the specificity of their particular personality and history, but emblematically, as archetypes. We have already seen important instances of this in the way that Büchner has Marie and the Drum-Major see one another as personifications of sexual potency: Marie the fecund brood-mare, the very image of voracious Woman ('Das ist ein

---

[1] See Monika Rössing-Hager, *Wortindex zu Georg Büchner: Dichtungen und Übersetzungen* (Berlin, 1970), 245–6. Apart from proper names and titles, the word 'Mensch' is in fact the most frequently used noun in all Büchner's poetic writing (cf. 'Häufigkeitsregister', ibid. 417 ff.; but note that the figures relating to Büchner's Victor Hugo translations have to be deducted, by reference to the main 'Alphabetisches Register'). Readers may wish to make a small bet with themselves as to the *second*-commonest noun in Büchner's poetic writings (see below, Ch. 19 n. 2).

Weibsbild guckt siebe Paar lederne Hose durch'); the Drum-Major sturdy as a tree, rampant as a lion, virile as an ox. In fact this perspective is emphasized again and again throughout the work. Thus the Drum-Major is given to vaunt his cocky, virile self-image in the scene with Marie: 'Wenn ich am Sonntag erst den großen Federbusch hab' u. die weiße Handschuh, Donnerwetter, Marie, der Prinz sagt immer: Mensch, er ist ein Kerl.' (364; *On Sundays when I've got me great plume of feathers and me white gloves, fair take your breath away it would, Marie, the Prince he always says 'Now there's a real feller!'*) When he picks a fight with Woyzeck and ritually humiliates him at the inn, he does so in his role as Macho Man:

Ich bin ein Mann! [*schlägt sich auf die Brust*] ein Mann sag' ich. Wer will was? Wer kein besoffen Herrgott ist der laß sich von mir. Ich will ihm die Nas ins Arschloch prügeln. Ich will—[*zu Woyzeck*] da Kerl, sauf, der Mann muß saufen [etc.] (384)

I'm a man, I am! [*Pounds his chest*] a man, I tell you. Anyone want to argue? Unless you're some pissdrunk God Almighty just keep your distance, or I'll ram your nose right down to your arsehole, I'll—[*to Woyzeck*] hey, you, drink! Real men have to drink [etc.]

As 'heroine' of the piece, Marie is clearly a much more complex figure; but again, this complexity is conveyed in emblematic terms: she is variously Mystery, Beauty-in-Rags, Venality, Sinfulness, Penitence (and it goes almost without saying that all these elements, with the possible exception of venality, were Büchner's invention: the real Johanna Christiane Woost appears to have been altogether unremarkable middle-aged slut). As for the rest of the characters, virtually all of them are of course presented as types, not individuals: The Hauptmann, The Doctor, and The Professor, for instance; The Innkeeper, The Journeymen, and The Jew; The Idiot, The Old Man, and The Grandmother.

One of the most telling devices encouraging us to see the story in archetypal terms is the succession of song-fragments interspersed through the text. Some of these fragments bear no particular or obvious relationship to the central story, and simply contribute to the general atmosphere. This is the case, for instance, with Andres' song at the start of H2, 1 and H4, 1 (Büchner's artistry is conspicuous here in the changes he makes when reworking H2, 1 to create H4, 1: the two stanzas in the earlier draft are too long and too jolly, and set the scene off on too cheerful a note; by choosing a brief, dislocated fragment, and placing it *after* Woyzeck's grim, mood-setting opener, Büchner makes the song far more atmospheric and menacing, with its unspoken hint of the two hares as potential prey). The snatch of song at the beginning of H2, 3 has a similar general effect (and is reminiscent of the Beggar's song in *Dantons Tod*, 34–5): 'Auf der Welt ist kein Bestand | Wir müssen alle sterben, das ist uns wohl bekannt!' (344; *In this world shall none abide, | All of us we have to die, and well we know it too!*) Much more importantly, however, there is a whole group of song-fragments that relate indirectly but unmistakably to Marie, and which lend great depth and intensity to her story by conveying a powerful sense of universality. We begin to see this within seconds of Marie's first appearance in H4, 2. First, her snatch of song 'Soldaten das sind schöne Bursch' effectively links the Drum-Major with the stock figure of the 'Handsome Soldier'; then, following Magreth's jibe about her x-ray eyes, Büchner has her slam the window and continue thus:

Komm mein Bub. Was die Leut wollen. Bist doch nur en arm Hurenkind und machst deiner Mutter Freud mit deim unehrliche Gesicht. Sa! Sa! [*singt.*]

> Mädel, was fangst du jezt an
> Hast ein klein Kind und kein Mann
> Ey was frag ich danach
> Sing ich die ganze Nacht
> Heyo popeio mein Bu. Juchhe!
> Giebt mir kein Mensch nix dazu. (340)

Come on lad. Don't know what these people're on about. You're just a poor little whore's kid and you makes your mum happy with your bastard face. There! There! [*sings.*]

> Hey lass what's this you're about
> You've got a young kid and no man
> But why oh why should I care
> All night long I'll just sing the same air
> Rockabye baby my lad, heigh ho!
> For me no one else gives a damn.

On a naturalistic reading of the text we might suppose that what we are meant to see here is a real person choosing to sing a song that fits her mood. But Büchner is doing something much bolder: Marie is not a real person but a dramatic persona, and that persona is conveyed to the reader/spectator just as much through the words of Marie's song as through her 'own' words. Indeed the song-words are even more powerful, in that they help us to get beyond the private and particular, and to recognize Marie as archetypal.

A similar effect is achieved by the song-fragment delivered through the 'Barbier' in H1, 10. Once again, the hyper-condensed narrative concerns a young girl whose sexuality carries her beyond the pale:

> Ach Tochter, liebe Tochter
> Was hast du gedenkt,
> Daß du dich an die Landkutscher
> Und die Fuhrleut hast gehängt? (385)
>
> Oh daughter, dearest daughter
> What ever was in your mind
> That made you run off with the carters
> And the coachmen and their kind?

The same essential story is recounted yet again in Marie's song in the earrings scene in H4:

> Mädel mach's Ladel zu
> S' kommt e Zigeunerbu
> Führt dich an deiner Hand
> Fort in's Zigeunerland. (358)
>
> Hey lass now shut up the house
> A gypsy boy's coming at last
> To lead you away by the hand
> Off into gypsy land.

The beginning of H1, 17—the highly charged inn scene that follows almost immediately after the murder—is particularly revealing because it so clearly demonstrates the complementarity of the song-plots and the main plot: Marie having been expunged as a 'whore' ('heiß, heiß Hurenathem', 399; *hot, hot breath of a whore*), *all* women now appear to Louis/Woyzeck in the same image—and their insatiable sexuality is duly hypostasized in the archetypal un-heroine of a song. Originally here, Büchner penned the first eight words of the 'Ach Tochter, liebe Tochter' song, but then immediately crossed them out and used another song instead:

Tanzt alle, immer zu, schwizt und stinkt, er holt Euch doch eimal Alle.

[*singt*] Frau Wirthin hat 'ne brave Magd
Sie sitzt im Garten Tag u. Nacht
Sie sitzt in ihrem Garten
Biß daß das Glöcklein zwölfe schlägt
Und paßt auf die Soldaten. *(401)*

Dance all of you, go on, sweat and stink, the devil'll take you all in the end.

[*sings*] The innkeeper's wife has a good little maid
She sits in the garden night and day
Sits there in her garden
Sits there till the bell strikes twelve
Waiting for the guardsmen.

In fact this is not the reader/spectator's first acquaintance with this particular song, for Büchner also reuses it in H4, 10, again in the context of visionary turmoil in Woyzeck, whirling dances, steaming women, the heat of unbridled sexuality (378; cf. also the corresponding scene H1, 4, 379).[2]

Songs were included very effectively in both *Dantons Tod* and *Leonce und Lena*, but they were essentially illustrative and atmospheric in function, no more, no less. In *Woyzeck*, however, the songs are at the heart of the work; they are part of a kind of rich, sombre polyphony in relation to which the surface action functions like a descant: it constitutes the most sustained and prominent melody, but one that derives its remarkable resonance and power from the counterpoint that underlies it.

We see this particularly clearly in H1, 4, 'Magreth mit Mädchen vor der Haustür' (397/9). Only the last dozen words in this relatively long scene directly concern the plot, when 'Louis' suddenly appears and summons 'Magreth' to leave on what proves to be her final journey. At first sight the rest of the scene might seem extraneous or at best atmospheric, but that is far from being the case. What we hear first is the song sung by one of the children (or perhaps more than one: the identifier 'Mädchen' is ambiguous):

---

[2] Büchner first used the song in an early draft of *Leonce und Lena*, I. i (139). Perhaps he decided not to retain it in the later version(s) of the comedy because it had meanwhile proved so apt for *Woyzeck*.

Emblems and Archetypes 341

Wie scheint d. Sonn St. Lichtmeßtag
Und steht das Korn im Blühn.
Sie gingen wohl die Straße hin
Sie gingen zu zwei u. zwein.
Die Pfeifer gingen vorn,
Die Geiger hinte drein.
Sie hatte rothe Sock

The sun shines bright at Candlemas
The corn it stands so high
They walked along the road they did
They walked out two by two
The pipers piping out in front,
The fiddlers fiddling close behind.
She wore red socks

For all its apparent air of brightness, warmth, fruition, festive gaiety, the song has an ominous ring. This is partly because of its context: given the whole thrust of the scenes that precede it, its merry tone cannot seem other than profoundly ironic; after all, it comes only seconds after Louis's climactic exclamation near the close of H1,13: 'Hörst du's nicht? Ich hör's den ganzen Tag. Immer zu. Stich! stich die Woyzecke todt.' (391; *Can't you hear it? I hear it the whole day long. 'Go on. Stab! Stab the Woyzeck woman dead.'*) But even within the song itself, there are disturbing features. The first is admittedly abstruse, but once recognized, it drastically alters the feel of the entire song. The fact is that Candlemas doesn't fit here at all: it falls on 2 February, when vivid sunshine is improbable and ripe corn impossible. But the very 'wrongness' of the allusion intensifies its poetic-dramatic expressiveness: Candlemas is the Feast of the Purification of the Virgin Mary following her encounter with sexuality in pregnancy and childbirth ('das Fest Mariä Lichtmeß')—and its mention here subtly foreshadows another imminent 'purification', namely the would-be conversion of Magreth/Marie's black sinfulness into spotless white via the extinction of her life ('Du warst schwarz davon, schwarz! Hab ich dich jezt gebleicht.', 405). In the ensuing lines we hear about an indeterminate 'them' processing along some indeterminate road to the apparently merry accompaniment of fiddles and fifes. But the resonances here are unmistakably grim: only a few scenes earlier (in H1, 6) it was fiddles and fifes—'die Geigen und die Pfeifen'—that heralded the subterranean voices telling Louis to 'stab, stab, stab the

Woyzeck woman dead' (383). The real punch of the song, however, comes in its final line, when the focus suddenly shifts from a genderless plurality to a particular female, startlingly identified through a single attribute: her 'red socks'.[3] It is perhaps difficult for us in the West to think ourselves back into a social code that regarded almost the entire female body as needing to be hidden from view—including ankles. But we might recall the Hauptmann overwhelmed by 'love' as he ogles the white stockings revealed when their owners go hopping over rain-puddles; and in any case, a pointer is supplied in the instant response of the 'First Child': 'S' ist nit schön' (*That's not nice*). What really gives the line its impact, though, is the fact that 'redness' is a motif repeatedly associated with Magreth/Marie—in respect of both her sexuality, and her death. In H1, 5, when the nameless He and She are dancing at the inn, Louis not only literally sees red, and sees a vision of all the dancers writhing in an 'ocean of blood', a 'red ocean'—Büchner also has him exclaim 'Sie hat rothe rothe Backe' (379; *She has red, red cheeks*). The murder itself is presaged in H1, 15 by the moon rising as red as a 'bloody steel' ('Was der Mond roth auf geht. / Wie ein blutig Eisen', 399). We are told that Magreth's corpse lies 'by the red cross' ('am rothen Kreuz', 403). And when Louis returns to recover the knife, the motif is rounded off with a final grim flourish: 'Was hast du eine rothe Schnur um d. Hals? Bey wem hast du das Halsband verdient, mit deinen Sünden?' (405; *Why the red line around your neck? Who did you earn this necklace from with all your sins?*) When in due course Büchner writes the H4 sequence, he further intensifies the motif: in the earrings scene we hear Marie vaunt the redness of her mouth, no whit diminished by her poverty ('doch hab' ich einen so rothen Mund als die großen Madamen'); and it is precisely her red mouth that becomes the visible symbol of her sin when Woyzeck confronts her in H4, 7: 'Du hast ein rothe Mund, Marie. Keine Blase drauf? Adieu, Marie, du bist schön wie die Sünde—. Kann die Todsünde so schön seyn?' (364; *You've a red mouth, Marie. No blisters on it? Goodbye, Marie, you're beautiful as sin. Can mortal sin be so beautiful?*)

Following the song, Büchner dashed down a succession of dialogue-snippets, which he must have meant as a preliminary

---

[3] We cannot be entirely sure about this. Lehmann prints 'Sock' in small letters, indicating uncertainty; Schmid prints 'Sck', but in normal-sized letters, indicating a confident reading (GS 6).

Emblems and Archetypes 343

sketch rather than as a finished sequence (there is little indication, for instance, of who says what); then at some later stage he added further snippets—certainly the 'Warum? / Darum! / Aber warum darum?' exchange, and very probably the two words 'König Herodes'.[4] Both these latter elements form part of the sombre counterpoint referred to earlier. The bald allusion to 'King Herod' (which Büchner presumably intended to enlarge on in a subsequent reworking of the scene) immediately conjures up visions of infamous acts of biblical butchery: Herod's murder of John the Baptist at Salome's behest, and the delivery of his head 'in a charger' (Matthew 14: 3–11); and the Slaughter of the Innocents perpetrated by Herod following the birth of Jesus (Matthew 2: 16). As for the 'Warum? / Darum! / Aber warum darum?' lines (*Why? / Because! / But why because?*): at one level they simply reflect the typical badinage of children; at a deeper level, however, they bear on central and fundamental questions of the work, as we see more plainly in the much more developed echo of the motif voiced through the drunken Handwerksbursche in H2, 4: 'Warum hat Gott die Mensche geschaffe? . . . Ja! Ja! Also!—Darum! auf daß! damit! oder aber [etc.]' (352; *Why did God create mankind? . . . Yes! Yes! That's it!—Because! for the sake of! in order to! on the other hand [etc.]*).

After the scraps of dialogue, Büchner delivers what is surely the most famous, most haunting passage he ever wrote: the Grandmother's tale:

Es war eimal ein arm Kind und hat kei Vater u. kei Mutter war Alles todt und war Niemand mehr auf der Welt. Alles todt, und es ist hingegangen u. hat greint Tag und Nacht. Und wie auf der Erd Niemand mehr war, wollt's in Himmel gehn, und der Mond guckt es so freundlich an und wie's endlich zum Mond kam, war's ein Stück faul Holz und da ist es zur Sonn gangen und wie's zur Sonn kam war's ein verwelkt Sonneblum und wie's zu den Sterne kam, warens klei golde Mück die waren angesteckt wie d. Neuntödter sie auf die Schlehe steckt u. wie's wieder auf die Erd wollt, war die Erd ein umgestürzter Hafen u. war ganz allein u. da hat sich's hingesetzt u. geweint u. da sitzt es noch u. ist ganz allein. (397/9, GS 6[5])

[4] Lehmann does not regard 'König Herodes' as an insertion. But Schmid's manuscript-facsimile (p. 6) clearly shows the words penned at a slightly lower level than the preceding ones; they also seem to be written in a different ductus—similar to that of the 'Warum? / Darum!' insertion.

[5] The first 'wie', and the reading 'verwelkt', are both derived from Schmid (in preference to Lehmann's 'weil' and 'verreckt'); the punctuation likewise follows

Once upon a time there was a poor child, had no father and no mother, everyone was dead and nobody was left in all the world. Everyone dead, so he[6] went and cried both day and night. And as there was nobody left on earth he wanted to go into heaven and the moon gave him such a friendly look and when in the end he came to the moon it was a lump of rotten wood and so he went to the sun and when he came to the sun it was a withered sunflower and when he came to the stars they were tiny golden insects stuck there as though by a butcher-bird on blackthorn and when he wanted to come back to earth again, the earth was an upturned crock and he was all alone so he sat down and cried and he's sitting there still, all alone.

As in the case of the Marion monologue in *Dantons Tod*, these lines derive their tremendous impact in part from the fact that they constitute an entire narrative complete of itself, interposed quite suddenly in the dramatic continuum, and spoken by a character who never otherwise appears. In keeping with the general tenor of *Dantons Tod*, Marion's tale was expansive, individualized, particularized; the Grandmother's, by contrast, could scarcely be more laconic or stark, more irreducibly essentialist. With its 'Es war einmal' it announces itself at once as a *Märchen*, a fairytale, and the authentic fairytales it variously echoes are easily identified;[7] yet in its extreme gauntness of style, its relentless succession of confounded hopes, its substitution of timeless agony for benign resolution, it amounts to a kind of *anti*-fairytale, a distillation of the fairytale form in negative terms. The story is extreme in every respect. Its setting is no particular place, nor even Planet Earth, but the entire infinitude of space—earth, moon, sun, stars, the universe. Its time-scale is likewise an infinitude, stretching from the timeless Then of 'Es war einmal' to the timeless Now of 'da sitzt es noch . . .'. The plot progresses—if that is the right word—from absolute isolation

Schmid. Note that Lehmann's 'greint' is dubious; Schmid prints 'g + + t', and other editors have plumped for 'gesucht', 'gerufen'; more recently the word 'gerrt' has been identified from 'gerren', dialect for 'to sob loudly' (cf. Schmid, *Lesartenverzeichnis*, 18; Thomas Michael Mayer, 'Zu einigen neuen Lesungen und zur Frage des "Dialekts" in den *Woyzeck*-Handschriften', in T. M. Mayer (ed.), *Georg Büchner Jahrbuch*, 7/1988–9, 174).

[6] In Büchner's German the personal pronoun throughout is the neuter 'es', referring back to 'das Kind'. 'It' doesn't work at all well in English, and in translating one has to choose between 'he' and 'she'. 'He' is chosen here because the child orphaned within the drama itself is a boy—but the choice remains arbitrary, and inevitably both alters and diminishes the thrust of the original. (In the two most likely source-fairytales, the child in both cases is a girl; cf. Hinderer, *Büchner-Kommentar*, 234.)

[7] Loc. cit.

Emblems and Archetypes 345

to even more absolute isolation. The 'poor child' is immediately established as central—but central within an absolute void, a world bereft of all other life as though after some ultimate holocaust; nowhere else in Büchner's writing is death–bereftness–isolation–nothingness more concentratedly, more implacably conveyed than here: 'kei Vater u. kei Mutter', 'Alles todt', 'Niemand mehr auf der Welt', 'Alles todt', 'auf der Erd Niemand mehr'. The forlorn orphan embarks on a quest implicitly driven by last-ditch hope; but every would-be celestial refuge proves to be decayed, withered, dead. So the child returns 'home'; but in the meantime 'home' has become yet worse than before: the earth is not only absolute deadness and emptiness, it is also absolute disarray and confusion ('ein umgestürzter Hafen'). The story finally reaches its climax with the child enthroned as the very image of a grief and loneliness that can never end: 'u. war ganz allein u. da hat sich's hingesetzt und geweint u. da sitzt es noch u. ist ganz allein'. The bleak vision here is much the same as in the ringing utterance of Danton's that brings down the curtain on the final gaol scene: 'Die Welt ist das Chaos. Das Nichts ist der zu gebärende Weltgott.' But instead of aphoristic grandiloquence, we are offered a graphic narrative, a parable of human existence so stark, so vivid, that we feel as though blasted by an icy wind.

How does the story connect with the drama as a whole? An obvious element is the sheer verbal one: the mordant, twice-repeated phrase 'Alles todt' is echoed at both beginning and end of the H4 fragment, to the point that it becomes in effect a leitmotif: in H4, 1, Woyzeck's final line is 'Still, Alles still, als wär die Welt todt.' (338; *Quiet, all quiet, as if the world was dead.*); in H4, 16, Marie's agonies over the Bible story of the woman taken in adultery culminate in her suddenly beating her chest and crying 'Alles todt!' (392). We perhaps hear another echo in H2, 7, when Woyzeck is stricken by the Hauptmann's insinuations about Louisel/Marie and the Drum-Major: his wrenching words 'ich bin ein arm Teufel,—und hab sonst nichts auf der Welt' (375) are reminiscent of the Grandmother's 'Es war eimal ein arm Kind . . . und war Niemand mehr auf der Welt.' But we need to be chary here. It is all too easy to see the Grandmother's tale as a summation of Woyzeck and *his* existential predicament. If it epitomizes the plight of any one figure in particular, then surely it is that of the infant Christian, whose father is about to murder his mother and then (so we can safely assume) die himself, be it at his own hand or the State's. But in fact it greatly diminishes the tale if we see it simply as a recapitulation of this or that element of the main action. Rather, it is the other way around: instead of seeing the tale in terms of the main action, we see the main action in terms of the tale. The existential, universalist perspective of the parable does much to condition our perception of the protagonists and their doings. This is starkly exemplified within the scene itself when Büchner has Woyzeck suddenly appear at the very end and initiate the brief exchange with 'Magreth':

LOUIS. Magreth!
MARGRETH [*erschreckt*] Was ist?
LOUIS. Magreth wir wolln gehn. S'ist Zeit.
MARGRETH. Wohinaus?
LOUIS. Weiß ich's?

LOUIS. Magreth!
MARGRETH [*frightened*] What's up?
LOUIS. We need to go, Magreth. It's time.
MARGRETH. Where to?
LOUIS. Who knows?

If these five lines had survived on their own (on a separate scrap of paper, let's say), they would have had no particular weight or impact. In their given context, however, and especially when performed on the stage, the lines are electrifying and portentous, and point far beyond themselves. Louis and Magreth do not come across to us here as poverty-stricken small-fry about to contribute a banal if sordid murder to the local crime statistics; they appear in the same perspective as the emblematic Child that travelled through the universe on its futile quest and now sits for ever crying and alone. The departure betokened by Woyzeck's 'wir wolln gehn' is of the same order as that signalled in the Grandmother's 'wollt's in Himmel gehn'; and it promises to take them into a bleak, nameless void: 'Wohinaus? / Weiß ich's?'

Few passages in Büchner's œuvre are as compellingly, unforgettably bleak as the Grandmother's tale. But it is certainly not the Definitive Statement of *Woyzeck*, any more than the 'Chaos ... Nichts' pronouncement enshrines the ultimate truth of *Dantons Tod*. Indeed the tale is relativized—with wonderful subtlety—by the very manner in which it is conveyed. If Büchner had wished to provide a visual 'objective correlative' for the story's message, he could easily have done so; for instance, he could have had the Idiot recount the story near the close of the play, with Christian in his arms as the palpable embodiment of the narrated child's plight. But of course he does no such thing. On the contrary, he chooses a scenic language that conveys a message directly opposite to that of the spoken words: we *hear* of a fictive child that is motherless, fatherless, infinitely alone; but we *see* actual children gathered around a Grandmother—an iconic tableau of security, communion, non-isolation. As in the opening scene of *Dantons Tod*, where Büchner achieved a similar dual effect, the contrary messages do not cancel one another out; they tend rather to confirm each other's figurative status as hyperbolic images of the negative and positive potential of human existence.

Dramaturgically speaking, the defining characteristic of the Grandmother episode is that it constitutes a kind of performance-within-the-performance: the plot is suspended, and a character who never otherwise appears makes a set-piece speech before an on-stage audience. Isolated examples of this procedure occurred in *Dantons Tod*: Marion's story recounted to Danton, and the Payne sub-scene at the start of Act III. In *Woyzeck*, however, such scenes become a recurrent and crucial component of the work.

We have already looked at the first of these, namely the fairground scenes, where the Barker and his animals are used to challenge the whole construct of human society, 'die menschlich Societät', to suggest that all its assumptions about 'education', 'civilization', 'progress', etc. are mere delusions, and that for all our masks and pretensions we remain essentially Nothings—'nix, gar nix'. We are ultimately no different from the performing horse: no matter how cultivatedly intelligent or decorously clothed we may appear, we piss and shit the same as he does. And the challenge is brought to a strikingly direct, almost homiletic climax: 'Das hat geheißt: Mensch sey natürlich. Du bist geschaffe Staub, Sand, Dreck. Willst du mehr seyn, als Staub, Sand, Dreck?' Now this is a pretty extreme reductivist view of human existence; but it is not presented to the reader/spectator as 'The Truth'. If Büchner had wished to do that, he would have conveyed it to us direct, using some convincingly authoritative mouthpiece. Instead, he relativizes and distances the proposition, and the argument as a whole, by setting it in a rumbustious fairground, and packaging it as the patter of a louche Barker flamboyantly working his crowd. We need to remember, too, that whereas in H1 the fairground episode comes first, thus functioning as a quasi-exposition and thereby setting the tone, in H2 and H4 it follows after two scenes that have already established a very different mood and dynamic.[8] What we see here is quite literally a sideshow: it bears scarcely at all on the plot; and instead of presenting a central or definitive truth, it helps to define the terms and tenor of the argument by offering a garish 'worst-case' view of human existence (and one that is taken up again later in H1 through the problematic figure of the 'Barbier'; cf. above, pp. 294ff.).

A further such episode is the mock-sermon delivered through the 'Handwerksbursch' in H4, 11 (and H2, 4). After the 'What?' of human existence, now the 'Why?': the Barbier asked '*Was* ist der Mensch?', and gave the answer 'Knochen! Staub, Sand, Dreck' (387); now Büchner has the Handwerksbursche ask '*Warum* ist der Mensch?'—and the (non-)reply offered here is no whit less bleak:

1. HANDWERKSBURSCH.[*predigt auf dem Tisch*] Jedoch wenn ein Wandrer, der gelehnt steht an dem Strom der Zeit oder aber sich d. göttliche Weisheit beantwortet u. sich anredet: Warum ist der Mensch? Warum ist der Mensch?—Aber wahrlich ich sage Euch, von was hätte der Landmann, der Weißbinder, der Schuster, der Arzt leben sollen, wenn Gott den Menschen nicht geschaffen hätte? Von was hätte der Schneider leben sollen, wenn er dem Menschen nicht die Empfindung der Schaam eingepflanzt, von was der Soldat, wenn Er ihn nicht mit dem Bedürfniß sich todtzuschlagen ausgerüstet hätte? Darum zweifelt nicht, ja ja, es ist lieblich u. fein, aber Alles Irdische ist eitel, selbst das Geld geht in Verwesung über.—Zum Beschluß meine geliebten Zuhörer laßt uns noch über's Kreuz pissen, damit ein Jud stirbt. (380)

FIRST JOURNEYMAN. [*preaches from a tabletop*] Yet if a wanderer leaning by the river of time, or perchance divine wisdom itself, should pose the question and provide the answer: Wherefore is man? Wherefore is man?— But verily I say unto you, how could the farmer, the cooper, the cobbler, the doctor have earned their living if God had not created man? How could the tailor have earned his living if He hadn't made man feel ashamed of his nakedness? How the soldier if he hadn't given man the urge to kill? Therefore doubt ye not, yea verily, it is sweet and lovely, but vanity of vanities, all is vanity, even money decays in the end.—In conclusion, dear brethren, let us now piss on the cross that a Jew might die.

[8] We don't of course know how Büchner would have handled the fairground scene in H4; but the fact that he left himself so much blank space after the scene-heading (one and a half manuscript pages) suggests that it would have been longer than H2, 3, and perhaps as long as H1, 1 and H1, 2 together.

It would be difficult to imagine a more sardonic, even savage piece of parody than this, in which the format of the sermon and the language of the Bible are used to flaunt a message directly antithetical to the one they inherently represent. 'God' and 'divine wisdom' are seemingly posited, but only in order to be ridiculed through the flagrantly circular and materialist proposition that God created man to give men a livelihood; and when the Cross and thereby the Passion are invoked at the close, it is only for the purpose of a brutal and calculated blasphemy. But it is even clearer here than in the case of the fairground that the message is not meant to be swallowed whole by the reader/spectator: the 'preacher' is an uncouth and drunken journeyman, his 'pulpit' an inn-table, his 'congregation' the raucous assembly of drinkers, musicians, whirling dancers. Moreover the speech is more blatantly than any other a performance-within-the-performance; we relish it as a virtuoso if scabrous burlesque, and as such it brings relief of a kind after the intensity of Woyzeck's rage and anguish immediately beforehand ('Warum bläßt Gott nicht die Sonn aus, daß Alles in Unzucht sich übernanderwälzt [etc.]').

There is one other episode where a character spouts before an on-stage audience, namely when the Professor addresses his students from his attic window in H3, 1. The philosophical perspective presented here is of course quite the opposite of those entailed in the passages discussed above: whereas the notion of God is conspicuously absent from the universe of the 'anti-fairytale', and implicitly derided by the Barker and the Handwerksbursche, it is blithely taken for granted by the establishment Professor:

Meine Herrn wir sind an der wichtigen Frage über das Verhältniß des Subjects zum Object. Wenn wir nur eins von d. Dingen nehmen, worin sich d. organische Selbstaffirmation d. Göttlichen, auf einem so hohen Standpunkte manifestirt u. ihr Verhältniß zum Raum, zur Erde, zum Planetarischen untersuchen, meine Herrn, wenn ich dieße Katze zum Fenster hinauswerfe, wie wird dieße Wesenheit sich zum centrum gravitationis u. d. eigenen Instinct verhalten. (394)

Gentlemen, we now come to the important question of the relationship of the subject to the object. If we but take one of those things in which the organic self-affirmation of the divine manifests itself at such an elevated level, if, gentlemen, I throw this cat out of the window, how will this embodiment of being behave in relation to the centre of gravity and to its own instincts?

Here as elsewhere, the Doctor/Professor is a grimly comic figure, and we can only laugh at his grandiose talk of 'das Verhältniß des Subjects zum Object' and 'die organische Selbstaffirmation des Göttlichen', especially as it is prefaced with a salacious reference to young girls' underwear, and rounded off with the comic-cruel defenestration of the allegedly divine cat. But although we don't swallow his pompous, complacent optimism, any more than we swallow the alcoholic negativism of the Handwerksbursche, the issues involved are indeed 'important'. We only have to remind ourselves of Büchner's critique of Descartes, written at around the same time, with its focus precisely on the Subject–Object relationship and the associated question of God:

Gott ist es [i.e. for Descartes], der den Abgrund zwischen Denken und Erkennen, zwischen Subject und Object ausfüllt, er ist die Brücke zwischen dem *cogito ergo sum*, zwischen dem einsamen, irren, nur einem, dem Selbstbewußtseyn, gewissen, Denken und der Außenwelt. Der Versuch ist etwas naiv ausgefallen, aber man sieht doch, wie instinctartig scharf schon Cartesius das Grab der Philosophie abmaß; sonderbar ist es freilich wie er den lieben Gott als Leiter gebrauchte, um herauszukriechen. (ii. 153; cf. above, pp. 34f.)

All the various 'interludes' in the *Woyzeck* drafts punctuate the main action with graphic and mostly grim interpretations of existence. But again: we should resist the temptation to detach them from their contexts and mistake them for definitive concretions of meaning; they function within the continuum of the play, and their impact and importance lie chiefly in the fact that they emphasize the existential tenor of the central action. The albeit futile quest of the child, the questions as to the 'What?' and 'Why?' of man, the problem of the subject–object relationship: these are the terms in which the story of Woyzeck and his unfolding agony is to be understood. Woyzeck is more profoundly anguished than any other of Büchner's protagonists by the 'gulf' between thinking and knowing, between subject and object, between the lonely, errant, solipsistic mind and the objective reality of the world outside; but unlike Descartes, he can build no 'bridge', find no 'ladder' with which to escape the philosophical 'pit' or 'grave' in which he finds himself.

This brings us back to the philosophizing Woyzeck, the Woyzeck 'eaten up' and driven close to derangement by too much thinking

Emblems and Archetypes 351

('er philosophirt wieder', 'Er schnappt noch über mit den Gedanken', 'Du denkst zuviel, das zehrt'). And we can seize the very moment at which his philosophical-existential anguish reaches its critical turning-point, namely when he hears from the Hauptmann of Marie's infidelity. Büchner doesn't have him react to this news in 'private', personal terms at all, but in terms of agonized reflections on hell and heaven, and the depths to which human kind is capable of sinking:

> H. Hauptmann, die Erd ist höllenheiß, mir eiskalt! eiskalt, die Hölle ist kalt, wollen wir wetten. Unmöglich, Mensch! Mensch! unmöglich. . . . Es ist viel möglich. Der Mensch! est ist viel möglich. Wir habe schön Wetter H. Hauptmann. Sehn sie so ein schön, festen groben Himmel, man könnte Lust bekomm, ein Kloben hineinzuschlagen und sich daran zu hänge, nur wege des Gedankenstrichels zwischen Ja und nein ja—und nein H., H. Hauptmann ja und nein? Ist das Nein am Ja oder das Ja am Nein Schuld? Ich will drüber nachdenke. [*geht mit breiten Schritten ab, erst langsam dann immer schneller*] (375; the first 'nein' is Schmid's conjecture, GS 16, in place of Lehmann's conjectural 'wieder')

> The earth's as hot as hell, sir, to me it's icy cold! Icy cold, hell is cold, d'you want to bet? Impossible. 'umans! 'umans! Impossible. . . . Lots of things are possible. 'umans! Lots of things are possible. Nice weather we're having sir. See what a nice, solid, rough-cast look the 'eavens have got, makes you want to drive a nail into 'em and hang yourself, just because of that tiny little line between yes and no, yes and no, sir, yes and no. Is No to blame for Yes, or Yes for No? I want to think about that. [*strides off, slowly at first, then faster and faster*]

The words are not readily comprehensible in all particulars, but this is quite fitting, for Woyzeck himself is plunged into the most anguished incomprehension by the apparent betrayal of his love—the only thing giving sense and substance to his life ('ich bin ein arm Teufel,—und hab sonst nichts auf der Welt'). Categories are thrown into confusion: hell and earth, hot and cold, the thinkable and the unthinkable. We cannot know what—if anything—Büchner specifically had in mind when he wrote the 'yes'/'no' lines. They perhaps hark back to the 'möglich'/'unmöglich' opposition; the 'Gedankenstrichel zwischen Ja und Nein' might refer to the thin line between resisting and yielding to temptation; the question whether No is to blame for Yes, or vice versa, may be asking what came first in the overall scheme of things: the positive, which then spawned the negative, or the negative, which then spawned the positive. But I doubt whether clarity should be sought or expected; what these lines bespeak is Woyzeck's profound and irremediable perturbation, the disintegration of his only hold on existence. He even contemplates killing himself; instead, he will kill Marie.

19
Choice or Compulsion?

THE clue to the essential issue underlying Woyzeck's tortured response to the news of Marie's infidelity is to be found at the beginning and end of the passage, in the double mention of 'hell', and the reference to 'Schuld' ('guilt', 'blame'). Büchner has him perceive Magreth/Marie as the very picture of mortal sin in its most alluring guise ('Adieu, Marie, du bist schön wie die Sünde—. Kann die Todsünde so schön seyn?', 364); and when he kills her, he eradicates not merely her physical existence, but the stain of her misdeeds: she was 'black' with sin, and he 'bleaches' her white ('Du warst schwarz davon, schwarz! Hab ich dich jezt gebleicht.', 405). As already suggested at the outset: at the heart of the work is the problem of crime and punishment, sin and retribution—and the even more fundamental problem of whether our notions of 'sin', 'moral choice', 'civilization' have substance in the first place, or are simply expedient fictions, a cloak with which to mask the brute reality of nature and its autonomous compulsions.

The opposite extremes on the spectrum of possibilities are plainly, even programmatically, marked out through the Barker and the Doctor, on both occasions in the context of the supremely natural process of excretion—the horse dumping its load on the stage, Woyzeck pissing against the wall 'like a dog'. At the negative end of the spectrum is the view that man, as part of nature, consists solely of 'dust, sand, dirt', and should not aspire to be anything more ('Das hat geheiße: Mensch, sey natürlich. Du bist geschaffe Staub, Sand, Dreck. Willst du mehr seyn, als Staub, Sand, Dreck?' 355). At the positive end of the spectrum is the view that man possesses free will, and so has the power to transcend the would-be imperatives of nature:

WOYZECK. Aber H. Doctor, wenn einem die Natur kommt.
DOCTOR. Die Natur kommt, die Natur kommt! Die Natur! Hab' ich nicht nachgewiesen, daß der musculus constrictor vesicae dem Willen unterworfen ist? Die Natur! Woyzeck, der Mensch ist frei, in dem Menschen verklärt sich die Individualität zur Freiheit. Den Harn nicht halten können! (366)

WOYZECK. But Doctor, when nature calls.
DOCTOR. When nature calls, when nature calls! Nature! Have I not proved that the musculus constrictor vesicae is subordinate to the will? Nature! Woyzeck, man is free, in man individuality is transfigured into freedom. Can't hold your water!

We need to be clear that these are extremes, and the play is not so managed as to 'prove' or bear out either the one viewpoint or the other: in *Woyzeck*, man is manifestly far more than 'dust, sand, dirt', yet equally manifestly does not possess transfigurative freedom of will giving ready control over powerful impulses. One could say that Büchner locates the play in the problematic space between the two extremes. But even this would be misleading, for it begs what is arguably the most fundamental question of all: the Doctor's standpoint is opposite to the Barker's in positing sovereign free will—but it shares the same essential premiss that nature is brutish and nasty. This negative reading of nature is indeed reflected in the action of the play—but so too are more positive possibilities.

For Georg Büchner, the area where nature most powerfully and persistently threatens to confound all our notions of civilization is, of course, the genital/excretory area. Nature asserts itself in the 'civilized' horse, and thus 'puts society to shame'; Woyzeck's contract-breaking piddle is likewise dictated by nature (and by the same token: when he wants to piss, he can't—'Woyzeck muß er nicht wieder pissen? . . . / Ich kann nit H. Doctor', 366). We decorously hide what Danton called 'das häßliche Ding', but we might as well leave it uncovered for dogs to lick, for beneath our masks and disguises—so the negativist argument goes—we are essentially animals, and do no more than eat, sleep, and fuck (71). At the beginning of H4, 2 the Drum-Major strides past at the head of his band, implicitly replete with baton and braid, but what Marie instantly recognizes is his animality, his lion-like bearing; and no matter how gaudy his Drum-Major's get-up, she has a penetrating eye for the only bit of him that really matters: she can 'see her way clean through seven pairs of leather breeches' (340).

We need to look at Marie more closely, however. We have already seen how Büchner figures her throughout the drafts as an emblematic personification of unbiddable, fathomless sexuality—her eye so penetrating, her mouth so red, her hair so wild; so black, too, that it makes her an infinite mystery, and seems to drag her into the depths 'like a heavy weight' ('wie ein Gewicht', 356). In this respect she is a magnificently realized companion-piece to her virtual namesake Marion in *Dantons Tod*. But she is also much more. For one thing she is dramaturgically a very different kind of figure. Marion is a single-scene character who moreover remains as it were fixed within the frame—not acting or interacting in the present, but recounting a history (in this specific sense she is directly analogous to the Grandmother). Marie by contrast is centrally involved in the action, and as such comes across as a quasi-real figure moving within a quasi-real-life continuum, with a home and next-door neighbours, a child, a husband of sorts, a distinct social station and context, and ordinary foibles such as her bedazzlement at the sight of the Barker with his tassels and the woman wearing trousers (347)—indeed it is just such a foible, seemingly quite innocent, that first brings her together with her lover-to-be in H1, 2, when she clambers into the front row to get a better view of the proceedings ('Das muß ich sehn', 355). At the same time, though, it has to be recognized that Büchner makes no attempt to flesh her out fully; on the contrary, he is economical to the point of mystification. In particular, we never discover what her precise relationship with Woyzeck might be. They are not married (362); they do have a (bastard) child (362); they are enough of a couple for Woyzeck and others to think of Marie as his 'wife' ('mei Frau', 368; 'Er hat eine brave Frau', 373); Woyzeck supports the 'Menage' with his earnings (368). But we learn nothing of any background or antecedents beyond the sole fact that they have been together for something less than two years (399).[1] And we learn precious little about their relationship in the present. We don't even know whether Woyzeck lives with Marie in a nuclear family, or merely visits her, with the military barracks serving as his main 'home'; and our uncertainty is made all the more acute since we are predisposed by Marie's first song to assume that she has neither a husband nor any other kind of provider ('Hast ein klein Kind und kein Mann . . . Giebt mir kein Mensch nix dazu.') There is another, more fundamental uncertainty: are we to suppose that Marie—like Marion—is a prostitute? When Woyzeck in the murder scene speaks of her 'hot, hot breath

---

[1] This 'less than two years' timespan is curious, in that it implies that the child could be no more than a year or so old, whereas he is clearly represented as being about three or four. As we have seen, this is by no means the only temporal oddity in *Woyzeck*. Cf. also Michael Patterson, 'Contradictions Concerning Time in Büchner's *Woyzeck*', *German Life and Letters*, NS 32 (1978–9), 115–21.

of a whore' (399), this is just as likely to be figurative as literal; but in H4, 2 (and H2, 2), Büchner has her specifically define herself as a 'whore' through her description of her child as 'en arm Hurenkind'. Or should we take this, too, as figurative, as a hyperbolic characterization of her status as an unmarried mother, which automatically makes her little or no better than a whore in the eyes of prevailing society? Needless to say, Büchner does not leave these things unclear by accident: it is all part of the overall pattern whereby Marie remains unfathomable, a 'giddying abyss', and at the same time an essentially archetypal figure.

There is another and even more vital respect in which Marie differs from Marion. Perhaps the most chilling trait in Marion is that she has no moral sense whatever; indeed Büchner has her explicitly dismiss morality as simply a disguised manifestation of the pleasure principle: there is no essential difference between the worshipper of Christ and the worshipper of carnality, so she claims, since both do what they do solely for the pleasure it affords them (22). In the case of Marie, however, Büchner makes the moral dimension critically important. It is instructive here to see how Büchner develops the persona from scene-sequence to scene-sequence. Magreth in H1 exhibits no such dimension—but that is because she scarcely exists as a character at all: she figures large only in the murder scene (H1, 15); apart from that, she makes a single brief utterance in each of the first three scenes, putatively dances past the window in H1, 5, speaks just fourteen words in the Grandmother scene, and is present only as a corpse in H1, 19 and H1, 20. In the H2 sequence, the character begins to acquire real substance, chiefly in H2, 2 and H2, 8, but also in H2, 5 (when we see her through the eyes of the Drum-Major and his sidekick). Nonetheless, it is only in the final scene (H2, 9) that Büchner begins to give the persona a moral dimension, and even then it is only hinted at in the single line of dialogue that he wrote before abandoning the H2 draft altogether: 'Und ist kein Betrug in seinem Munde erfunden. Herr Gott!' (391; *And neither was guile found in his mouth. Lord God!*)

In H4, Marie appears in six of the seventeen scenes. The first of these, H4, 2, is a reworking of an earlier scene (H2, 2), and we get no sense here of a troubled conscience; on the contrary, we find Marie rejecting the moral censure flung at her by her 'bitch' of a neighbour ('Luder! . . . Komm mein Bub. Was die Leut wollen. Bist doch nur en arm Hurenkind'); indeed her song even suggests a touch of defiant insouciance in its depiction of the response of the 'Mädel' to the strictures of society ('Ey was frag ich danach | Sing ich die ganze Nacht'). At this stage, of course, her sexual entanglement with the Drum-Major has scarcely even begun; but things are very different by the time we come to H4, 4—a completely new scene. H1, 2, H1, 3, and H2, 5 all pointed to some kind of louche encounter between the pair, which Büchner may well have intended to incorporate into his H4 revision of the fairground scene (left blank in the manuscript except for the heading). Be that as it may, an encounter of some sort has clearly already taken place by the beginning of H4, 4, which shows Marie admiring herself in the mirror with her new earrings—a reward or an inducement, so we must assume, from the lustful Drum-Major; and in the ensuing monologue, it is precisely her sexuality that she vaunts in the synecdoche of her 'red mouth' ('doch hab' ich einen so rothen Mund als die großen Madamen', 358). When Woyzeck challenges her over the earrings, Büchner originally had her respond with the words 'Was willst Du?'—an echo of her earlier 'Was die Leut wollen'; but he immediately crossed this out, and substituted a response at once startling and enigmatic: 'Bin ich ein Mensch?' This could arguably mean something like 'I'm only human, aren't I?' But it is far more likely that 'Mensch' is used here in its alternative neuter form ('das Mensch', 'die Menscher'), still common in Büchner's day—a term for a woman ranging in its connotations from the mildly derogatory 'wench' right through to the strongly pejorative 'trollop' or 'harlot' (see Grimm, *Deutsches Wörterbuch*); on this assumption, therefore, Marie is saying something like 'So I'm a tart, am I?' This reading is confirmed almost beyond doubt by the fact that Büchner has Marie explicitly use the neuter form when she harks back to her earlier question in her closing lines following Woyzeck's departure—and it is here, for the first time in the various drafts, that Büchner endows his character with an unmistakable, even strident conscience (whilst simultaneously prefiguring her death by the knife): 'MARIE [*allein nach einer Pause*] ich bin doch ein schlecht Mensch. Ich könnt' mich erstechen.' (360; MARIE *[alone, after a pause] I really am a no-good tart. Stab meself dead I could.*) Her conscience does not have the last word, however, for it is countered at once by an equally strident attempt at self-justification: '—Ach! Was Welt? Geht doch Alles zum Teufel, Mann u. Weib.' (—*Oh, sod it! In a world like this? Everything's going to the devil, after all—man, woman, everything.*) We can detect a similar pattern in H4, 6 (an entirely new scene, like H4, 4). Marie at first resists the Drum-Major's sexual embrace, then seems to let herself go; and although the language here is supremely laconic, we can reasonably infer that Büchner means to show her resisting on account of her conscience, then shrugging it off and letting the devil inside her have his way: 'Laß mich! . . . Rühr mich an! / Sieht Dir der Teufel aus d. Augen? / Meintwegen. Es ist Alles eins.' (364; *Let go of me! . . . Just touch me! / Is that the devil in your eye? / Don't care if it is. It's all the same in the end.*)

In the confrontation scene that follows (a reworking of H2, 8), Büchner incorporates no signs of conscience at all; indeed he has Marie respond to Woyzeck's raging indignation by being at first intimidated ('verschüchtert'), but then dismissive and cheeky ('keck'). It is psychologically convincing that she should react with such spirit to accusations from others, just as she did in the face of Magreth's angry insults in H4, 2. When she is alone, however, Büchner has her conscience speak—just as he did in the case of Danton, Robespierre, and Barrère in *Dantons Tod*. We have already seen a brief example of this at the close of H4, 2 ('ich bin doch ein schlecht Mensch [etc.]'); but we also find an entire scene devoted to it, namely H4, 16, the penultimate scene of the draft. What Büchner does here is to take up the solitary last line of the H2 sequence, and build on it to create a scene of intense poignancy:

MARIE [*allein blättert in der Bibel*]. Und ist kein Betrug in seinem Munde erfunden. Herrgott! Herrgott! Sieh mich nicht an. [*blättert weiter:*] aber die Pharisäer brachten ein Weib zu ihm, im Ehebruch begriffen u. stelleten sie in's Mittel dar.—Jesus aber sprach: so verdamme ich Dich auch nicht. Geh hin und sündige hinfort nicht mehr. [*schlägt d. Hände zusammen*] Herrgott! Herrgott! Ich kann nicht. Herrgott gieb mir nur soviel, daß ich beten kann. . . . Und trat hinein zu seinen Füßen und weinete u. fing an seine Füße zu netzen mit Thränen u. mit den Haaren ihres Hauptes zu trocknen u. küssete seine Füße und salbete sie mit Salben. [*schlägt sich auf d. Brust*] Alles todt! Heiland, Heiland ich möchte Dir die Füße salben. (390/2)

MARIE [*alone, leafing through the Bible*]. 'Neither was guile found in his mouth'—Lord God, Lord God! Don't look at me! [*turns more pages*] 'And the scribes and Pharisees brought unto him a woman taken in adultery, and set her in the midst.—And Jesus said unto her, Neither do I condemn thee; go, and sin no more.' [*claps her hands together*] Lord God! Lord God! I can't. Lord, just give me strength enough to pray. . . . 'And stood at his feet weeping, and began to wash his feet with tears, and did wipe them with the hairs of her head, and kissed his feet and anointed them with ointment.' [*strikes herself on the chest*] Everything's dead! Saviour, o Saviour, I wish I could anoint your feet.

Büchner draws here on three different passages in the New Testament, with sin being the pivotal issue in every case. The first quotation is from Peter's first epistle, and refers in its original context specifically to Christ, 'Who did no sin, neither was guile found in his mouth'—to quote the relevant verse in its entirety (I Peter 2: 22). But needless to say, the quotation in Marie's mouth is not about Christ and his guilelessness as such, but instead conveys an awareness on Marie's part of her own 'guile'—in the full sense of the word (more vividly apparent in the German term 'Betrug') as 'insidious cunning, deceit, treachery' (*OED*). The abjectness of her sense of deceit and shame is expressed through her telling God not even to look upon her, as though his gaze might destroy her. Then in the second quotation, her deceit is given its particular name through the story of the 'woman taken in adultery' (John 8). What makes this so poignant is that Büchner has Marie reveal not only a consuming sense of being an adulteress, a grievous sinner, but also an equally powerful sense that she cannot help herself, cannot obey the command to 'go, and sin no more' ('Herrgott! Herrgott! Ich kann nicht'); she hopes at best for the strength to pray. This is the burden, too, of the third quotation, taken from the story in Luke 7 of the abundant sinner who came in to Jesus as he 'sat at meat in the Pharisees' house', and who earns forgiveness through her abundant love of him ('Wherefore I say unto thee, Her sins, which are many, are forgiven; for she loved much', Luke 7: 47). If only Marie could earn the same forgiveness through the same act of love towards her Saviour: 'Heiland, Heiland, ich möchte dir die Füße salben.' But she cannot; and so, in the shocking image Büchner puts into her mouth, the world for her is suddenly quite dead: 'Alles todt!' The phrase is poignant enough in itself; with its leitmotival resonances it is almost unbearable, harking back as it does to the opening scene and Woyzeck's 'Still, Alles still, als wär die Welt todt', and forward to the Grandmother's 'Alles todt'—and to Marie's own death ('Bist du todt? Todt! Todt!'; 338, 397, 401).

Marie's declaration of hopelessness, 'Herrgott! Herrgott! Ich kann nicht', exemplifies a particularly subtle feature running through all the various drafts, namely Büchner's telling use of modal verbs. As in this case here, 'können' is especially prominent in the negative. This is typified in H1, 2 when the Barker talks of his performing horse: 'es kann rechnen u. kann doch nit an d. Finger herzählen, warum? Kann sich nur nit ausdrücke, nur nit explicirn, ist ein verwandelter Mensch!' (355; *he can add up but he still can't count on 'is fingers. And why? Just can't express 'isself, just can't explain 'isself, he's a 'uman being in all but shape!*) Another striking instance occurs in H2, 6, in the context of Woyzeck's illicit piss, and the Doctor's remonstrations: 'Aber H. Doctor wenn man nit anders kann? / Nit anders kann, nit anders kann. Aberglaube, abscheulicher Aberglaube! . . . Woyzeck der Mensch ist frei [etc.]' (367; *But Doctor, if you can't help it? / Can't help it, can't help it. Superstition, abominable superstition! . . . Woyzeck, mankind is free [etc.]*). It is instructive to compare *Woyzeck* and *Leonce und Lena* in point of modal usage. In the comedy, the most frequently used modal is 'wollen', as typified in Leonce's final speech of the play, when he wonders what he and Lena might want to do with all the 'puppets and playthings' now at their disposal as King and Queen of Bum: the verb 'wollen' recurs no fewer than five times within a few lines (133–4). We find only one such cascade of 'wollen' forms in *Woyzeck*—where they neatly serve to emphasize the wanton pugnacity of the Drum-Major in the fight scene ('Wer will was? . . . / Ich will ihm die Nas ins Arschloch prügeln. Ich will—[*zu Woyzeck*] da Kerl, sauf, der Mann muß saufen, ich wollt die Welt wär Schnaps, Schnaps', 384). In *Leonce und Lena*, 'wollen' occurs nearly twice as often as 'müssen'; but in *Woyzeck* it is 'müssen' that occurs most frequently—almost 50 per cent more often than 'wollen'. This intensive use of 'müssen' helps not least to define the persona of Marie. Prior to the murder sequence in H1, 'Magreth' makes only three brief utterances, namely one in each of the first three scenes—and in every case Büchner has her use the verb 'müssen' (347, 355, 359). In H2, 5, the inevitability, the 'must-ness' of her perdition is beautifully suggested through the remark of the 'Unterofficier': 'Wie sie den Kopf trägt, man meint das schwarz Haar müßt sie abwärts ziehn, wie ein Gewicht' (356; *How she carries her head! You'd think her black hair must drag her down, like a heavy weight*). But needless to say it is Woyzeck that is mainly identified with—and through—the verb 'müssen'.

Choice or Compulsion? 361

In the early stages of H2 and H4, it is Woyzeck's 'drivenness' that is conveyed—but drivenness as a function of his abjectly subordinate position in society. Thus in H4, 1 (and H2, 1), when the drum sounds, he and Andres must instantly get going: 'Sie trommeln drin. Wir müssen fort.' (338, 341). In the following scene he bangs on Magreth's window and she invites him in; but he has to get back for roll-call: 'Kann nit. Muß zum Verles. . . . Ich muß fort.' (342; cf. 343). Again at the end of the earrings scene, Büchner has him go rushing off: 'Ich muß fort.' (360). There is even a suggestion in H1 that Büchner envisaged this as a specific element in Magreth's unfaithfulness: she is impressed by a boss-man lording it over his underling: 'Der andre hat ihm befohlen und er hat gehn müssen. Ha! Ein Mann vor einem Andern.' (359). The general sense that the underclass are permanently subjected to intolerable compulsions is mordantly epitomized in Woyzeck's famous comment to the Hauptmann in the shaving scene: 'Unseins ist doch einmal unseelig in der und der andern Welt, ich glaub' wenn wir in Himmel kämen so müßten wir donnern helfen.' (362; *Our sort just don't have no chance in this world or the next; I reckon if we ever got to heaven we'd have to help with the thunder*.) As the action progresses, however, Woyzeck's drivenness increasingly displays a quite different dynamic. Büchner still has him use the same tell-tale language: 'Ich muß fort, muß sehn! . . . Ich muß fort'; 'Ich muß hinaus. . . . Ich muß fort. . . . Ich muß hinaus' (379: H1; 378: H4); but what chiefly drives him now is not the external, social world with its various dictates, but his own inner visions, thoughts, compulsions. This is summed up at the close of H1, 11 with yet another use of the verb 'müssen', when Woyzeck is haunted once again by his vision of a knife, and declares that he *must* get hold of it: 'Ich muß das Ding haben' (389).

In due course Woyzeck's compulsion to kill proves irresistible, and Magreth is brutally murdered. But in the meantime the compulsion does not go unchallenged. Indeed Büchner sets up a crucial tension through the very next words that he has Woyzeck utter: his exclamation 'Ich muß das Ding haben' at the close of H1, 11 is immediately followed in H1, 12 (the briefest of brief scenes) by a recital of the Seventh Commandment: 'Du sollst nicht tödten', whereupon he rids himself of the knife by putting it in a cave and running away (391). This tension is brought into the sharpest possible focus in the H4 draft, when Büchner reworks H1, 6 to create H4, 12. The new scene mostly echoes the earlier one—but it also includes an entirely new element, namely a starkly contrasted pair of modal verbs: 'Ha was, was sagt ihr? Lauter, lauter,—stich, stich die Zickwolfin todt? stich, stich die Zickwolfin todt. Soll ich? Muß ich?' (382). When this passage was quoted earlier, the last four words were expediently translated as 'Should I? Must I?' This captures the punchiness of the original, but not its full import. For Büchner's 'Soll ich? Muß ich?' spotlights a central issue of the work: in expunging Marie, is Woyzeck essentially doing right by enacting an ethical imperative, a kind of unspoken but quasi-divine commandment—'Thou shalt kill her' ('Soll ich?')? Or is he following a blind compulsion ('Muß ich?')?

Büchner returns here to the critical question that burned at the heart of *Dantons Tod*, and found expression above all in the 'September' scene, when Danton hears his 'vile sins' screaming at him in the night, and finds dubious refuge only in the idea of 'das Muß': 'Es muß, das war dieß Muß. Wer will der Hand fluchen, auf die der Fluch des Muß gefallen? Wer hat das *Muß* gesprochen, wer? Was ist das, was in uns hurt, lügt, stiehlt und mordet?' (41). Indeed in H1, 20, when Woyzeck is trying to get rid of the tell-tale knife after the murder, there are even distinct resonances of the 'September' scene itself: Woyzeck's 'Will denn die ganze Welt es ausplaudern?' (405) is actually not very Woyzeckian—but it plainly echoes words and cadences voiced through Danton: 'Will denn das nie aufhören? . . . will's denn nie still und dunkel werden . . .?'; '. . . wenn so die Wände plaudern' (40). In H1, 20, too, there is a distinct reminiscence of the 'bloody finger' and 'bloody hands' that so haunted Robespierre and Danton, when, at the close of the scene, we see Woyzeck feverishly trying to wash away the accusing bloodstains: 'Bin ich noch blutig? ich muß mich waschen. Da ein Fleck und da noch einer.' (405; cf. also 403, where it is his bloodstained hand that betrays him).

However, the connections between *Woyzeck* and *Dantons Tod* run deeper still. We have already seen how Woyzeck's raging vision of universal, pullulating lechery in the dancing scene (H4, 11) carries echoes of the earlier play: Woyzeck's 'Warum bläßt Gott nicht die Sonn aus, daß Alles in Unzucht sich übernanderwälzt' is strongly reminiscent of Danton's 'es ist als brüte die Sonne Unzucht aus'; the image of gnats copulating on one's very hands is an unmistakable echo of the same image voiced through Lacroix in the

Marion scene ('Thut's am hellen Tag, thut's einem auf den Händen, wie die Mücken.' / 'die Mücken treiben's ihnen sonst auf den Händen'; 380, 23). In Chapter 9 I argued that at the deepest levels of *Dantons Tod* Büchner conveys a picture of the world as almost irredeemably corrupt—a world of ubiquitous depravity and disease. And it is essentially the same vision that increasingly prevails in *Woyzeck* as Büchner progresses from draft to draft (intriguingly encapsulated in the incomplete—and as yet unsourced—French quotation that Büchner originally penned at the beginning of H2, 9, and then crossed out: 'La corruption du siècle est parvenue à ce point, que pour maintenir la moral', 391). In *Woyzeck* as in the earlier play, it is the genitals and their doings that constitute the central focus of interest. As we noted earlier, Büchner makes his protagonist's stance in this regard profoundly contradictory. When he is upbraided by the Hauptmann and then by the Doctor for improperly using his penis—by fathering a bastard, and pissing in the street—he puts all the blame on nature, thus echoing the argument expressed through the Barker (and likewise through Marion: 'Meine Natur war einmal so, wer kann da drüber hinaus?', 22). Never for a moment, however, does he see the genital cavortings of Marie in such terms: Marie in his eyes is not a helpless innocent driven by the irresistible compulsions of nature, by what Danton called 'das Muß', but a grievous sinner guilty of 'a sin so big and so fat', so 'noisome' that it could 'drive the angels out of heaven' (364); a sinner who can be cleansed of her vileness only through death ('Du warst schwarz davon, schwarz! Hab ich dich jezt gebleicht.', 405).

Woyzeck is of course by no means the first character in Büchner to seek to 'clean away' supposed moral 'filth' through the expedient of death: this is precisely what Robespierre sought to do; in the accusing words of Danton: 'Hast du das Recht aus der Guillotine einen Waschzuber für die unreine Wäsche anderer Leute und aus ihren abgeschlagnen Köpfen Fleckkugeln für ihre schmuzzigen Kleider zu machen...?' (27; *Do you have the right to use the guillotine as a washtub for other people's dirty linen, and to use their severed heads to scour the stains from their grubby clothes...?*) Within his specific, parochial environment, Woyzeck is indeed a kind of pocket Robespierre. And we see this not only in his murderous 'cleansing' of Magreth/Marie, and in the consequent accusing blood that he cannot seem to wash away, but also in his vision of a kind of universal canker of lecherous corruption. We see this latter element most graphically in his raging response to the whirling dancers in the relevant inn scene: whereas in the H1 version his response is relatively tame, and targets only the one pair of dancers, in H4 it is eloquently emphatic and anguished, and embraces virtually the whole of creation: God, sun, man, animals, insects ('Warum bläßt Gott nicht die Sonn aus, daß Alles in Unzucht sich übernanderwälzt, Mann und Weib, Mensch u. Vieh. Thut's am hellen Tag, thut's einem auf den Händen, wie die Mücken', 380). In this instance, the vision of lechery is explicit; but we find it mediated just as powerfully, albeit more obliquely, in the opening two scenes of H2 and H4, and especially in the latter: what Büchner has Woyzeck envision here is no less than the destruction of Sodom and Gomorrah, which God caused to be 'consumed' for their 'iniquity' and 'because their sin was grievous'. The H4 formulation 'Ein Feuer fährt um den Himmel und ein Getös herunter wie Posaunen' (338) carries clear echoes of Genesis 19: 24: 'Then the Lord rained upon Sodom and upon Gomorrah brimstone and fire from the Lord out of heaven.' Woyzeck's warning to Andres not to look back ('Sieh nicht hinter dich', 338, 339) echoes the Lord's warning to Lot: 'Escape for thy life; look not behind thee' (Genesis 19: 17). The clearest pointer of all is the addition Büchner made in the manuscript to Woyzeck's second speech in H4, 2: 'steht nicht geschrieben, und sieh da ging ein Rauch vom Land, wie der Rauch vom Ofen?' (342)—for this is a direct quotation from the description of the burning ruins of Sodom and Gomorrah in Genesis 19: 28 ('and, lo, the smoke of the country went up as the smoke of a furnace').

On this level of the work, Woyzeck is no delusion-prone local nut-case on the brink of going berserk, but a true visionary mediating the same kind of grim vision already so powerfully conveyed at various junctures in *Dantons Tod*. And the fact that this dimension is established so emphatically at the very beginning of the H2 and H4 drafts serves in effect to set the parameters and tone of the entire work, and predisposes us to see the protagonists in all their ensuing deeds and sufferings not as paltry, happenstance individuals, but as archetypal, emblematic figures—a perspective that is then repeatedly reinforced, as we have seen. One further and momentous aspect of this process needs to be recognized, however, and that is Büchner's persistent and often atmospheric use of religious imagery, associations, and allusions.

Choice or Compulsion? 365

One of the most conspicuous manifestations of this pattern is to be found in the 'interlude' scenes, where Büchner has his characters refer to God on almost every occasion. In H1, God is invoked through the Barker in the very first sentence of the manuscript ('Meine Herren! Meine Herren! Sehn sie die Creatur, wie sie Gott gemacht, nix, gar nix', 343). Again, God figures in the first sentence spoken by the 'Barbier' in H1, 10 ('Was kann der liebe Gott nicht, was?', 385). The 'Handwerksbursche' in H2, 4 repeatedly mentions God, asking in particular why God created man ('Warum hat Gott die Mensche geschaffe?', 352); and this passage is duly reworked to great effect in the mock sermon following Woyzeck's rage at the lechery of the dancers (380). In H3, 1 the Professor speaks of organic nature as 'God's self-affirmation' ('d. organische Selbstaffirmation d. Göttlichen', 394). And God is Woyzeck's crucial weapon when he trounces his master in the shaving scene ('Der Herr sprach: Lasset die Kindlein zu mir kommen', etc., 362).[2]

Within the main action, Büchner frequently has the characters come out with exclamations which in ordinary life are buzz-words emptied of meaning, but which in this highly charged and laconic context almost invariably recover their true resonance and burden. When the Hauptmann splutters 'Teufel Sargnagel' or 'Teufel. 4 Wochen?' (370, 373), this is conventional phatic language. But the spectre of the devil himself is evoked by Woyzeck's cries of 'Teufel!' when he espies the lascivious dancers, challenges Marie in the confrontation scene, rushes from the inn because of the blood on his hand (379, 366, 403). Marie is involved in two of these instances, and indeed she is repeatedly linked with the devil. She herself justifies her new liaison with the Drum-Major on the grounds that 'the entire world's going to the devil anyway' ('Ach! Was Welt? Geht doch Alles zum Teufel, Mann u. Weib', 360). The Drum-Major's very first word in the H2 sequence is 'Teufel', uttered as he salivates over the exuberant sexuality of 'Louisel' ('Teufel zum Fortpflanzen von Kürassierregimenter [etc.]', 356); and in their scene together, Büchner has him see the devil in her very eyes ('Sieht Dir der Teufel aus d. Augen?', 364). Where there is the devil, there is also hell—and it is hell that Woyzeck immediately speaks of when he first hears of Marie's infidelity (375); then at the inn soon after

---

[2] One of the most fascinating revelations afforded by Monika Rössing-Hager's *Wortindex* is the fact that, after 'Mensch', the noun most commonly used by Büchner in his poetic œuvre is 'Gott'/'Herrgott'.

the murder, he talks obsessively of hell and the devil ('Tanzt alle, immer zu, schwizt und stinkt, er holt Euch doch eimal Alle.... d. Teufel holt die eine und läßt die andre laufen.... man kann auch ohne Schuh in die Höll gehn', 401). Needless to say, these various allusions serve to complement and amplify the central motif of sin, introduced first of all towards the close of H1 ('Bey wem hast du das Halsband verdient, mit deinen Sünden?', 405), and greatly intensified in H4, both in the penitence scene ('Geh hin und sündige hinfort nicht mehr [etc.]', 390), and also in the confrontation scene—so different in this key respect from its H2 prototype ('Eine Sünde so dick und so breit... du bist schön wie die Sünde—. Kann die Todsünde so schön seyn?', 364). In this context we might note that Woyzeck is Robespierre-like even to the extent that he, too, sees himself as a kind of 'Heaven's policeman'—to borrow the trenchant term that Danton flung at his antagonist ('Bist du der Policeysoldat des Himmels?', 27).

The effect of these various allusions (and there are numerous others of the same order) is that the drama constantly unfolds within a religious framework of reference. To some extent this could arguably be explained by the requirements of verisimilitude: given that religion loomed large amongst the cultural furniture of the period, one might say that it necessarily had to be included in any faithful evocation of underclass life. But Büchner goes far beyond any such requirements, particularly in the way that he includes so many allusions that are quite gratuitous with respect to the plot and the fictive psychology of the characters. The double mention of the name 'Christian' in H3, 2, and the shift in H4 from 'Magreth/ Louisel' to 'Marie', are typical of this, as is the veiled allusion to the Purification of the Virgin Mary in the children's song ('St. Lichtmeßtag', 397), or the fact that Büchner has Woyzeck identify his birthday as 'Mariä Verkündigung' (392)—Lady Day, the Feast of the Annunciation.[3] Even the specific age that he bestows on Woyzeck carries strong religious resonances: whereas the real Woyzeck was 41 at the time of the murder, our protagonist gives his age as precisely '30 Jahr 7 Monat u. 12 Tage'—Christian numbers in every case (the twelve disciples; the seven loaves/baskets/brethren etc.; 30 is commonly held to have been Christ's age at the time of his death).

[3] As with the reference to Candlemas in the children's song, Büchner curiously gets the date wrong: the proper date is 25 March, but Woyzeck gives it as 'd. 20. Juli' (as deciphered by Schmid; Lehmann reads only 'd. 20. J+').

Another eloquent detail of this kind is the physical location of the murder; it cannot conceivably be a random choice of place when Büchner has one of the children in H1, 18 declare—quite gratuitously—that Marie's body is lying 'by the red cross' ('am rothen Kreuz', 403). And of course this is not the only allusion to the crucifixion. The mock sermon delivered by the 'Handwerksbursche' ends with the defiantly blasphemous exhortation that he and his 'beloved listeners' should 'piss on the cross that a Jew might die' (380; cf. 352). Above all, there is the uniquely moving final scene of the H4 draft, in which Woyzeck divests himself of every last meagre possession—including a family crucifix ('Das Kreuz is meiner Schwester', 392)—and then recites sacral verses (the first of them already used in *Lenz*, 84) in which suffering is fervently embraced, transfigured into worship, actively besought of God as a means of sharing in the supreme Passion of Christ 'red and raw' on the cross:

> Leiden sey all mein Gewinst,
> Leiden sey mein Gottesdienst.
> Herr wie dein Leib war roth u. wund
> So laß mein Herz seyn aller Stund. (392)[4]

> May suffering be my sole reward,
> May suffering be my praise to God.
> Lord as thy flesh was red and raw
> So let my heart be ever more.[4]

It is galling that we can never know how Büchner meant to continue his H4 draft, or even whether he was clear in his own mind as to how he would proceed. And yet the last two scenes with their ritualistic tableaux of heroine and hero existentially *in extremis* are a fitting and strangely satisfying climax to the *Woyzeck* project as a whole. Resolution is denied to us both aesthetically and philosophically; but this is apt. Woyzeck is not like Danton or Leonce: he cannot be magicked into the role of King, nor escape into comic irony; nor can he find solace in comradeship, or in the promise of reunion with his beloved beyond death. He is also unlike the Haupt-

---

[4] For the source of these lines—part quotation, part invention—see Heinrich Anz, ' "Leiden sey all mein Gewinnst". Zur Aufnahme und Kritik christlicher Leidenstheologie bei Georg Büchner', in T. M. Mayer (ed.), *Georg Büchner Jahrbuch*, 1/1981, 160–8.

mann: he cannot take refuge in specious moral posturing or in sheer activity ('Aber Woyzeck, die Tugend, die Tugend! Wie sollte ich dann die Zeit herumbringen?'; 'Beschäftigung, Woyzeck, Beschäftigung!'; 362, 360). Like all Büchner's protagonists, Woyzeck sees more than is good for him; but he alone knows no respite—he can never avert his gaze, never close his eyes to the abyss. His particular misfortune is that the abyss as represented by Marie is utterly unfathomable, a chasm as black as 'a well or a chimney'. The specific image of the abyss occurs at precisely that moment in the text when his visionary gaze suddenly fails him. Marie's sin, her 'Sünde so dick und so breit', should be visible, palpable—but he can see no mark of it at all ('Ich seh nichts, ich seh nichts. O, man müßt's sehen, man müßt's greifen könne mit Fäusten', 364, and cf. 377). Instead, she seems like innocence personified ('Sie geht wie die Unschuld', 377)—and hence the image of the giddying abyss: 'Weib!—Nein es müßte was an dir seyn! Jeder Mensch ist ein Abgrund, es schwindelt einem, wenn man hinabsieht.' (377; *Woman!—No, there should be some sign! Everyone's an abyss, it makes you giddy looking down.*)

The essential questions remain unanswered—perhaps because they are unanswerable. Which is truer or more powerful, Nature or Civilization? Is mankind mere 'dust, sand, dirt', or an 'organic self-affirmation of the divine'? Is man driven by irresistible compulsions, or free to choose? And in the meantime, the outcome for the play's particular exemplars of humanity is bleak indeed: Marie is brutally murdered; Christian is orphaned like the child in the Grandmother's tale; Woyzeck puts himself irredeemably beyond the pale, and is doomed to perdition in one guise or another.

One might expect this to leave us with a chilling sense of gloom. And yet it does not. To read the *Woyzeck* drafts, and especially to see a composite version performed on the stage, paradoxically inspires in us a warmer, deeper sense of involvement and sympathy than anything else that Büchner wrote. The key to this paradox may be readily found in the aesthetic that Büchner so emphatically spelled out in *Lenz*. There, he scornfully rejected those authors who sought to 'transfigure' reality, and whose supposedly 'idealist' characters were mere 'wooden puppets'. Instead of trying to 'improve' reality—so Büchner has Lenz declare—writers should enter into the innermost being of the very lowliest of men, and then recreate that being in all its subtlety and vitality: 'Man versuche es einmal und

Choice or Compulsion? 369

senke sich in das Leben des Geringsten und gebe es wieder, in den Zuckungen, den Andeutungen, dem ganz feinen, kaum bemerkten Mienenspiel' (87). Or again, later on the same page:

> es darf einem keiner zu gering, keiner zu häßlich seyn . . . ; das unbedeutendste Gesicht macht einen tiefern Eindruck als die bloße Empfindung des Schönen, und man kann die Gestalten aus sich heraustreten lassen, ohne etwas vom Äußern hinein zu kopiren, wo einem kein Leben, keine Muskeln, kein Puls entgegen schwillt und pocht.

> no one should be considered too lowly, no one too ugly . . . ; the most ordinary of faces makes a deeper impression than any mere semblance of beauty, and one can let the characters' own inner being emerge quite naturally, without introducing anything copied from outside, where no life, no pulse, no muscles surge and throb.

All of this is magnificently exemplified in Woyzeck and Marie, of whom Büchner could easily be speaking when he has Lenz refer to the characters in his plays *Der Hofmeister* and *Die Soldaten*:

> Es sind die prosaischsten Menschen unter der Sonne; aber die Gefühlsader ist in fast allen Menschen gleich, nur ist die Hülle mehr oder weniger dicht, durch die sie brechen muß. Man muß nur Aug und Ohren dafür haben. (87)

> They are the most everyday people in the world; but the pulse of feeling is the same in almost everyone, the only difference is the thickness of the covering that it has to penetrate. One simply needs eyes to see it and ears to hear it.

Indeed the 'pulse of feeling' beats even more strongly in Woyzeck and Marie than in any of the other figures in the work, who are all much less red-blooded, and in some cases more carapaced in convention or status. Both of them are more vivid, more passionate, above all more real—and it is this that moves us so deeply; Büchner thus fully lives up to his own canon of art: 'Der Dichter und Bildende ist mir der Liebste, der mir die Natur am Wirklichsten giebt, so daß ich über seinem Gebild fühle, Alles Übrige stört mich.' (88; *The writers and artists I like the most are those that most strongly convey to me the reality of nature, with the result that their work inspires me with feeling; everything else troubles me.*)

It is their very 'prosaicness' and extreme, unadorned 'naturalness' that lends both hero and heroine a tragic grandeur still unique within German theatre, and helps to make them doubly moving. At one level, they move us as particular individuals caught up in a particular history that they can neither master nor evade. And the drastic economy of means is such that the simplest utterance or gesture can carry a force more searing than the grandest rhetoric. Woyzeck's 'sie war doch ein einzig Mädel', or: 'ich bin ein arm Teufel,—und hab sonst nichts auf der Welt H. Hauptmann', or: 'Was du heiße Lippen hast! . . . und doch möcht' ich den Himmel geben sie noch eimal zu küssen'; Marie's 'Herrgott! Herrgott! Ich kann nicht. Herrgott gieb mir nur soviel, daß ich beten kann'; Christian's scream and double rejection of his murderer-father in H3, 2: such touches have an emotional impact inversely proportional to their seeming artlessness. At one and the same time, however, we are even more profoundly and more subtly moved by the protagonists not as particular individuals, but as exemplars of human existence in its most universal and most defenceless mode—a perspective reinforced again and again through the successive 'interludes', and brought to a supremely poignant climax at the end of the H4 sequence in the invocation of the Passion, and its solemn rite of suffering wholeheartedly embraced—but without the faintest expectation or glimmer of redemption. Is it any exaggeration to say that in Georg Büchner's *Woyzeck*, unfinished though it is, we see not only his own supreme achievement, but also one of the greatest and most original achievements of modern European drama?

Conclusion

HAVING been thrilled, baffled, and generally haunted by Georg Büchner throughout my adult life, first as a student and then as a teacher, I thought that by writing a book I would surely succeed in getting him out of my system. Although of course I could not hope to find any 'ultimate truth', I reckoned that I would come to terms with Büchner's work at long last, and arrive at a rounded, coherent critique that fixed him so to speak in the frame—in my own eyes if in no one else's. I should have known better. Ten years on, despite having written many more words about the man than he wrote himself, and translated and annotated almost his entire output, I find Büchner if anything more haunting and elusive than ever. My central 'wholist' argument seemed compelling when I started; it now seems merely plausible: whereas once it seemed to offer a key to the ark, in practice it has afforded only a perspective—a revealing one, I hope, but a perspective all the same. Nonetheless I feel no regrets, offer no apologies, and take nothing back. Georg Büchner is a genius whose work remains beyond measure, ultimately unamenable to the analytical, freeze-frame procedures and pretensions of the critic. To take *Woyzeck* as an example: although in writing the final section of this book I have spent many months reading and rereading Büchner's drafts, they have never palled, never solidified as it were into definitive shapes and interconnections; on the contrary, they seem not only as fresh and vivid as ever, but increasingly rich in resonance and portent.

The immeasurable quality of Büchner's writing derives from a whole variety of factors: the sheer subtlety and complexity of his poetic vision; his compulsion to explore questions rather than present answers; above all, perhaps, his dedication to vitality and 'feltness' in his whole artistic practice. In seeking the meaning of his work, I used to suppose that one might find it at an essentially intellectual level, in a set of rational propositions, however diverse. Throughout his writing there is indeed a bewildering array of rationalizations and interpretations, each offering a fleeting fix on existence. But his meaning never lies in these apparent meanings: it resides above all in the vigour and pulse and tireless energy of his works. This is why *Woyzeck* is such a consummate achievement. In its story-line with its neon-lit outcomes of betrayal, murder, extreme isolation, *Woyzeck* is almost unbearably bleak and forbidding; in its throbbing pace and lustiness, in the depth and full-bloodedness of its central characters, it is magnificently vivid and heartening. Even when its words proclaim the most chilling despair, Georg Büchner's work conveys a powerful and warming sense of the 'ebb and flow of human emotions', 'the glow, the hum, the radiance of creation regenerating itself in and around us each second of the day', that 'infinite beauty that passes from form to form, eternally changed and revealed afresh'. Büchner well knew how difficult it was for even the truest artist to seize and communicate this wondrous beauty: 'man kann sie aber freilich nicht immer festhalten und in Museen stellen und auf Noten ziehen' (87; *but of course you can't always capture it and stick it in museums or put it into music*); in the more graphic image voiced through Leonce: 'Die Nachtigall der Poesie schlägt den ganzen Tag über unserm Haupt, aber das Feinste geht zum Teufel, bis wir ihr die Federn ausreißen und in die Tinte oder die Farbe tauchen.' (116; *The nightingale of poetry wings above us the whole day long, but the best of her has gone to the devil by the time we've ripped out her feathers and dipped them in paint or ink.*) And yet few writers have caught the essence more vividly than Georg Büchner. To appreciate this fully we need to 'see' and 'hear' in an appropriate way. Critical analysis is valid and necessary, but it gets us only so far. Büchner's art lives as art; and we attune to it fully only when we recognize it as being—in the terms applied by Louis Jouvet to the plays of Molière—not so much 'un texte littéraire' as 'une *transcription physique*'.[1]

---

[1] Louis Jouvet, *Témoignages sur le théâtre* (Paris, 1952), 229. I am indebted to Gerry McCarthy for this reference.

Bibliography

I BÜCHNER'S WORKS

(a) Collected Works

Nachgelassene Schriften, [ed. Ludwig Büchner] (Frankfurt, 1850).
Sämmtliche Werke und handschriftlicher Nachlaß. Erste kritische Gesammt-Ausgabe, ed. Karl Emil Franzos (Frankfurt, 1879).
Sämtliche Werke und Briefe, ed. Fritz Bergemann (Leipzig, 1922).
Sämtliche Werke und Briefe. Historisch-kritische Ausgabe mit Kommentar, ed. Werner R. Lehmann, i. *Dichtungen und Übersetzungen mit Dokumentation zur Stoffgeschichte* (Hamburg, 1967); ii. *Vermischte Schriften und Briefe* (Hamburg, 1971); = 'Hamburg Edition'; two further volumes planned, but subsequently abandoned; later editions of vols. i and ii published in Munich.
Gesammelte Werke. Erstdrucke und Erstausgaben in Faksimiles, ed. Thomas Michael Mayer (Frankfurt, 1987; 10 vols.).
Werke und Briefe. Münchner Ausgabe, ed. Karl Pörnbacher, Gerhard Schaub, Hans-Joachim Simm, and Edda Ziegler (Munich, 1988).
Sämtliche Werke, Briefe und Dokumente, ed. Henri Poschmann, i. *Dichtungen* (Frankfurt, 1992); ii. *Schriften, Briefe, Dokumente*: not yet published.

(b) Collected Works in English

Complete Works and Letters, translated by Henry J. Schmidt, edited by Walter Hinderer and Henry J. Schmidt (New York, 1986).
The Complete Plays, translated by various hands, edited and introduced by Michael Patterson (London and New York, 1987).
Complete Plays, 'Lenz' and Other Writings, translated, introduced, and annotated by John Reddick (London, 1993).

(c) Individual works

Georg Büchner: Danton's Tod. Entwurf einer Studienausgabe, ed. Thomas Michael Mayer, in Peter von Becker (ed.), *Georg Büchner: Dantons Tod. Die Trauerarbeit im Schönen. Ein Theaterlesebuch* (Frankfurt, 1980); 2nd rev. edn., under the title *Georg Büchner: Dantons Tod. Kritische*

Studienausgabe des Originals mit Quellen, Aufsätzen und Materialien (Frankfurt, 1985); this latter edition is not in print, and is not generally available in libraries. (The 1980 edn. is referred to here as TMM.)
Dantons Tod. *Faksimile der Erstausgabe von 1835 mit Büchners Korrekturen*, ed. Erich Zimmermann (Darmstadt, 1981) = 'Darmstadt Copy'.
'Dantons Tod' and 'Woyzeck', ed. Margaret Jacobs (Manchester, 1971; 3rd rev. and reset edn.); German play-texts, English apparatus.
Leonce und Lena. Ein Lustspiel. Kritische Studienausgabe, ed. Thomas Michael Mayer, in Burghard Dedner (ed.), *Georg Büchner. Leonce und Lena. Kritische Studienausgabe. Beiträge zu Text und Quellen* (Frankfurt, 1987). (Referred to here as BD.)
'Woyzeck'. Texte und Dokumente, ed. Egon Krause (Frankfurt, 1969).
'Woyzeck'. Kritische Lese- und Arbeitsausgabe, ed. Lothar Bornscheuer (Stuttgart, 1972; numerous reprints); for companion commentary volume, see under 'Bornscheuer' in Secondary Literature section.
'Woyzeck'. Faksimileausgabe der Handschriften, ed. Gerhard Schmid (Leipzig and Wiesbaden, 1981); comprises 'Faksimile. Transkription. Kommentar. Lesartenverzeichnis'. (Referred to here as GS.)
'Woyzeck'. Nach den Handschriften neu hergestellt und kommentiert, ed. Henri Poschmann (Leipzig, 1984; 4th edn.: Frankfurt, 1991).
Woyzeck, ed. John Guthrie (Oxford and New York, 1988); German play-text, English apparatus.
Lenz. Studienausgabe, ed. Hubert Gersch (Stuttgart, 1984; numerous reprints).
Georg Büchner and Friedrich Ludwig Weidig, *Der Hessische Landbote. Texte, Materialien, Kommentar*, ed. Gerhard Schaub (Munich, 1976).

II BIBLIOGRAPHIES

SCHLICK, WERNER, *Das Georg-Büchner-Schrifttum bis 1965. Eine internationale Bibliographie* (Hildesheim, 1968).
PETERSEN, KLAUS-DIETRICH, 'Georg-Büchner-Bibliographie', *Philobiblon*, 17 (1973), 89–115.
KNAPP, GERHARD P., 'Kommentierte Bibliographie zu Georg Büchner', in Arnold (ed.), *Georg Büchner I/II* (1979), 426–55.
MAYER, THOMAS MICHAEL (ed.), 'Georg Büchner-Literatur 1977–1980', in T. M. Mayer (ed.), *Georg Büchner Jahrbuch*, 1/1981, 319–50.
BISCHOFF, BETTINA, MAYER, THOMAS MICHAEL, and WISSKIRCHEN, HANS, 'Georg Büchner-Literatur 1981–1984 (mit Nachträgen)', in T. M. Mayer (ed.), *Georg Büchner Jahrbuch*, 4/1984, 363–406.
LIETZ, CHRISTINE, MAYER, THOMAS MICHAEL, and STOCKMANN, KRISTINA, 'Georg Büchner-Literatur 1985–87 (mit Nachträgen)', in T. M. Mayer (ed.), *Georg Büchner Jahrbuch*, 6/1986–7, 407–56.

———— ————, 'Georg Büchner-Literatur 1988–89 (mit Nachträgen)', in T. M. Mayer (ed.), *Georg Büchner Jahrbuch*, 7/1988–9, 415–37.

III SECONDARY LITERATURE

ABUTILLE, MARIO CARLO, *Angst und Zynismus bei Georg Büchner* (Berne, 1969).
ADEY, LOUISE, 'Leonce und Lena: Time, Love and Language', in Keith-Smith and Mills (eds.), *Büchner in Britain*, 19–28.
ANON. (ed.), *Georg Büchner 1813–1837. Revolutionär, Dichter, Wissenschaftler* (Basel and Frankfurt, 1987); catalogue of exhibition in Darmstadt, 1987.
ANTON, HERBERT, *Büchners Dramen. Topographien der Freiheit* (Paderborn, 1975).
ANZ, HEINRICH, ' "Leiden sey all mein Gewinnst". Zur Aufnahme und Kritik christlicher Leidenstheologie bei Georg Büchner', in T. M. Mayer (ed.), *Georg Büchner Jahrbuch*, 1/1981, 160–8.
ARMSTRONG, WILLIAM BRUCE, ' "Arbeit" und "Muße" in den Werken Georg Büchners', in Arnold (ed.), *Georg Büchner III*, 63–98.
ARNOLD, HEINZ LUDWIG (ed.), *Georg Büchner I/II*, special number of *Text + Kritik* (Munich, 1979); 2nd edn., rev. and with Index (Munich, 1982).
———— (ed.), *Georg Büchner III*, special number of *Text + Kritik* (Munich, 1981).
BACH, ANNELIESE, 'Verantwortlichkeit und Fatalismus in Georg Büchners Drama "Dantons Tod" ', *Wirkendes Wort*, 6 (1955/6), 217–29.
BARK, JOACHIM, 'Bibelsprache in Büchners Dramen. Stellenkommentar und interpretatorische Hinweise', in Dedner and Oesterle (eds.), *Zweites Internationales Georg Büchner Symposium 1987*, 476–505.
BATTAFARANO, ITALO MICHELE, 'Der Traum der Revolution: Wilhelm Zimmermanns *Masaniello* (1833) und Georg Büchners *Dantons Tod* (1835)', in Dedner and Oesterle (eds.), *Zweites Internationales Georg Büchner Symposium 1987*, 203–22.
BAUMANN, GERHART, *Georg Büchner. Die dramatische Ausdruckswelt* (Göttingen, 1961).
BECKER, PETER VON (ed.), *Georg Büchner: Dantons Tod. Die Trauerarbeit im Schönen. Ein Theaterlesebuch* (Frankfurt, 1980); includes Thomas Michael Mayer's 'Entwurf einer Studienausgabe'.
———— 'Die Trauerarbeit im Schönen. "Dantons Tod"—Notizen zu einem neu gelesenen Stück', ibid. 75–90.
———— (ed.), *Georg Büchner. Dantons Tod. Kritische Studienausgabe des Originals mit Quellen, Aufsätzen und Materialien* (Frankfurt, 1985); = 2nd rev. edn. of *Georg Büchner: Dantons Tod* (1980).

BECKERS, GUSTAV, *Georg Büchners 'Leonce und Lena'. Ein Lustspiel der Langeweile* (Heidelberg, 1961).

BEHRMANN, ALFRED, and WOHLLEBEN, JOACHIM, *Büchner: Dantons Tod. Eine Dramenanalyse* (Stuttgart, 1980).

BENN, MAURICE B., *The Drama of Revolt: A Critical Study of Georg Büchner* (Cambridge, 1976).

BERNS, JÖRG JOCHEN, 'Zeremoniellkritik und Prinzensatire. Traditionen der politischen Ästhetik des Lustspiels *Leonce und Lena*', in Dedner (ed.), *Georg Büchner. Leonce und Lena*, 219–74.

BOA, ELIZABETH, 'Whores and Hetairas. Sexual Politics in the Work of Büchner and Wedekind', in Mills and Keith-Smith (eds.), *Georg Büchner—Tradition and Innovation*, 161–81.

BOCKELMANN, ESKE, 'Von Büchners Handschrift oder Aufschluß, wie der *Woyzeck* zu edieren sei', in T. M. Mayer (ed.), *Georg Büchner Jahrbuch*, 7/1988–9, 219–58.

BOHN, VOLKER, 'Dokumente der Frührezeption von "Dantons Tod" ', in Arnold (ed.), *Georg Büchner III*, 99–103.

—— ' "Bei diesem genialen Cynismus wird dem Leser zuletzt ganz krankhaft pestartig zu Muthe". Überlegungen zur Früh- und Spätrezeption von "Dantons Tod" ', ibid. 104–30.

BOLTEN, JÜRGEN, 'Geschichtsphilosophische Einsicht, Langeweile und Spiel. Zu Büchners "Leonce und Lena" ', *Archiv für das Studium der neueren Sprachen und Literaturen*, 222 (1985), 293–305.

BORMANN, ALEXANDER VON, '*Dantons Tod*. Zur Problematik der Trauerspiel-Form', in Dedner and Oesterle (eds.), *Zweites Internationales Georg Büchner Symposium 1987*, 113–31.

BORNSCHEUER, LOTHAR, *Erläuterungen und Dokumente. Georg Büchner: 'Woyzeck'* (Stuttgart, 1972; numerous reprints).

—— (ed.), *Georg Büchner: Leben, Werk, Zeit* (Marburg, 1985); catalogue of an exhibition celebrating the 150th anniversary of *Der Hessische Landbote*.

BUCH, WILFRIED, *Woyzeck. Fassungen und Wandlungen* (Dortmund, 1970).

BUCK, THEO, ' "Man muß die Menschheit lieben". Zum ästhetischen Programm Georg Büchners', in Arnold (ed.), *Georg Büchner III*, 15–34.

—— *Grammatik einer neuen Liebe. Anmerkungen zu Georg Büchners Marion-Figur* (Aachen, 1986).

—— 'Das Groteske bei Büchner', *Études germaniques*, 43 (1988), 66–81.

—— 'Liebe, Revolution und Tod. Zur Lucile-Figur in Büchners Drama "Danton's Tod" ', in H. Kaspar Spinner and Frank-Rutger Hausmann (eds.), *Eros—Liebe—Leidenschaft. Meisterwerke der Weltliteratur*, ii (Bonn, 1988), 132–50.

—— *Charaktere, Gestalten. Büchner-Studien I* (Aachen, 1990).

BÜTTNER, LUDWIG, *Büchners Bild vom Menschen* (Nuremberg, 1967).

CLOSS, AUGUST, 'Nihilism in Modern German Drama: Grabbe and Büchner', in August Closs, *Medusa's Mirror: Studies in German Literature* (London, 1957), 147–63.

COWAN, ROY C., 'Identity and Conscience in Büchner's Works', *Germanic Review*, 43 (1968), 258–66.

DAASE, CHRISTOPHER, ' "Da läugne einer die Vorsehung". Zur komischen Bedeutung der Valerio-Figur in *Leonce und Lena*', in Dedner and Oesterle (eds.), *Zweites Internationales Georg Büchner Symposium 1987*, 379–98.

DEDNER, BURGHARD, 'Legitimationen des Schreckens in Georg Büchners Revolutionsdrama', *Jahrbuch der Deutschen Schillergesellschaft*, 29 (1985), 343–80.

—— (ed.), *Georg Büchner. Leonce und Lena. Kritische Studienausgabe, Beiträge zu Text und Quellen* (Frankfurt, 1987).

—— 'Bildsysteme und Gattungsunterschiede in *Leonce und Lena, Dantons Tod* und *Lenz*', ibid. 157–218.

—— 'Büchners Lachen: Vorüberlegungen zu *Leonce und Lena*', in Anon. (ed.), *Georg Büchner 1813–1837*, 296–305.

—— 'Georg Büchner: *Dantons Tod*. Zur Rekonstruktion der Entstehung anhand der Quellenverarbeitung', in T. M. Mayer (ed.), *Georg Büchner Jahrbuch*, 6/1986–7, 106–31.

—— 'Die Handlung des *Woyzeck*: wechselnde Orte—"geschlossene Form" ', in T. M. Mayer (ed.), *Georg Büchner Jahrbuch*, 7/1988–9, 144–70.

—— (ed.), *Der widerständige Klassiker. Einleitungen zu Büchner vom Nachmärz bis zur Weimarer Republik* (Frankfurt, 1990).

—— and OESTERLE, GÜNTER (eds.), *Zweites Internationales Georg Büchner Symposium 1987. Referate* (Frankfurt, 1990).

DIERSEN, INGE, 'Louis und Franz. Magreth, Louisel, Marie. Zur Genesis des Figurenkreises und des Motivgefüges in den Woyzeck-Texten', in Werner (ed.), *Studien zu Georg Büchner*, 147–92.

DÖHNER, OTTO, 'Georg Büchners Naturauffassung', typescript Dr. Phil. thesis, Marburg, 1967.

—— 'Neuere Erkenntnisse zu Georg Büchners Naturauffassung und Naturforschung', in Gersch, Mayer, and Oesterle (eds.), *Georg Büchner Jahrbuch*, 2/1982, 126–32.

DRUX, RUDOLF, ' "Eigentlich nichts als Walzen und Windschläuche." Ansätze zu einer Poetik der Satire im Werk Georg Büchners', in Dedner and Oesterle (eds.), *Zweites Internationales Georg Büchner Symposium 1987*, 335–52.

ELM, THEO, 'Georg Büchner: Individuum und Geschichte in "Dantons Tod" ', in Theo Elm and Gerd Hemmerich (eds.), *Zur Geschichtlichkeit der Moderne. Der Begriff der literarischen Moderne in Theorie und Deutung. Ulrich Fülleborn zum 60. Geburtstag* (Munich, 1982), 167–84.

FINK, GONTHIER-LOUIS, 'Volkslied und Verseinlage in den Dramen Büchners', in Martens (ed.), *Georg Büchner*, 443–87.
—— 'Leonce und Lena'. Komödie und Realismus bei Georg Büchner', ibid. 488–506.
—— 'Georg Büchner et la Révolution Française', *Recherches germaniques*, 19 (1989), 69–101.
—— 'Das Bild der Revolution in Büchners *Dantons Tod*', in Dedner and Oesterle (eds.), *Zweites Internationales Georg Büchner Symposium 1987*, 175–202.
FISCHER, HEINZ, *Georg Büchner. Untersuchungen und Marginalien* (Bonn, 1972).
GERSCH, HUBERT, MAYER, THOMAS MICHAEL, and OESTERLE, GÜNTER (eds.), *Georg Büchner Jahrbuch*, 2/1982 (Frankfurt, 1983); = Part I of the proceedings of *Internationales Georg Büchner Symposium: Ergebnisse und Perspektiven der Forschung*, held in Darmstadt in June 1981.
—— —— —— (eds.), *Georg Büchner Jahrbuch*, 3/1983 (Frankfurt, 1984); = Part II of the proceedings of *Internationales Georg Büchner Symposium: Ergebnisse und Perspektiven der Forschung*, held in Darmstadt in June 1981.
GILLE, KLAUS F., 'Büchners "Danton" als Ideologiekritik und Utopie', in Arno Herzig, Inge Stephan, and Hans G. Winter (eds.), *"Sie, und nicht Wir". Die Französische Revolution und ihre Wirkung auf Norddeutschland und das Reich*, ii. *Das Reich* (Hamburg, 1989), 607–23.
GILLMANN, ERIKA, MAYER, THOMAS MICHAEL, PABST, REINHARD, and WOLF, DIETER (eds.), *Georg Büchner an 'Hund' und 'Kater'. Unbekannte Briefe des Exils* (Marburg, 1993).
GLÜCK, ALFONS, 'Der "ökonomische Tod": Armut und Arbeit in Georg Büchners *Woyzeck*', in T. M. Mayer (ed.), *Georg Büchner Jahrbuch*, 4/1984, 167–226.
—— 'Militär und Justiz in Georg Büchners *Woyzeck*', ibid. 227–47.
—— ' "Herrschende Ideen": Die Rolle der Ideologie, Indoktrination und Desorientierung in Georg Büchners *Woyzeck*', in T. M. Mayer (ed.), *Georg Büchner Jahrbuch*, 5/1985, 52–138.
—— 'Der Menschenversuch: Die Rolle der Wissenschaft in Georg Büchners *Woyzeck*', ibid. 139–82.
——, 'Der historische Woyzeck', in Anon. (ed.), *Georg Büchner 1813–1837*, 314–24.
—— 'Der *Woyzeck*. Tragödie eines Paupers', ibid. 325–32.
—— 'Woyzeck—Clarus—Büchner (Umrisse)', in Dedner and Oesterle (eds.), *Zweites Internationales Georg Büchner Symposium 1987*, 425–40.
GOLTSCHNIGG, DIETMAR (ed.), *Materialien zur Rezeptions- und Wirkungsgeschichte Georg Büchners* (Kronberg/Taunus, 1974).
—— *Rezeptions- und Wirkungsgeschichte Georg Büchners* (Kronberg/Taunus, 1975).

GÖRLICH, BERNARD, and LEHR, ANKE, 'Materialismus und Subjektivität in den Schriften Georg Büchners', in Arnold (ed.), *Georg Büchner III*, 35–62.

GRANDIN, JOHN M., 'Woyzeck and the Last Judgement', *German Life and Letters*, NS 31 (1977–8), 175–9.

GRAY, RICHARD T., 'The Dialectic of Enlightenment in Büchners *Woyzeck*', *German Quarterly*, 61 (1988), 78–96.

GREINER, BERNHARD, ' "Ich muß lachen, ich muß lachen": Wege und Abwege des Komischen in Büchners "Leonce und Lena" ', *Jahrbuch der deutschen Schillergesellschaft*, 32 (1988), 214–34.

GRIMM, REINHOLD, 'Cœur und carreau. Über die Liebe bei Georg Büchner', in Arnold (ed.), *Georg Büchner I/II*, (1979), 299–326.

—— 'Georg Büchner und der moderne Begriff der Revolte', in T. M. Mayer (ed.), *Georg Büchner Jahrbuch*, 1/1981, 22–67.

—— *Love, Lust and Rebellion: New Approaches to Georg Büchner* (Madison, Wis., 1985).

GUNDOLF, FRIEDRICH, 'Georg Büchner', in Martens (ed.), *Georg Büchner*, 82–97.

GUTHRIE, JOHN, 'The True Dialectic of *Dantons Tod*: A Reply', *New German Studies*, 10 (1982), 151–74.

—— *Lenz and Büchner: Studies in Dramatic Form* (Frankfurt, Berne, and New York, 1984).

HAENEL, HANS-DIETER, *Kettenkarussell und Spiegelkabinett. Determinanz der Form im Drama Georg Büchners* (Frankfurt, Berne, and Las Vegas, 1978).

HAMBURGER, MICHAEL, 'Georg Büchner', in Michael Hamburger, *Reason and Energy: Studies in German Literature* (London, 1957), 179–208.

HASUBEK, PETER, ' "Ruhe" und "Bewegung". Versuch einer Stilanalyse von Georg Büchners "Lenz" ', *Germanisch-romanische Monatsschrift*, NS 19 (1969), 33–59.

HAUSCHILD, JAN-CHRISTOPH, *Georg Büchner. Studien und neue Quellen zu Leben, Werk und Wirkung* (Königstein, 1985).

—— 'Büchners *Aretino*. Eine Fiktion?', in Anon. (ed.), *Georg Büchner 1813–1837*, 353–5.

—— (ed.), *Georg Büchner. Bilder zu Leben und Werk* (Düsseldorf, 1987); catalogue of an exhibition celebrating the 150th anniversary of Büchner's death.

—— 'Neudatierung und Neubewertung von Georg Büchners "Fatalismusbrief" ', *Zeitschrift für deutsche Philologie*, 108 (1989), 511–29.

—— 'Schiffbruch und Lebensplan. Büchners Vaterbeziehung im Prozeß der Literarisierung', in Dedner and Oesterle (eds.), *Zweites Internationales Georg Büchner Symposium 1987*, 37–52.

—— *Georg Büchner in Selbstzeugnissen und Bilddokumenten* (Hamburg, 1992); replaces earlier 'Rowohlts Monographien' volume by Ernst Johann first published 1958.

HERMAND, JOST, 'Der Streit um *Leonce und Lena*', in Gersch and Mayer (eds.), *Georg Büchner Jahrbuch*, 3/1983, 98–117.

HIEBEL, HANS H., 'Georg Büchners heiter-sarkastische Komödie "Leonce und Lena" ', in Winfried Freund (ed.), *Deutsche Komödien. Vom Barock bis zur Gegenwart* (Munich, 1989), 110–28.

—— 'Allusion und Elision in Georg Büchners *Leonce und Lena*. Die intertextuellen Beziehungen zwischen Büchners Lustspiel und Stücken von Shakespeare, Musset und Brentano', in Dedner and Oesterle (eds.), *Zweites Internationales Georg Büchner Symposium 1987*, 353–78.

HILDESHEIMER, WOLFGANG, 'Büchners Melancholie', in Wolfgang Hildesheimer, *Das Ende der Fiktionen. Reden aus fünfundzwanzig Jahren* (Frankfurt, 1984), 87–101.

HILTON, JULIAN, *Georg Büchner* (London and Basingstoke, 1982).

HINCK, WALTER, 'Büchner und Brecht', in Arnold (ed.), *Georg Büchner III*, 236–46.

HINDERER, WALTER, ' "Wir stehen immer auf dem Theater, wenn wir auch zuletzt im Ernst erstochen werden". Die Komödie der Revolution in Büchners *Dantons Tod*', in Wolfgang Rothe (ed.), *Schnittlinien für HAP Grieshaber* (Düsseldorf, 1959), 250–6.

—— *Büchner-Kommentar zum dichterischen Werk* (Munich, 1977).

—— 'Pathos oder Passion: Die Leiddarstellung in Büchners "Lenz" ', in Walter Hinderer, *Über deutsche Literatur und Rede. Historische Interpretationen* (Munich, 1981), 168–90.

HÖLLERER, WALTER, 'Georg Büchner', in Walter Höllerer, *Zwischen Klassik und Moderne. Lachen und Weinen in der Dichtung einer Übergangszeit* (Stuttgart, 1958), 100–42.

HOLMES, TERENCE M., 'The Ideology of the Moderates in Büchner's "Dantons Tod" ', *German Life and Letters*, NS 27 (1973–4), 93–100.

—— 'Georg Büchners "Fatalismus" als Voraussetzung seiner Revolutionsstrategie', in T. M. Mayer (ed.), *Georg Büchner Jahrbuch*, 6/1986–7, 59–72.

—— 'Die Befreiung der Maschine: Büchners Kritik der bürgerlichen Teleologie', in Dedner and Oesterle (eds.), *Zweites Internationales Georg Büchner Symposium 1987*, 53–62.

HORTON, DAVID, ' "Die gliederlösende, böse Liebe". Observations on the Erotic Theme in Büchner's *Dantons Tod*', *Deutsche Vierteljahresschrift für Literaturwissenschaft und Geistesgeschichte*, 62 (1988), 290–306.

—— 'Modes of Consciousness Representation in Büchner's *Lenz*', *German Life and Letters*, NS 43 (1988–9), 34–48.

ISSA, HODA, *Das 'Niederländische' und die 'Autopsie'. Die Bedeutung der Vorlage für Georg Büchners Werke* (Frankfurt, Berne, New York, and Paris, 1988).

JAMES, DOROTHY, *Georg Büchner's 'Dantons Tod': A Reappraisal* (London, 1982).
JANCKE, GERHARD, *Georg Büchner. Genese und Aktualität seines Werkes. Einführung in das Gesamtwerk* (Kronberg/Taunus, 1975).
JANSEN, JOSEF, *Erläuterungen und Dokumente. Georg Büchner: Dantons Tod* (Stuttgart, 1969; numerous reprints).
JENS, WALTER, *Euripides. Büchner* (Pfullingen, 1964).
KEITH-SMITH, BRIAN, and MILLS, KEN (eds.), *Büchner in Britain: A Passport to Georg Büchner* (Bristol, 1987).
KITTSTEINER, HEINZ-DIETER, and LETHEN, HELMUT, 'Ich-Losigkeit, Entbürgerlichung und Zeiterfahrung. Über die Gleichgültigkeit zur "Geschichte" in Büchners *Woyzeck*', in Gersch and Mayer (eds.), *Georg Büchner Jahrbuch*, 3/1983, 240–69.
KLINGMANN, ULRICH, ' "Ich wollte mich an mein Volk erinnern". Utopie und Praxis in Georg Büchners "Leonce und Lena" ', *Germanisch-romanische Monatsschrift*, NS 37 (1987), 280–90.
KLOTZ, VOLKER, 'Büchners gebrochene Wirkungen', in Volker Klotz, *Dramaturgie des Publikums. Wie Bühne und Publikum aufeinander eingehen, insbesondere bei Raimund, Büchner, Wedekind, Horváth, Gatti und im politischen Agitationstheater* (Munich and Vienna, 1976), 89–137.
KNAPP, GERHARD P., *Georg Büchner. Eine kritische Einführung in die Forschung* (Frankfurt, 1975).
—— *Georg Büchner* (Stuttgart, 1984; 2nd rev. edn.).
—— *Georg Büchner: Dantons Tod* (Frankfurt, 1987; 2nd, enlarged edn.).
KNIGHT, A. H. J., *Georg Büchner* (Oxford, 1951).
KOBEL, ERWIN, *Georg Büchner. Das dichterische Werk* (Berlin and New York, 1974).
KOHLENBACH, MARGARETE, 'Puppen und Helden. Zum Fatalismusglauben in Georg Büchners Revolutionsdrama', *Germanisch-romanische Monatsschrift*, NS 38 (1988), 395–410.
KOOPMANN, HELMUT, 'Dantons Tod und die antike Welt. Zur Geschichtsphilosophie Georg Büchners', *Zeitschrift für deutsche Philologie*, 84 (1965), Special Number, 22–41.
KRAPP, HELMUT, *Der Dialog bei Georg Büchner* (Darmstadt, 1958).
KUBITSCHEK, PETER, 'Die tödliche Stille der verkehrten Welt—Zu Georg Büchners "Lenz" ', in Werner (ed.), *Studien zu Georg Büchner*, 86–104.
KURZENBERGER, HAJO, 'Komödie als Pathographie einer abgelebten Gesellschaft. Zur gegenwärtigen Beschäftigung mit "Leonce und Lena" in der Literaturwissenschaft und auf dem Theater', in Arnold (ed.), *Georg Büchner III*, 150–68.
LEHMANN, SUSANNE, 'Der Brand im Haus der Büchners 1851. Zur Überlieferung des Darmstädter Büchner-Nachlasses', T. M. Mayer (ed.), *Georg Büchner Jahrbuch*, 6/1986–7, 303–13.

LEHMANN, WERNER R., *Textkritische Noten. Prolegomena zur Hamburger Büchner-Ausgabe* (Hamburg, 1967).

—— 'Repliken. Beiträge zu einem Streitgespräch über den *Woyzeck*', *Euphorion*, 65 (1971), 58–83.

LEHR, ANKE, 'Georg Büchner, deutscher Patriot und Ideologe einer Bauernrevolution? Einige Bemerkungen zu M. Smulovic', in Arnold (ed.), *Georg Büchner III*, 216–17.

LEVESQUE, PAUL, 'The Sentence of Death and the Execution of Wit in Georg Büchner's *Dantons Tod*', *German Quarterly*, 62 (1989), 85–95.

LIPMANN, HEINZ, *Georg Büchner und die Romantik* (Munich, 1923).

LOPE, HANS-JOACHIM, ' "Fama" / "Fame" und kein Ende. Neue Randbemerkungen zur "Vorrede" von Büchners *Leonce und Lena*', in T. M. Mayer (ed.), *Georg Büchner Jahrbuch*, 6/1986–7, 276–9.

LUKÁCS, GEORG, 'Der faschistisch verfälschte und der wirkliche Georg Büchner', in Martens (ed.), *Georg Büchner*, 197–224.

LÜSCHER, ROLF, *Einige Versuche in Grundlosem um Georg Büchners 'Lenz'* (Berne and Frankfurt, 1982).

MAASS, CHRISTIAN, 'Georg Büchner und Johann Bernhard Wilbrand. Medizin in Gießen um 1833/34', in Anon. (ed.), *Georg Büchner 1813–1837*, 148–54.

MCCOLGAN, M., 'The True Dialectic of *Dantons Tod*', *New German Studies*, 6 (1978), 151–75.

MCINNES, EDWARD, 'Scepticism, Ideology and History in Büchners *Dantons Tod*', in Derek Attwood, Alan Best, and Rex Last (eds.), *For Lionel Thomas: A Collection of Essays Presented in his Memory* (Hull, 1980), 53–69.

MANN, GOLO, 'Georg Büchner und die Revolution', *Neue Rundschau* [unnumbered volume] (1969), 1–12.

MANTHEY, JÜRGEN, 'Abschied von der Revolution: Georg Büchner', *Neue Rundschau*, 98/3 (1987), 93–111.

MARTENS, WOLFGANG (ed.), *Georg Büchner* (Darmstadt, 1965).

—— 'Zum Menschenbild Georg Büchners. *Woyzeck* und die Marionszene in *Dantons Tod*', in Martens (ed.), *Georg Büchner*, 373–85.

—— 'Büchner: *Leonce und Lena*', in Walter Hinck (ed.), *Die deutsche Komödie. Vom Mittelalter bis zur Gegenwart* (Düsseldorf, 1977), 145–59, 382–3.

MAY, KURT, 'Büchners "Woyzeck" ', in Martens (ed.), *Georg Büchner*, 241–51.

MAYER, HANS, *Georg Büchner und seine Zeit* (Wiesbaden, [1960]; 2nd edn.).

—— 'Prinz Leonce und Doktor Faust. Büchners Lustspiel und die deutsche Klassik', in Hans Mayer, *Zur deutschen Klassik und Romantik* (Pfullingen, 1963), 306–14.

MAYER, THOMAS MICHAEL, 'Umschlagporträt. Statt eines Vorworts', in Arnold (ed.), *Georg Büchner I/II* (1979), 5–15.

—— 'Büchner und Weidig—Frühkommunismus und revolutionäre Demokratie. Zur Textverteilung des "Hessischen Landboten" ', ibid. 16-298.
—— 'Zu einigen neueren Tendenzen der Büchner-Forschung. Ein kritischer Literaturbericht (Teil I)', ibid. 327-56.
—— 'Georg Büchner. Eine kurze Chronik zu Leben und Werk', ibid. 357-425.
—— (ed.), *Georg Büchner Jahrbuch*, 1/1981 (Frankfurt, 1981).
—— 'Bausteine und Marginalien', ibid. 187-223; includes *inter alia* 'Zu August Lewalds "Lustspiel-Preisaufgabe" und zu Datierung und "Vorrede" von *Leonce und Lena*', 201-10.
—— 'Zu einigen neueren Tendenzen der Büchner-Forschung. Ein kritischer Literaturbericht (Teil II: Editionen)', in Arnold (ed.), *Georg Büchner III*, 265-311.
—— ' "Wegen mir könnt Ihr ganz ruhig sein ..." Die Argumentationslist in Georg Büchners Briefen an die Eltern', in Gersch, Mayer, and Oesterle (eds.), *Georg Büchner Jahrbuch*, 2/1982, 249-80.
—— (ed.), *Georg Büchner: Leben, Werk, Zeit. Katalog* (Marburg, 1985); catalogue of an exhibition celebrating the 150th anniversary of *Der Hessische Landbote*.
—— (ed.), *Georg Büchner Jahrbuch*, 4/1984 (Frankfurt, 1986).
—— (ed.), *Georg Büchner Jahrbuch*, 5/1985 (Frankfurt, 1986).
—— (ed.), *Georg Büchner. Insel-Almanach auf das Jahr 1987* (Frankfurt, 1987).
—— (ed.), *Georg Büchner Jahrbuch*, 6/1986-7 (Frankfurt, 1990).
—— (ed.), *Georg Büchner Jahrbuch*, 7/1988-9 (Tübingen, 1991).
—— 'Zu einigen neuen Lesungen und zur Frage des "Dialekts" in den *Woyzeck*-Handschriften', ibid. 172-218.
MEIER, ALBERT, *Georg Büchner: 'Woyzeck'* (Munich, 1980).
—— *Georg Büchners Ästhetik* (Munich, [1983?]).
—— 'Georg Büchners Ästhetik', in Gersch, Mayer, and Oesterle (eds.), *Georg Büchner Jahrbuch*, 2/1982, 196-208.
—— '*Dantons Tod* in der Tradition des Politischen Trauerspiels', in Dedner and Oesterle (eds.), *Zweites Internationales Georg Büchner Symposium 1987*, 132-45.
MICHELSEN, PETER, 'Die Präsenz des Endes. Georg Büchners *Dantons Tod*', *Deutsche Vierteljahresschrift für Literaturwissenschaft und Geistesgeschichte*, 52 (1978), 476-95.
—— 'Das Leid im Werk Georg Büchners', *Jahrbuch des Freien Deutschen Hochstifts* (1989), 281-307.
MILLS, KEN, and KEITH-SMITH, BRIAN (eds.), *Georg Büchner—Tradition and Innovation: Fourteen Essays* (Bristol, 1990).
MOSER, SAMUEL, 'Robespierre, die Ausgeburt eines Kantianers. Immanuel Kants Philosophie als Schlüssel zum Verständnis der Robespierre-Figur in

Georg Büchners Drama "Dantons Tod" ', in Arnold (ed.), *Georg Büchner III*, 131–49.

MÜHLHER, ROBERT, 'Georg Büchner und die Mythologie des Nihilismus', in Martens, *Georg Büchner*, 252–88.

MÜLLER-SEIDEL, WALTER, 'Natur und Naturwissenschaft im Werk Georg Büchners', in Eckehard Catholy and Winfried Hellmann (eds.), *Festschrift für Klaus Ziegler* (Tübingen, 1968), 205–32.

OEHLER, DOLF, 'Liberté, Liberté Chérie. Männerphantasien über die Freiheit. Zur Problematik der erotischen Freiheits-Allegorie', in Becker (ed.), *Georg Büchner: Dantons Tod. Die Trauerarbeit im Schönen*, 91–105.

OESTERLE, GÜNTER, 'Das Komischwerden der Philosophie in der Poesie. Literatur-, philosophie- und gesellschaftsgeschichtliche Konsequenzen der "voie physiologique" in Georg Büchners *Woyzeck*', in Gersch and Mayer (eds.), *Georg Büchner Jahrbuch*, 3/1982, 200–39.

PABST, REINHARD, 'Zwei unbekannte Berichte über die Hinrichtung Johann Christian Woyzecks', in T. M. Mayer (ed.), *Georg Büchner Jahrbuch*, 7/1988–9, 338–50.

PASCAL, ROY, 'Büchner's *Lenz*—Style and Message', *Oxford German Studies*, 9 (1978), 68–83.

PATTERSON, MICHAEL, 'Contradictions Concerning Time in Büchner's *Woyzeck*', *German Life and Letters*, NS 32 (1978–9), 115–21.

PEACOCK, Ronald, 'A Note on Georg Büchner's Plays', *German Life and Letters*, NS 10 (1956–7), 189–97 (reprinted, in German, in Martens (ed.), *Georg Büchner*, 360–72).

PETERSEN, JÜRGEN H., 'Die Aufhebung der Moral im Werk Georg Büchners', *Deutsche Vierteljahresschrift für Literaturwissenschaft und Geistesgeschichte*, 47 (1973), 245–66.

POSCHMANN, HENRI, 'Büchners *Leonce und Lena*. Komödie des status quo', in T. M. Mayer (ed.), *Georg Büchner Jahrbuch*, 1/1981, 112–59.

—— 'Probleme einer literarisch-historischen Ortsbestimmung Georg Büchners', in Gersch, Mayer, and Oesterle (eds.), *Georg Büchner Jahrbuch*, 2/1982, 133–43.

—— *Georg Büchner. Dichtung der Revolution und Revolution der Dichtung* (Berlin and Weimar, 1988; 3rd edn.).

—— 'Textgeschichte als Lesergeschichte. Zur Entzifferung der "Woyzeck"-Handschriften', *Weimarer Beiträge*, 35 (1989), 1796–805.

—— ' "Wer das lesen könnt". Zur Sprache natürlicher Zeichen im *Woyzeck*', in Werner (ed.), *Studien zu Georg Büchner*, 193–206; the same with minor variations in Dedner and Oesterle (eds.), *Zweites Internationales Georg Büchner Symposium 1987*, 441–52.

PROSS, WOLFGANG, 'Naturgeschichtliches Gesetz und gesellschaftliche Anomie: Georg Büchner, Johann Lucas Schönlein und Auguste Comte', in Alberto Martino (ed.), *Literatur in der sozialen Bewegung. Aufsätze und Forschungsberichte zum 19. Jahrhundert* (Tübingen, 1977), 228–59.

—— 'Die Kategorie der "Natur" im Werk Georg Büchners', *Aurora. Jahrbuch der Eichendorff-Gesellschaft*, 40 (1980), 172–88.

—— '*Was wird er damit machen?* oder "Spero poder sfogar la doppia brama, De saziar la mia fame, e la mia fama." ', in T. M. Mayer (ed.), *Georg Büchner Jahrbuch*, 1/1981, 252–6.

REDDICK, JOHN, 'Mosaic and Flux: Georg Büchner and the Marion Episode in *Dantons Tod*', *Oxford German Studies*, 11 (1980), 40–67.

—— ' "Ihr könntet einen noch in die Lüge verliebt machen." Georg Büchner and the Agony of Authenticity', *Forum for Modern Language Studies*, 23 (1987), 289–324.

—— 'The Shattered Whole: Georg Büchner and *Naturphilosophie*', in Andrew Cunningham and Nicholas Jardine (eds.), *Romanticism and the Sciences* (Cambridge, 1990), 322–40.

REUCHLEIN, GEORG, *Das Problem der Zurechnungsfähigkeit bei E. T. A. Hoffmann und Georg Büchner. Zum Verhältnis von Literatur, Psychiatrie und Justiz im frühen 19. Jahrhundert* (Frankfurt, Berne, and New York, 1985).

RICHARDS, DAVID G., 'Anmerkungen zur Hamburger Büchner-Ausgabe, den *Woyzeck* betreffend', *Euphorion*, 65 (1971), 49–57.

—— *Georg Büchner and the Birth of the Modern Drama* (Albany, NY, 1977).

RIEWOLDT, OTTO F., ' ." . . . der Größten einer als Politiker und Poet, Dichter und Revolutionär." Der beiseitegelobte Georg Büchner in der DDR', in Arnold (ed.), *Georg Büchner III*, 218–35.

RINGGER, KURT, 'Georg Büchner zwischen FAMA und FAME', *Archiv für das Studium der neueren Sprachen und Literaturen*, 213 (1976), 100–4.

RÖSSING-HAGER, MONIKA, *Wortindex zu Georg Büchner: Dichtungen und Übersetzungen* (Berlin, 1970).

ROTHE, WOLFGANG, 'Georg Büchner: Dantons Tod', in Wolfgang Rothe, *Deutsche Revolutionsdramatik seit Goethe* (Darmstadt, 1989), 45–64.

RUCKHÄBERLE, HANS-JOACHIM, 'Georg Büchners *Dantons Tod*—Drama ohne Alternative', in T. M. Mayer (ed.), *Georg Büchner Jahrbuch*, 1/1981, 169–76.

—— '*Leonce und Lena*. Zu Automat und Utopie', in Gersch and Mayer (eds.), *Georg Büchner Jahrbuch*, 3/1983, 138–46.

SCHAUB, GERHARD (ed.), *Erläuterungen und Dokumente. Georg Büchner: Lenz* (Stuttgart, 1987; numerous reprints).

SCHINGS, HANS-JÜRGEN, 'Im Zeichen des Mitleids. Zum Realismus Georg Büchners', in Hans-Jürgen Schings, *Der mitleidigste Mensch ist der beste Mensch. Poetik des Mitleids von Lessing bis Büchner* (Munich, 1980), 68–84.

SCHMID, GERHARD, 'Der Nachlaß Georg Büchners im Goethe- und Schiller-Archiv Weimar. Überlegungen zur Bedeutung von Dichterhandschriften für Textedition und literaturwissenschaftliche Forschung', in T. M. Mayer (ed.), *Georg Büchner Jahrbuch*, 6/1986–7, 159–72.
—— 'Probleme der Textkonstituierung bei Büchners "Woyzeck" ', in Werner (ed.), *Studien zu Georg Büchner*, 207–26.
SCHMID, PETER, *Georg Büchner. Versuch über die tragische Existenz* (Berne, 1940).
SCHMIDT, HENRY J., *Satire, Caricature and Perspectivism in the Works of Georg Büchner* (The Hague and Paris, 1970).
—— 'Frauen, Tod und Revolution in den Schlußszenen von Büchners *Dantons Tod*', in Dedner and Oesterle (eds.), *Zweites Internationales Georg Büchner Symposium 1987*, 286–305.
SCHRÖDER, JÜRGEN, 'Revolution und Dichtung. Georg Büchners Straßentheater', in Hansgerd Delbrück (ed.), *'Sinnlichkeit in Bild und Klang'. Festschrift für Paul Hoffmann zum 70. Geburtstag* (Stuttgart, 1987), 279–303.
SCHWEDT, ERNST-HENNING, 'Marginalien zu "Woyzeck" ', in Arnold (ed.), *Georg Büchner III*, 169–79.
SENGLE, FRIEDRICH, 'Georg Büchner', in Friedrich Sengle, *Biedermeierzeit. Deutsche Literatur im Spannungsfeld zwischen Restauration und Revolution 1815–1848*, iii (Stuttgart, 1980), 265–331, 1093–7.
SIESS, JÜRGEN, *Zitat und Kontext bei Georg Büchner. Eine Studie zu den Dramen 'Dantons Tod' und 'Leonce und Lena'* (Göppingen, 1975).
SMULOVIC, M., 'Georg Büchners Weltanschauung und ästhetische Ansichten', in Arnold (ed.), *Georg Büchner III*, 195–215.
STERN, J. P., 'A World of Suffering: Georg Büchner', in J. P. Stern, *Reinterpretations. Seven Studies in Nineteenth-Century German Literature* (London, 1964; 2nd, identical edn.: Cambridge, 1981), 78–155.
—— 'Georg Büchner: Potsherds of Experience', in J. P. Stern, *Idylls and Realities: Studies in Nineteenth-Century German Literature* (London, 1971), 33–48.
STROHL, JEAN, *Lorenz Oken und Georg Büchner. Zwei Gestalten aus der Übergangszeit von Naturphilosophie zu Naturwissenschaft* (Zurich, 1936).
SWALES, MARTIN, 'Ontology, Politics, Sexuality: A Note on Georg Büchner's Drama *Dantons Tod*', *New German Studies*, 3 (1975), 109–25.
THORN-PRIKKER, JAN, *Revolutionär ohne Revolution. Interpretationen der Werke Georg Büchners* (Stuttgart, 1978).
—— ' "Ach die Wissenschaft, die Wissenschaft!" Bericht über die Forschungsliteratur zu Büchners "Lenz" ', in Arnold (ed.), *Georg Büchner III*, 180–94.
UEDING, CORNELIE, *Denken—Sprechen—Handeln. Aufklärung und Aufklärungskritik im Werk Georg Büchners* (Berne and Frankfurt, 1976).

—— 'Dantons Tod—Drama der unmenschlichen Geschichte', in Walter Hinck (ed.), Geschichte als Schauspiel. Deutsche Geschichtsdramen: Interpretationen (Frankfurt, 1981), 210–26.

ULLMAN, BO, 'Der unpolitische Georg Büchner. Zum Büchner-Bild der Forschung, unter besonderer Berücksichtigung der "Woyzeck"-Interpretationen', Studier i modern språkvetenskap, NS 4 (1972), 86–130.

VIËTOR, KARL, Georg Büchner, Politik, Dichtung, Wissenschaft (Berne, 1949).

—— 'Die Tragödie des heldischen Pessimismus. Über Büchners Drama "Dantons Tod" ', in Martens (ed.), Georg Büchner, 98–137.

—— 'Woyzeck', ibid. 151–77.

VIETTA, SILVIO, 'Am Anfang der literarischen Moderne in Deutschland: Georg Büchner', in Silvio Vietta, Neuzeitliche Rationalität und moderne literarische Sprachkritik. Descartes. Georg Büchner. Arno Holz. Karl Kraus (Munich, 1981), 73–127, 230–6.

—— 'Sprachkritik bei Büchner', in Gersch, Mayer, and Oesterle (eds.), Georg Büchner Jahrbuch, 2/1982, 144–56.

VÖLKER, LUDWIG, 'Woyzeck und die "Natur" ', Revue des langues vivantes, 32 (1966), 611–32.

—— 'Die Sprache der Melancholie in Büchners Leonce und Lena', in Gersch and Mayer (eds.), Georg Büchner Jahrbuch, 3/1983, 118–37.

VOLLHARDT, FRIEDRICH, 'Das Problem der "Selbsterhaltung" im literarischen Werk und in den philosophischen Nachlaßschriften Georg Büchners', in Dedner and Oesterle (eds.), Zweites Internationales Georg Büchner Symposium 1987, 17–36.

VOSS, E. THEODOR, 'Arkadien in Büchners Leonce und Lena', in Dedner (ed.), Georg Büchner. Leonce und Lena, 275–436.

WALTER, URSULA, 'Der Fall Woyzeck. Eine Quellen-Dokumentation (Repertorium und vorläufiger Bericht)', in T. M. Mayer (ed.), Georg Büchner Jahrbuch, 7/1988–9, 351–80.

WENDER, HERBERT, 'Anspielungen auf das zeitgenössische Kunstgeschehen in Danton's Tod', in Dedner and Oesterle (eds.), Zweites Internationales Georg Büchner Symposium 1987, 223–44.

—— Georg Büchners Bild der Großen Revolution. Zu den Quellen von 'Danton's Tod' (Frankfurt, 1988).

WERNER, HANS-GEORG (ed.), Studien zu Georg Büchner (Berlin and Weimar, 1988).

—— ' "Dantons Tod". Im Zwang der Geschichte', ibid. 7–85.

—— 'Büchners aufrührerischer Materialismus. Zur geistigen Struktur von "Dantons Tod" ', Weimarer Beiträge, 35 (1989), 1765–79.

WETZEL, HEINZ, 'Die Entwicklung Woyzecks in Büchners Entwürfen', Euphorion, 74 (1980), 375–96.

—— 'Ein Büchnerbild der siebziger Jahre. Zu Thomas Michael Mayer:

"Büchner und Weidig—Frühkommunismus und revolutionäre Demokratie" ', in Arnold (ed.), *Georg Büchner III*, 247–64.

—— 'Das Ruinieren von Systemen in Büchners *Leonce und Lena*', in T. M. Mayer (ed.), *Georg Büchner Jahrbuch*, 4/1984, 154–66.

WIESE, BENNO VON, 'Georg Büchner. Die Tragödie des Nihilismus', in Benno von Wiese, *Die deutsche Tragödie von Lessing bis Hebbel* (Hamburg, 1958; 4th edn.), 513–34.

WITTKOWSKI, WOLFGANG, *Georg Büchner. Persönlichkeit. Weltbild. Werk* (Heidelberg, 1978).

—— 'Stufenstruktur und Transzendenz in Büchners *Woyzeck* und Grillparzers Novelle *Der arme Spielmann*', in Gersch and Mayer (eds.), *Georg Büchner Jahrbuch*, 3/1983, 147–65.

—— 'Sein oder Nichtsein. Zum Streit um die religiöse Büchnerdeutung', in Wolfgang Frühwald and Alberto Martino (eds.), *Zwischen Aufklärung und Restauration. Sozialer Wandel in der deutschen Literatur (1700–1848). Festschrift für Wolfgang Martens zum 65. Geburtstag* (Tübingen, 1989), 429–50.

WOHLFAHRT, THOMAS, 'Georg Büchners Lustspiel "Leonce und Lena": Kunstform und Gehalt', in Werner (ed.), *Studien zu Georg Büchner*, 105–46.

WÜLFING, WULF, ' "Autopsie". Bemerkungen zum "Selbst-Schauen" in Texten Georg Büchners', *Weimarer Beiträge*, 35 (1989), 1780–95.

ZONS, RAIMAR ST., *Georg Büchner. Dialektik der Grenze* (Bonn, 1976).

Index

abyss 33–4, 51, 52, 57, 98, 130–1, 158, 235, 237, 245, 256, 318, 328, 356, 368
aesthetic (Büchner's) 8, 56–9, 60–75, 139, 368
animals:
  Dantons Tod 105, 106, 107, 108, 114, 117, 121, 131, 136, 148, 150, 151–2, 174, 182, 183, 184, 185, 191–2, 202, 237, 310, 362–3
  Leonce und Lena 227, 263–4, 271, 284
  Woyzeck 48, 308–9, 310–12, 316, 318, 338, 347, 350, 354, 360, 364
animality, *see* animals
anti-classical (Büchner) 6, 13
  see also classicism
Arcadia 223, 224 n., 255, 282, 283
  see also Cockaigne
archetypes 72, 194, 201, 311, 316, 336–40, 346, 347, 354, 356, 364, 370
Aristotle 16
Arnim, Achim von 207
automata, *see* puppets

Bacon, Francis 20, 22
Baudelaire, Charles 73, 167
beauty 9, 12–13, 26, 28, 29, 37, 39, 40, 42, 67, 68, 72–3, 74, 125, 128, 172, 185, 190–1, 201, 202, 203, 229, 252, 256, 259, 260, 266, 274, 308, 342, 353, 372
being 9–10, 31–3, 74, 84, 163, 164 n., 189, 190, 202, 203, 259, 260, 267, 274, 275–6, 285
Benn, Maurice B. 12, 119, 134 n.
Bergemann, Fritz 306, 307
Bible 69–71, 96, 187, 266, 321, 349, 358–9, 345, 364
Biermann, Wolf 5

blood:
  Dantons Tod 95, 97–8, 103, 107, 108, 109, 131, 132, 134, 137, 170, 173, 175, 178, 264
  Woyzeck 319, 362, 363
Boa, Elizabeth 179 n., 200
Böll, Heinrich 4
Bonaventura 217
Bonnet, Charles 16
boredom, *see* ennui
Brecht, Bertolt 4, 5
Brentano, Clemens 207, 217
Bruford, W. H. 18
Brutus, Lucius Junius 135
Brutus, Marcus Junius 135, 136
Buch, Wilfried 293
Büchner, Georg (characters in his works)*
  Andres 79
  Barker (Marktschreier, Ausrufer) 48, 277
  Brion, Friederike 75, 164 n., 258
  Barrère 358
  Camille 31, 57, 58–9, 65, 232, 237, 243, 249, 252, 260, 283, 329
  Danton 9, 13, 17, 63, 74, 226, 237, 239, 244, 255, 260, 262, 283, 330, 332, 335, 345, 347, 358, 362, 363, 366, 367
  Doctor/Professor 47–50, 98, 253
  Hauptmann 34, 47, 48, 50–6, 81, 238–9, 253, 256
  Hérault-Séchelles 283
  Julie 74, 228, 262, 330
  King Peter 43–6, 50, 98, 155, 157
  Lacroix 9
  Lena 50, 74, 164 n., 289
  Lenz 13, 31, 65, 69, 74, 75, 162, 164 n., 191, 216, 228, 232, 238, 239, 242, 253, 258, 260, 265, 266, 328–9, 369
  Leonce 9, 13, 50, 74, 79, 82, 164 n., 289, 332, 335, 367, 372

*References are *not* given here to that Part of the book in which the play to which a character belongs is the main object of interest.

390 Index

Lucile 243, 256, 257
Marie 186
Marion 7, 9, 31, 74, 228, 249, 252,
    257, 261, 267, 344, 347, 355
Oberlin 238, 239, 329
Payne 347
Robespierre 50, 264, 358, 363, 366
Rosetta 74
Simon 81, 244
Tutor 79
Woyzeck 48, 50, 51, 52, 53–6, 79,
    81, 238
Büchner (family):
    Alexander 38
    Ernst Karl (father of GB) 62, 139
    Ludwig 3 n., 179 n., 207, 208, 215,
        290
    Luise 208
    Wilhelm 59 n., 289
Buffon, Georges Louis Leclerc, comte
    de 16

Caesar, Julius 135, 142–3
Caligula 253, 254
Carus, Carl Gustav 24
Cato of Utica 135, 142–4
chaos 13, 74, 150, 153, 165, 229,
    259, 260, 266, 345
child 13, 202, 226, 227–8, 265–6,
    305, 340, 343, 345, 346, 347
Clarus, Johann Christian August
    324–8
classicism 3, 8, 13, 18, 19, 109, 223
Closs, August 12
Cockaigne 281, 283
    see also Arcadia
Coleridge, Samuel Taylor 16, 17, 18,
    20
commedia dell'arte 47, 217, 281
communion 69, 71, 83, 84, 182, 199,
    202, 203, 259–60
community, see communion
confusion 10–11, 16, 45, 50, 54, 152,
    155, 214, 232, 345, 351–2, 354
conscience 52, 53, 102–3, 129–31,
    134, 136–7, 140, 141, 173, 333,
    356–9
corruption:
    Dantons Tod 79, 96–7, 99–101, 111,
        123, 142, 144, 148, 162, 167,
        169, 170, 172–3, 175–9, 181–3,
        184–5, 192, 202, 203, 312
    Der Hessische Landbote 312–13

letters 61
Woyzeck 312, 362–4
    see also sexuality
crucifixion, see Passion (of Christ)
Cuvier, Georges 16, 22, 24, 36 n.

Darwin, Charles 15, 16, 18, 40, 140
David, Louis 65
death:
    Dantons Tod 74, 85, 130, 131,
        134–6, 167–8, 175, 192–3,
        195–9, 196, 228
    Leonce und Lena 220–1, 227–9,
        246, 248–9, 255–6, 262–7, 284
    letters 27, 28
    Woyzeck 228, 321, 343, 345, 358–9
Dedner, Burghard 64 n.
Descartes, René 31–3, 34–5, 36, 98,
    140, 157, 158, 159, 160, 277, 350
despair 30, 185, 372
    Dantons Tod 28, 83, 125, 126–7,
        129, 146, 148, 150, 152, 154,
        166, 237, 249
    Leonce und Lena 237, 241, 252
    letters 27, 134
determinism 29, 30, 119
devil 226, 318, 357–8, 365–6
dreams:
    Dantons Tod 130–1, 137, 201, 202
    Leonce und Lena 220, 222, 225,
        227–8, 247, 249, 266–7
    see also visions

Eckermann, Johann Peter 3
Eichendorff, Joseph 222
emblems, see archetypes
emotion, see feeling
empiricism 18, 20, 21, 22, 23, 25
energy 115, 145, 241
Enlightenment 16, 17, 30
ennui:
    Dantons Tod 114, 124–5, 126–7,
        129, 149, 203
    Lenz 238
    Leonce und Lena 226, 236, 237,
        245, 247, 250, 251, 253, 254,
        255, 256, 259, 267, 269, 275,
        278, 283
enthusiasm 37–8, 241, 255, 270, 272,
    273
Epicureanism 99–102, 119, 151, 163,
    171, 172, 239–40, 250

Index

fatalism 8, 25 n., 29, 109, 133, 144
fear 50–1, 57, 115, 131, 214, 215,
   225, 230, 250, 260, 272, 273
feeling 371, 372
   Dantons Tod 58, 162, 189, 201–2
   Lenz 67, 68, 71, 73, 83, 329
   Leonce und Lena 241, 257, 271,
   280
   Spinoza 35–6, 159
   Woyzeck 369
Fichte, Johann Gottlieb 19, 141
flight 129, 235
   see also refuge

fluidum:
   Dantons Tod 165, 188–9, 191, 192
   Lenz 164 n., 260
   Leonce und Lena 196–7, 223, 229,
   252–3, 258–9, 260, 284–5
food:
   Dantons Tod 104–8, 115, 121, 128,
   166, 200
   Leonce und Lena 212–13, 218,
   270–1, 272, 274, 278, 281, 282
   Woyzeck 48
fragmentation 8–9, 11, 18, 20
   Dantons Tod 97, 128, 190, 193
   Leonce und Lena 252, 256
Franzos, Karl Emil 10 n., 62 n., 290,
   300, 306, 307
freedom:
   Dantons Tod 89, 91, 93–5, 98, 103,
   105, 106, 109, 110–14, 119,
   120, 129, 131, 141–4
   Leonce und Lena 50, 234
   Woyzeck 49
free will 44, 49–50, 56, 200, 327,
   353–4, 368
Frei, Felix (pseud.) 14 n.
functionalism (critique of) 11, 39, 40,
   41, 46, 89, 140, 203, 234, 274
   see also mechanistic, the (critique of)

Geist 19, 164–5, 256–7, 258, 259, 329
Glück, Alfons 303 n.
God 5, 23, 33–5, 98, 350
   Dantons Tod 58, 61, 96–7, 98, 157,
   158–9, 160–2, 164, 165
   Lenz 69, 238
   Leonce und Lena 226, 264
   Woyzeck 55, 308, 343, 348, 349,
   358–9, 364, 365, 367

Goethe, Johann Wolfgang von 3, 4, 5,
   15, 19–21, 23, 25, 26, 31, 36 n.,
   38, 39, 66, 217, 222
Grass, Günter 4
Grimm, Reinhold 148 n., 191 n.
guillotine 86, 97, 102, 105, 118, 119,
   149, 174, 175, 192, 197–9
Gutzkow, Karl 14 n., 30, 43, 62, 94,
   106, 207, 208, 210, 215, 218,
   230, 290

harmony 12–13, 26, 27–8, 29, 30, 39,
   42, 72, 125–6, 152, 164, 165,
   185, 203, 227, 261, 274
Hauptmann, Gerhart 5
Hegel, Friedrich 19, 95–6, 98
Heine, Heinrich 171 n.
Herzog, Werner 4
Hinderer, Walter 217
history 61, 119, 131, 336
   Büchner as 'scribe' of 60, 63, 64,
   138
   Büchner's changing of 90, 93, 102,
   131 n., 139–40, 200, 337
   'fatalism' of 29, 108–9, 144
Hoffmann, E. T. A. 26, 33 n., 72,
   167, 222, 274–5, 282
Holberg, Ludvig 217
Hölderlin, Friedrich 203
Holmes, T. M. 89
hunger, *see* food
Huxley, Thomas Henry 15, 39

idealism 18, 19, 21, 22, 25, 26
   Büchner's anti-idealism 58–9, 61–2,
   64, 65, 82, 139, 232, 329, 368
   Büchner's idealism 37, 38, 40, 72,
   81, 85, 89, 91, 93, 94, 109–10,
   119, 163, 181, 200–1, 202–3,
   274
   gulf ideal/real 127, 128, 146, 166,
   182, 283
   Leonce und Lena 255–6, 257, 259,
   270–1, 273, 274, 275
identity 44, 45–6, 213–15, 229–30,
   231, 232, 234, 239–40, 242, 243,
   245, 254, 261, 275–6, 279
ideology 89, 92
   Dantons Tod 87, 98, 102, 103,
   105, 119, 144, 170
'immorality' of *Dantons Tod* 61,
   62–3, 80, 138

individual 39–40, 41, 46, 109, 140, 185
Dantons Tod 87–90, 147, 150, 196
Leonce und Lena 46
Woyzeck 49–50, 309
insight:
  in the arts 58, 66–7, 68, 71, 73, 329–30
  Danton 79, 85, 122
  Hauptmann 52
  Leonce 240
  Lucile 194
  Robespierre 102
  Woyzeck 314–22, 335, 368
  see also visions
intellect, critique of 30, 33, 35, 39, 71, 157, 158, 162, 164, 194, 241, 309
  see also mind (critique of), rationalism (critique of), thought (critique of)
intuition 33, 38–9, 44, 71, 92, 185, 194–5, 201, 257, 322
isolation 13, 83, 84, 193, 203, 227–8, 250, 253, 263, 265, 343, 344–5, 346, 350, 372

Jean Paul 217, 222
Jaeglé, Minna 3 n., 26, 29, 36, 109, 208, 260, 274, 276
James, Dorothy 7 n.
Jens, Walter 6
Jesus 69–71, 100, 101, 138, 175, 264, 358–9, 366
  see also Passion (of Christ)
Jouvet, Louis 372

Kafka, Franz 4, 73
kaleidoscopic 6, 93, 123, 146, 314
Kant, Immanuel 19, 21, 31
Kästner, Erich 4
Kaufmann passage 65, 79, 139, 162–3
Klasse (die große), see Volk
Kleist, Heinrich von 73, 167
Knapp, Gerhard 12 n.
Knight, A. H. J. 7, 13
Koeppen, Wolfgang 5
Krapp, Helmut 8

Lamarck, Jean-Baptiste de Monet, chevalier de 16
language (as motif) 96, 116–19, 124, 150, 154, 251, 270
laughter 148, 182, 196, 280
Lavater, Johann Kaspar 37, 38

Lehmann, Werner R. 9 n., 268 n., 291, 292, 293, 295 n., 297, 298, 300, 324 n., 343 n.
Liebig, Justus von 22–3, 38
lies (as motif) 81, 103, 137, 149, 183
life (as principle) 31, 33, 36, 39, 40, 42, 44, 56, 64, 65, 66, 67, 68, 73–4, 98, 158, 232–3, 371
Linnaeus, Carl 16, 25
love:
  Dantons Tod 80, 85, 171–2, 193–4, 199
  Lenz 66, 67, 233
  Leonce und Lena 9, 220–1, 233, 247–50, 251–3, 254, 256, 259, 262, 263, 265, 267, 272, 274, 278, 283–5
  Woyzeck 56, 315–16, 342, 351, 359
Lukács, Georg 6, 97 n.

McCarthy, Gerry 372
madness:
  Doctor 47, 49, 323
  Lenz 74, 216, 237, 328–9
  Leonce 253, 274
  Lucile 154, 195
  Valerio 242–4
  Woyzeck 49, 313, 323–9, 332, 334, 364
Maes, Nicolaes 68 n.
mantle, see masks
marionettes, see puppets
Marx (and the Marxian) 6, 18, 89
masks:
  Dantons Tod 65, 79, 80, 81, 82, 83, 85, 102–3, 147, 150–1, 153, 165, 173, 181, 183–4, 185, 189, 199, 214–15, 237, 310
  Lenz 73
  Leonce und Lena 211, 214–15, 216, 220, 221, 222, 224, 230, 236, 245, 251, 275, 276, 279
  Woyzeck 52–3, 335–6, 347, 353, 354
mass, see Volk
Mayer, Hans 12, 13, 119, 207
Mayer, Thomas Michael 9 n., 29, 30 n., 171 n., 208
mechanistic, the (critique of):
  Dantons Tod 58–9, 86, 89–90, 140–1

Index

Leonce und Lena 44, 50, 276, 278, 285
letters 26–7
Trial Lecture 36–7, 39–40, 41, 42
Woyzeck 50, 277
see also functionalism (critique of)
Medawar, P. B. 15, 24
melancholy 51, 52, 233, 236, 241, 246, 248, 249, 250, 259, 315, 327
Menzel, Wolfgang 14 n.
Messiah, see Jesus
metaphysical, see mystical
Mill, John Stuart 15
mind (critique of) 29, 30, 31, 35–6, 40, 158, 159, 257
   Dantons Tod 57, 84, 92, 98, 157, 161, 164, 201
   Lenz 71
   Leonce und Lena 43, 44–5, 46, 258, 259, 270
   Woyzeck 49, 56, 350
   see also intellect (critique of), rationalism (critique of), thought (critique of)
Minnigerode, Carl 62
mirrors 150, 215, 226, 239, 281, 282, 305, 357
Molière 274, 372
morality 61, 63–4, 73, 80–1, 138, 139–40
   Dantons Tod 81–2, 87, 95, 99, 100–1, 102, 129, 142, 144, 161–2, 163, 172–3, 175, 177, 189, 200
   Leonce und Lena 278
   Woyzeck 44, 52–3, 54–5, 306, 307–8, 313, 326, 335–6, 356, 363, 368
mosaic 8–9, 11, 18, 115, 190
Mühlher, Robert 6, 12
Müller, Johannes 14, 24
Müller-Seidel, Walter 25, 29
multiplicity 7, 8, 17, 18, 121, 131, 302, 340, 371
   see also perspective
multivalence, see multiplicity
music 26–7, 38
   Dantons Tod 27–8, 125–6, 152–3
   Lenz 68–9, 164 n., 258
   Leonce und Lena 9, 247, 283
   Woyzeck 320, 337–42

müssen 133–4, 137–8, 184, 360–2, 363
Musset, Alfred de 217, 222
Muston, Alexis 69 n.
mystical 21–2, 36–7, 38, 39
   Dantons Tod 164–5, 182, 192, 201, 202, 203
   Leonce und Lena 223, 247, 258, 259–60, 275
   Woyzeck 328–9

nature 10–12, 20–1, 30–1, 36, 42, 67, 70, 109, 369
   Dantons Tod 82, 87, 90, 95, 98, 100, 163, 175, 183, 189–90
   Leonce und Lena 203, 210, 227, 239, 241, 261, 271
   Woyzeck 49, 56, 307–8, 309–10, 313, 316, 322–3, 327, 335, 347, 353–4, 363, 368
Naturphilosophie 19, 21–5, 26, 37
Nero 135, 253, 254
Newton, Isaac 15, 20, 23
Nichts 13, 150, 153, 161, 165, 220, 214–15, 345, 347
night 130, 137, 224, 225, 227, 247, 265, 266–7, 273, 331
nightmares, see dreams
nihilism 6, 8, 12, 63, 150, 153, 165
Novalis 19

Oken, Lorenz 10, 14, 15, 21, 22, 23, 24, 38, 39
ontology 42, 73, 214, 249, 270, 275–7, 278, 309, 333

pain 35–6, 159–60, 212
Paradise 227, 229, 265, 285
paradox 7, 8, 13, 108, 198, 368
Passion (of Christ) 71, 138, 264, 348, 349, 367, 370
   see also Jesus
Peacock, Ronald 7
perspective 7
   Dantons Tod 114, 130, 150, 152, 169, 184–5, 196
   Leonce und Lena 209, 216, 219, 224, 226, 227, 239, 254, 272, 277, 279, 285
   Woyzeck 315, 331–2, 349
pessimism 8, 12, 13, 63, 83, 109, 153
philosophy 30, 43, 44, 46
Platen, Graf August von 222

Popper, Karl 24
poverty 48, 55, 104, 105–6, 170, 303–6
'primordial type' 11, 20, 39
progress (as motif) 10, 57, 85–6, 96, 103–4, 127–8, 310, 316, 347
puppets:
  Dantons Tod 58, 102, 133, 156, 189, 200
  Lenz 65, 368
  Leonce und Lena 44, 45, 50, 210, 214, 231–2, 232, 233, 234, 240, 276–7, 278, 280, 335
  letters 61, 64, 109
  Woyzeck 49, 50, 56, 323
Pygmalion 65, 74, 191

Raphael 67
rationalism (critique of) 30–3, 36, 39, 98, 155, 157, 158
  see also intellect (critique of), mind(critique of), thought (critique of)
reality 21, 25, 31
  in the arts 58–9, 60–8, 73, 329, 368
  Dantons Tod 58–9, 64–5, 93, 123, 150, 183–4, 185, 191
  Leonce und Lena 13, 43, 229, 251, 268, 275
  Woyzeck 353
Reed, T. J. 21
refuge 52–3, 58–9, 131–2, 234, 243, 285, 336, 362, 367–8
  see also flight
Rembrandt 68 n.
Rimbaud, Arthur 73
resurrection 28, 74–5, 246–7, 256, 265–7
revolutionary (Büchner as) 6, 8, 30, 94
robots, *see* puppets
Roget, P. M. 17 n.
Romantics, Romanticism 22, 68, 207, 211, 222, 241, 271, 274
Rousseau, Jean-Jacques 86, 94, 233

sacrifice 141–4, 263–4, 284
sadism 152, 165, 200
Saint-Hilaire, Geoffroy 22, 36 n.
Savoy, Carel van 69
Schelling, Friedrich 19, 24
Schiller, Friedrich 8, 19–21, 31, 38, 87 n., 109

Schlegel, Friedrich 19, 217
Schmid, Gerhard 290, 291, 292, 293, 295, 300, 343 n.
Schopenhauer, Arthur 12, 25 n., 153
Schöpfung 64–5, 66, 68, 74, 125, 165–6, 185, 191, 229, 252, 259, 260, 266, 329–30, 372
science (Büchner's) 8, 10–11, 14, 25, 38, 40
sexuality:
  Dantons Tod 79–80, 81–2, 85, 147–8, 151–2, 156, 167–71, 173–4, 176, 177, 178–84, 187–90, 192, 195, 202
  Woyzeck 56, 308, 311–12, 316–18, 336–7, 339, 340, 341, 342, 354, 355–6, 357–8, 362–4
  see also corruption
Shakespeare, William 5 n., 66, 217, 234, 281
sin 130, 131, 169, 175, 308, 341, 342, 353, 358–9, 362, 363, 364, 366, 368
Spinoza, Baruch 33–4, 35, 98, 157, 158, 159, 160, 161, 162
Stern, J. P. 13
Sterne, Laurence 217
Stifter, Adalbert 72, 167
Strohl, Jean 21
suffering, *see* pain
suicide 134, 135, 141–4, 193, 199, 200, 274
systems (critique of):
  Dantons Tod 86, 89–90, 98, 119, 127, 129, 143, 201, 203
  Leonce und Lena 45, 50

'teleological' (approach in sciences) 41
thought (critique of) 31–3, 43, 46, 84, 158, 161, 256–7, 333–4, 350–1
  see also intellect (critique of), mind (critique of), rationalism (critique of)
Tieck, Ludwig 217
time (as motif):
  Dantons Tod 125
  Lenz 238
  Leonce und Lena 223, 224, 227, 244, 248, 250, 261, 262, 278, 281, 282, 283, 285
  Woyzeck 34, 51–2, 53, 238–9
time (disparities concerning) 341, 355 n., 366 n.

totality, *see* wholeness
truth 81, 82, 131, 137, 276

ugliness 66, 73

Viëtor, Karl 12, 40, 88
Virgil 222, 223, 224
virtue:
  Dantons Tod 82, 99–102, 103,
    138–9, 163, 172, 176, 179
  Woyzeck 53, 55, 56, 306, 335, 368
visions 13, 26, 39, 70
  Dantons Tod 181, 184, 191, 314
  Leonce und Lena 220–1, 223, 225,
    226, 227, 229, 242–3, 248–9,
    265, 275, 277, 281, 282,
    283
  Woyzeck 321–2, 325, 328–32, 342,
    361, 364
  see also dreams, insight
Volk 6, 41, 88, 89, 94, 105–9, 116,
  176, 177–8, 180, 203, 212, 334

Voltaire 17
Voss, E. Theodor 222
Voss, Johann Heinrich 222

Wedekind, Frank 5, 81, 186
Weidig, Ludwig 92, 213
wholeness 6–7, 8–9, 10–11, 13, 15,
  20, 40, 81, 274, 371
  Dantons Tod 91, 201
  Lenz 70
  Leonce und Lena 252, 266, 267,
    285
wholism, *see* wholeness
Wilbrand, Johann Bernhard 23, 39 n.
windows 68–9, 130, 131, 137, 226,
  228, 314–15, 334, 349
Wolf, Christa 5
Woost, Johanna Christiane 324,
  327
Woyzeck, Johann Christian 324–8

Zons, Raimar St. 25